[illegible]

MONTESQUIEU

A Critical Biography

Oxford University Press, Amen House, London E.C.4

GLASGOW NEW YORK TORONTO MELBOURNE WELLINGTON
BOMBAY CALCUTTA MADRAS KARACHI KUALA LUMPUR
CAPE TOWN IBADAN NAIROBI ACCRA

Montesquieu

MONTESQUIEU

A Critical Biography

By

ROBERT SHACKLETON
Fellow of Brasenose College, Oxford

OXFORD UNIVERSITY PRESS
1961

Printed in Great Britain by
The Camelot Press Ltd., London and Southampton

TO MY MOTHER

TO THE MEMORY OF MY FATHER

PREFACE

IT is a rash enterprise, in the twentieth century, to write an account of the life and ideas of a man of many interests who lived before the age of specialization. It requires a multiplicity of competences, scientific, philosophical, legal, historical, and literary, rarely to be found today in one man, and to which I could certainly not lay claim. Specialists will find here shortcomings which they will feel disposed to censure. I would ask them, in the words of Montesquieu's own Preface to *L'Esprit des lois*, 'd'approuver ou de condamner le livre entier et non pas quelques phrases'. I have tried not to analyse and evaluate the thought of Montesquieu, but to write his biography; and his life being a life of ideas rather than events, I have tried to study the genesis of those ideas and to show how his works grew out of his reading, his travels, and his friendships.

The preparation of this book has taken me into more than sixty libraries, public or private, in five countries, and in these, almost without exception, I have been courteously and helpfully received. My first duty is to acknowledge the gracious permission given to me by Her Majesty the Queen to cite documents to be found at Windsor Castle, to which my attention was very kindly drawn by the Librarian, Sir Owen Morshead, and his successor, Mr. R. C. Mackworth-Young. I am grateful for facilities offered to me by the Duke of Buccleuch and Sir David Scott in relation to documents at Boughton House, by the Duke of Richmond and Gordon in relation to documents now deposited in the County Record Office at Chichester, by the Earl and Countess Waldegrave at Chewton, and by the Earl of Harrowby. I am grateful for leave to inspect and cite documents in the libraries of the Royal Society of London and of the Royal College of Surgeons of England, and in the private collection of the late Dr. and Mrs. Manfred Altmann of London, and for the loan of a copy of a remote manuscript to Sir Charles Petrie. I have a particular debt, for guiding my steps to English archives, to Mr. L. C. Hector of the Public Record Office.

In France, I gladly acknowledge my indebtedness to the kindness of Monsieur R. Schuman, who has allowed me access to his collection of manuscripts at times when his preoccupations were pressing; to Monsieur P. Cornuau, for allowing me to study manuscripts passing through his hands; to the Father Superior of the Collège libre de Juilly, for allowing me to inspect the archives of his college; to Madame Latapie of Naujan-et-Postiac (Gironde), for a most amiable reception and access to her family papers; to Monsieur X. Védère, for the unfailing courtesy of his welcome to the Archives municipales de Bordeaux; and to Monsieur L. Desgraves, Conservateur-en-chef de la Bibliothèque municipale de Bordeaux, for the waving aside of formalities and for the most frequent and tireless assistance.

Almost all Montesquieu scholars, and a very large number of eighteenth-century specialists, have become known to me during the last few years, and from none have I had anything but the most helpful and friendly treatment. To enumerate them would be well-nigh impertinent. They all have my grateful thanks. Four of them have pride of place for work and for friendship: Jean Brethe de La Gressaye, Sergio Cotta, François Gebelin, and André Masson.

For courtesy, kindness, and assistance I am much indebted to Baron Raoul de Montesquieu of Raymond and to Baron Philippe de Montesquieu of Agen and Villegongis. To the Comtesse de Chabannes, *châtelaine* of La Brède, I have the greatest debt of all, for an invariably amiable welcome at La Brède and for unrestricted access to the library and manuscripts of her illustrious ancestor, of whom she is a worthy descendant.

I wish to thank for financial assistance the Cassel Educational Trust, the Board of the Faculty of Modern Languages at Oxford, and the French Government's department of Relations culturelles. I thank finally my colleagues at Brasenose College for the grant of sabbatical leave, for the provision of secretarial assistance, and by no means least, as individuals, for forgiving and answering my importunate questions in fields other than my own.

R. S.

OXFORD
1 January 1961

CONTENTS

LIST OF PLATES

NOTE ON BIBLIOGRAPHICAL REFERENCES

I. *To the text of Montesquieu*

The best edition of Montesquieu is:

Œuvres complètes de Montesquieu, publiées sous la direction de M. André Masson, Paris (Nagel), 3 vols., 1950, 1953, and 1955.

It is referred to as Nagel I, II, and III. The first volume, which is a photographic reprint of the 'vulgate' edition of the *Œuvres complètes*, Amsterdam and Leipzig (=Paris), 1758, has three sequences of pagination. These are referred to as A, B, and C.

The most widely diffused edition is:

Œuvres complètes de Montesquieu; texte présenté et annoté par Roger Caillois, Paris (N.R.F.: Bibliothèque de la Pléiade), 2 vols., 1949 and 1951.

It is referred to as Pléiade I and II. It lacks some material which is found in the Nagel edition, notably the correspondence.

References are given as follows:

Lettres persanes	e.g. *L.P.* 24. The number is that of the letter as in H. Barckhausen's critical edition (Paris, 1897), which is followed by most subsequent editions including Pléiade I, and which differs little from Nagel I.
Considérations sur les causes de la grandeur des Romains et de leur décadence	e.g. *Romains*, ch. xi, followed by page references to Nagel I and Pléiade II.
De l'Esprit des lois	e.g. *Lois*, XIX, 4. The references are to book and chapter, the text used being that of Nagel I which is in general use.
Pensées	e.g. *Pensée* 2124 (Bkn. 1355). The first number is that of the paragraph in the

	order of the manuscript, as shown in Nagel II; the second number is that of the paragraph in *Pensées et fragments inédits*, ed. H. Barckhausen, Bordeaux, 1899–1901 (roughly followed in Pléiade I).
Spicilège	e.g. *Spicilège* 331 (MS., pp. 293–4). The first number is that of the paragraph as in Nagel II; the second number is that of the page in the manuscript as shown in Pléiade II.
Correspondence	e.g. Montesquieu to Venuti, 22 July 1749. In the absence of any further indication, the letter appears in its chronological place in Nagel III.
All other works	e.g. Nagel III, p. 283; Pléiade I, p. 875.

II. *To other printed material*

The sources and authorities differing considerably from chapter to chapter, no general bibliography of works consulted is given.[1] Bibliographical details of a work are given only, in most cases, in the first reference to it, and that reference is indexed.

In references to articles in periodicals, the year only is normally given.

III. *To manuscript material*

A reference to a manuscript is given only when I have myself seen it, and I have not knowingly failed to mention its publication when manuscript material used has been published.

Eighteenth-century spelling and punctuation have been modernized.

All dates are given in New Style except those of events occurring in England, which are in Old Style.

[1] A most useful bibliography of works dealing with Montesquieu is given by D. C. Cabeen, *Montesquieu: a Bibliography*, New York, 1947, and brought up to date by D. C. Cabeen, 'A supplementary Montesquieu bibliography' (*Revue internationale de philosophie*, 1955).

ABBREVIATIONS

Arch. dép. Gironde	Archives départmentales de la Gironde.
Arch. hist. Gironde	The journal entitled *Archives historiques du département de la Gironde.*
Arch. mun. Bx	Archives municipales de Bordeaux.
B.M.	British Museum.
B.N.	Bibliothèque nationale.
Bodl.	Bodleian Library.
Bx	Bibliothèque municipale de Bordeaux.
Congrès 1955	*Actes du Congrès Montesquieu réuni à Bordeaux du 23 au 26 mai 1955*, Bordeaux, 1956.
Cortona	Biblioteca dell'Accademia etrusca di Cortona.
FS	*French Studies*, Oxford, 1947 sq.
HMC	Historical Manuscripts Commission.
Lettres familières	*Lettres familières du président de Montesquieu baron de la Brède à divers amis d'Italie*, s.l., 1767.
Lettres familières (1768)	*Lettres familières de M. le président de Montesquieu*, nouvelle édition, Florence et se trouvent à Paris, 1768.
RHBx	*Revue historique de Bordeaux et du département de la Gironde*, Bordeaux, 1908 sq.
RHLF	*Revue d'histoire littéraire de la France*, Paris, 1894 sq.
RLC	*Revue de littérature comparée*, Paris, 1921 sq.
Secondat, *Mémoire*	Jean-Baptiste de Secondat, *Mémoire pour servir à l'éloge historique de M. de Montesquieu*, as in Vian.
Vian	L. Vian, *Histoire de Montesquieu d'après des documents nouveaux et inédits*, deuxième édition, Paris, 1879.

I

EARLY YEARS, 1689–1721

I. FAMILY AND BIRTH

THE name Montesquieu is of mixed Latin and Frankish origin and means a wild or barren mountain, and it is of fairly frequent occurrence in the south-west of France. There are several places of this name in the vicinity of Toulouse; but the hamlet which was to make the name famous lies a little further north. Nearly ten miles west of Agen, and two miles south of the Garonne, stands a small, unimpressive hill, which is still large enough to dominate the surrounding flat country. The land is not fertile. Poultry and sheep are its most prominent products, but some poor vines creep up the side of the hill. The ruins of a castle crown the eminence. Walls of stout stone, built on foundations of rock, are now overgrown with moss and thickly girt with nettles. Two withered palm trees stand in isolation. Peasants' cottages have grown up against the walls. Countless dogs bark at the unknown visitor, and children doff their caps to him. This dismal and desolate scene is the village of Montesquieu as it stands today; but when the walls were whole and a lord lived within them, the spot was scarcely less remote from civilization. It is the south-west of France in its least smiling aspect.

From the isolation of this barren hill to the refinement of political doctrine and to the glitter of style in *L'Esprit des lois* the distance is not small.

The founder of the family of Secondat de Montesquieu was Jacob de Secondat, who was born at Agen in 1576, and was baptized as a Protestant. His family was one of minor *noblesse d'épée*, four of his brothers being killed in battle as young men. He was the sixth, but second surviving, son of Jean de Secondat, whose ancestors had left their native Berry and settled at Agen in the previous century. Jean de Secondat was chamberlain to Jeanne D'Albret, Queen of Navarre, who expressed her gratitude for his services by giving him, in 1561, the sum of 10,000 *livres* that he might buy from her the lordship of Montesquieu. In 1606 this lordship was by Henri IV promoted to a barony, in favour of Jacob de Secondat, with the courtesy title of marquis, which, however, was never used.[1] Though the family was not one of great eminence, it had connexions of unusual interest. A first cousin of Jacob's grandfather had married the renowned philologist, Julius-Caesar Scaliger, who had settled at Agen, and his son, Josephus-Justus, likewise a celebrated scholar, was thus a kinsman of the Secondat family. Jacob's mother, Eléonore de Brénieu, was of English extraction and lineally descended, through Margaret Pole, Countess of Salisbury, from Edward III. The blood of the Plantagenets thus flows in the house of Secondat.

Jacob's eldest son, Jean-Baptiste-Gaston, married Anne-Jeanne Du Bernet, daughter of a prominent member of the legal nobility of the south-west, and used her dowry to buy a legal office for himself. He had ten children,[2] including three sons who became ecclesiastics and three daughters who became nuns. His third son, Jacques, was Montesquieu's father. He was an active soldier, handsome, bronzed, and sensual, if his portrait can be relied on; and according to his son he had a noble and charming face, much wit and good sense, and very little wealth.[3] In 1686 he married Marie-Françoise de Pesnel, an heiress who owned vast acres of land and who, as well as being of English origin through the noble houses of D'Albret and Bourbon, was descended from Saint-Louis. Montesquieu declares that his mother, having much property, had many debts and many lawsuits.[4] Her husband, in a memoir[5] which he wrote after her death, credits her with an acute business sense: 'elle avait l'esprit d'un habile

[1] O'Gilvy, *De Secondat de Montesquieu*, Bordeaux, 1858 (extracted from *Nobiliaire de Guienne et de Gascogne*); E. de Perceval, 'La Baronne de Montesquieu', in *Actes de l'Académie de Bordeaux*, 1932–3, p. 30; and Jean-Baptiste de Secondat, *Mémoire pour servir à l'éloge historique de M. de Montesquieu.* This last document, which is the primary source of information about Montesquieu, is printed in L. Vian, *Histoire de Montesquieu*, Paris, 1878 (second edition), pp. 396–407. It will be referred to as Secondat, *Mémoire*, followed by the page reference from Vian; but where necessary I correct the text from the original manuscript which is at La Brède.

[2] To the nine listed by O'Gilvy must be added Nicole de Montesquieu, whose existence is disclosed by papers at La Brède. She was the superior of the convent of Notre Dame at Agen, a religious house very closely connected with the Montesquieu family.

[3] Nagel, III, p. 1564. [4] Ibid., p. 1565.

[5] The text of the manuscript, which is at La Brède, has been published incompletely and inaccurately by Vian (p. 18, second edition only), after Tamisey de La Roque (*Revue critique*, 27 April 1878).

homme pour les affaires sérieuses, nul goût pour les bagatelles'. She had a great affection for her children, a keen sense of duty, and was devoted to the succour of the poor. She was a woman of great piety; her favourite reading was the New Testament; and when she died her husband discovered that she had made frequent use of a scourge and an iron girdle.

It was she who brought to the family of Secondat the castle of La Brède.

To reach La Brède the traveller must proceed south-westwards from Bordeaux along the main road, built by the Romans, which leads to Agen and eventually to Toulouse, and advances along the left bank of the Garonne through gently undulating acres of vines with scattered houses. Ten miles from the city and shortly before reaching the tiny river port of Beautiran, the road passes through the hamlet of La Prade. Here a branch road goes off westwards and after two miles reaches a few houses grouped around a romanesque church. This is the village of La Brède, and less than a mile further along the road is the castle which has given its name to the village.

The Château de La Brède is not a modest country house pretentiously named. It is a real castle, built and fortified at the beginning of the fifteenth century, on the site of a previous construction. From its oldest recorded owners, the noble family of La Lande, it passed late in the sixteenth century to the family of Pesnel, and from them to the family of Secondat. It is surrounded by a moat and access is given by three drawbridges. Its mass, solid but graceful, rises into four turrets capped with conical roofs, the largest of them girt with machicolations. The same conical structure is repeated in outhouses which resemble the *trulli* of Apulia. The rooms of the castle, whether they look on to tiny courtyards or, through walls of immense thickness, on to the smooth sheet of water, are cool in summer, but far from warm in winter. The entrance hall with its twisted columns of dark wood, the sombre dining-room with elaborately carved panelling, the kitchen from which a regiment of retainers can be fed, and the *salon* hung with ancestral portraits, striking as they all are, yield in significance to the enormous guardroom with its gigantic tunnel vault, its antique frescoes about the fireplace, its door leading to the chapel, and its window commanding the inner drawbridge. This room, lined with books, is the workshop from which *L'Esprit des lois* will emerge. From the loftier rooms one's glance surveys the countryside. This is one of the last outposts of the fertile vine-growing region of Bordeaux. The dry white wine of La Brède, the red wine of Rochemorin, more highly reputed in that day, and more widely sold, than Médoc or Saint-Emilion, constitute the riches of the property, and not far away are the sweet white wines of Sauternes. Beyond the vineyards extend the broad, monotonous, sparsely peopled acres of the *landes*, and the forest, on some sides, reaches almost to the moat of the castle.

In this castle, on 18 January 1689, the *châtelaine*, Marie-Françoise de Pesnel, gave birth to a son, who on the same day was baptized in the parish church of La Brède, and received the name of Charles-Louis.[1] His godfather was a beggar of the village, Charles by name, selected in order that the child might ever be reminded of his obligations to the poor. Montaigne, likewise, was held at the font by paupers: the similarity between the careers of the two great Gascon authors begins with the beginning of their lives. And as Montaigne's first years were spent in a village house, so the young Charles-Louis was sent to nurse at the flourmill of La Brède where he passed the first three years of his life, eating simple foods and learning to speak with the rustic accent which he never forsook.

He had two sisters who became nuns, Marie who was his elder by sixteen months, and Thérèse who was born on 31 August 1691. A younger brother, Joseph, was born on 9 November 1694, and Charles-Louis stood godfather for him. He became an ecclesiastic of some distinction, and will be mentioned again in these pages. Another brother and sister died in infancy, and in giving birth to the younger of these in 1696 their mother died. Charles-Louis was then seven, and when the example of the domestic virtues and the piety for which his mother was renowned in the province was removed from him by her death, he inherited her wealth and the title of Baron de La Brède.

Until the age of eleven, Charles-Louis was educated at home

[1] The parish registers for 1689 are not extant. The evidence for the date of birth is the memoir of Secondat, and for the date of baptism, F. de P. Latapie, 'Notice de la paroisse de La Brède' in Baurein, *Variétés bordeloises* (Bordeaux, 1876, 4 vols.), III, p. 8, of dubious reliability.

and in the village, being taught to write by the schoolmaster of La Brède, by name Souvervie.[1] In 1700, his father decided to send him away to school, and selected the Collège de Juilly 370 miles away, in the diocese of Meaux where Bossuet was still bishop.

II. EDUCATION

The renown of Juilly was great. Situated in a most agreeable park, with spacious grounds and noble buildings, yet near to Paris, being but twenty miles distant from Notre-Dame, Juilly had and retains to this day a real charm. Established by letters-patent of Louis XIII in 1638, and controlled by the Congregation of the Oratory, it had already in Montesquieu's day a solid tradition while being modern in outlook. Not many schools in the north-east of France attracted pupils from remote provinces,[2] but Juilly was in different case. Although it cost 60 *livres* to travel from Bordeaux to Paris in the public coach,[3] many boys from the south-west of France were sent to Juilly, as the registers testify,[4] partly on account of the decline of the Collège de Guyenne, where Montaigne had been educated. From Bordeaux there are found to be at Juilly in 1700 two brothers called La Boyrie, two Loyac brothers, cousins of Montesquieu, Marans who was his kinsman and was eventually to attend him on his death-bed. One pupil bears the name Saucats, which is the property immediately adjacent to La Brède. Jean-Jacques Bel, who until his premature death was to remain a close friend of Montesquieu, went to Juilly in 1703, and other less known names from Bordeaux are numerous. Nor did the great disdain to send their sons to Juilly. The name of Trudaine is frequently listed. Three years senior to Montesquieu was a scion of the Brancas family; the Marquis de Bassompierre was matriculated in 1702; and the Duke of Berwick himself, natural son to James II of England, was an alumnus.

[1] Bx MS. 1913 contains a loose slip of paper, signed by Montesquieu, which gives this information.

[2] F. de Dainville, 'Effectifs des collèges et scolarité aux XVIIe et XVIIIe siècles dans le nord-est de la France' (*Population*, 1955).

[3] G. d'Avenel, *Histoire économique de la propriété*, Paris, 1894–1912, VI, p. 632.

[4] The manuscript *dossier des pensions* is still preserved at Juilly.

The young Baron de La Brède entered Juilly on 11 August 1700, his Loyac cousins accompanying him. The journey between Juilly and Bordeaux he made on horseback, attended by a manservant.[1] His fees amounted to 342 *livres* a year, not a light charge on his father's income. On 4 May 1702, his younger brother Joseph, at this time known as Monsieur de Martillac, came to join him. From February 1704, a further payment of 50 *livres* a year was made, in order that the boys might drink wine. The elder brother was praised as being industrious, but Joseph, despite his great amiability, was backward and needed special attention.[2] Charles-Louis remained at Juilly until 11 August 1705, but Joseph stayed three and a half years longer.

The education imparted at Juilly was a valuable one, though the pressure on the pupils was great.[3] The day's activities began at five in the morning when the boys left their beds. Prayers were said at 5.15, and private study followed until 7.30. Half an hour was now devoted to breakfast and recreation, and mass was said at eight o'clock. From 8.30 until 11 classes were held, the subject being changed in the interest of variety every half hour. An early dinner was consumed to the accompaniment of readings from either the lives of the saints or the *Annals* of Baronius, and an hour of private study followed. Classes were resumed at 1.30 and were followed by a break for tea and recreation at four o'clock. The rest of the evening, apart from supper at seven o'clock, was devoted to study and the writing of letters home, until prayers and bed at 8.30.

The instruction itself was thorough. Latin and French were the languages mainly studied, Greek being at all times subordinate; and although it was deemed necessary to be proficient in the speaking of Latin, the actual language of instruction was French. Geography, history, and mathematics were in the timetable, and instruction was given also in such subjects as drawing, music, riding, fencing, and dancing. Education was a subject to which several priests of the Oratory had given very serious

[1] *Montesquieu (catalogue de l'exposition)*, Bordeaux, 1955; no. 86.

[2] Ibid., no. 91; *Bulletin de l'Alliance des arts*, December 1843, p. 190; Vian (p. 19, first edition only).

[3] C. Hamel, *Histoire de l'abbaye et du collège de Juilly*, Paris, 1888, is the most useful book on Juilly.

thought. The *Entretiens sur les sciences* of Bernard Lamy[1] express the principal ideas of the Oratorians, who, while piety and the cult of religion were their main object, were advanced and progressive in their day; and if the Jesuits and the schools of Port-Royal produced men more learned in the classics, Juilly produced more all-round men. Their ideas were judicious and balanced, and though Montesquieu later declared himself dissatisfied with his education,[2] it was as liberal an education as France could afford.

Though the influence on Montesquieu's literary activity of the instruction received at Juilly may well have been extensive,[3] the surviving corpus of his works shows but two undoubted vestiges of his schooldays. The library of La Brède contains a notebook in a child's hand, deemed to be that of Montesquieu, and entitled *Historia Romana*. This consists of some 78 pages of question and answer in elementary form:

> Q. A quibus condita est urbs Roma?
> R. A Troianis.[4]

It is simple, factual and insignificant; but it shows the first interest in Rome of one who was to treat its history memorably. The other relic of his days at Juilly is a tragedy in verse, entitled *Britomare*, of which some hundred lines remain. That it is not for intrinsic reasons that its disappearance is to be regretted, is made sufficiently clear by lines such as these:

> Dans l'état où je suis, hélas! te puis-je dire
> Et pourquoi je me trouble, et pourquoi je soupire?

But already the style and sentiments of the mature Montesquieu can be foreseen when he writes:

> Je défendais encore ma liberté mourante,

and

> La raison ne voit rien dans cette épaisse nuit.[5]

[1] The first edition of this work appeared at Grenoble in 1683. The catalogue of Montesquieu's library shows that he eventually possessed, as well as the *Entretiens*, six other works by Lamy.

[2] This judgement was reported by Montesquieu's son to an eminent foreign traveller (*Archiva del General Miranda*, IV, Caracas, 1930, p. 244), and is confirmed by L.-B. Castel, *L'Homme moral opposé à l'homme physique* (in J.-J. Rousseau, *Œuvres complètes*, Geneva, 1782, 33 vols. 12mo, XXXII, p. 183).

[3] A valuable study of this problem is H. Roddier, 'De la composition de l'*Esprit des lois*: Montesquieu et les oratoriens de l'académie de Juilly' (*RHLF*, 1952).

[4] Pléiade II, pp. 1443–5; not in Nagel.

[5] *Pensée* 359 (Bkn. 477).

The greatest influence of Juilly on Montesquieu, however, was the regard which he learned to acquire for the most illustrious member of the Congregation, the philosopher Malebranche who, if he but rarely visited Juilly, was none the less greatly revered there.[1]

From his return to the south-west until 1708 Charles-Louis appears to have studied law at the University of Bordeaux.[2] His masters bore names well-known in Bordeaux's history, but their instruction was far from effective. A report on the faculty of Law in 1709[3] reveals that the Dean, Tanesse, was ninety-eight years of age, while his son, also a professor, was an absentee. D'Albessard, of an old legal family which will enter Montesquieu's life again, was eighty and blind, and his lectures were dictated by a student. Blaise Fresquet, the first professor of French law, which was a new subject in the University and had been but recently introduced by order of Louis XIV,[4] appointed as his deputy an Irishman innocent of all acquaintance with the French language. The instruction received by Charles-Louis at Bordeaux, where in 1708 he took the degrees of bachelor and *licencié* and was admitted advocate, can hardly have been adequate and it is comprehensible that he should now leave Bordeaux to seek practical experience of the law in Paris.

III. INTRODUCTION TO PARIS

The young man's stay in Paris, which appears to have lasted from 1709 to 1713, is the least known period of his life. Not a single letter from these years survives, either written or received by Montesquieu, and it is only from isolated comments contained in his notebooks that it is possible tentatively to reconstruct

[1] E.-A. Blampignon, *Etude sur Malebranche*, Paris, 1841, p. 6; Sainte-Beuve, *Port-Royal*, Paris (Bibliothèque de la Pléiade), 1953–5, III, pp. 359–60.

[2] R. Céleste, 'Montesquieu à Bordeaux' (*Deux opuscules de Montesquieu*, Bordeaux and Paris, 1891), pp. 67–68.

[3] Laplace (intendant) to Contrôleur-général, 5 October 1709 (*Correspondance des contrôleurs-généraux des finances*, ed. A. M. de Boislisle and P. de Bretonne, Paris, 1897, III, pp. 227–8).

[4] *Statuts et règlements de l'ancienne université de Bordeaux 1441–1793*), ed. H. Barckhausen, Libourne and Bordeaux, 1886, pp. 89–92; and cf. A. de Curzon, *L'Enseignement du droit français dans les universités de France aux XVIIe et XVIIIe siècles*, Paris, 1920.

in a very limited way the society in which he lived. He returned to Paris before the end of the decade, possibly for a few months early in 1717, possibly on other occasions also, though for not more than short visits.

His mentor in Parisian society appears to have been Pierre-Nicolas Desmolets. This amiable and learned cleric, whose father was known to Montesquieu, was born in 1678, and in 1701, while the future author of the *Lettres persanes* was still at Juilly, became a priest of the Oratory. He may well, for a time, have taught at Juilly, and it was doubtless there that he made the acquaintance of Montesquieu. He was a man of solid learning. Succeeding the bibliographer Lelong as librarian of the Paris Oratory, he edited at different times two journals, the more important, entitled *Continuation des mémoires de littérature*, revealing to the reading public new, rare and important documents. It was Desmolets who here, for the first time, published two works of Pascal, *De l'esprit géométrique* and the *Entretien avec M. de Sacy*, and his contribution to the history of literature was a great one. He was a broad-minded, tolerant man, able to close his eyes, as Montesquieu was to discover to his advantage, to the short-comings of his fashionable friends.

One of the first services rendered by Desmolets to the young Montesquieu was to lend to him a scrapbook containing the most diverse information on innumerable topics, grave and gay alike. Montesquieu caused extracts from this collection to be copied out at the beginning of a large quarto volume. It contains scientific notes on the thermometer and the barometer, on rainfall, mines, vegetation; historical notes on religious orders, Mahomet, Roman dress and currency, on slavery and on the foundation of Christ Church; extracts from the writings of the ancients; a lampoon on Madame de Maintenon; a long discussion of quietism, and several paragraphs on religious doctrine. This *recueil* was made no later than 1715 and probably a little earlier, and having received it, Montesquieu continued to add to it from his own reading. He gave to it the title of *Spicilège* and continued to make entries in it until almost the end of his life.[1]

It is the *Spicilège* that discloses that Montesquieu from time to time attended, during these early years in Paris, meetings of

[1] The *Spicilège* remained unknown until 1944, and is the most useful recently published collection of material on Montesquieu's life and works.

two of the royal academies. The Académie des Sciences and the Académie des Inscriptions held two public meetings each year, after Easter and in November after the feast of St. Martin, at which it was customary for the perpetual secretary to deliver a eulogy of any academician recently dead. Montesquieu specifically refers to having been present on one of these occasions, and references to other *éloges* make it probable that he was present on two others. The meetings in question were the November sessions of each academy in 1712, when he heard the *éloge* of the antiquary Tallemant in the Académie des Inscriptions and that of the renowned astronomer Cassini in the Académie des Sciences.[1] The *éloge* of the botanist Blondin he certainly heard in 1713, the date of that session of the Académie des Sciences being Wednesday, 15 November.[2] Since Montesquieu was not, and never became, a member of either of these academies, it is unlikely that he had access to their private meetings; but a detailed account of a paper read on 26 January, 1717, found in the *Spicilège* at a time when the paper in question had not yet been published, suggests that his contacts with academic circles were close enough for him to be acquainted with their major occupations. Both the academies were in fact passing through a phase of appreciable activity. In the Académie des Sciences, though the great days of Huygens and Cassini were ended, astronomy was still advanced by La Hire and Cassini's son. Varignon was busy with mathematical topics, and Réaumur, later to become Montesquieu's friend, was beginning his distinguished career with papers on the most varied of subjects, from geometrical theorems to the ancient problem of the blue dye to be found in the ocean. The Académie des Inscriptions was debating such questions as the history of the Vestal Virgins, and the prodigies of the ancient world. The perpetual secretaries of the two academies were Fontenelle and Gros de Boze, both of them eventually well-known to Montesquieu. Available evidence does not disclose whether he had made the acquaintance of either of them at this time, though it is certainly likely that he already knew Fontenelle. But at a quite early date he knew Nicolas Fréret.[4] Parisian by

[1] *Spicilège* 25 and 260 (MS., pp. 204 and 206–8).
[2] Ibid., 263 (MS., pp. 209–10).
[3] Ibid., 259 (MS., p. 206).
[4] *Eloge*, in *Œuvres complètes de Fréret*, ed. Leclerc de Septchênes, Paris, 1796, 20 vols., I, pp. 1–54.

birth, scholarly by temperament, Fréret had been a pupil of Rollin, and was ardently working on problems of ancient history, archaeology, and chronology. He is said by the age of sixteen to have read and made notes on the works of Scaliger, Dodwell, Petavius and Usher. By 1709 (he was born in 1688) he was actively producing memoirs on Greek mythology, and in 1714 he was admitted with the status (appropriate, it was thought, to his age but not to his reputation) of pupil, to the Académie des Inscriptions. Later, he was to be recognized as one of the most learned men of the age, displaying vast erudition in such fields as oriental religion and ancient chronology; but in his youth Fréret was a controversial figure and a man of advanced views. Even the Bastille was not unknown to him. Denounced by the historian Vertot for writing against the Bull *Unigenitus*, and for delivering a notorious critique—of which Montesquieu was later to copy an analysis into the *Spicilège*[1]—of the Jesuit Daniel's *Histoire de France*, he spent the first six months of 1715 in confinement.[2] Montesquieu knew Fréret in 1716 at the latest,[3] probably through Desmolets, and their friendship shows that Montesquieu was associating, at this very early stage of his career, with the pioneers of the Enlightenment.

These pioneers did not content themselves with audacious ideas, but devoted themselves often to the serious study of the most recondite subjects. Fréret's chosen field of specialization was China. Not only did he learn Chinese, but made plans actually to visit China in 1714. Although unable to realize this project, he had frequent contact with the Chinese, and when a young Chinese Christian named Arcadio Hoange or Hoam-gé visited France, Fréret became his friend. Hoange was placed in charge of Chinese books at the Bibliothèque du Roi, and Fréret introduced him into the intellectual society of Paris. It was in this way that Montesquieu met Hoange. The *Spicilège* contains a report of a conversation in which Hoange expressed his naïve astonishment on discovering that crime and punishments existed in Europe.[4] In his notebook *Geographica tome II*, moreover, Montesquieu

[1] *Spicilège* 585 (MS., pp. 539–42).

[2] F. Funck-Brentano, *Les Lettres de cachet à Paris*, Paris, 1903, no. 2282; A. Brûlé, 'Le P. Tournemine et l'arrestation de Fréret' (*RHLF*, 1932).

[3] Montesquieu to Desmolets, 4 April 1716.

[4] *Spicilège* 368 (MS., p. 326).

records in minute detail discussions he had had with Hoange.[1] Fascinated by the details of the religion of Confucius, baffled by the Chinese alphabet and grammar but making valiant efforts to understand them, noting the absolute nature of the royal power in China and the confusion of secular and religious authority, Montesquieu shows in these conversations the unflagging interest in the east which never left him.

Another man of vigorous and independent mind whom Montesquieu met about this time, and in this same society, was the Abbé Bernardo Lama.[2] Neapolitan by birth, he had hastened in his youth to Paris in order to make the acquaintance of Malebranche. His subsequent career was to take him to a chair at Turin, exile at Vienna, and finally to a chair at Naples. Montesquieu records conversations with him on ancient Greek historians, and on the establishment of the Old Testament canon, and this last subject Lama treated in a spirit quite other than reverential. Montesquieu also could learn from Lama that the Pope, in relation to other bishops, was no more than *primus inter pares*, that the Bull *Unigenitus* was deplorable and invalid, and that the Jesuits were enemies of the Gospel and followers of the devil.[3]

Montesquieu's acquaintance with the exponents of these daring and heterodox ideas is important in itself, but it is important also to his biographer because of another association to which it points: that with the Comte de Boulainvilliers.

Fréret was closely associated with the mysterious Boulainvilliers;[4] a recently discovered document in the Archives of Turin discloses that Lama's address in Paris was *chez Monsieur le comte de Boulainvilliers*.[5] The probability of Montesquieu's having known Boulainvilliers becomes a strong one, the more so since he cites some of Boulainvilliers's ideas before the works

[1] Nagel II, pp. 927–43; not in Pléiade. On Hoange, see especially A. Masson, Nagel II, pp. xxv–xxxi.

[2] Lama is referred to twice in the *Spicilège* (365 and 392, MS., pp. 324–5 and 336–7); both passages being prior to 1728 and contemporary with references to Fréret, they must refer to the period of Lama's stay in France, which ended in 1720. On Lama see F. Nicolini, *Un grande educatore italiano, Celestino Galiani*, Naples, 1951, and F. Venturi, *Saggi sull'Europa illuminista, I: Alberto Radicati di Passerano*, Turin, 1954.

[3] Venturi, op. cit., pp. 113–14.

[4] R. Simon, *Henry de Boulainviller*, Paris [1941], pp. 87–88.

[5] Venturi, op. cit., p. 111.

in which they were embodied had been published.[1] Belonging to a family of ancient lineage but little fortune, Boulainvilliers had an intellect which knew no limits. Held by some to have written the notorious *Traité des trois imposteurs*,[2] he was certainly the author of a life of Mahomet, and of a refutation of Spinoza which clarified rather than refuted his ideas.[3] A learned historian and a venturesome astrologer (which provoked from Fleury the sardonic comment, repeated by Montesquieu,[4] that he knew neither past, present, nor future), his almost legendary reputation spread even to the popular songs of his age,[5] and when he died in 1722, it was held even by the cynical Saint-Simon that he had predicted accurately the year, month, day and hour of his death.[6] His most enduring fame is owed to his theory of feudal origins, which he supported with immense learning. In his own day, his intellect was feared and his character praised, and years later Montesquieu was to pay him a warm tribute, the more telling since it was probably based on personal knowledge, in expressing his admiration for 'cette simplicité, cette franchise, et cette ingénuité de l'ancienne noblesse dont il était sorti'.[7]

IV. PRIVATE AND PUBLIC LIFE IN THE SOUTH-WEST

The death, at the age of fifty-eight, of his father called Montesquieu back to La Brède. He was still in Paris when his father died on 15 November 1713. On the next day Jacques de Secondat was interred in the village church, in his own pew near the lectern, beside his wife and his infant daughter Marianne, and in the presence of his kinsmen Loyac, Queynac, and Salligourde.[8] His

[1] *Spicilège* 364 (MS., p. 324).

[2] I. O. Wade, *The Clandestine Organisation and Diffusion of Ideas in France from 1700 to 1750*, Princeton, 1938, pp. 124–40.

[3] Marais to Bouhier, 4 May 1732 (*Journal et mémoires de Mathieu Marais*, ed. M. de Lescure, Paris, 1863–8, IV, pp. 360–1.

[4] *Pensée* 2156 (Bkn. 1346).

[5] *Chansonnier historique du XVIIIe siècle*, ed. E. Raunié, Paris, 1879–84, II, pp. 25 and 290.

[6] Saint-Simon, *Mémoires*, ed. A. M. de Boislisle, Paris, 1879–1930, XXVI, p. 248.

[7] *Lois*, XXX, 10.

[8] *Extrait d'état civil* (at La Brède); Arch. dép. Gironde, catalogue, série E. suppl., t. I, p. 211.

eldest son now came to take possession of his heritage.

Montesquieu—for so he had begun to call himself though his title was still Baron de La Brède—was a feudal proprietor of some substance, with seignorial rights and obligations; he was a qualified advocate; he was without parents and unmarried, and La Brède thus lacked a *châtelaine*. He was almost twenty-five, and it was time for him to settle down, and in particular for him to marry. Casting his eyes first on the daughter of a Bordeaux wine merchant named Denis,[1] he thought better of the project, and contracted instead a more dignified and perhaps not less lucrative alliance. His bride was Jeanne Lartigue or de Lartigue, and although there is controversy about her right to the particule, she is known to have belonged to a family recently ennobled and wealthy, living at Clairac, some ten miles from the hamlet of Montesquieu, and possessing also a house in the close vicinity of La Brède.[2] The marriage contract was signed at Clairac on 11 March 1715, and made over to the husband a dowry of 100,000 *livres*, and on 30 April following the wedding was celebrated at Bordeaux in the church of Saint-Michel.[3] The ceremony was quiet and inconspicuous, one of the witnesses being illiterate, and not even the closest relatives of either bride or bridegroom were present. Jeanne de Lartigue was in fact a Huguenot, and remained loyal to the reformed faith until her death. The marriage seems to have had but a meagre basis of affection. Montesquieu's fortune was strengthened, and he acquired a mother for his children and an efficient steward for his estates.

The following year, on 10 February, a son was born to them, and was given the name Jean-Baptiste; he was followed, on 22 May 1717, by a daughter Marie-Catherine, and another daughter, Marie-Josèphe-Denise, known as Denise, was born in 1727.

Soon after the birth of his son, a great change took place in the fortunes of Montesquieu. This was brought about by the death of his uncle Jean-Baptiste, who was head of the family and had inherited from his father both the barony of Montesquieu and the office of president in the Parlement of Bordeaux. He was

[1] A. Grellet-Dumazeau, *La Société bordelaise sous Louis XV*, Bordeaux and Paris, 1897, p. 70, n. 1, citing a manuscript *sottisier*, now lost, belonging to the counsellor Raoul.

[2] E. de Perceval, loc. cit.

[3] The entry in the church register is reproduced in J. Starobinski, *Montesquieu par lui-même*, Paris, 1953, p. 7.

childless, and his will, dated 11 January 1716,[1] after bequests to his sister and to his three-surviving brothers, all of them ecclesiastics, left his entire fortune to his nephew Charles-Louis. On 24 April 1716[2] the uncle died, and was succeeded in his estates, his title, and his office by his nephew.[3]

Montesquieu's territorial interests thus received an eastward extension into the area of the middle Garonne and the Lot; the hamlet of Montesquieu fell into his personal possession; his wife's family at Clairac, and the family of his third cousin Godefroy, Baron de Montagnac, later to marry his daughter Denise, became his neighbours. But more important that these accessions of fortune was Montesquieu's entry into the office of *président à mortier* in the Parlement of Bordeaux.

The *parlements* of France were institutions of considerable antiquity. Each was manned by a *premier président*, several *présidents à mortier*, and a considerable number of counsellors. The *premier président* was a royal nominee, but the office of *président à mortier*, so called from the flat-topped cylindrical hat, resembling a mortar board, which was the official headgear, was a hereditary and marketable commodity, which brought its owner a moderate income and considerable prestige. The less elevated post of counsellor was likewise bought and sold. The first in rank of the *parlements* was that of Paris, which shared a vigorous corporate consciousness with the provincial courts. Originally established as sovereign courts of law, the *parlements* began to arrogate to themselves political functions, and this happened early enough for Machiavelli to be able to describe them as the guardians of the fundamental laws and institutions of the French monarchy.[4] In the seventeenth and eighteenth centuries, the desuetude of the States-General caused the political significance of the *parlements* inevitably to increase.

The fourth in seniority of the *parlements* was that of Guyenne,

[1] A copy is preserved in the archives of La Brède.

[2] *Registre secret du Parlement de Bordeaux* (*recueil Verthamon*) (Arch. mun. Bx), vol. 41, p. 502.

[3] Documents preserved in the archives of La Brède show the extent to which this succession strengthened Montesquieu's financial position. From different friends he borrowed 2,000 *livres* in 1714, 9,000 in 1715, and 9,000 again (of which 6,000 were lent by La Caze, *premier président* or a relative of the *premier président* of that name) in 1716. This total sum of 20,000 he repaid in its entirety by the end of 1720.

[4] *Discorsi*, III, 1.

usually known as the Parlement of Bordeaux. Founded by Louis XI in 1462, its sway extended from Limoges to Bayonne. It was divided into five chambers, and comprised at the eve of the Revolution no fewer than nine *présidents à mortier* and ninety-one counsellors.[1] Its routine legal functions were intricate and extensive, since in addition to French law and Roman law, it administered several customary systems, and the office of president was far from being a sinecure. But the Parlement of Bordeaux was by no means a docile legal tribunal. During the agitation of the Fronde it had been exiled to Agen. Returning to Bordeaux in 1654, it enjoyed twenty years of relative tranquillity, but when the fiscal policy of the government provoked agitation and rioting in Bordeaux, it was once more expelled, and from 1675 held its sessions first at Condom, then at Marmande, and finally (for twelve years) in the diminutive town of La Réole. It was during the exile of the Parlement that Montesquieu's uncle Jean-Baptiste became *président à mortier* in succession to his father, and began a magisterial career of great distinction. After the reconciliation of the Parlement with Louis XIV in 1690 (effected by its agreement to establish a new presidency and six new counsellorships, and to sell them for 400,000 *livres* for the benefit of the government), there were sufficient internal troubles to keep him preoccupied. It was before him, in 1703, that Dalon, the newly nominated *premier président*, took the oath; and ten years later, when the same Dalon was dispossessed by royal order,[2] it was he who presided over the company during the vacancy. When Dalon's successor, the Marquis de La Caze, took office in 1714, it was once again Montesquieu's uncle who presided over the ceremony and pronounced a speech, which survives in a manuscript copy in his nephew's hand, and which is eloquent, loyal both to the monarch and to the Parlement, and showing a true love of justice.[3] Its author has been described, in words undoubtedly inspired by

[1] A. Communay, *Le Parlement de Bordeaux*, Bordeaux, 1886, p. 4. The most complete authority is C.-B.-F. Boscheron des Portes, *Histoire du Parlement de Bordeaux*, Bordeaux, 1878, 2 vols.

[2] Uncertainty about the nature of Dalon's transgression is dispelled by an unpublished passage in the memoir on Montesquieu by his son, contained in the archives of La Brède: 'le premier président . . . vendait la justice et s'était vendu à la faveur et . . . pour sauver sa tête fut obligé de se démettre de sa charge'.

[3] Pléiade II, pp. 1441–2; not in Nagel. The MS. is in the Bibliothèque de l'Université de Paris (*fonds* V. Cousin, V, no. 34).

Montesquieu, as "un des plus beaux génies et peut-être l'homme le plus libre et le plus juste de son temps.'[1]

The discussions provoked by the Bull *Unigenitus* of 1713, from which the Parlement of Bordeaux was bold enough, under the guidance of Montesquieu's uncle, to excise an article,[2] the death of Louis XIV and the Regent's initially conciliatory attitude to the *parlements*, whose help he needed to quash that monarch's will, strengthened and encouraged the members of the *parlementaire* class. They display a zealous devotion to their privileges which they often equate with the rights of the people; they insist on the right of presenting remonstrances to the King; they argue that the King, not less than the people, is bound by fundamental laws of great antiquity; they profess Gallican and often Jansenist sympathies. They are beginning a period of activity and enthusiasm, when Montesquieu becomes one of them.

He had already been appointed counsellor on 24 February 1714, being on the same day dispensed from the prohibition imposed by his being related to a president.[3] Two years later he succeeded to the presidency on the death of his uncle, secured a dispensation from the age limit,[4] sold his counsellorship,[5] and (in July 1716) took the oath.

Montesquieu was not unprepared for legal office. Later in his life he declared that he had studied law unceasingly:

> Au sortir du collège on me mit dans les mains des livres de droit; j'en cherchai l'esprit, je travaillai, je ne faisais rien qui vaille.[6]

A nineteenth-century visitor to La Brède discovered there, along with a variety of legal extracts, a manuscript essay, now lost, on the mode of studying jurisprudence;[7] and there still survive six

[1] Secondat, *Mémoire*, p. 397.

[2] No. XCI, dealing with unjust excommunication. (Boscheron des Portes, op. cit., I, pp. 258–9).

[3] Arch. dép. Gironde, catalogue, série B, p. 154.

[4] Ibid., p. 156. The rule required presidents to be forty years of age, or to have ten years' standing as counsellors.

[5] Ibid., p. 157. The purchaser was Pierre-François de La Salle de Canens.

[6] Montesquieu to Solar, 7 March 1749.

[7] M. Labat, 'Le Château de La Brède' (*Recueil des travaux de la Société d'agriculture, sciences, et arts d'Agen*, III, 1834, p. 183). The following extract from the essay, given by Labat, has never appeared in the works of Montesquieu: 'Quand on a appelé d'un juge à un autre, c'est un grand abus de permettre de recourir à un troisième, parce que l'esprit de l'homme est fait de manière qu'il

quarto volumes, almost entirely in Montesquieu's own hand, of notes on Roman law, entitled *Collectio juris.*[1] The closely written pages of these notebooks contain detailed analyses of the *Digest*, the *Code*, and the first of the *Novellae*. There is no commentary. Nowhere is there any trace of a personal opinion of Montesquieu. Though occasionally reproducing an observation by the seventeenth-century jurist Mornac, whose works he possessed in an edition of 1660, ordinarily he contents himself with the bare, factual analysis of the text. In the middle of the last volume, however, he abandons the *Corpus iuris civilis* to give accounts of several cases which had claimed his attention. Such headings are to be read as 'Entre M. de La Cour des Bois maître des requêtes et M. de Vauvré' and 'Entre l'archevêque de Reims d'une part . . . et les moines de l'Abbaie de Saint-Remy de Reims de l'autre'. He copies out an extract from the custom of Brittany. He enumerates various legal maxims. He reports several cases which came before him in the Parlement of Bordeaux. There is abundant testimony of the seriousness with which he gave his mind to the duties of his legal office.

Montesquieu, none the less, was not a great magistrate. There are but three remembered interventions by him in the affairs of the Parlement. One of these was a rhetorical exercise consisting of a formal speech at the opening session of 1725;[2] one is the act less of a magistrate than of a wine-grower, when happening to be in Paris he represents to the government the Parlement's opposition to a proposed tax on wine;[3] the third is a claim which he made, in 1721, for himself and his colleagues, that *présidents à mortier* should in no case be compelled to attend afternoon sessions.[4] He was indeed unhappy in court; some years later he writes:

Quant à mon métier de président, j'avais le cœur très droit; je

n'aime pas à suivre les idées des autres, qu'il se porte naturellement à réformer ce qui a été fait par ceux à qui il croit des lumières inférieures. Multipliez les degrés des tribunaux, vous les verrez moins occupés à rendre la justice aux citoyens qu'à se corriger les uns les autres.'

[1] These are now in the Bibliothèque Nationale, where they have the shelf-mark n.a.f. 12837–42.

[2] Nagel III, pp. 209–19; Pléiade I, pp. 44–52.

[3] Boscheron des Portes, II, pp. 248–9; Montesquieu to Gillet de La Caze, February 1723.

[4] Ibid., II, pp. 247–8.

comprenais assez les questions en elles-mêmes; mais, quant à la procédure, je n'y entendais rien. Je m'y étais pourtant appliqué; mais, ce qui m'en dégoûtait le plus, c'est que je voyais à des bêtes ce même talent qui me fuyait, pour ainsi dire.[1]

Montesquieu's legal office was important, not in itself, but for the dignity and status which it gave him.

It was important especially because it enabled him to meet and form a friendship with the Duke of Berwick.

This brave and dignified nobleman, natural son of James II of England, was a cosmopolitan figure. A general in the English and Spanish armies, and a Marshal of France, a duke in the English and French peerages, and a grandee of Spain, he was at home anywhere in western Europe. Exiled from England, he awaited the return of the Stuarts, says Saint-Simon, as the Jews await their Messiah.[2] Living in France, he was a prominent figure at court, and a much respected man. In 1716 he was appointed military governor of Guyenne, and came to Bordeaux to take up his command. He continued to hold this appointment until early in 1724, but did not reside continuously after 1719.[3]

Montesquieu narrates in the usually more arid pages of his *Collectio juris* a visit paid by Berwick to the Parlement of Bordeaux on 12 November 1717.[4] The Marshal, although he had already been present three times at meetings of the Parlement, was uncertain of procedure, and in passing into the council chamber took precedence of the *présidents à mortier*. The company debated this breach of protocol, and charged the *premier président* with the task of drawing the Marshal's attention to this innovation. Berwick replied that he was very sorry, and that since he had done this in public he would find an occasion of repairing his offence in public. Ten days later, he attended the Parlement again, and gave way to the *présidents à mortier*. On later occasions he had more serious and less easily repaired quarrels with the Parlement. Neither military training nor Stuart blood could equip a man to deal with a self-conscious legal assembly. But his personal relations were more happy. It is Montesquieu himself who in an *éloge* of Berwick describes the impression he made in Bordeaux: modesty

[1] *Pensée* 213 (Bkn. 4).
[2] Saint-Simon, *Mémoires*, ed. Boislisle, XIX, p. 377.
[3] See Sir Charles Petrie, *The Marshal Duke of Berwick*, London, 1953.
[4] VI, f.141v.

and severity, good sense and balance, tranquillity and happiness, were his characteristics. It was impossible to see him and not to love virtue.[1]

Montesquieu praises also his loyalty to his friends, and indeed profited from that quality. The prestige of a royal friend helped Montesquieu greatly in his travels, and also in his entry into Parisian society. If there is a great difference between the obscurity of his early visits to Paris, and his penetration in the 1720s into the society of the court, it is the patronage and support of Berwick which is mainly responsible.

V. THE ACADEMY OF BORDEAUX

Legal and social life had not prevented Montesquieu from having literary and intellectual ambitions, and from seeking tentatively to realize them. In 1711 he had written a treatise, now lost, or surviving at most in fragments,[2] on the idolatry of the pagans, in which, doubtless under the influence of Bayle, he sought to show that they did not merit eternal damnation.[3] He had written also, probably about the same time, an essay on Cicero which, though it is a simple eulogy, is interesting in that it praises Cicero for his attacks on superstition and for his support of liberty against the tyrant Caesar.[4] Of a different nature is a *Mémoire sur les dettes de l'Etat*, composed late in 1715 or soon after, and addressed to the Regent.[5] Here Montesquieu examines the problem of the indebtedness of the State, and seeks to devise a method of reducing the national debt without increasing taxation. The method proposed is ingenious. He advocates a partial repudiation of the debt by means of a capital levy, the amount to be confiscated from each individual varying inversely with the proportion of his holding of government stock, so that a man who has three-quarters of his wealth in public funds will lose a quarter of that holding, while a man who has only one-quarter of his capital so placed will lose three-quarters of that amount. To this is added a compulsory conversion scheme based on the acceptance of the fact that government stock has fallen to 50 per cent. of the

[1] Nagel III, pp. 392–4; Pléiade II, pp. 1230–1.
[2] *Pensée* 1946 (Bkn. 673). [3] Secondat, *Mémoire*, p. 397.
[4] Nagel III, pp. 15–21; Pléiade I, pp. 93–98.
[5] Nagel III, pp. 24–31; Pléiade I, pp. 66–71.

par value. The memoir is interesting particularly in view of its refusal to countenance any increase in taxation and its willingness to accept the notion of repudiation of the debt. It stands alone as Montesquieu's only political writing of this period of his life.[1]

Intellectual life in Bordeaux, in the early years of the century, was becoming organized. A number of magistrates and literati had been in the habit of meeting in one another's houses in order to hear music and to discuss the progress of literature. Their gatherings soon began to assume a scientific rather than a literary basis, and in due course, inspired by the example of the Paris Académie des Sciences and the newly founded academies at Montpellier and Toulouse, they sought letters-patent from the crown. These were granted in 1712, and the Academy of Bordeaux was constituted.[2] Its original members were De Gascq, *président à mortier* in the Parlement, Le Berthon, counsellor, in 1715 *président à mortier*, and in 1735 *premier président* of the Parlement, Caupos, César and Navarre who were counsellors, Melon who was *inspecteur des fermes*, and two brothers, patrons of literature and music, Sarrau de Boynet and Sarrau de Vésis. It is not surprising that Montesquieu was soon thought of as a possible member, and indeed, on 3 April 1716, the 'Sieur de La Brède' was elected on the motion of Navarre, who was then acting as secretary, and who had known Montesquieu since their schooldays at Juilly.[3]

The new member passed into a society which was by no means strange to him; but he made two acquaintances of particular importance. The first of these was Melon, who was by no means an unknown figure. He was to become secretary to the Scotsman John Law, who was minister of finance, and later, in his *Essai politique sur le commerce* of 1734, was to establish his reputation as an economist. His influence on the work of Montesquieu was appreciable. The other significant acquaintance was Dortous de Mairan, a native of Béziers, who stood at the threshold of a

[1] It is possible that the *Mémoire sur la Constitution Unigenitus* was written, or drafted, in 1717, but M. Védère's reasons for attributing it to a much later moment in Montesquieu's career seem to me valid (Nagel III, pp. 269–71).

[2] See P. Barrière, *L'Académie de Bordeaux*, Bordeaux and Paris, 1951, based on a study of the voluminous archives of the Academy, which are preserved in the Bibliothèque municipale of Bordeaux.

[3] P. Courteault, *Un ami bordelais de Montesquieu*, Bordeaux, 1938.

scientific career of great eminence. A young man with whom Malebranche himself had not disdained to correspond, he won the Academy's prizes in three successive years and was admitted to associate membership in 1717 in order (it was said) to prevent him from competing for any more. His progress to fame was rapid. In 1718 he moved to Paris and was rapidly elected to the Académie des Sciences where he was eventually to succeed Fontenelle as perpetual secretary. Montesquieu's election to the Academy of Bordeaux thus gave him the friendship of a prominent figure in the society of the metropolis.

On 18 April 1716, Montesquieu was installed as a member of the Academy, and on the same day delivered a *discours de réception* which is in no way memorable. His first paper to the Academy was read on 18 June 1716, and is entitled *Dissertation sur la politique des Romains dans la religion.* Inspired in part, without doubt, by his conversations with Fréret, but also by the *Discorsi* of Machiavelli, this treatise is one of the most interesting of the minor works of Montesquieu. Its opening words illustrate Montesquieu's concern, maintained throughout his life, with religion as a social phenomenon:

> Ce ne fut ni la crainte ni la piété qui établit la religion chez les Romains, mais la nécessité où sont toutes les sociétés d'en avoir une.[1]

He takes this idea further in a passage quoted, as Bayle before him had quoted it, from the *De civitate Dei*, in which Saint Augustine records the aphorism of Scaevola, that there are three kinds of gods, those established by poets, those established by philosophers, and those established by magistrates.[2]

This dissertation was received with no more than very moderate enthusiasm[3] by the Academy, whose interests were much more scientific than historical or philosophical. There had, indeed, been a proposal by Navarre, in 1715, that the work of the Academy should be systematically planned, each member undertaking certain specific fields of investigation. He envisaged the natural and literary history of Guyenne as the framework and the objective

[1] Nagel III, p. 38; Pléiade I, p. 81.

[2] Cf. P. Bayle, *Continuation des Pensées diverses*, Rotterdam, 1705 (the edition possessed by Montesquieu), I, p. 225. See my article 'Bayle and Montesquieu' (*Pierre Bayle, le philosophe de Rotterdam*, ed. P. Dibon, Amsterdam, etc., 1959).

[3] Barrière, op. cit., pp. 59–60.

of their labours, and though his aim was never realized, it remained as an ideal and a stimulus throughout the century, and a personal responsibility was placed on members to prosecute work of their own. This work proved in the majority of cases to be scientific, and Montesquieu, abandoning for the present political and historical writing, turned to science himself. On 28 September 1716, he founded an annual prize of 300 *livres* for anatomical research,[1] and, perhaps in some measure as a recompense for this benefaction, he was selected to be *directeur* of the Academy for the year 1718, although there were two founder members, Navarre and Melon, still active in the Academy, who had not held that office.

Montesquieu's first duty as *directeur* was to pronounce the *discours de la rentrée* on his entry into office in November 1717. His speech was eloquent and polished, but has no great merit. Its most interesting passage expresses an opinion to which he is consistently faithful in his mature age: he castigates prejudices as 'ces véritables monstres de l'esprit.'[2] Experimentalism and hatred of the *a priori* and the undemonstrated in science were characteristic of the Academy. Sarrau de Boynet had already asserted: 'c'est à présent une espèce d'attentat que de vouloir soumettre les esprits, en matière de science, par les opinions des autres.'[3] Experiment and independence of judgement were prized by the Academy, and Montesquieu's mind was directed into a channel which it was not going to leave.

As *directeur* Montesquieu had to act as spokesman for his colleagues in assessing the entries for the prize competitions which were held from time to time; also it fell to him from time to time to give a summary or a *résomption* of communications submitted to the Academy by its members. Several of these short discourses survive, treating such subjects as the cause of echo, the function of renal glands, the transparency of bodies, and the causes of weight. If they disclose no original thought on the part of their author, at least they show his willingness seriously to inform himself about problems which were strange to him.

More ambitious intentions are revealed by a notice published in 1719 in the *Mercure* and the *Journal des savants*, announcing an *Histoire de la terre ancienne et moderne* which was being prepared

[1] This was converted in 1719 into a prize for physics.

[2] Nagel III, p. 52; Pléiade I, p. 7.

[3] Barrière, op. cit., p. 145.

at Bordeaux. An annotation reported as appearing on some manuscript fragments, now lost,[1] suggests that this was envisaged as a personal work of Montesquieu, not as a collective enterprise of the Academy; but information from all parts of the world was solicited, and was to be addressed to Montesquieu. That a geological work of this scope should be envisaged thirty years before the appearance of Buffon's treatment of the same theme shows Montesquieu as a pioneer, at least so far as intentions were concerned; but the work never saw the light of day, and it is improbable that it was ever very far advanced.

The only remaining piece of scientific writing which came from Montesquieu's pen at this period of his life is more important. Known now under the title *Essai d'observations sur l'histoire naturelle*, it was read by its author to the Academy of Bordeaux on 20 November 1721. It relates experiments which Montesquieu had made at different moments during the three years preceding, assisted by his secretary the Abbé Duval.[2] These experiments, made both on animals and on plants, were rigorous and ruthless. In some cases, such as the vivisection of a frog, they were made with the assistance of a microscope; in others they involved the drowning of ducks and geese. In all cases they were undertaken with great seriousness. Montesquieu draws some general conclusions from his experiments, and in these he is seen to lean on the scientific pronouncements of others.[3] Discussing plants, which are the subject of his most interesting pronouncement, he asserts that they are nothing more

[1] Nagel III, p. 89.

[2] Duval had previously served Montesquieu's uncle Jean-Baptiste and witnessed his will. He was not Montesquieu's first secretary; the *Spicilège* shows the handwriting of another in its earlier pages; yet another, borrowed perhaps from the Academy or lent to the Academy, since his hand appears also in its archives, served Montesquieu between 1715 and 1726. From 1715 onwards Montesquieu appears never to have been without at least one secretary, except while travelling. See my article, 'Les Secrétaires de Montesquieu' (Nagel II, pp. xxxv–xliii).

[3] In one case he paradoxically inverts the ordinary opinion. Discussing the uniformity and diversity of nature, he discerns 'la variété dans la fin et la simplicité dans des moyens' (Nagel III, p. 109; Pléiade I, p. 37). The more usual view is that of Fontenelle: "on ne saurait guère attribuer à la nature trop d'uniformité dans les règles générales et trop de diversité dans les applications particulières" (*Histoire de l'Académie des Sciences*, 1702, p. 52). One is tempted to ask if Montesquieu is simply guilty of a slip of the pen which has been perpetuated by copyists and editors.

than the fortuitous result of the general movement of matter. He turns to this theme again, decrying those who oppose his view and insisting on the mechanical structure of the vegetable world. He proudly claims Descartes as his master, declaring:

> Ceux qui suivent l'opinion que nous embrassons peuvent se vanter d'être cartésiens rigides, au lieu que ceux qui admettent une providence particulière de Dieu dans la production des plantes, différente du mouvement général de la matière, sont des cartésiens mitigés qui ont abandonné la règle de leur maître.[1]

This is, in fact, less the doctrine of Descartes himself, who was not greatly concerned with plants, than of his successors.

La Hire the younger and Dodart (whose grandson was a friend of Montesquieu) fill many pages of the memoirs of the Académie des Sciences in the first decade of the century with detailed and systematic descriptions of the mechanical operations of plants. Fontenelle, summarizing a botanical paper by the younger Geoffroy, expresses the characteristic view:

> Les plus surprenantes variétés, dès qu'elles sont approfondies, n'attaquent point l'uniformité du système général de la nature.[2]

But it is the illustrious Malebranche who is the author of the opinions adopted by Montesquieu. The renowned son of the Oratory, in his *Entretiens sur la métaphysique*, distinguishes between *la providence générale* and *une providence extraordinaire*; the natural universe, in which he expressly includes the vegetable creation, taking many of his examples from plants, is governed only by the first of these, and the *lois générales des communications des movements*, which are a part of God's ordinary providence, control its daily operations.[3] To be a Cartesian, then, for Montesquieu in 1721, is to be a disciple of Malebranche; and a disciple of Malebranche who concentrated on the laws of movement, forgot the spirituality of the soul, and was very far from seeing all things in God, was accepting of Cartesianism that part which is philosophically and was historically most conducive to materialism. Montesquieu's mechanistic approach to biology, *a priori* in

[1] Nagel III, p. 112; Pléiade I, p. 39.

[2] *Histoire de l'Académie des Sciences*, 1711, p. 41.

[3] *10e entretien*, in *Œuvres*, ed. J. Simon, Paris, 1859, I, pp. 207–11, 223–4, and see P. Schrecker, 'Malebranche et le préformisme biologique' (*Revue internationale de philosophie*, 1938).

spite of his ostensible insistence on experiment, shows him to be a vigorous enemy of the teleological school in natural history, of which in the next decade the Abbé Pluche was to become the most popular exponent, and shows that in spite of tributes paid to providence he has something in common with the nascent materialism of the age.

II

LETTRES PERSANES, 1721

I. THE LITERARY TRADITION

MONTESQUIEU'S activities at Bordeaux, whether in the Parlement or in the Academy, offer no indication at all of unusual intellectual powers or literary skill. Other magistrates were more distinguished, and other academicians were more assiduous; and the public and disclosed occupations of Montesquieu during the first thirty-two years of his life give promise of nothing more than a respectable and useful provincial career. Privately, however, and unostentatiously, perhaps with the advice of two Bordeaux friends, Barbot and Jean-Jacques Bel,[1] he was engaged in the composition of a work, the publication of which in 1721 was to be a landmark not simply in the author's career but also in the history of French literature and of the whole movement of the Enlightenment.

It was probably soon after 1717 that Montesquieu began work on the *Lettres persanes*.[2] Either in 1720 (in summer or autumn) or the spring of 1721, he carried with him to Paris the completed manuscript, and showed it to his friend Desmolets. The broad-minded cleric read the manuscript and announced to Montesquieu, 'Président, cela sera vendu comme du pain.'[3] The Abbé Duval, Montesquieu's secretary, was despatched to Amsterdam,[4] where he found a publisher in Jacques Desbordes, a French Protestant whose family had left Bordeaux after the revocation of the Edict of Nantes. Desbordes, printing on the title page no author's name, a false place, and a non-existent publisher, brought out, in the spring or early summer of 1721, the first published work of Montesquieu, the *Lettres persanes*. It enjoyed at once an enormous success. Montesquieu himself reports that its sale was

[1] C. Denina, *La Prusse littéraire*, Berlin, 1790–1, I, p. 377, and *Discorso sopra le vicende della letteratura*, Turin, 1761, p. 142. D'Alembert goes so far as to claim that the printer had inserted some letters which were not by Montesquieu (*Eloge*, in Nagel I, A, p. vii), but Montesquieu's own writings offer no support for this view.

[2] See my article, 'The Moslem Chronology of the *Lettres persanes*' (*FS*, 1954).

[3] Guasco, *Lettres familières*, XIII.

[4] Ibid., II.

so great that the booksellers of Holland pulled by the sleeve everyone whom they met in the street, saying, 'Monsieur, faites-moi des *Lettres persanes*.'[1]

Usbek and Rica, two wealthy Persians, set off westwards from Ispahan in search of wisdom. Their journey is to last for ten years. They proceed by land to Smyrna, thence by sea to Leghorn, and from Leghorn to Paris, passing through Marseilles. They maintain a frequent correspondence with friends left behind in Persia, and also with their friend Rhedi, likewise travelling in Europe, though in different towns. In their letters, which are dated according to the Islamic calendar, they communicate their impressions of European society, drawing from time to time comparisons with Eastern usages and institutions, and thus presenting a novel satirical picture of France in the early eighteenth century. At the same time, especially in the early letters, written before they have left Asia, and in the abundant correspondence which Usbek maintains with the guardians of his harem, a detailed picture of oriental society is given to the western reader.

No literary work is made out of nothing; and no work so immediately successful as the *Lettres persanes*, of which some ten editions appeared in the first year, can constitute a complete break with all existing literary tradition. Montesquieu had a variety of antecedents. The most important of these, if the *Lettres persanes* be considered as a work of social description and satire, is *Les Caractères* of La Bruyère, itself the finest example of a literary *genre* which had already been illustrated by innumerable examples. Published for the first time in the year before the birth of Montesquieu. *Les Caractères* enjoyed a great vogue in the ensuing years. The fineness of its psychological analysis, the occasional salutary asperity of its judgements and the independence of its outlook make it a work still read for the excellence of its literary qualities and for its value as a document throwing light on the reign of Louis XIV.

The epistolary form which Montesquieu uses in the *Lettres persanes* was not new. Letters had played a great part in many of the prose romances written in France in the seventeenth century and even before, and sometimes these letters had been printed in separate volumes. Such was the case with the well-known story of *Amadis de Gaule*. As early as 1560 there was published

[1] *Pensée* 2033 (Bkn. 112).

Le Trésor des douze livres d'Amadis de Gaule, which contains the letters, speeches and harangues which are scattered throughout the original work. In 1616 the first publication of the works of Peter Abelard made known not only his theological and philosophical writings, but also his love letters to Eloisa, and these established a tradition of novels in letter form, of which Rousseau's *La Nouvelle Héloïse* is the culminating point, and of which the most significant example before Montesquieu is the *Lettres d'une religieuse portugaise*, published in 1669 and translated, it is claimed, by Lavergne de Guilleragues, who combined the distinctions of French ambassador at Constantinople and president of the Cour des Aides at Bordeaux.

The self-sufficient splendour of the reign of Louis XIV did not prevent an interest from developing in the civilizations and histories of the East.[1] The Koran was translated into French by Du Ryer in 1647, and his version was the principal form in which that work was known in Europe (apart from a Latin rendering published in 1698) until the English translation of George Sale in 1734. Montesquieu possessed Du Ryer's translation, and also an Italian version of the sixteenth century. In the course of the seventeenth century there appeared accounts of the travels of a number of European merchants, and to the present day these are an unfailing source of delight. Most prominent in their number are the voyages of Chardin and of Tavernier, both of them giving detailed and exact relations of the circumstances of travel and also of the civilization and history of the countries they traversed. Montesquieu possessed their works and leaned on them heavily for the oriental documentation of the *Lettres persanes*. The timetable of the itinerary of Usbek and Rica is based on Tavernier, while the Islamic dating of the letters follows the data afforded by Chardin.

The translation of the *Arabian Nights* by Galland, its publication beginning in 1704, stimulated French interest in exoticism. In the years following, there occurred a number of events likely to have provoked on the part of Montesquieu an interest in remote foreign lands, or to have predisposed public opinion in

[1] See on this subject P. Martino, *L'Orient dans la littérature française au dix-septième et au dix-huitième siècle*, Paris, 1906, and (dealing with a more limited aspect) M. L. Dufrenoy, *L'Orient romanesque en France (1704–1789)*, Montreal, 1946–7, 2 vols.

favour of the work he was to write. The first of these was the visit to Europe in 1710 of Te Yee Neen Ho Ga Prow, emperor of the Iroquois Indians, accompanied by three subordinate kings.[1] Their stay in Europe had great repercussions in the literature of the day, inspiring most notably an essay by Addison in No. 50 of the *Spectator*, on 27 April 1711, which contains a letter deemed to be written by one of the kings, satirically descriptive of English political life, and which was translated into French as early as 1714. In 1715 there arrived in Paris an ambassador sent by the Shah of Persia, and his odd demeanour and strange judgements on French life provoked the curiosity of the public.[2] Two years later Peter the Great arrived in person in Paris, and the French were enabled, as very few had been seen before, to set eyes on a Scythian despot. The *Spicilège* shows that this visit interested Montesquieu and the *Lettres persanes* themselves reflect the thoughts which it provoked.[3] Meanwhile Montesquieu, as has been seen, had made the acquaintance of the Chinese visitor Hoange and had by him been enabled to see France through foreign eyes.

Nor were there lacking, in the field of literature, examples of the technique of selecting a foreign basis for comparison. Pierre Bayle, in the second edition of his *Dictionnaire historique et critique* of 1702, had remarked[4] on the interest which would be found in an account of western civilization by a Japanese or a Chinese who had lived in Europe. Our Christian missionaries, he says, mock the usages of the primitive peoples of the East; but let them remember the words of Horace,

> Quid rides? mutato nomine de te
> Fabula narratur,

words which indeed might serve as epigraph for the *Lettres persanes*.

In 1708 Malebranche, much revered by Montesquieu, published his *Entretien d'un philosophe chrétien et d'un philosophe*

[1] R. P. Bond, *Queen Anne's American Kings*, Oxford, 1952.

[2] M. Herbette, *Une ambassade persane sous Louis XIV*, Paris, 1907.

[3] *Spicilège* 239 (MS., p. 180); *L.P.* 51, 81.

[4] s.v. Japon, rem. A. See J. Ray, 'Du *Dictionnaire* de Bayle aux *Lettres persanes*' (*Revue philosophique*, 1945), where it is claimed, with less than conclusive evidence, that Montesquieu had read this article and refers to it in *Pensée* 104 (Bkn. 1327).

chinois. Already under the false mantle of Saint-Evremond had appeared a *Lettre italienne écrite par un Sicilien à un de ses amis*,[1] in which a description of the Paris hospital for the blind in terms very close to those used in the 32nd *Lettre persane* suggests that it was known to Montesquieu. Already the entertaining pages of Dufresny's *Amusements sérieux et comiques*,[2] soon to be plagiarized in England by Tom Brown, had included a gay letter ostensibly written by a Siamese visitor to Paris. Already too there had been Persian letters, from the pen of J. F. Bernard, the title of whose work[3] suggests La Bruyère as his model, and by the unhappy Joseph Bonnet, whose *Lettre écrite à Musala*[4] caused its author to be imprisoned in the Bastille.

Montesquieu's intention may have been in part shaped by some or all of these works, and on some of them he most probably drew. But of greater moment than they, and of greater literary merit than any except the *Amusements sérieux et comiques*, is the celebrated and widely read collection of letters published by the Italian Giovanni Paolo Marana. In Italian known as *L'Esploratore turco*, in French as *L'Espion dans les cours*, this work in the many editions of its English translation was entitled *Letters writ by a Turkish Spy*. The Bibliothèque Nationale possesses a manuscript of the Italian text, its binding lavishly adorned with crescents and *fleurs-de-lis*; according to its dedication it was presented to Louis XIV as a genuine translation from the Arabic, discovered in 1683. The first edition appeared a year later, and it was forthwith translated into French. Its text consists of letters, deemed to be written by one Mahmoud who for forty-five years was a secret representative in Paris of the Sublime Porte. He was undiscovered in spite of his turban, and if the frontispiece is to carry authority

[1] Paris, 1700, attributed to Cotolendi.

[2] Paris, 1699. Certain passages of this work suggest that Montesquieu knew it, but they are not passages in the Siamese letter, and it is clearly an exaggeration to attribute to it a determining role in the genesis of the *Lettres persanes*.

[3] *Réflexions morales, comiques et satiriques sur les mœurs de notre siècle*, Cologne, 1715. Attention has been drawn to this work by G. L. Van Roosbroeck, *Persian Letters before Montesquieu*, New York, 1932, in which the text is partly republished. What is significant is that the letters are Persian. No sources can be established.

[4] Barbier knows two letters with this title, both of 1716; a third, without date, is to be found in the Bodleian. This last contains several resemblances in style and manner to Montesquieu (the Pope, for example, is called the Mufti of Rome); but there are no clear sources.

he inhabited a room lined with books in whose number the attentive eye can distinguish Tacitus, the Koran and Saint Augustine, and with a portrait of Masaniello, the Neapolitan fisherman and revolutionary, hanging on the wall.

The indebtedness of Montesquieu to Marana, asserted by Voltaire in *Le Siècle de Louis XIV*, was tacitly admitted already in 1721 when a reprint of the first edition declared itself, on the title-page, to be "dans le goût de l'*Espion dans les cours*.'[1] The affinity between Montesquieu and Marana is made sufficiently clear by such passages as this:

I hear the philosophers talk of immortality, the poets of Elysium, the Christian priests of heaven, hell, and purgatory, the Indians Brahmins of transmigration: but I know not what or which I have reason to believe of all these . . . I see men everywhere professing some religion or other, paying divine honours to some superior being or beings, according as they have been educated: which many times tempts me to think that religion is nothing but the effect of education . . .

When I behold mankind divided into so many innumerable different religions in the world, all vigorously propagating their own tenets, either by subtlety or violence, yet few or none seeming by their practice to believe what they with so much ardour profess, I could almost think that these various ways of worship were first invented by politicians, each accommodating his model to the inclinations of the people whom he designed to circumvent.[2]

The demonstration of an Italian scholar of the last century, Pietro Toldo, leaves little doubt of Montesquieu's debt to Marana,[3] and his argument is reinforced by the fact that Montesquieu is now known to have possessed the 1717 edition of *L'Espion dans les cours*.

One of the first characteristics which make the *Lettres persanes* significant in French literary history is the fidelity of the local colour in the picture they give of the East. The works of both Chardin and Tavernier, it has been seen, were possessed by Montesquieu, and were seriously used by him in the letters. Of Chardin he had two copies, the second and fuller edition being acquired, according to the bookseller's receipt which is preserved

[1] L. Vian, *Montesquieu: bibliographie de ses œuvres*, Paris, 1872, p. 7.

[2] *Letters writ by a Turkish Spy*, London, 1730, IV, pp. 163–4.

[3] 'Dell'*Espion* di Giovanni Paolo Marana e delle sue attinenze con le *Lettres persanes* del Montesquieu' (*Giornale storico della letteratura italiana*, 1897), substantiated by A. Adam (ed., *Lettres persanes*, Geneva and Lille, 1954).

at Bordeaux, between 10 May 1720, and 22 May 1722. He made extracts from Chardin and from the Koran, as well as an analysis of Brisson's *De regio Persarum principatu*. This last survives at La Brède, and is seen to be in the handwriting of Duval, while the others, now lost, were made at early date and in all probability during the preparation of the *Lettres persanes*.[1] The topography and religion of Persia and Asia Minor are accurately described, and the care with which oriental detail was studied by the author won for him the praise, which must be held authoritative, of no less renowned a traveller than Lady Mary Wortley Montagu:

> Montesquieu, in his *Persian Letters*, has described the manners and customs of the Turkish ladies as well as if he had been bred up among them.[2]

The development in France of what is known as *sensibilité* was appreciably advanced by the *Lettres persanes*. This was the cult of passion in literature, the creation and study of situations in which passion was unrestrained, blindly following its own course. Various ethical notions from time to time accompanied this interest in passion: the belief that passion was natural and that what was natural could not be wrong; the insistence that passionate self-expression was the chief good; that the greatest men are those who have the most violent passions. *Sensibilité* so understood is in the main a phenomenon later than the *Lettres persanes*. Its main exponents in France are Prévost, Rousseau and Diderot, while the ethical ideas associated with it are expressed by them and by Helvétius. These writers are the pre-Romantics of the eighteenth century, the precursors of Victor Hugo and of Stendhal. But before them there are writers to whom can be attributed *un cœur sensible*. There is Racine, in whom, however, as was fitting in even a lapsed pupil of the solitaries of Port-Royal, the force of violent passion was never vested with moral worth. There is Madame de La Fayette; but love for her was austere and controlled; there is Fénelon, for whom however passion was sublimated into religious zeal. The most significant forerunners of the *Lettres persanes* from the point of view of *sensibilité* are the *Aloysia Sigea* of Chorier, written in Latin but translated into French with the title of *Académie des dames*[3] and

[1] *Pensée* 41 (Bkn. 1761).
[2] Joseph Spence, *Anecdotes*, ed. S. W. Singer, London, 1820, p. 230.
[3] See A. Adam, op. cit., p. xxvi.

the scurrilous though not ill written *Vénus dans le cloître, ou la Religieuse en chemise.* This latter work, by the Abbé Barrin, which Montesquieu was later to buy in English translation, contains some serious study of the relationship between the passions and the body; but it is so written that when it leaves the borderline between the decent and the indecent, it is to plunge on to the pornographic side. The *Lettres persanes* are concerned, in the passages dealing with the harem, with the same kind of theme, and this is an essential part of the work. It is these passages which provide a framework and a plot, and it is this same spirit which characterizes the several *récits* or stories within the story, formal survivals of what had been a popular device in seventeenth-century novels and died hard in the age of Marivaux and Lesage. The sixth letter shows Montesquieu's interest in the psychology of jealousy, letter 67 examines the notion of incest, while frequently throughout the book there is discussion of the harem and of the reactions of eunuchs. In all these various preoccupations, the confines of the decent and the indecent are Montesquieu's country; but more restrained and more skilful than the author of *Vénus dans le cloître*, he never transgresses the border of decency. The emotional part of the *Lettres persanes* is handled by Montesquieu in such a way that he was able, at least in the rakish society of the Orléans Regency, to make *sensibilité* respectable, to give it *droit de cité* in literature. He was certainly not the first author of an almost licentious work to be elected to the Academy, which he was to join in 1728; but was the first whose sole claim was constituted by such a work.

II. SOCIETY AND GOVERNMENT

Rica describes to an unnamed friend, in letter 132, a visit which he had paid to a café and the people whom he had met there. There was an impecunious country gentleman visiting Paris, who deplored the fate which compelled him to live in the provinces on his illusory *quinze mille livres de rente*, a character whom Montesquieu doubtless depicted with sympathy. There was a Parisian who lamented his poverty, for though he had in his house vast sums in banknotes and in coin, he possessed no real estate and craved for a small property in the country. A genealogist and an old soldier complete the company, along with a philosopher who was plunged into dismay by the appearance of a sunspot. This gallery of despondents, for only the genealogist was happy, is briefly described by Rica in simple, sardonic detail. Elsewhere in the work there are descriptions, from his pen or from Usbek's, of tax-farmers, of journalists, of translators, of Jesuits, and inevitably of doctors. These portraits are all satirical and at least moderately hostile: there is no description of the *honnête homme.* There are comments on social institutions, on the theatre, on card-playing; there is a discussion of fashion. There is a comment on the Quarrel of Ancients and Moderns; there is a hostile description of the French Academy. There are cynical observations on the relations between husbands and wives. It is this aspect of the *Lettres persanes* which evokes the recollection of La Bruyère, not because the comments are the same—Montesquieu, for example, was on the other side in the Quarrel of Ancients and Moderns—but because of the subjects treated. The social criciticism in the *Lettres persanes*, however, goes on to take a form which it did not assume in *Les Caractères.* La Bruyère does not depict by name specific individuals living in his own day. Montesquieu on the other hand does this readily, and the political history of France during the nominal period of the letters, from 1711 to 1720, is clearly reflected in the *Lettres persanes.* The Persian envoy in Moscow writes to Usbek a description of the character of the Tsar Peter; Rica gives a brief account of Charles XII of Sweden; Usbek refers to Prince Eugene as the Grand Vizir of Germany. After Usbek has declared in letter 37 that no form of government would please Louis XIV better than that of the Turks, Rica asserts in letter 107 that that monarch was entirely governed by women. In letter 92, meanwhile, a description is given of the struggle for power which occurred when he died. The Regent is at this stage praised for the favour he showed initially to the Parlement of Paris; but in letter 140 the banishment of that body to Pontoise is alluded to in terms which could give no pleasure to Orléans.

Nor does Montesquieu limit himself to commenting on the political events and the manners of his age. He is emboldened to comment on religious and philosophical problems, and to examine questions of legal and political theory. It is true that La Bruyère does this also. It has been found possible to construct what is almost a system of social and political thought from *Les Caractères*.[1] It is in the difference between the approaches of the two writers that basic contrast reveals itself most clearly. La Bruyère in all his judgements is guided by absolute standards which are never placed in doubt. He has a fixed conception of monarchy, differing, it is true, in some respects from that of Louis XIV as it was seen in action, but none the less despotic in its power. He has a fixed conception of religion, which is that of the Roman Catholic Church. He has a fixed conception of reason, immutable and universally valid: 'la raison est de tous les climats.'[2] Montesquieu's attitude to reason will be discussed later; of the fixed standards of monarchy and religion it may be said that he does not accept them, but does more than simply discard them. He discredits them by making them the subject of debate and by setting up against them, for purposes of comparison, the Persian monarchy and the Islamic faith. Instead of the absolute standards of La Bruyère he adopts the method of relative comparison.

Usbeck discusses in several places the different forms of government which are found in the world.[3] He approves the opinion that virtue, honour and reputation have their true seat in republics, where virtue can best flourish; he admits that freedom and the love of glory are to be found more abundantly in France than in Persia (letter 89). Monarchy, however, is always liable to degenerate into despotism or into a republic, since the balance of power is not easily maintained (letter 102). The English monarchy differs from others in Europe because it is based on consent and because the power of the prince is limited (letter 104). Usbek's considered view about the relative merits of the various forms of government is simply expressed: the best government is the one which most easily secures its end ('celui qui va à son but à moins de frais,' letter 80).

[1] M. Lange, *La Bruyère, critique des conditions et des institutions sociales*, Paris, 1909.

[2] 'Des jugements', §22, in *Œuvres*, ed. G. Servois, Paris, 1865, II, p. 88.

[3] For a discussion of the political and religious ideas expressed in the *Lettres persanes*, see S. Cotta, *Montesquieu e la scienza della società*, Turin, 1953, ch. 3, and two articles by A. S. Crisafulli, 'Parallels to ideas in the *Lettres persanes*,' and 'Montesquieu's story of the Troglodytes: its background, meaning and significance' (*Publications of the Modern Language Association of America*, 1937 and 1943).

This empirical and untheoretical decision does not prevent Montesquieu from examining the problem of the growth of societies. This he does mainly in an allegorical fable put into the mouth of Usbek.[1] The Troglodytes were a small people of Arabia, who overthrow their foreign king, determined henceforth to dispense with government and to be guided only by natural instinct, each one seeking his own good and caring nothing for the good of the others. The adoption of this principle led to the extinction of their society. The strong man stole the weak man's wife. The man whose fields were fertile was expelled by an alliance of two who were jealous; they soon quarrelled themselves, and the stronger killed the weaker, but was himself soon afterwards murdered by two others. Eventually plague descended twice on the country. The first time a doctor from a neighbouring land cured the victims. But since they refused him all payment, he allowed them to perish when the plague returned, and the society of the Troglodytes became extinct. Or it was almost extinct, for there survived two families who resolved in all things to follow the path of virtue. They refounded the community; they practised frugality; they instituted the worship of the gods; they regarded at all times the interests of their neighbours as being at least as important as their own. Guided by this new spirit, their society grew and prospered and was happy, and even, through the force of its example, was no longer exposed to attack by warlike neighbours. But as the people became more numerous, it was felt that it was expedient to select a king. Their choice fell on an old man, noted for the practice of virtue, and to him the crown was offered. He accepted, but with sorrow in his heart at the thought that society would now be governed by authority, and he wept at the thought that another discipline than virtue was found necessary.

In this simple story it is not hard to discern the representation of the theory of Hobbes, that man is by nature evil and is a wolf to man, and the theory of Shaftesbury, that virtue is natural to man. These theories are tested by Montesquieu in allegorical experiment, and the results are clear. A society based on the Hobbesian principle is not viable. It contains the seeds of its own destruction and perishes. A society based on virtue, however, is in different case. It does not become extinct; it can survive. But

[1] This is contained in letters 11–14, while its continuation, eventually discarded, is found in *Pensée* 1616 (Bkn. 120).

it is bound to transform itself. It cannot last in its original simple condition. Institutions of government will inevitably prove themselves necessary; but when government has been set up, virtue is not less necessary than before: it is more necessary, because new temptations have been created. The continuation of the story, discarded by Montesquieu but still valuable for the light it throws on his intentions, relates that after the death of the first king, who reigned only for a short time, his successor was asked if commerce and riches might be introduced into the State. He reluctantly assented to this request, pointing out that virtue was now more necessary than ever before; and one of his subjects said to him,

> Vous connaissez, Seigneur, la base sur quoi est fondée la vertu de votre peuple: c'est sur l'éducation.

These words contain the final lesson of the allegory. Hobbes is indeed wrong, since a community inspired entirely by the self-interest of its individual members perishes. The good Troglodytes, on the other hand, were not good by their nature; they were made good by the example of a few. It is the force of education, and not the innate qualities of mankind, which make a society virtuous or evil; and as civilization develops and mutual relationships become more complicated, virtue on the part of citizens becomes increasingly necessary, and challenges to it become increasingly menacing. The story of the Troglodytes does not explain the origin of society, nor was it intended to do so. Speculation on that point Usbek expressly describes as ridiculous (letter 94).

The complications of modern society do not escape Montesquieu's attention. It was fitting that the young *président à mortier* should make some observations on the subject of law. Letter 100 contains a discussion of the history of French law and of the diverse elements of which it is composed; letters 94 and 95 discuss the development of international law; penal law is considered in letter 80, where it is pointed out that more terrifying penalties are needed in the despotisms of the East than in European countries; natural law in relation to the position of women is more than once Montesquieu's concern (letters 38, 62), and the problem of the relationship between law and manners, particularly significant in view of the discussions on this theme which will eventually appear in *L'Esprit des lois*, is alluded to in letters 14 and 129. Economics is seen also to interest Montesquieu, a subject in which he had doubtless been guided, in the pursuit both of ideas and of information, by his colleague Melon. The story of the Troglodytes contains some mention of the division of labour; the financial experiments of John Law are discussed, behind the most penetrable of allegorical veils, in letter 142; the relative values of gold and paper money are considered in letter 24, and in several other places it is stressed, sometimes with particular reference to Spain, that gold is but a symbol and has no intrinsic worth. Montesquieu is interested both in economic theory in general terms, and in special and technical problems such as that of the issue of currency.

III. RELIGION, PHILOSOPHY, AND HISTORY

In considering the evidence afforded by the *Lettres persanes* for the religious ideas of Montesquieu, it may be noted first that in connexion with one problem where religion and politics met, he expresses the views which one would expect from the president of a Parlement in the early eighteenth century. The Jansenist controversy was vigorous in 1721, and it does not escape mention in the letters. Usbek finds it paradoxical that the head of the Church should prohibit or at least discourage the reading of the sacred canon on which the Church is founded.[1] An anti-Jansenist bishop who in drawing up his *mandement* has relied greatly on the clandestine assistance of a Jesuit is described in letter 101 as 'un gros homme avec un teint vermeil', a probable echo of the servant's description of Tartuffe in Molière's play: 'gros et gras, le teint frais, et la bouche vermeille.' The same tone of badinage is used in letter 143, in a passage later discarded, when Montesquieu gives, in French or in Latin, some satirical medical nostrums in which the names of Jesuit doctors, among others, are amusingly invoked. The prescription for a lenitive, for example begins: 'Recipe Molinae anodyni chartas duas; Escobaris relaxativi paginas sex; Vasquii emollientis folium unum . . .' Montesquieu displays some hostility towards the Bull *Unigenitus*, but there is no trace of enthusiasm for Jansenist doctrine.

[1] This is a reference (in letter 24) to the 80th proposition condemned by the Bull *Unigenitus*: 'lectio sacrae Scripturae est pro omnibus.'

Of the more general religious ideas of the President, the most important positive relief which can be discerned in the work is the belief in the existence of God. This is asserted by Usbek in letter 69. It is true, he says, that the ontological argument for God's existence is unsound; it is true that doctors have rightly pointed out the incompatibility of the infinite prescience of God with the freedom of men's wills. These are irrelevancies: 'mon cher Rhedi, pourquoi tant de philosophie?' God is so high that we cannot even perceive his clouds.

If the claim that God exists is founded, that does not mean that his worshippers are exempt from error or worthy of respect. Above all, the Roman Catholic Church is denounced, through the Moslem mouths of Usbek and Rica. The Pope, says the memorable letter 24, is a magician, who teaches that three and one are the same, that bread is not bread, that wine is not wine. He is but an old idol, says Rica in letter 29, worshipped through force of habit. The Catholic religion, unless it abandons the celibacy of the clergy, cannot survive for 500 years (letter 117). The practices and institutions of the Church are attacked in a variety of ways. Sometimes they are condemned outright through the mouth of a Mohammedan; sometimes a comparison is drawn between a Christian and a non-Christian usage; sometimes a comment is made only on the non-Christian usage, and the reader is left to effect his own comparison. So the widow-burning of the Hindus is treated as a practice required by the God Brama (letter 125); so Usbek is made to admit that the Koran is fallible (letter 97); the ablutions of the Moslems are mocked in letter 31, and in letter 17 a fantastic explanation is afforded of their prohibition of pork, an explanation which succeeds in making fun of the Old Testament story of the deluge. Monks are more than once described as dervishes, and in letter 93 there is a relatively serious discussion of the opinions about the origin of monasticism, 'sensible Christians' regarding most of these histories as allegorical. The tone of the comments on most religious institutions is one of scepticism and disrespect.

The juxtaposition and equal comparison of Christianity and other religions was in itself a daring procedure, and one for which even thirty years later, the Abbé de Prades was to be severely censured by the Sorbonne. When Montesquieu writes in letter 60 that the Jewish religion is a trunk which has produced two branches, Mohammedanism and Christianity, he was coming near to the ancient blasphemy of the horoscope of religion, and to the clandestinely circulating doctrine of the three impostors. It is not surprising that Usbek asks his cousin, who is a dervish, if the invincible ignorance of the Christians will excuse their unbelief and give them access to heaven when they die. Montesquieu already had written a dissertation to disprove the eternal damnation of the pagans. If the details of religious conviction are then indifferent, the case for religious toleration is irresistible, and it is, moreover, reinforced by reasons of political expediency (letter 85). In fine—and this is Montesquieu's ultimate counsel in religious matters—it is morality and not faith which is important. Disputes about religion do not, it is said in letter 46, make men either better Christians or better citizens. The first object of a religious man should be to please God, and he can please God in no surer way than by observing the rules of society and the duties of humanity. Compared with these obligations, the practices, rites and ceremonies of all religions are trifling and insignificant.

The principal intellectual aim of Montesquieu in the *Lettres persanes* was to destroy prejudice. He attacked the absolute ideal of monarchy and the absolute ideal of Roman Catholicism as they were found in the work of La Bruyère. But what of La Bruyère's third absolute? Does Montesquieu attack the prejudice of reason itself? Does he show himself as a disciple of the constructive rationalism of Descartes, or of what then seemed the newer empiricism of Locke?

There is no clear and simple answer to this question. His belief in justice as an absolute and immutable concept ('la justice est éternelle et ne dépend point des conventions humaines,' letter 83) is *a priori* and rationalist. He insists in letter 97 that two principles explain all philosophy: that any body, if unimpeded, tends to describe a straight line, and that any body which moves around a centre tends to move further away from it. These laws were laid down by Descartes in his *Principia*,[1] and both in having selected these rather than other laws, and in the attempt itself to explain all the workings of the universe by reference to physical laws, Montesquieu reveals himself to be Cartesian. On

[1] II, §39; cf. also Malebranche, *De la recherche de la vérité*, VI, 2e partie, ch. IV (ed. G. Lewis, Paris, 1945, II, pp. 210–11).

the other hand he insists in letter 59 that aesthetic judgements are all subjective (for the negroes the colour of the devil is a dazzling white while their Gods are black; if the triangles were to give themselves a God, he would have three sides). All judgements of purity and impurity similarly are individual and empirical: 'les sens . . . doivent être les seuls juges de la pureté ou de l'impureté des choses', letter 17). Montesquieu hesitates and is undecided between rationalism and empiricism in the *Lettres persanes*. It is arguable that his treatment of the first cause is rational while his treatment of second causes is empirical;[1] but he shows no consciousness of making such a distinction and if he did he would have found it hard to justify. This hesitation characterizes Montesquieu's thought also in the years succeeding the *Lettres persanes*, and traces of it are found even in *L'Esprit des lois*. There are reasons for it, however, and one of the reasons is that at the time of the *Lettres persanes* he was beginning to interest himself in a problem of a different sort.

This is the problem of historical causation. When discussing reason and the senses, Montesquieu was walking in tracks which had already been beaten. In dealing with historical causation, he was handling a topic which was relatively new, and one which the nature of his mind particularly fitted him to treat. He deals sometimes with the question on the individual level, in his discussion, for example, of the physical causes of religious sentiment in letter 75; but his ideas are more amply exposed in letters 112–22, where he examines the reasons for the decline in the population of the earth.

Rhedi, travelling in Italy, writes to Usbek to say how greatly he has been struck by the smallness of populations in various countries which he has visited. Italy, Greece, Spain, the countries of the North, Poland, Turkey and Egypt, all appear to him to be supporting now a population far smaller than they possessed in ancient times. He asks Usbek how this can be explained, and if one is obliged to assume an internal vice in Nature, which causes mankind so to decline. Usbek rebuts this notion. He insists that the earth is not incorruptible, nor indeed the heavens; but the laws of movement govern all. In the history of the earth there have been great calamities which have sometimes come near to

[1] This analysis is hinted at but not formally suggested by S. Cotta, op. cit., pp. 129–30.

eliminating completely the human race. After this exordium he addresses himself to the specific problem raised by his correspondent.

In Europe and that part of Asia which was included in the Roman Empire, the religion of the Romans has been replaced by two religions, Christianity and Islam. The Roman religion forbade polygamy and permitted divorce. The Mohammedan faith permits polygamy, and the Christian faith forbids divorce. Now it is claimed the birthrate is lower in a polygamous society than in one which is monogamous, because the reproductive power of one man is dissipated among several females simultaneously. The rate of reproduction therefore in the monogamous Roman society was higher than in the Mohammedan societies which have succeeded it in the East. If a man, however, for the whole of his life is tied to one woman, of whom he may tire after three years, the number of his children will be smaller than if he had been able to divorce her and marry another. For this reason Roman society was more reproductive than the Catholic Christian societies which have succeeded it in the West. To this should be added that the particular form of slavery which existed in the Roman Empire caused the slave population to increase greatly; while the existence of innumerable eunuchs in modern Moslem lands and of multitudes of ecclesiastics, pledged to continence, in Christendom, draws from reproduction a substantial proportion of the population. To these main reasons other subsidiary observations are added. The unremitting hope that a Messiah will be born urges the Jews continually to reproduce and thus has enabled them to survive repeated persecutions; the belief that procreation in itself is pleasing to God sustained the population of the ancient Persians; ancestor-worship among the Chinese leads each man to seek to multiply the number of his potential worshippers. The other-worldliness of the Moslems discourages them from establishing large families, while in Christian countries the law of primogeniture has the same effect. The population of Africa is kept low by the Moslem faith of the Arabs, and by the disappearance of large numbers of negroes who are sold into slavery in America. The small population of lands inhabited by savages is due to the inability of the untilled land to support many inhabitants, and to the prevalence of abortion, practised by women who fear that pregnancy makes them unattractive to their husbands. The existence of colonies, finally, is a drain on population, while moderate government encourages the birthrate.

It is pointless to judge these observations of Montesquieu in the light of modern demographical science. Their errors, their naïveté and their equivocations are sufficiently clear. What is important, however, is the fact that Montesquieu was engaged in speculation on the problem and attacked it with some ingenuity. It was only towards the end of the previous century that Sir William Petty had seriously established the study of 'political arithmetic'. Voltaire was later to mock Montesquieu for his preoccupation with this theme,[1] but Hume was to praise him, and both the Scottish philosopher in his essay *Of the Populousness of ancient Nations*[2] and Beccaria in his *Elementi di economia politica*[3] were to show themselves extensively influenced by this part of the *Lettres persanes*.

In examining this question at greater length than any other question in the *Lettres persanes*, Montesquieu shows himself as one of the pioneers of modern economic thought.

The general nature of the explanations he suggests is also highly significant. To the physical effect, the size of populations, he assigns moral causes which are connected with either religious practice or religious belief. The inter-relationship of the moral and the physical is stressed by Montesquieu repeatedly in *L'Esprit des lois*, and it is here seen to be stressed too in the *Lettres persanes*. The interest in the harem which is apparent in the work is now seen to be not something separate from Montesquieu's more serious thought, but closely connected with it; not only does it appeal to the *sensibilité* of his reading public; it is closely linked to his social theories. But it is in the attitude to religion displayed in demographic discussion that Montesquieu is most interesting. He shows a greater willingness to inquire about the historical effects of religion and the social consequences of religious belief, than about the intrinsic truth of doctrine. This attitude has already been shown by him in his early *Dissertation sur la politique des Romains dans la religion*, but it is now taken further. He com-

[1] *Essai sur les mœurs* (*Œuvres*, ed. L. Moland, Paris, 1877–85, 52 vols., XIII, p. 183).

[2] First published in his *Political Discourses*, Edinburgh, 1752.

[3] *Illuministi italiani*, ed. F. Venturi, III, Milan and Naples, 1958, pp. 153–68.

pares different religions, and in particular, having already hinted at the physical causation of religions (letter 75), he now considers their physical and social effects.

It has been seen that the *Lettres persanes* is of great importance in the history of imaginative literature. This does not prevent the work from containing a mass of ideas. They are ideas which are often confused, undeveloped, and inconsistent, but they are the elements from which twenty years later *L'Esprit des lois* will be created. There are few ideas in the greater work of which there is no trace already in the *Lettres persanes.* But it is not simply in its position as the precursor of *L'Esprit des lois* that the *Lettres persanes* are noteworthy; they have a remarkable position of their own in the history of the French Enlightenment. The new and advanced ideas which were to become celebrated during the century were, before 1721, to be found in the pages of the *Dictionnaire historique et critique* and in other works of Pierre Bayle. They had not, hitherto, with the solitary exception of the works of the cautious and unoutspoken Fontenelle, been united with *belles-lettres*. With the *Lettres persanes* they were brought out of clandestine circulation and made available for all to read. The Persian device was the means of defence which Montesquieu used in order to give himself greater freedom of expression; but also it was a genuine instrument of objectivity and relativism. The introduction of relativism into French thought is the most complete achievement of the work; the adumbration of notions of historical causation is its greatest originality.

III

PARIS SOCIETY, 1721–8

I. THE COURT

THE fame of the *Lettres persanes* made Montesquieu ambitious to receive in person plaudits from people more in the public eye than those who had congratulated him in Bordeaux. His visits to Paris became more frequent. In 1721 he lived first in the Rue Dauphine, in a house called the Hôtel de Flandre, and later in the Rue de la Verrerie in the Marais, then a very fashionable quarter of Paris. In 1722 he did not leave Bordeaux, but in each of the next two years he spent six months in the metropolis. Returning to the Left Bank, he stayed first for a short time in the Hôtel de Transylvanie on what is now the Quai Voltaire—a house made famous by the Abbé Prévost in *Manon Lescaut*, where it is described as a gambling den where Des Grieux lives for a time. Perhaps it was here that Montesquieu won 275 *livres* at play which lasted until seven in the morning.[1] He moved subsequently to the neighbouring Rue de Beaune, where Madame Du Deffand was later to receive her friends. Some of the President's time was occupied by business which he undertook on behalf of friends in Bordeaux. Once he represented the interests of the Parlement, several times those of the Academy. But his main interest was in penetrating into metropolitan society.

It did not take Montesquieu long to make a successful entry both into Court circles and into the intellectual society of Paris.

At Court the rule of the Regent, the Duc d'Orléans, was at its height. By reaction from the later years of Louis XIV, life both at Versailles and at the Court in Paris was of great debauchery. Orléans united with undoubted political talent extreme sensuality, which was to lead him to a premature death, and the morals of his coadjutor, Cardinal Dubois, were scarcely better. The examples set by the highest in rank were followed, less extravagantly, by humbler figures at Court. This was the society that Montesquieu entered, separated from his wife whom he left in Bordeaux.

His mentor at Court was the powerful Duke of Berwick, who seems neither to have participated in its excesses, nor to have

[1] Bulkeley to Montesquieu, 10 September 1723.

disapproved of them. Through Berwick, his son the Duke of Liria, and his kinsman Lord Bulkeley, who was the close and faithful friend of the President throughout his life, Montesquieu became acquainted with several members of the old military nobility of France, and especially with the family of Goyon de Matignon. The aged Maréchal de Matignon had fought for James II in Ireland where he made the acquaintance of Berwick, then a boy. Their names had often been linked subsequently. A popular song of 1709 laments Louis XIV's dependence on Madame de Maintenon, and deplores France's poverty in great men:

> La ressource de la France,
> Les Berwick et les Matignon,
> Les dévots et les poltrons.[1]

Montesquieu's closest acquaintances in the Matignon family were the Maréchal's son, the Comte de Gacé, and his daughter Marie-Anne, who was married to the Marquis de Grave. The President's relations with Madame de Graves, so far as they can be deduced from extant letters, were affectionate and provoked her husband's jealousy. The Comte de Gacé, described by Bulkeley as the *maquereau* of the royal Duc de Bourbon, had been unfortunate in his married life. His first wife died early, and his second wife was the central figure in an orgy of drunkenness and promiscuity in 1717, which led to her being incarcerated in a convent, and which was frequently narrated and much discussed in the memoirs of the day.

The Matignons were an ancient family of the *noblesse d'épée*, allied by marriage to the Prince of Monaco, to the ducal family of Franquetot, to the powerful and distinguished official families of Le Tellier (the family of Louvois) and Colbert, and indirectly to that of D'Argenson. They had also contracted an alliance of a very different character. The Maréchal had married a Berthelot,[2] and the Berthelot family was new, rich, unscrupulous, scandalous: in the words of Saint-Simon, 'gens du plus bas peuple qui s'enrichissent en le dévorant.'[3] François Berthelot, who died in

[1] B.N., MS. fr. 12694, p. 355.

[2] This was regarded by their equals as a *mésalliance*; cf. Caumartin de Boissy to Mme de Balleroy, 12 April 1721 (E. de Barthélemy, *Les Correspondants de la marquise de Balleroy*, Paris, 1883, II, p. 318).

[3] *Mémoires*, XLI, p. 62.

1712, had acquired in Canada enormous riches and the title of Comte de Saint-Laurent. He succeeded in marrying a daughter to Matignon, while both his son Berthelot de Jouy and his grandson Berthelot de Montchesne married members of the Bégon family, important functionaries allied by marriage to Colbert.[1] Berthelot de Pléneuf, younger brother of Berthelot de Jouy, held the office of *directeur des poudres et salpêtres de France*, and not only used its opportunities mainly for his personal enrichment, but did so in so flagrant a manner, starving to death the unhappy patients in military hospitals,[2] that an inquiry was held. The result was that he was driven into exile and bankruptcy. He was one of the richest and most squalid characters of the eighteenth century.

His wife enjoyed a different notoriety. Lampoons described her as the Messalina of the age, and her lovers (who included the Comte de Gacé) were numerous and influential. She gave her husband a daughter Agnès, who by marrying a diplomat of an old though impoverished family became at the age of thirteen Marquise de Prie. Her husband was severely hit by Pléneuf's bankruptcy. He was French Ambassador in Turin, and his father-in-law took refuge with him. Prie found it extremely difficult to maintain his state at the Sardinian Court, and eventually sent his wife to Paris in order that she might make her fortune, a step which could have only one result. Thus the celebrated Madame de Prie was launched on her career.[3] With characteristic vigour Saint-Simon sums up her personality:

> Avec de la beauté, l'air et la taille de nymphe, beaucoup d'esprit, et pour son âge et son état de la lecture et des connaissances, c'était un prodige de l'excès des plus funestes passions: ambition, avarice, haine vengeance, domination, sans ménagements, sans mesure.[4]

More ambitious than her mother, she found her way into the bed not simply of John Law at the height of his power, but of the Regent himself, and among other princes of the blood royal, the Comte de Clermont and the Comte de Charolais sought her favours. Her greatest success was with the head of the House of Condé,

[1] Michel Bégon was known to Montesquieu (*Spicilège* 393, MS. p. 337).
[2] Hénault, *Mémoires*, Paris, 1911, p. 78.
[3] See H. Thirion, *Madame de Prie*, Paris, 1905.
[4] *Mémoires*, XXXIV, p. 306.

the ineffective, undistinguished, debauched, and devout Duc de Bourbon, generally known as Monsieur le Duc, second in rank only to Orléans. She became his acknowledged mistress, which made her the most powerful figure in his semi-exiled court at Chantilly, and the little restraint (for example, the abstention from meat on Fridays)[1] which was found at Chantilly, was absent from Madame de Prie's own house at Bellébat near Fontainebleau.

The society of Bellébat was famous. Voltaire celebrated its merrymaking in a verse dialogue entitled *La Fête de Bellébat*,[2] in which the interlocutors are several of the Berthelot family, including Madame de Prie, Hénault, and above all the Curé de Courdimanche, the licentious and drunken parish priest. A chorus of the inhabitants of Bellébat sings a poem of eight stanzas, each of them ending 'Dites votre *Confiteor*', in celebration of the multitudinous vices of this ecclesiastic. Montesquieu likewise celebrated him in verse. Apostrophizing him as the Anacreon of village priests, he praises his unlimited natural appetites, evokes his friendship for the numerous tribe of the Berthelots, and describes him as the universal father of his village and as an unequalled drinker.[3]

At least fourteen members of the Berthelot family were known to Montesquieu, including Madame de Prie herself, to whom he addressed two indifferent quatrains. He stayed at Bellébat, and was well acquainted with its habitués, some of whom were of more respectable character than the Berthelots.[4] Hénault was a man of learning and wit. Bulkeley was sensible in outlook and could talk about books. Dodart, son and grandson of eminent physicians, was an engaging person. He was gay and entertaining: he announces to Montesquieu the death of the chief minister Dubois in the words, 'The Grand Vizir is dead.' Intelligent, and possessing wide interests, he could discuss Lucretius or contemporary science with the President, and he collected manuscript copies of the clandestine works of the day,

[1] Montesquieu writes, 'Je disais, étant à Chantilly, que je faisais maigre par politesse: Monsieur le Duc était dévot' (*Pensée* 1001, Bkn. 46).

[2] *Œuvres*, II, pp. 277 sq.

[3] Nagel III, p. 563; Pléiade II, p. 1472.

[4] Mme Du Deffand, in 1726, knew Mme de Prie (*Correspondance complète de la marquise Du Deffand*, ed. M. de Lescure, Paris, 1865, I, pp. xxviii–xxix). But there is no evidence of Montesquieu's knowing Mme Du Deffand well before 1742.

for example, as he tells Montesquieu, those of Boulainvilliers.[1] Montesquieu's own distant cousin, Madame d'Herbigny, was an *habituée* of Bellébat; she was born an Estrades—a family in which the mayoralty of Bordeaux was hereditary—and she had an intelligent grasp of political developments in France. She appears, moreover, to have been acquainted with Saint-Simon.[2] Another cousin of Montesquieu was in the Bellébat circle, the worthy and faithful Marans, who was to attend the President on his death-bed and whom, almost alone among his acquaintance, he addressed as *tu*. It is surprising that people like these should have been close friends of the Berthelots; but if an unpublished poem at Bordeaux is worthy of credence, even the Duchess of Berwick knew and admired the Curé de Courdimanche.[3] The success of their family is remarkable even in the generally undiscriminating society of the Regency. But granted that success and their popularity, it is not surprising that Montesquieu also, a novice at Court and with his own character not yet finally moulded, should ally himself to them. Living in these years in a rakish society, he lived the life of a rake. Strict faithfulness to his wife was not one of his qualities, and at no time did he depart from it more than in his early years in court circles. Various notes in his correspondence, not more specifically addressed than to 'mon petit amour', 'mon cher cœur', or 'belle comtesse' show that his life was in harmony with his surroundings, and it was not for nothing that Bulkeley wrote,[4] 'courtisane, c'est-à-dire suivante de la Cour'.[5]

[1] Dodart to Montesquieu, 23 November 1723.

[2] Mme d'Herbigny to Montesquieu, 13 June 1725.

[3] *Réponse de Mme la maréchale de Berwick à M. le curé de Courdimanche*, to be found in Barbot's *sottisier* (Bx MS. 693, p. 612). This is a collection of occasional pieces, largely scurrilous, made by Barbot; it is the source of the two poems of Montesquieu mentioned above. The text of Mme de Berwick's *Réponse* has neither merit nor interest.

[4] Bulkeley to Montesquieu, 10 December 1723.

[5] Uniquely different from most members of this society was the mysterious Aïssé. A Circassian slave, bought at Constantinople by the French ambassador Ferriol, she was brought up in France by his sister-in-law who was a sister of Mme de Tencin. Compelled to become Ferriol's mistress, since it was for that that he had bought her, she fell in love with the Chevalier d'Aydie, and though they never married, their love was celebrated for its simplicity and sincerity. Montesquieu is said to have known Aïssé, but evidence is lacking. They certainly had several acquaintances in common, and Montesquieu in 1748 was a close friend of D'Aydie; but Aïssé died in 1733. It is possible that she inspired *Lettre persane* 79.

A prominent figure in French social life was Mademoiselle de Clermont. The lady who was known by this title was the Princesse Marie-Anne de Bourbon, sister to Monsieur le Duc and a granddaughter of Louis XIV. After the marriage of Louis XV she was appointed Surintendante de la Maison de la Reine, but she was most conspicuously associated with the Bourbon household at Chantilly. She was of great beauty and it was suspected, reports Toussaint,[1] that her heart was not always idle. Her accepted lover, indeed, as Montesquieu himself discloses,[2] was the Duc de Melun, who met his end in a hunting accident in July 1724. In this same month, it was proposed by the Government that she should be married to a Spanish prince,[3] and this project was the occasion for a letter, partly in prose and partly in verse, which Montesquieu addressed to her.[4] He writes in a respectful style, but with considerable freedom in relation to subject matter; he praises the beauty of her body; he deplores her approaching marriage; he makes bold to say that he would love her himself if he dared.

These few and mediocre verses are not the only tribute Montesquieu was to pay to the Court of Chantilly. Guasco reports[5] that it was the society of Mademoiselle de Clermont which inspired a polished and more memorable work, the first to be published by Montesquieu since the *Lettres persanes* had appeared in Holland: *Le Temple de Gnide*.[6]

It was in 1725, during Holy Week, that *Le Temple de Gnide* appeared.[7] Unlike Montesquieu's other works, it was published in Paris, with royal approbation and privilege. It constitutes a volume of 82 pages. The preface explains the elaborate fiction adopted by the author. A French Ambassador to the Sublime

[1] Toussaint, *Anecdotes curieuses de la Cour de France sous le règne de Louis XV*, ed. P. Fould, Paris, 1908, p. 40.

[2] *Spicilège* 746 (MS., pp. 739–40). [3] Marais, *Journal*, III, p. 120.

[4] Montesquieu to Mlle xxx, 1724 (Nagel III, pp. 770–2).

[5] *Lettres familières*, VII (Nagel III, p. 1017, n.f.).

[6] See on this subject the skilful argument of F. Gebelin, 'La Clef du *Temple de Gnide*'' (*Congrès 1955*). Gebelin's contention that Gnide is an allegorical representation of Chantilly is well maintained; I find less convincing his identification of Thémire with Mme de Grave. The opinion of Vian (p. 75) and of Gebelin himself in 1914 (*Correspondance de Montesquieu*, I, p. 62, n. 1), that *Le Temple de Gnide* was written for Mlle de Clermont, and the claim that she is its central figure, have not been decisively refuted.

[7] Marais, *Journal*, III, pp. 312–13.

Porte (perhaps an echo of Ferriol) returned to France with several Greek manuscripts. Among them is an anonymous prose poem which is now translated into French. It is an account of the passions of the author, who was the son of a priest of Venus and was born at Sybaris. Leaving his native town because of the unsubtle nature of its pleasures, he travels to Crete, Lesbos, Lemnos, Delos, and finally to Gnidus in search of true happiness. It is at Gnidus that he finds it, on the breast of Thémire. A brief fragment of a similar nature, usually now entitled *Céphise et l'amour*, appears at the end of the volume.[1]

Le Temple de Gnide is not an obscene work. It is skilfully written, rich and luxuriant in manner, passionate and sophisticated. It is an artistic representation of the life of court circles in the early years of Louis XV's reign, though no doubt a less accurate picture than Voltaire's coarser *Fête de Bellébat*. While its wealth of stylized classical allusion enabled it to retain its appeal into the age of Chénier and David,[2] and though an Italian was later to see in it much of the Gothic and the Chinese,[3] its heated *sensibilité* ensured for it great success when it appeared. Matthieu Marais, though himself deploring it as an attempt and (what made it worse) a successful one, to veil obscenity under allegory, so that it might well have come from the library of Ninon de Lenclos, reports that the ladies of Paris are now anxious to learn Greek because in that language one finds such attractive things.[4]

Marais did not at this stage know who had written *Le Temple de Gnide*. A few days later he reports that some attribute the work to Montesquieu, and that they may be right, while others

[1] Another work of the same kind appeared in the *Mercure de France* in 1727, under the title *Voyage à Paphos*. This has sometimes been attributed to Montesquieu and may, indeed, be by him. There are some similarities in phraseology (for example, 'chaque dieu a ses autels, et chaque autel a ses faux prêtres; la politique, l'ignorance et la corruption en forment tous les jours') (Nagel III, p. 252; Pléiade II, p. 1459). But there is no conclusive evidence, and Montesquieu's reputation will gain more from a denial than from the assertion of his authorship of this very mediocre work.

[2] It was turned into verse by Léonard and by Colardeau; it was translated into Latin by Michael Clancy, and at least five times into Italian (once by Carlo Vespasiano), and it was imitated in Italian by Algarotti in his *Congresso di Citera*.

[3] 'Non poco del gotico e del cinese' (Vespasiano to Metastasio, 25 June 1768; Modena, Biblioteca Estense, MS. γ V. 5.1).

[4] Marais to Bouhier, 5 April 1725 (Marais, *Journal*, loc. cit.).

say that Hénault is the author; but this Marais will not have: Hénault, he says, is much too French to have written this work.[1] Montesquieu did not acknowledge the work, and even denied it. To one of the Berthelots he writes in the month of its appearance, 'Je ne suis point l'auteur du *Temple de Gnide*', while to another correspondent he says that he is grateful to the author of *Le Temple de Gnide* for having caused her to write to him. Barbot, meanwhile, writes from Bordeaux to say that he will not pay Montesquieu the 192 *livres* he owes him, until the President has told him all he knows about the new work; and he prudently refuses to express an opinion about the book until he knows whether Montesquieu is its author.

Finally, a long and interesting letter from Desmolets—who is revealed as Montesquieu's agent for the publication of the work—discloses that it was not an immediate success, only 600 copies out of the 2,000 printed having been sold. Even at Court, it met with no immediate success. But when it had been praised by the Duc de Bourbon, many purchasers decorated with the *cordon bleu* of the Order of the Holy Ghost flocked to the publisher to buy, and Monsieur le Duc himself sent to ask who the author was. Speculation was rife about the authorship. By some people the work was attributed to the same Mirabaud who, forty-five years later, was involuntarily to lend his posthumous name to D'Holbach's *Système de la nature*. But at last, says Desmolets, the President's Thémire herself declared that Montesquieu was the author and had read the work to her before publication, and for most people the secret now existed no more.

Trivial literary composition and dissipated revelry are not the only things which in Montesquieu's career mark these years of his association with the Court. For this is the only period of his life when he was in close touch with the government of France. Le Blanc was in office as minister for war under Cardinal Dubois, and his mistress was Madame de Pléneuf. Madame de Pléneuf's daughter, Madame de Prie, had quarrelled with Le Blanc, and interested the Duc de Bourbon in her quarrel. Bourbon succeeded in July 1723 in procuring the disgrace of Le Blanc, and on the death of Orléans later in the same year, assumed the office of chief minister, but without provoking widespread enthusiasm. The memorialist Barbier wrote that the new first minister was

[1] Marais to Bouhier, 10 April 1725 (ibid., p. 315)

to no one's taste, possessing neither common sense nor any experience of affairs.[1] His period of office was short, and when Fleury replaced him, Madame de Prie was driven into exile in Normandy and the political importance of the household at Chantilly came to an end. While it lasted, however, it had given Montesquieu the only direct contact he was to have with monarchical government in action in France. Certain of his minor political writings were composed at this time and in this atmosphere. The most important of them bears the title *Lettres de Xénocrate à Phérès* and in it is to be found the same kind of classical allegory as in *Le Temple de Gnide*. Its five letters constitute an *éloge* of the Duc d'Orléans, lightly disguised under the name Alcamène. A dream, in which Alcamène thinks he owns all the treasures of the universe, symbolizes the financial experiments of John Law. 'A man of obscure birth' received into Alcamène's household is Cardinal Dubois. The young monarch, whose personal rule after the death of Alcamène promises a bright future for the State, is Louis XV. These letters give a percipient character study of Orléans, whose aptitudes Montesquieu admires; but politically they are a naïve work—much more so than the *Lettres persanes*—and they are written from the standpoint of a courtier who despises politicians. They are far from giving a foretaste of *L'Esprit des lois*.

Montesquieu however made about this time the acquaintance of a celebrated figure of international renown, whose influence on his later political writings was destined to be very great. This was Viscount Bolingbroke. Exiled from England since the death of Queen Anne, he had identified his fortunes temporarily with those of the Jacobite cause. He was a friend of Matignon and of Berwick, as well as of several of Montesquieu's intellectual acquaintances. He did not return permanently to England until April 1725. Montesquieu declares that he knew Bolingbroke, though without greatly respecting him.[2] The exiled statesman is known to have been a close friend of Matignon and of Berwick, and Bulkeley writes of him to Montesquieu in 1723.[3] The *Spicilège* reports two conversations between Montesquieu and the

[1] E. J. F. Barbier, *Journal historique et anecdotique du règne de Louis XV*, Paris, 1847–56, 4 vols., I, p. 196.

[2] *Pensée* 2127 (Bkn. 1351).

[3] Bulkeley to Montesquieu, 10 September 1723.

second Lady Bolingbroke, and refers to her as Madame de Villette,[1] which suggests that Montesquieu knew her before her marriage to Bolingbroke in 1722, when she was living with him as his mistress, or at least soon enough after her marriage for the use of her previous name still to be easy. Finally, in a letter written in 1752 but published only in 1955, Montesquieu declares that he made his acquaintance thirty years before.[2]

II. MADAME DE LAMBERT

Not content with the society of the Court, of Chantilly and of Bellébat, Montesquieu sought to pursue in Paris those intellectual ambitions which had caused his election to the Academy of Bordeaux; and if, with the success of the *Lettres persanes* behind him, he was now concerned more with literature and less with pure science, that reorientation of interest was less important then than it would have been in a later age. For men of science and men of letters were not separate and distinct groups. The genial and learned Desmolets and the vigorous and more quarrelsome Mairan, both of whom provided Montesquieu with books when he was in the country, were now able to sponsor him in intellectual society. It was undoubtedly through the one or the other that he met their common friend Fontenelle. This celebrated man of letters, already sixty-four years of age when the *Lettres persanes* appeared, was destined to live thirty-five years more. He had published all his most famous works before Montesquieu was born. He had participated in the Quarrel of Ancients and Moderns and written his celebrated *Histoire des oracles* and yet more famous *Entretiens sur la pluralité des mondes* before he was thirty-five, and was perpetual secretary of the Académie des Sciences as well as being a member of the Académie Française and of the Académie des Inscriptions. Prudent, cautious, and benevolent, he was on good terms with most men of letters. Montesquieu's relations with him were uniformly amiable and courteous throughout his life; and when someone in conversation accused Fontenelle of heartlessness, Montesquieu sprang to his defence with

[1] *Spicilège* 754, 757 (MS., pp. 749–50, 752–3).

[2] Montesquieu to Warburton, 4 July 1752 (*Autographes de Mariemont*, ed. M.-J. Durry, Paris, 1955, II, pp. 499–502).

the rejoinder, which became famous, 'Eh bien! il en est plus aimable dans la société!'[1]

A society in which the gifts of Fontenelle were extensively displayed was that of the Marquise de Lambert, one of the most remarkable personages of the early eighteenth century.[2] Born in 1647, stepdaughter of the *esprit fort* Bachaumont by whom she was brought up, left a widow and by no means a wealthy one in 1686, she did not inaugurate her salon until late in her life. Then, in her house in the Rue de Richelieu, at the northern extremity of the Bibliothèque de Roi, she held her receptions on Tuesdays and Wednesdays. More intellectual than the Court, less devout than the circle which had gathered around Madame de Maintenon, less disreputable than Ninon de Lenclos's society in the Temple, her gatherings became celebrated, not least because they enjoyed the patronage, and occasionally received the visits, of the Duchesse du Maine, the habitués of whose court at Sceaux were scarcely inferior in rank to those of Versailles and Chantilly, whom they certainly outshone in intellect. Described by Matthieu Marais as 'ce bel esprit qui protège les beaux esprits du nouveau style',[3] she attracted to her house a varied assembly of nobles and men of letters. Among the regular visitors were Fontenelle and La Motte, seconded by the sardonic Mairan, whom La Motte defined as 'une exactitude, une précision tyrannique'.[4] The Abbé Mongault, tutor to the son of the Regent, and Monsieur de Sacy, both of them academicians, were to be found there, along with Hénault, at home in all societies, Marivaux, Crébillon, Dubos, Madame Dacier, and, surprisingly, the actress Adrienne Lecouvreur. The Duc de Nevers, her friend and the owner of her house, the Marquis d'Argenson and the Marquis de Saint-Aulaire (whom eventually, according to Hénault, she married), represented the nobility. Melon of Bordeaux and Bouhier of Dijon were sometimes present, when they were in residence in Paris.

[1] Raynal, *Anecdotes littéraires*, III, The Hague, 1766, p. 269.

[2] See on her E. de Broglie, 'Les Mardis et mercredis de la marquise de Lambert' (*Le Correspondant*, 10 and 25 April 1895); J.-P. Zimmermann, 'La Morale laïque au commencement du XVIIIe siècle' (*RHLF*, 1917); H. La Perrière, *La Marquise de Lambert*, Troyes, 1935; and R. Dauvergne, *La Marquise de Lambert à l'hôtel de Nevers*, Paris, 1947.

[3] Marais, *Journal*, III, p. 144.

[4] La Motte to Duchesse du Maine, s.d. (La Motte, *Œuvres*, Paris, 1754, X, p. 14).

The salon enjoyed a great reputation. Its meetings, which occurred on Tuesdays (mainly but not exclusively for the nobility) and Wednesdays (for men of letters), gave intense pleasure to those who frequented them. The Duchesse du Maine poured forth her feelings with lyrical enthusiasm:

O mardi respectable! mardi imposant! mardi plus redoutable pour moi que tous les autres jours de la semaine! mardi qui avez servi tant de fois au triomphe des Fontenelle, des La Motte, des Mairan, des Mongault! mardi auquel est introduit l'aimable abbé de Bragelonne; et pour dire encore plus, mardi où préside Madame de Lambert![1]

To be admitted on either day was a title of respect. Gambling was not allowed, and the most scandalous members of French society were excluded. The salon had indeed received some initial encouragement from Fénelon. Its one vice was a venial delight in intrigue, especially in intrigue which might determine an election to the Academy, and Madame de Lambert's salon was a potent force in many elections to the ranks of the immortals.

Introduced doubtless by Fontenelle, probably in 1724, Montesquieu sent Madame de Lambert some Persian letters in order to win her esteem. A letter of 29 July 1726 shows that he had then become a regular attender at her Tuesday gatherings. Later in the same year, she praises him to a correspondent, remarking, 'Souvent il nous apporte des manuscrits de sa façon, infiniment approuvés par Messieurs de Fontenelle et de La Motte.'[2] When she urges him to return from Bordeaux to Paris, he promises to come, saying that the pleasure of seeing her again is almost his sole motive. And in 1728, writing to her from abroad, he says:

Parlez de moi aux mardis, c'est-à-dire aux amis les plus chers que j'aie au monde; parlez-en aux mercredis, ce jour n'est pas moins heureux que l'autre quand on peut en jouir.[3]

[1] Duchesse du Maine to La Motte, s.d. (ibid., p. 10).

[2] Mme de Lambert to Morville, 5 August 1726 (Nagel III, pp. 1537–8). Montesquieu was an enthusiastic admirer of La Motte: "M. de La Motte est un enchanteur, qui nous séduit par la force des charmes" (*Pensée* 116, Bkn. 450). On another occasion he likens him to Rembrandt (*Pensée* 1215, Bkn. 893). He was present at the first night of *Inès de Castro* on 6 April 1723 (*Pensée* 143, Bkn. 916) where he may have met Voltaire (*Voltaire's Correspondence*, ed. Th. Besterman, Geneva, 1953 sq., I, p. 202).

[3] Montesquieu to Mme de Lambert, 20 April 1728.

It is not hard to discover what intellectual interests predominated in the salon of this 'woman of a superior understanding and knowledge of the world', as she was described by Lord Chesterfield, who seems to have known her.[1] The inventory of her books, brief and selective only as was the usage of the times, shows that she owned works by Malebranche and Descartes as well as Plato and Cicero; but Charron and La Mothe Le Vayer also were on her shelves; and it is more significant that she possessed the *Histoire des Incas* of Garcilaso de la Vega and the *Histoire des Sévarambes*, than the *Dictionnaire pratique du bon ménager*. It is her own works, however, which give most information about the discussions in her house. Though her *Avis d'une mère à son fils* first came out in 1726, being published by Desmolets in his periodical *Continuation des mémoires de littérature*, and was several times reprinted against her wishes, most of her works appeared only after her death, Fontenelle seeing them through the press. They illustrate the activity of her salon, and reveal the nature of the inspiration behind many of Montesquieu's writings of these years.[2]

Duty, taste, love, friendship, happiness: such were the topics discussed in Madame de Lambert's apartment in the Hôtel de Nevers. They were simple moral problems, calling for no especial competence or experience, but rather for a clear mind and for good will. The Marquise, says Montesquieu, studied how the love of men for women might be purified and made socially useful.[3] Happiness[4] was one of the first problems discussed, and echoes of the philosophy of Shaftesbury were heard in her salon. An essay by Fontenelle, entitled *Du bonheur*, appeared for the first time in the 1724 edition of his works. A subtle and delicate psychological study, not lacking an element of paradox, it shows finesse rather than decision and has no real profundity.

[1] Chesterfield to his son, 6 June 1751 (*The Letters of Philip Dormer Stanhope, 4th Earl of Chesterfield*, ed. Bonamy Dobrée, London, 1932, 6 vols, IV, p. 1744).

[2] Soon after the publication of the *Lettres persanes* Montesquieu began to write down reflections, notes from reading, and projects of future works, in quarto notebooks, eventually three in number, known as the *Pensées*. It is possible, with an element of uncertainty, to date approximately most pages in the *Pensée* (and likewise in the *Spicilège*). See R. Shackleton, 'La Genèse de l'*Esprit des lois*' (*RHLF*, 1952).

[3] *Pensée* 1207 (Bkn. 1955).

[4] See C. Rosso's intelligent essay *I Moralisti del 'bonheur'*, Turin, 1954.

Montesquieu's writings on happiness are to be found in the *Pensées*, and the date of the insertion of the first fragments leaves little doubt that they were intended for the discussions in Madame de Lambert's salon.[1] His doctrine, which can be summed up in his own words,[2] 'le bonheur fondé sur la machine', is a materialist one. Happiness and unhappiness, he explains, consist of a certain organic disposition of the body. They are the moral effects of physical causes. Unhappy men are of two sorts, those who suffer from languor and those who suffer from impatience, and both languor and impatience depend on the organs of the body. Similarly there are two kinds of happy men, those who have lively desires, and are vigorously stimulated by easily accessible external objects, and those whose physical constitution causes them to be gently stimulated and easily satisfied. Happiness and unhappiness are relative and not absolute. When we say that a man is unhappy, we mean that if we, with our organs, were in his situation, we should be unhappy.

An anchorite finds a new pleasure in his accustomed vegetables when he returns to them after fasting. And though the soul itself can undoubtedly, through the faculty of imagination, magnify happiness and unhappiness, the main cause lies in the body. The arguments which most affect our happiness or unhappiness are those (like the immensity of the universe) which appeal to our senses rather than to pure mind.

Traces of materialism in Montesquieu's thought are here manifest. They have already been seen in the *Lettres persanes*, and they are seen again in a discourse, presented to the Academy of Bordeaux in November 1723, on relative movement. Though the text of this essay is not extant, it is known through other people's accounts[3] that the President here asserts that movement is essential to matter. This anti-Cartesian notion (which shows a rapid evolution in the allegiance, if not in the substance, of his thought since the *Essai d'observations sur l'histoire naturelle* read in 1721) was conceived as a refutation of the Aristotelian argument for the existence of God as the Unmoved Mover. If matter

[1] *Pensée* 30 (Bkn. 549) is the most important passage and belongs to the period 1722–5. Other passages appearing in the third volume (*Pensée* 1675, Bkn. 551) suggest that Montesquieu returned to this theme late in life; he was frequently to take up again in old age the occupations of his youth.

[2] *Pensée* 58 (Bkn. 996).

[3] Nagel III, pp. 125–7; and cf. Dodart to Montesquieu, 28 December 1723.

by its nature is in motion, there is no need for an external creator to give an initial impulse; and the contention that motion is inseparable from matter was regarded as an argument to disprove the existence of God. Toland, in his *Letters to Serena*,[1] gave one of the most celebrated expositions of this theory; and Montesquieu, in arguing on the same lines, and in his frequent use of the still audacious word *machine* for body, places himself clearly—as the *Lettres persanes* also have shown him to be placed—in the nascent materialist movement in France.

Taste was one of the subjects to which Madame de Lambert's guests turned their minds, and their hostess herself wrote some *Réflexions sur le goût*. In the late summer of 1726 Jean-Jacques Bel sent Montesquieu the manuscript of a critique which he was about to publish of the theory of taste outlined by Dubos in his *Réflexions critiques sur la poésie et sur la peinture* of 1719. Montesquieu replied, advancing some ideas of his own on the topic, but checking himself finally, saying that the subject needs much reflection.[2] This is the beginning of the President's *Essai sur le goût*, which, though finally revised for publication in the *Encyclopédie* where it appeared after its author's death, existed in part before 1728.[3] Undoubtedly influenced by discussions at the Hôtel de Nevers, and perhaps read there, this essay too shows traces of a bold materialism:

> Un organe de plus ou de moins dans notre machine nous aurait fait une autre éloquence, une autre poésie.[4]

A projected *Histoire de la jalousie*, fragments of which are scattered about the *Pensées*, may have been suggested to Montesquieu by discussions in Madame de Lambert's salon; and the extent to which enthusiasm found there for Cicero had its effect on him will be seen later. But meanwhile it must be noted that in 1725 Montesquieu presented to the Academy of Bordeaux a discourse entitled *De la considération et de la réputation*, an extract from which was published in the following year in the periodical *Bibliothèque française*. The collected works of Madame de Lambert include an essay, first published in 1748, with the title

[1] London, 1704, later translated into French by D'Holbach.

[2] Montesquieu to Bel, 29 September 1726

[3] See my 'Montesquieu et les beaux-arts' (*Actes du Cinquième Congrès de la Fédération internationale des langues et littératures modernes*, Florence, 1954).

[4] Nagel I, C, p. 614; Pléiade II, p. 1241.

Discours sur la différence qu'il y a de la considération à la réputation. The similarity between this work and Montesquieu's is too great to be fortuitous, and has been much discussed. But speculation on the relationship between these two works was ended with the publication of the *Pensées*, where one reads:

C'était pour mon écrit sur la *Considération*: 'il y a environ vingt-cinq ans que je donnai ces réflexions à l'Académie de Bordeaux. Feu Madame la marquise de Lambert, dont les grandes et rares qualités ne sortiront jamais de ma mémoire, fit l'honneur à cet ouvrage de s'en occuper. Elle y mit un nouvel ordre, et par les nouveaux tours qu'elle donna aux pensées et aux expressions, elle éleva mon esprit jusqu'au sien. La copie de Madame de Lambert s'étant trouvée après sa mort dans ses papiers, les libraires, qui n'étaient point instruits, l'ont insérée dans ses ouvrages, et je suis bien aise qu'ils l'aient fait, afin que, si le hasard fait passer l'un et l'autre de ces écrits à la postérité, ils soient le monument éternel d'une amitié qui me touche bien plus que ne ferait la gloire.'[1]

This generous tribute, which does not less honour to the President than to the Marquise, enables the historian of Montesquieu to identify one of the influences which transformed the *habitué* of Bellébat into the author of *L'Esprit des lois*.

III. PRIVATE ACADEMIES

In certain of the houses of Paris, periodical gatherings of individuals sharing the same interests were held, more formally than in the salon of Madame de Lambert, but still privately and unofficially. Desmolets presided over one of these bodies, where literary memoirs were read, but eventually the opposition of the Jesuits caused its dissolution.[2] Another such gathering met in the house of the Cardinal de Rohan, a vast palace of which the construction was completed in 1716, and which today houses the Archives Nationales. Montesquieu at one time frequented this society, where Fréret may have been his sponsor. Its organizer was an Italian, the Abbé Oliva, who, having been a protégé of Clement XI, was secretary of the conclave of 1721 which resulted in the election of Innocent XIII. It was then that he made the

[1] *Pensée* 1655 (Bkn. 128), written after 1748.
[2] Guasco, *Lettres familières* (1768), XL (Nagel III, p. 1344).

acquaintance of Rohan, who brought him to Paris to act as his private librarian. Oliva was a man of intelligence and charm, well acquainted with the literati of his day. In Montesquieu's career he is a significant figure on account of his nationality. The President had a large number of Italian friends, most of them clerics and scholars, Cerati, Niccolini, Venuti, and Guasco being the most important, Bernardo Lama being the first. Oliva is the first whose close acquaintance with Montesquieu is attested;[1] and through Oliva Montesquieu may have known the celebrated Abbé Antonio Conti, who was in France from 1718 to 1726. This Venetian polymath[2] was a friend of Oliva, dedicated some of his works to him, and often, in Paris, would spend the whole night with him discussing history and antiquities. He had known Malebranche and corresponded with Leibniz, and was a close acquaintance of Newton himself. Mairan, Réaumur, Fréret, Desmolets, and Fontenelle were his friends. It is more than likely that he knew Montesquieu in the years following the publication of the *Lettres persanes*; and in 1728 when the President was in Venice, it was Conti who acted as his cicerone.

Oliva's *conversazioni* were mocked by some of his contemporaries, and Barbot reports to Montesquieu a song directed against them, beginning:

> Dieux, quelle est cette académie
> Où Fréret passe pour savant,
> Et dont, pour comble d'infamie,
> Tournemine est le président?[3]

The Jesuit Tournemine, who was editor of the *Mémoires de Trévoux*, was lacking in common sense and tact, though not in learning. Voltaire (who had been his pupil at the Collège Louis-le-Grand) made famous an epigram which circulated among his brother Jesuits:

> C'est notre Père Tournemine
> Qui croit tout ce qu'il imagine.[4]

[1] Montesquieu to Guasco, 5 December 1750.

[2] See the *notizie* (by G. Toaldo) in Conti, *Prose e poesie*, Venice, I, 1739 and II, 1756.

[3] Barbot to Montesquieu, 11 April 1725.

[4] Voltaire to Duclos, 7 June 1762 (*Œuvres*, XLII, p. 130; *Correspondence*, ed. Besterman, no. 9694).

Montesquieu was so antagonized by Tournemine's assertiveness that he ceased to attend the gatherings of the Hôtel de Rohan, and retained throughout his life a consistent hostility towards him, which was an unusual departure from his normal good humour. 'Qui est-ce que le Père Tournemine? Je n'en ai jamais entendu parler', he used to say to his friends, according to Guasco,[1] while Rousseau relates a more benevolent *mot*: 'Believe neither Tournemine nor me, speaking of the other; for we have ceased to be friends.'[2]

A private academy of greater reputation and more unconventional ideas, in connexion with which Montesquieu's name has often been mentioned, was the Club de l'Entresol, presided over by the learned Abbé Alary. This is one of the most interesting organizations in the whole of the French eighteenth century.

Alary, who had been a tutor of the young Louis XV, was a member of the Academy and a member of the salon of the Marquise de Lambert. He had an apartment in the house of the Président Hénault in the Place Vendôme. Here, on Saturdays, he used to give tea to his friends, who were among the most illustrious citizens of France. They gathered to read the gazettes and to discuss the topics of the day, and to their society, on account of the position of Alary's rooms, they gave the name Club de l'Entresol. The nobility, both of sword and robe, and the middle classes used to meet here on terms of equality; and they formed the first society for the discussion in a free spirit of political topics. The most important contributions to the study of political theory in France, between Bossuet's *Politique tirée de l'Ecriture sainte* and *L'Esprit des lois*, come from the members of the Entresol. They were not concerned with the abstract moral themes debated in the salon of Madame de Lambert. They flung themselves instead into acutely controversial political, social, and historical problems; and some apparently innocuous themes were in reality pregnant with danger. The Marquis d'Argenson,[3] for example—the most celebrated of its members, at least in retrospect—began by treating public law but later narrowed his

[1] Guasco, loc. cit.

[2] *Confessions*, ed. B. Gagnebin and M. Raymond, in *Œuvres complètes*, Paris, 1959, I, p. 497.

[3] D'Argenson gives in his memoirs the fullest available account of the activities and membership of the Entresol (*Journal et mémoires du marquis d'Argenson*, Paris, 1859–67, 9 vols., I, pp. 91–111).

scope and dealt simply with French ecclesiastical law. This was a highly dangerous subject at a time when Gallicanism and Jansenism were united in opposition to the policy of the chief minister Fleury, and D'Argenson's contribution, read to a society one of whose members, the Abbé de Pomponne, was a great-nephew of Antoine Arnauld himself, was important enough for the Abbé, later Cardinal, de Bernis to write a précis of it in his own hand. Alary himself treated the history of Germany, likewise a controversial subject since it involved, at this time when Boulainvilliers's ideas were in at first clandestine and then open circulation, the problem of feudal origins and the rights of the nobility in relation to the crown. Diplomatic history and genealogical history were discussed, as were economic history, the mixed State, Italian governments, and forms of government in general.

The prestige of the Entresol was at first high, and membership of it was a great recommendation in diplomatic and administrative circles, and Fleury treated it with respect. But later indiscretions were committed. Alary too frequently spoke of the Entresol in conversations with outsiders. It was alleged that the Entresol was the real government of France. It is not surprising that in the end ministers' suspicions were aroused; and in 1731, after seven years of existence, the Entresol was dissolved by the ever-cautious Fleury.

Did Montesquieu belong to the Entresol?

It was customary, relates D'Argenson, for members to deposit with Alary the manuscripts of their communications. A nineteenth-century editor of Montesquieu declares that the manuscript of Montesquieu's *Dialogue de Sylla et d'Eucrate*, first published in the *Mercure de France* in 1745, was found with Alary's papers.[1] This account, if true, and there is no serious reason for calling it in doubt, provides strong circumstantial evidence for Montesquieu's membership.

Four members, at least, of the Entresol were members also of Madame de Lambert's salon, D'Argenson himself, Alary, until for an unknown reason he quarrelled with her in 1731, the Abbé Bragelonne and the Marquis de Lassay. D'Argenson, whose uncle was from 1719 to 1728 Archbishop of Bordeaux, Montesquieu certainly knew, though how well and at what stage cannot

[1] Montesquieu, *Œuvres*, Paris (Belin), 1817, I, p. xxi.

be said. Alary he knew; and the *Spicilège* discloses that he knew Lassay and visited his house.[1] The family connexions of some members of the Entresol make likely their acquaintance with Montesquieu. The Maréchal de Matignon had a son, a son-in-law, and a nephew who were members: the Marquis de Matignon, the Marquis de Balleroy (who was also cousin to D'Argenson), and the Duc de Coigny. The gallant and intelligent Comte de Plélo, soon to be killed in action, was allied to many noble houses and his daughter was later to marry the son of Montesquieu's neighbour in the south west, the Duchesse d'Aiguillon; he was a close friend and intimate companion of the Abbé Conti and of Mairan.[2] Lévesque de Champeaux and Pallu were both to perform services for Montesquieu in 1748, but nothing reveals the date of their acquaintance with him. The Abbé de Saint-Pierre, a protégé of Madame de Lambert, was, with D'Argenson, the most advanced political thinker of the club, and a prophet of international union. He was a friend of Fontenelle (who cast a solitary vote against his exclusion from the Academy) and is from time to time mentioned by Montesquieu and always with respect: 'l'illustre Abbé de Saint-Pierre', 'l'excellent Abbé de Saint-Pierre', 'le meilleur honnête homme qui fût jamais'.[3] The cosmopolitan Andrew Michael Ramsay, deist, Roman Catholic and freemason at once, the friend, disciple and biographer of Fénelon, novelist and political theorist, *persona grata* in Jacobite circles, was known to the President: 'J'ai connu Ramsay; c'était un homme fade, toujours les mêmes flatteries.'[4] Finally, Bolingbroke himself, a close friend of Alary, had attended the Entresol in its early days,[5] and was at that time known to Montesquieu.

The extent of Montesquieu's acquaintance, certain and possible, among the members of the Entresol is further circumstantial evidence in favour of the claim that he attended its meetings. But why then does D'Argenson, anxious to throw lustre on his

[1] *Spicilège* 434 and 642 (MS., pp. 369–71 and 606).

[2] See E. R. Briggs, 'L'Incrédulité et la pensée anglaise en France au début du XVIIIe siècle' (*RHLF*, 1934).

[3] *Pensées* 1295, 1718, 1876, 1940 (Bkn. 910, 407, 408, 198).

[4] *Pensée* 2122 (Bkn. 911).

[5] Bolingbroke to Alary, 6 October 1723 and 2/13 July 1724 (*Lettres historiques . . . de Henri Saint-John Lord Vicomte Bolingbroke*, ed. Grimoard, Paris, 1803, III, pp. 206–7, 193).

society, make no mention of Montesquieu, who in the end outshone all its members?

The nature of Montesquieu's supposed contribution to the proceedings of the Entresol throws some light on this problem. Inspired by some scenes from Corneille,[1] Montesquieu began to write the *Dialogue de Sylla et d'Eucrate* in 1724,[2] and two years later submitted it to Jean-Jacques Bel for his criticism.[3] The work cannot be called a masterpiece. The style is polished but conventional. It is interesting to see the President return to his early enthusiasm for Roman history, and to see him consider despotism, already denounced in the *Lettres persanes*, in relation to Rome. But the members of the Entresol, accustomed to discuss bulls and cartularies, cannot have thought highly of this dialogue. They can have seen it only as an essay in rhetoric, and not even as a very successful essay; as a triviality not worth very serious thought. If that was their attitude, indeed, they were not greatly wrong. Montesquieu had misjudged his audience, and had read to them something which with his prestige he could have lived down in the Academy of Bordeaux,[4] but which the intelligentsia of Paris would deem a failure.

It may be concluded, then, but with only tentative assurance, that Montesquieu was not lengthily associated with the Entresol; that he probably read the *Dialogue de Sylla et d'Eucrate* to it in 1727; that the reading was a failure and that the occasion was either so insignificant that D'Argenson forgot it, or so inauspicious (the members of the Entresol perhaps deriding a man who was later to become greater than any of them) that he chose not to refer to it.

The main interest of the *Dialogue de Sylla et d'Eucrate* lies in the variety of judgements which it has provoked. It incurred the disapproval of Napoleon. 'Rien de cette pompeuse analyse n'est

[1] *Pensée* 1948 (Bkn. 90).

[2] Barbot to Montesquieu, July 1724.

[3] Montesquieu to Bel, 29 September 1726. Montesquieu, then in Bordeaux, went to Paris early in 1727, and the reading of the dialogue to the Entresol occurred (if at all) either in 1727 or in the first three months of 1728. It is likely to have been not later than the autumn of 1727, because Montesquieu then acquired special reasons for not wishing to annoy Fleury.

[4] It may indeed have been read to the Academy of Bordeaux (Nagel III, p. 765, n.b.).

vrai,' said the Emperor, 'et la faire admirer, c'est fausser de jeunes esprits.'[1] Gibbon, on the other hand, praises its 'spirited and even sublime manner'.[2]

[1] Cited from Villemain, *Souvenirs contemporains*, I, p. 150 by C. Jullian, ed. of *Considérations sur les Romains*, Paris, s.d., p. xiii.

[2] *Decline and Fall of the Roman Empire*, ed. J. B. Bury, London, 1896, I, p. 183.

IV

ESSAYS AND AMBITIONS, 1721–8

I. THE *TRAITÉ DES DEVOIRS*

MONTESQUIEU'S loyalty to the Academy of Bordeaux continued vigorous and active, if not unabated, during his stays in Paris, and there was business to be undertaken both with the protector, the Duc de La Force, and with the government; for the Academy having a royal charter, the assent of the government was required for a large number of often insignificant acts. Several times Montesquieu was granted full powers by the Academy on the eve of departure to Paris.[1] The first business he had to discharge related to a donation of 60,000 *livres* which La Force made in 1720 to enable the Academy to acquire premises. After the securities constituting the gift had been handed over, in part to Montesquieu himself, the failure of Law's financial policy greatly reduced their value without reducing the commitments which had been entered into, and Montesquieu, along with Caupos and Sarrau de Boynet, found himself in a very delicate situation. Negotiations, not made easier by the frequent inaccessibility of La Force, had to be undertaken, and eventually Montesquieu found a way out by presenting to the Academy a share in the Compagnie des Indes. But the Academy obtained no permanent premises until it inherited a house from Jean-Jacques Bel in 1738.

Early in 1726 Montesquieu arranged to accompany La Force to see Morville, who was Secretary of State, with a view to obtaining from the Government further privileges for the Academy, such as exemptions from taxation. La Force himself was disposed to make a further benefaction, and in order to induce him to make it generous, by showing him that existing resources were husbanded with prudence, the Academicians resolved that two gold medals, both presented as prizes, one by La Force and the other by Montesquieu, should be turned into money and the proceeds invested. While these discussions were in progress, La Force died, and Montesquieu was thrown into long and

[1] 15 May 1720, 7 August 1722, 21 January 1725, 30 March 1727 (Bx MS. 1699 (1), pp. 70, 78, 87, 108).

awkward negotiations with the new Duke. At one stage there was even question of legal action by the Academy to secure its due. Its members, meanwhile, with greater prudence than ever, had elected Morville as the new protector, and Madame de Lambert was called on to act as intermediary and induce him to accept this expensive honour. In 1727 Montesquieu reopened his talks with Morville, seeking now to secure royal endowment of the Academy. He was most assiduous in his mission, carefully entertaining Morville's secretary the scholar Hardion, and proposing him for election to the Academy. It was proposed, in order to flatter Morville, to publish a volume of proceedings and dedicate it to him. But these steps led to no tangible result. The most that Morville did was to say that he would be prepared to approve a lottery.

In Bordeaux too the President was active in the affairs of the Academy. He had read his significant paper on movement in 1723.[1] He was appointed director for the year beginning on Saint Martin's day 1725, and on his entry into office on 15 November read a paper entitled *Discours sur les motifs qui doivent nous encourager aux sciences*: an intrinsically unimportant exercise, interesting because it shows Montesquieu more concerned now with the utility of the sciences than with the sciences themselves, and because he argues for the cultivation of literary graces in scientific writing. A more difficult task which fell to him during his year of office was to deliver an obituary address on the Duc de La Force. Tact was needed, for La Force had died in disgrace; but the Academy had something to hope for from his son. Here Montesquieu was admirable:

> Monsieur le Duc de La Force arriva aux temps critiques de sa vie; car il a payé le tribut de tous les hommes illustres: il a été malheureux. Il abandonna à sa patrie jusqu'à ses justifications mêmes.

The literary skill which had made the *Lettres persanes* famous had not deserted their author.

It was on 1 May 1725 that Montesquieu made what was to be the most valuable contribution of his life to the activities of the Academy of Bordeaux. On that day he read to that body as much as then existed of his *Traité des devoirs*. This work is not extant and, though it can be partially reconstructed, the lack of it constitutes

[1] See above, p. 59.

one of the unhappiest gaps in the corpus of Montesquieu's writings.[1]

Writing many years later to Berwick's son the Bishop of Soissons, Montesquieu tells the story of its composition. He discloses that he had formed the intention of writing a work on duties under the inspiration of Cicero's *De officiis*, and to this end had studied the writings of the Stoics, and especially the moral reflections of Marcus Aurelius. He read to the Academy of Bordeaux some fragments of what he had written, and extracts which appeared in journals were generally well received. But later, he confesses, his confidence waned as he began to find Cicero's division of duties unsatisfactory. He feared a rival treatise on the same theme, and abandoned the work.[2]

One of the President's earliest writings, it has been seen, was a *Discours sur Cicéron*; he had for some time been an admirer of the Roman. This enthusiasm was greatly encouraged by Madame de Lambert. Her collected works include a *Traité de l'amitié* and a *Traité de la vieillesse*, and her protégé Sacy also wrote and dedicated to her a treatise *De l'amitié*.[3] From the *De amicitia* and the *De senectute* to the *De officiis* was not a surprising move, and the works of the Marquise show much discussion on the theme of duty. In the *Avis d'une mère à sa fille* she declares that the order of duties is to know how to live with one's superiors, one's equals, one's inferiors, and with oneself, that above all other duties is the duty of worshipping God, and that the first duty of civil life is to think of others.[4] It was undoubtedly under her influence and with her encouragement that Montesquieu embarked on the preparation of his *Traité des devoirs*, and with the model afforded by Cicero in his mind.

[1] It is not, perhaps, lost for all time. In 1818 a large collection of manuscripts was dispatched to England, where Montesquieu's grandson was living at Canterbury. The catalogue of manuscripts sent includes 'un cahier intitulé: *Traité des devoirs*, mis au net' (Nagel III, p. 1575). Most of these manuscripts were burnt by the grandson, but a few returned to France, and in their number appeared a 'carton ou portefeuille . . . intitulé *Devoirs, lois, réputation*, contenant divers cahiers'. (Nagel III, p. 1581). This manuscript, no longer at La Brède and not mentioned in the catalogues of the two sales which have taken place, is probably elsewhere in France.

[2] Montesquieu to Mgr de Fitz-James, Bishop of Soissons, 8 October 1750.

[3] The Abbé Mongault, also of her salon and known to Montesquieu, had translated into French Cicero's *Letters to Atticus*.

[4] *Œuvres*, Paris, 1808, pp. 13 and 90.

If an attempt is made from all available sources to reassemble the elements of the *Traité des devoirs*,[1] a task made easier by the survival of the table of contents,[2] the nature of the work can be discerned. Beginning with a refutation of the fatalism of the disciples of Spinoza, Montesquieu goes on to insist on the existence and the benevolence of God, and thereafter on the nature of duties towards other men, which involves him in a discussion of justice. He proceeds to a critique of Hobbes and Spinoza, and then eulogizes the principles of the Stoics. Returning to the discussion of justice, he elucidates the notion of the hierarchy of duties,[3] and concludes with a discussion of political duty, illustrated from the Spanish conquests in America, in which he inserts a discussion of the contribution of Christianity to ethics.

From these vestiges of what was intended to be Montesquieu's first large-scale enterprise since the *Lettres persanes*, and his first wholly serious book, it can be seen at once that the influence of Cicero in the execution of the work is not a large one, however important it was in the initial conception. There is no sign here of the plan of the *De officiis*, no definition of the *utile* or of the *honestum*, no analysis of the four cardinal virtues; and the President shows a nascent political and social interest not displayed in the *De officiis*. There are signs of the influence of Samuel Clarke, and more frequent traces once again of his reading of Malebranche, on this occasion of the *Traité de morale*, but not sufficient to suggest that the Oratorian Father was his chief or continuous guide.

[1] See my article, 'La Genèse de l'*Esprit des lois*' (*RHLF*, 1952), where this reconstruction is attempted.

[2] Nagel III, p. 1581.

[3] This is particularly expressed in a passage from the *Pensées* (741, Bkn. 11), which has become famous: 'Si je savais quelque chose qui me fût utile et qui fût préjudiciable à ma famille, je la rejetterais de mon esprit. Si je savais quelque chose utile à ma famille, et qui ne le fût pas à ma patrie, je chercherais à l'oublier. Si je savais quelque chose utile à ma patrie, et qui fût préjudiciable à l'Europe, ou bien qui fût utile à l'Europe et préjudiciable au genre humain, je la regarderais comme un crime.' This closely resembles an anecdote told about Fénelon by Montesquieu's acquaintance Andrew Michael Ramsay: '[Fénelon] was above the little distinctions of country or religion, and used to say, "that he loved his family better than himself; his country better than his family; and mankind better than his country; for I am more a Frenchman," added he, "than a Fénelon, and more a man than a Frenchman" ' (Joseph Spence, *Anecdotes*, pp. 26–27).

For a model Montesquieu seems to have had recourse to the short treatise *De officio hominis* of the German Pufendorf, a work which he possessed in the French translation of Barbeyrac, entitled *Devoirs de l'homme et du citoyen.* Pufendorf has chapters headed 'Des devoirs de l'homme envers Dieu', 'Des devoirs de l'homme par rapport à lui-même', 'Des devoirs mutuels de l'homme', 'De l'état de nature', 'Des motifs qui ont porté les hommes à former des sociétés civiles'. In broad outline and in minute detail alike, the resemblance of Pufendorf's treatise to the *Traité des devoirs* is a striking one,[1] and this fact is of great moment in view of the future literary activity of the President. For Pufendorf's *De officio hominis* is an abridgement, concerned mainly with moral philosophy, of his vaster and more famous work, *De jure naturae et jure gentium*, which was second in importance only to the work of Grotius in the development of the political theory of the natural law school. Montesquieu in due course studied the larger work. The copy in the library at La Brède, again Barbeyrac's French translation, has several annotations in his hand. To find him already in 1725 reading, studying and using Pufendorf is of capital importance. It serves to date the beginning of his systematic interest in political philosophy.

The attitude to the Stoics disclosed in the *Traité des devoirs* is one of admiration and respect, and Montesquieu retains it at later moments in his life. He speaks favourably of Stoicism in the *Considérations sur les Romains*, but this is not all. The contemporary account of the *Traité des devoirs* contains this reflection by Montesquieu:

> Si je pouvais un moment cesser de penser que je suis chrétien, je ne pourrais m'empêcher de mettre la destruction de la secte de Zénon au nombre des malheurs du genre humain; elle n'outrait que les choses dans lesquelles il n'y a que de la grandeur: le mépris des plaisirs et de la douleur . . . Nés pour la société, [ils] croyaient tous que leur destin était de travailler pour elle; d'autant moins à charge que les récompenses étaient toutes dans eux-mêmes, et qu'heureux par leur philosophie seule, il semblait qu'ils crussent que le seul bonheur des autres pût augmenter le leur.[2]

These very words were used again by Montesquieu twenty-three

[1] For a detailed comparison, see my article last cited.

[2] Nagel III, p. 160; Pléiade I, pp. 109–10.

years later in *L'Esprit des lois*;[1] nor are they the only passage of *L'Esprit des lois* to come from the *Traité des devoirs*. For at the very beginning of the great work there is a vigorous denial of the fatalism of the Spinozists in words borrowed from the earlier treatise. There can be little doubt that if the complete text of the *Traité des devoirs* were before our eyes, other borrowings, and perhaps many, would be disclosed.

To assail and to refute the philosophies of Spinoza and Hobbes was a cardinal aim in the *Traité des devoirs*. The fifth chapter, 'Quelques principes de philosophie', its contents being largely inferred from the *Pensées*,[2] examines their teaching. Spinoza is first dealt with, and Montesquieu, though not denying him the title of genius, accuses him of asserting that man will die as an insect dies, since he is but a modification of matter, of eliminating personality from his system, drawing no distinction between Charlemagne and Chilperic, of denying the freedom of the will and thus of annihilating all moral philosophy. Hobbes, less extreme than Spinoza, is for that reason proclaimed more dangerous. He denies the existence of justice or reduces it to man-made law. He has wrongly described the state of nature as a state of war. Even animals, asserts Montesquieu, do not make war against their own species.[3]

These are strange arguments from the pen of a man who was toying with materialism himself. Montesquieu had, indeed, six years before in the *Lettres persanes* and in his *Essai d'observations sur l'histoire naturelle*, two years before in his *Discours sur le mouvement relatif*, and more or less simultaneously in his fragments on happiness and in the first draft of his *Essai sur le gout*, himself expressed materialist ideas. And if in, a passage perhaps intended for the *Traité des devoirs*, he abandons the belief that motion is essential to matter,[4] about the same time he cites with

[1] *Lois*, XXIV, 10. [2] *Pensées* 1266–7 (Bkn. 615–16.)

[3] Camille Jullian (who also has stressed Montesquieu's indebtedness in this argument to Samuel Clarke's *Discourse concerning the Being and Attributes of God*) points out that Cicero, in the *De divinatione*, finds himself constrained to make the same structures on the determinism of the Stoics, as Montesquieu makes here on the determinism of Spinoza. The President indeed was not the only writer who has admired the moral philosophy of the Stoics while ignorant of their metaphysics, of which (if not ignorant) he would have disapproved.

[4] *Pensée* 1096 (Bkn. 672). He could read a sustained refutation of this doctrine in Samuel Clarke's *Discourse*.

approval a *mot* of Madame de Lambert's friend Saint-Aulaire that opposition to materialism is caused by ignorance.[1]

Materialism and anti-materialism; determinism and liberty; expediency and absolute morality: when these beliefs co-exist in the mature Montesquieu they present either a problem to be solved or a paradox to be admitted. Co-existing in him in 1725, they show that his principles are not yet established and that his mind is not yet made up. They show that the uncertainty and immaturity seen in his social relations are reflected also in his intellect. This Montesquieu himself later admitted:

> Je suivais mon objet sans former de dessein; je ne connaissais ni les règles ni les exceptions; je ne trouvais la vérité que pour la perdre.[2]

Hesitation, wavering, and trial and error are seen too in the diversity of the other literary projects with which Montesquieu toyed in the decade after the *Lettres persanes*. The *Pensées* are filled with scattered reflections, with the suggestions of possible works, with prefaces and introductions, with discarded material which had been collected for works either completed or abandoned. Notes on fables, on miracles, on the Greeks and the Carthaginians, on chronology, are flanked by remarks on the Quarrel of Ancients and Moderns, on commerce, on slavery, on populations. At one point he records his intention of writing a history of the Society of Jesus,[3] at another he lists what he regards as the *Principes fondamentaux de politique*.[4] He completes a *Dialogue de Xantippe et de Xénocrate*[5] which might have pleased Madame de Lambert, and sketches a brief *Dialogue de Vulcain et de Vénus*[6] which is likelier to have pleased his friends at Bellébat. A fragment entitled *Histoire d'une île*[7] might have grown into an imitation of *Robinson Crusoe*, recently translated into French. A series of dialogues, largely erotic, was envisaged at one moment,[8] at another a collection of letters which were to receive the title *Lettres de Kanti*.[9] A work called *De la politique*[10] belonged, eventually if not originally, to the *Traité des devoirs*, and various

[1] *Pensée* 712 (Bkn. 2068). [2] Preface to *Lois*.
[3] *Pensée* 237 (Bkn. 537). [4] *Pensée* 278 (Bkn. 1911).
[5] Nagel III, pp. 119–24; Pléiade I, pp. 508–12.
[6] *Pensée* 564 (Bkn. 487). [7] *Pensée* 209 (Bkn. 489).
[8] *Pensées* 330–9 (Bkn. 478–86). [9] *Pensée* 640 (Bkn. 488).
[10] Nagel III, pp. 165–73; Pléiade I, pp. 112–18.

fragments on *Princes*[1] were associated with the same work, though Montesquieu was slow to abandon them and they recur in his later years. Finally, a longer essay and more important than these, bearing the title *Considérations sur les richesses de l'Espagne*,[2] was written and put on one side. It was twice taken up again, the second time to be incorporated in *L'Esprit des lois*, where it became chapter 22 of Book XXI. It contains serious and independent thought on economics, and would have been a much worthier contribution to the discussions of the Entresol than was the *Dialogue de Sylla et d'Eucrate*. It is the largest and most valuable part of *L'Esprit des lois* which can be shown to have existed before 1730.

From all this great variety of works projected and abandoned, as well as the relatively few which were carried to a conclusion, it is possible, especially after the *Traité des devoirs*, to see a growing interest in questions of political theory. He displays no finished doctrine but there are a number of recurrent ideas or habits of mind which present themselves several times. The anteriority of justice to the establishment of society is insisted on in the *Traité des devoirs* as it had been earlier in the *Lettres persanes*: 'la justice est éternelle et ne dépend point des conventions humaines.'[3] In the fragment *De la politique* there is prefigured the notion of the *esprit général*, which has been called the central doctrine of *L'Esprit des lois*:

> Dans toutes les sociétés, qui ne sont qu'une union d'esprit, il se forme un caractère commun. Cette âme universelle prend une manière de penser qui est l'effet d'une chaîne de causes infinies, qui se multiplient et se combinent de siècle en siècle. Dès que le ton est donné et reçu, c'est lui seul qui gouverne.[4]

Virtue and patriotism are identified: 'de toutes les vertus, celle qui contribue le plus à nous donner une réputation invariable, c'est l'amour de nos concitoyens.'[5] The ancient world is idealized and nostalgically admired:

> C'est l'amour de la patrie qui a donné aux histoires grecques et

[1] Nagel III, pp. 173–4, 536–51; Pléiade I, pp. 118–19, 519–31.
[2] This is a different work from the *Considérations sur les finances de l'Espagne* which is not by Montesquieu though it has sometimes been attributed to him.
[3] *L.P.* 83. [4] Nagel III, pp. 168–9; Pléiade I, p. 114.
[5] Nagel III, p. 205; Pléiade I, p. 123.

romaines cette noblesse que les nôtres n'ont pas. Elle y est le ressort continuel de toutes les actions, et on sent du plaisir à la trouver partout, cette vertu chère à tous ceux qui ont un cœur . . . Il semble que, depuis que ces deux grands peuples ne sont plus, les hommes se sont raccourcis d'une coudée.[1]

Finally Montesquieu refuses to regard liberty as a great political good: at the end of a long disparagement of freedom, he announces, 'Au reste, je compte pour très peu de chose le bonheur de disputer avec fureur sur les affaires d'Etat, et de ne dire jamais cent mots sans prononcer celui de *liberté*, ni le privilège de haïr la moitié de ses citoyens.'[2]

Some of the ideas of *L'Esprit des lois*, it is seen, are already present in Montesquieu's mind. Others, and they are not the least important, still have to be learnt.

II. PERSONAL MATTERS

The paucity of the information available about the general state of Montesquieu's health[3] suggests that he suffered from no grave maladies. It is well known however that his eyesight was imperfect. François de Paule Latapie, who in his youth served Montesquieu as his father had done before him, reports that from the President's earliest years his eyes were afflicted with myopia and ophthalmia.[4] From about 1724 onwards he bathed them daily, and the *Spicilège* contains several recipes for lotions. Even before then, he sought the acquaintance of eye specialists, one whose name has survived being John Thomas Woolhouse,[5] who, formerly oculist to James II, had followed his master into exile in 1688 and now lived in Paris, residing in the Hôpital des Quinze-Vingts

[1] *Pensée* 221 (Bkn. 598). [2] *Pensée* 32 (Bkn. 1302).

[3] The earliest, and almost the only, mention of illness is in July 1714, when a fever prevented him from paying homage for La Brède; he sent with his excuses a medical certificate signed Réaud (Arch. dép. Gironde, cat. série C, t. II, p. 408).

[4] Latapie to Campenon, 5 May 1817 (L. Cosme, 'A propos d'autographes de Montesquieu', *Revue philomathique de Bordeaux*, 1903, pp. 9–12). For a medical account of Montesquieu's eye trouble, see J. M. Eylaud, 'Montesquieu et ses yeux' (*Journal de médecine de Bordeaux*, 1956).

[5] *Spicilège* 362 (MS., p. 323), where his name is spelt Volouse. I am indebted to Mlle F. Weil for this identification.

which is described in the thirty-second *Lettre persane*. Montesquieu lived all his life in fear of blindness, of all afflictions the most redoubtable for a wide reader of books.

Anecdote illustrative of his character abounds in Montesquieu's later years, and his geniality, affability, generosity and simplicity, as well as his absent-mindedness, are the subjects of unnumbered stories. It is not so in the 1720's. One knows *a priori* that the friend of Fontenelle could not lack wit, that the friend of Madame de Lambert could not lack charm, that the protégé of Berwick could not be without honour. But direct evidence about the character of Montesquieu at this early moment of his life is meagre.

It is a young Irishman visiting Bordeaux who gives the first sustained account of the President's personality. Michael Clancy,[1] a medical student of Trinity College, Dublin, whose early education had been received in Paris, was seeking his fortune in France. While being entertained in Bordeaux by a visiting English peer, Lord Teynham, he met a young Englishman called Sully who had worked under John Law and later had been appointed clockmaker to the Duc d'Orléans.[2] Sully though well dressed was poor, and succeeded in persuading Clancy to lend him three *louis d'or*. Being engaged in research and wishing to acquaint the scientists of Bordeaux with his investigations, he contrived to obtain an invitation to address the Academy, and invited Clancy to accompany him. In the course of the discussion Barbot asked some questions about the activities of the Royal Society. Sully asked Clancy to answer them, and he did so. At this stage, writes Clancy,

> the President de Montesquieu, who sat opposite to me, fixed his eyes directly on me, and when I had done speaking the little I had to say, he suddenly arose from his seat, went round the gentlemen, who were seated about a large table, came up to me, and straight returned to his place.[3]

At the end of the meeting Montesquieu sent a message by Sully,

[1] See his *Memoirs*, Dublin, 1750, 2 vols., P. Courteault, 'Un traducteur latin du *Temple de Gnide*' (*Bulletin de la Société des bibliophiles de Guyenne*, 1939), and T. P. C. Kirkpatrick, 'Michael Clancy, M.D.' (*Irish Journal of Medical Science*, 1938).

[2] On Sully and his visit to Bordeaux, see Bx MS. 1699 (3), pp. 406–20; his own *Description abrégée d'une horloge*, Paris, 1726; and various papers in the B.N. (MSS. fr. 22233, ff. 210–34).

[3] Clancy, *Memoirs*, II, p. 46.

inviting the Irishman to call on him at his house in Bordeaux. He did so the next day, at an appropriate hour, and found the President in bed, reading, and annoyed at seeing the visitor whom he summarily dismissed. A few days later, Montesquieu renewed the invitation, Clancy was very amiably received, and discussed Terence and Congreve with his host. Montesquieu went on to discuss the British nation, saying that they were the only people who had ever been able to unite empire and commerce. 'In everything he advanced,' says Clancy, 'he rather seemed modestly to propose the question, than to have conceived the least opinion of a positive knowledge in himself.' He talked for two hours, and then invited his visitor to stay for dinner, the party consisting also of Montesquieu's brother, of two young men of quality, and of two or three members of the Academy of Bordeaux. The conversation after dinner lasted for four hours. This was the prelude to regular daily visits on the part of Clancy. These had lasted some three weeks when, one morning, as he approached the house, the young man saw Montesquieu departing in his carriage. The President stopped on seeing Clancy whom he had entirely forgotten, bade him enter the carriage, and bore him away there and then to La Brède where he kept him for some six months, employing him more or less as a secretary. The preoccupied air, the forgetfulness, the amiable condescension of Montesquieu, and his boundless enthusiasm, are well illustrated by this story, as is the admiring gratitude which he won from Clancy. For the Irishman regarded his encounter with Montesquieu as the greatest event of his career. Later, when he had become blind, he wrote of himself in these words:

> Though dark in sight, yet clear his mental view,
> Brightened by Boyle, Cerati, Montesquieu;[1]

and later still, he translated *Le Temple de Gnide* into Latin verse.

As for the impecunious Sully, one would wish to believe the story told on the presumed authority of the widow of Montesquieu's son. He wrote to the President, saying that he wished to hang himself, but perhaps would not hang himself if he had a hundred crowns; and Montesquieu replied, 'I send you a hundred crowns, do not hang yourself, my dear Sully, but come and see

[1] Prologue to his *Hermon, Prince of Chorea*, Dublin, 1746.

me.'[1] Sully received, in fact, a less substantial but more dignified recompense for his labours. He was elected corresponding member of the Academy of Bordeaux.[2]

A less amiable side of Montesquieu's character is seen in his relations with his wife, but the fault was perhaps not wholly his. He writes from La Brède to Madame de Grave in March 1725 describing life in the country:

Il y a [ici] une femme que j'aime beaucoup, parce qu'elle ne me répond pas lorsque je lui parle, qu'elle m'a déjà donné cinq ou six soufflets, par la raison, dit-elle, qu'elle est de mauvaise humeur.

It is early in the *Pensées* that Montesquieu asks who would ever marry, if concubinage were permitted.[3] He had the utmost confidence in his wife, however, as a business partner, and during his many absences left her with full powers for the management of his estates.

Within two months of each other, in the early summer of 1726, Montesquieu lost his two surviving uncles, both of them ecclesiastics. He inherited half the estate of the elder, Joseph, but this involved him in a net loss of almost 300 *livres*.[4] There was a compensation, however, for the uncle two years previously had renounced the abbacy of Faize, eight miles north-east of Libourne, in favour of Montesquieu's younger brother Joseph, and the President had successfully petitioned the Duc de Bourbon to permit the transfer. The benefice was a lucrative one: in his request to Monsieur le Duc, Montesquieu admitted only to a revenue of 2,000 *livres*, but when Barbot writes his word of congratulation he puts it much higher: five or six thousand livres are a good establishment, he says, for a Jansenist.[5] A year later, to Montesquieu's great delight, the brother received also the office of dean of the Church of Saint-Seurin in Bordeaux, an old church which had been a halting place on the pilgrimage route to Santiago de Compostela. This, said the President, was the best benefice in the province, though worth only 3,000 *livres* a year.[6]

[1] *Œuvres de Montesquieu*, Paris (Plassan), 1796, IV, p. 484.

[2] P. Barrière, *L'Académie de Bordeaux*, p. 68.

[3] *Pensée* 60 (Bkn. 1930).

[4] The will and a financial statement are to be found in the archives of La Brède.

[5] Barbot to Montesquieu, July 1724. On this abbacy see J.-A. Garde, *Histoire de Lussac et de l'abbaie cistercienne de Faize*, Libourne, 1953.

[6] Montesquieu to Mme de Grave, 17 July 1725.

The brother Joseph was no longer a financial charge to the President; indeed, he was the reverse, for Montesquieu now was able to dispose of his house in Bordeaux and thereafter, until Joseph died in 1754, stayed with him in the Deanery whenever he had occasion to visit Bordeaux.[1] His two sisters presented only a minimal burden. Both Marie and Thérèse were nuns, and received from the President pensions of the modest amount of 150 *livres* each.[2]

The only appreciable family expense was caused by the education of Montesquieu's son Jean-Baptiste. He was not entrusted to the Oratorians of Juilly, but was sent instead to the Collège Louis-le-Grand, which was an establishment of the Jesuits, and was placed in the particular care of Père Castel, a learned scientist as well as a theologian, whose acquaintance Montesquieu had made through a common acquaintance whom Castel describes as 'une dame fort noble et fort vertueuse.'[3] An active contributor to the *Mémoires de Trévoux*, and one of the precursors, in his *Clavecin oculaire* of the theorists of the symbolists, Castel was destined to play a significant role at different moments in Montesquieu's life. It was probably in the spring of 1724 that the President accompanied his eight-year-old son to Paris, where he left him in the hands of a servant called Doyenart who was subsequently ordained and became an unscrupulous and grasping priest.[4] A little more than a year later Montesquieu had doubts about the wisdom of leaving his son at Louis-le-Grand, and corresponded with Castel about this. The reason may have been dissatisfaction with his progress, for Jean-Baptiste made but little progress, either physical or intellectual, during his first months of residence, though he improved considerably when he had become accustomed to being away from home.[5] Montesquieu may, on the other hand, have been uneasy about leaving his son in the hands of the Jesuits, whom he had always distrusted. If the

[1] Montesquieu's residences in Bordeaux were in Rue des Lauriers (until 1715), Rue Margaux (1715–19), and Rue du Mirail (1719–25), in each case close to the busy Rue Sainte-Catherine (R. Céleste, 'Montesquieu à Bordeaux', in *Deux Opuscules de Montesquieu*, Bordeaux, 1891, pp. 67–70).

[2] Receipts for these pensions, from 1718 to 1740 for Marie, and from 1742 to 1744 for Thérèse, are preserved in the archives of La Brède. The story of Marie's marriage to D'Héricourt, intendant of Marseilles, is unfounded.

[3] L.-B. Castel, *L'Homme moral*, p. 183.

[4] Guasco, *Lettres familières*, LI (Nagel III, p. 1522, n.b).

[5] Castel to Montesquieu, 7 August 1725.

testimony reported by Grimm's friend Jacques-Henri Meister is to be held reliable, there is some reason for thinking that the President withdrew Jean-Baptiste and transferred him to the Collège d'Harcourt, whose tendencies were Jansenist, confiding him to the Abbé Quesnel, himself, as befits the bearer of his name, hostile to the Jesuits.[1] If Jean-Baptiste did in fact move from Louis-le-Grand to Harcourt, his education bears a curious similarity to that of Diderot, who, three years older than Montesquieu's son, seems to have been transferred from the one school to the other at a later stage of his career.[2]

Montesquieu's aims for his son are revealed by Meister's account. On a later visit to Paris the President closely questioned Quesnel about Jean-Baptiste's progress. The Abbé reported favourably on the boy's morals and character, to the father's great satisfaction, and went on to praise his intellectual application, and above all his devotion to natural history. At this Montesquieu became pale, and flung himself into an armchair with all the signs of the deepest despair. He exclaimed that all his hopes were now frustrated; the son would never hold the legal office for which he was intended; he would never be anything but a man of letters, an eccentric like his father; they would never be able to make him into anything else.

The President was not mistaken. His son showed no taste for the law, but spent his life in devotion to natural science, in which he made modest but useful contributions.[3]

Montesquieu's financial situation was not at this time a healthy one. There exists in the archives of La Brède a balance sheet which he drew up at the end of 1725, showing his economic position at that moment.[4] He owed his Bordeaux banker, a Jew called Pexotto, no less than 31,000 *livres*, his private friends, Barbot among them, were his creditors to the extent of 13,000 *livres*, and he had also some relatively small personal obligations amounting to some 2,500 *livres*. On the credit side 12,000 *livres* were due to him from his mother-in-law Madame de Lartigue. Against the resultant deficit he could set little but wine. He had

[1] Meister, in Grimm, *Correspondance littéraire*, ed. M. Tourneux, Paris, 1879, XI, p. 281.

[2] J. Pommier, *Diderot avant Vincennes*, Paris, 1939, p. 9.

[3] See J. Delpit, *Le Fils de Montesquieu*, Bordeaux, 1888.

[4] Printed in Nagel III, pp. 1565–6.

corn on one of his farms to the value of 2,000 *livres*, a certain amount of realizable farm equipment, and a credit of 3,500 *livres* in Sweden; otherwise his assets were represented by 125 casks of wine (on all but forty of which duty remained to be paid).

He possessed, it is true, considerable wealth in real property: land and houses at La Brède, Martillac in the close vicinity, Baron in Entre-deux-mers, and Montesquieu itself. But it was out of the question to realize these. If he sold any part of them his income would be reduced in proportion, and he would suffer a great loss of prestige. He was anxious to hand on to his children at least an undiminished patrimony, and in fact sought to increase his territorial holding and was vigorous in defence of his interests.[1] His financial difficulties were simply the result of his living above his income. All would have been well had he been prepared to settle down to a tranquil existence at La Brède. But Paris was attractive, his friends relentlessly urged him to return, and life in Paris was costly.

'Mon cher Usbek,' writes Dodart, 'Misérable enfant de la terre,' writes Bulkeley: 'come back and join us.' Berthelot de Duchy, Gacé, Madame de Grave, Madame d'Herbigny, Desmolets, Madame de Lambert, Berwick himself, urge him to return to *la bonne ville*.

But responsibilities, shortage of money,[2] and the necessity of obtaining leave of absence from the Parlement, granted always with the wish 'bon voyage et prompt retour',[3] tie Montesquieu to Bordeaux and to La Brède. On at least one occasion the Premier Président La Caze writes to the Government asking that Montesquieu be ordered to return, and in fact he is compelled to regain Bordeaux.[4]

His parliamentary office thus gave little joy to Montesquieu. Even its financial rewards were precarious. In 1724, 1725 and 1726 he had to write to Lalanne, paymaster of the Parlement,

[1] He made a lengthy and witty protest, to the anger of the intendant Boucher, against an order of the Government forbidding further planting of vines in Guyenne in 1725, having immediately before acquired for this purpose land in the commune of Pessac (Nagel III, pp. 263–71; Pléiade I, pp. 72–78).

[2] 'J'ai si mal vendu mon vin que je ne sais si je pourrai partir si tôt que je croyais' (Montesquieu to Bulkeley, 1 January 1724, misprinted as 1726 in Nagel).

[3] *Registre secret du Parlement de Bordeaux*, vol. XLII, pp. 579, 799. vol. XLIII, p. 326 (Arch. mun. Bx).

[4] Montesquieu to Mme de Graves, 22 June 1726.

asking for his stipend, and in 1725 at least it was two years in arrear.

His presidency was however a marketable commodity, and it is not surprising that early in 1726 Montesquieu sounded his friend Barbot about the possibility of arranging a sale.

Barbot, an able and intelligent man, though prone to be idle,[1] and a president himself, though of the Cour des Aides and not of the Parlement, reacted vigorously. He despatched on 9 April 1726 an exceedingly long letter of remonstration.

Non, mon cher Président, et je l'espère, vous ne vendrez point cette charge de président. Vous la devez à vos ancêtres, à votre postérité, à vous-même, à la province enfin qui jouit depuis longtemps de présidents de votre maison.

The splendid scolding continues. What are you going to do with your time? How can you renounce public life at your age? What will your family think? Do not worry about your creditors: they would all gladly engage themselves further. Two years' residence at La Brède would put an end to your debts. Reflect that in the public eye you will simply become an idle, useless citizen.

His protest made, however, Barbot addressed himself to the task, jointly with Sarrau de Vésis. Montesquieu did not wish to effect a sale outright, for he was anxious that his son should be able in due course to assume the *mortier*, and this fact diminished the attractiveness of the proposed terms for some of the possible buyers.

A buyer in due course was found, however, in Jean-Baptiste d'Albessard, a member of a prominent legal family of Bordeaux, a reliable man and (unlike Montesquieu's kinsman Marans who also was interested) able to pay.[2] The treaty of sale was signed at Bordeaux on 7 July 1726. Montesquieu surrendered the presidency for the life-time of the purchaser, whereafter it was to revert to Montesquieu or to his son. In the event of their predecease D'Albessard was to have the opportunity of outright purchase for whatever was then the normal figure, and it was expected that this would be in the vicinity of 100,000 *livres*. Meanwhile, while holding the office, D'Albessard was to pay to

[1] 'Si Barbot voulait travailler . . .; mais en vérité il faudrait qu'il travaillât' (Montesquieu to Sarrau de Boynet, June 1727) (Nagel III, p. 883).

[2] Berthelot de Duchy to Montesquieu, 30 July 1726.

Montesquieu or his sucessor the annual sum of 5,200 *livres*.[1]

The stipend of the office was 1,875 *livres*, from which tax of 450 *livres* was deducted at the source.[2] To this should be added a further sum known as the *épices*, consisting of payments made to the judges by litigants. It is hard to determine the value of the *épices* and other special fees; they depended in part on the extent of the professional activity of the individual magistrate, and were more modest in the criminal court known as the Tournelle than in the senior Grand'Chambre.[3] It is unlikely that Montesquieu, who usually sat with the Tournelle, and was an inactive magistrate, received a large sum from fees and *épices*. At most a few hundred livres were added to his net stipend of 1,425 *livres*. The sale of his office procured for him a substantial increase in income, probably exceeding 3,000 *livres*. There is little doubt that the desire for financial gain was his main reason for selling, though in years to come his son (followed by Maupertuis and D'Alembert), Mirabeau, and Condorcet were to dignify his motive.[4]

His responsibilities were reduced, his attachment to Bordeaux was relaxed, and his dignity was lessened, though not for long. For though his friends began for a time to address him as 'Monsieur' or 'mon cher Baron', and though on one occasion he goes out of his way to describe himself simply as an advocate at the Parlement of Bordeaux,[5] the title clung to him. The normal French practice of the indelibility of titles was followed, and Montesquieu remained 'Monsieur le Président' for the rest of his life and beyond.

The transaction completed, Montesquieu remained in the south-west to settle some other outstanding matters. At the beginning of the new year he travelled to Paris and did not return to Bordeaux or La Brède, or see his wife again, for over four years.

[1] *Arch. hist. Gironde*, LVIII.

[2] Arch. dép. Gironde, C 4066–7.

[3] F. L. Ford, *Robe and Sword*, Cambridge (Mass.), 1953, pp. 154–5. This book is a most useful guide to the finance of legal office.

[4] Secondat, *Mémoire*, p. 398: 'pour se livrer à l'inspiration de son génie et jouir de toute sa liberté'; Mirabeau to Vauvenargues, 7 February 1739: 'pour satisfaire son goût pour les sciences' (Vauvenargues, *Œuvres posthumes et œuvres inédites*, ed. D.-L. Gilbert, Paris, 1857, p. 114); Condorcet to Voltaire, 23 April 1776: 'Montesquieu . . . quitta son corps dès l'instant où il se sentit du talent' (Voltaire, *Œuvres*, XLIX, p. 593).

[5] Montesquieu to Lamoignon de Courson, 6 August 1726.

III. THE FRENCH ACADEMY

Helvétius reports that Montesquieu once said that he was favourably received in French society as a man of wit, until the *Lettres persanes* showed that perhaps he was in fact such; thereafter he suffered a thousand ills.[1] In Parisian society he still lacked official recognition, and in his attempt to obtain it by election to the Academy, he ran into serious difficulty. Non-residence in Paris was a great handicap, but not insuperable, as is shown by the election of Jean Bouhier, President of the Parlement of Dijon, 1727. But Montesquieu, even with Madame de Lambert's backing, was a much more controversial figure than that respected Burgundian scholar. It is by no means impossible that the sale of his office was in part designed to promote the appearance of residence in Paris.

Many legends have grown around the circumstances of Montesquieu's election to the Academy;[2] but if those facts only are

[1] Helvétius, *De l'esprit*, Paris, 1758, pp. 202–3.

[2] It has been claimed that Montesquieu was in fact elected to the Academy in 1725 or 1726 and that Fontenelle, who as *directeur* was to receive him into membership, had written his speech of welcome. But Montesquieu's enemies raised the question of his non-residence and the election was held invalid. The President, it is claimed, thereupon returned to Bordeaux, sold his office, and returned to be elected in 1727 (Vian, pp. 80 and 100; E. de Broglie, 'Les Mardis et les mercredis de la marquise de Lambert', in *Correspondant*, 10 and 25 April 1895). The only evidence produced for this claim is an entirely inconclusive passage from Trublet's memoir on Fontenelle (in *Œuvres* of Fontenelle, Amsterdam, 1764, XII, pp. 21–22). Fontenelle's only period of office as *directeur* in these years was from July to October 1726, and the only vacancy over which he had to preside was that created by the death of the Duc de La Force on 20 July 1726. The Academy met to elect a successor on 19 August, and adjourned until 22 August, the ostensible reason (which may in fact veil another) being the absence of a quorum. On 22 August Mirabaud was elected, the whole election being much more expeditious than any other in those years. It is certainly possible that there was a question of electing Montesquieu at this time; but if the reason for his non-election was non-residence, it would have been hard ten months later to elect Bouhier; and Montesquieu's sale of his office cannot have been the consequence of failure to be elected on this occasion, since the negotiations for that sale had already been begun early in April at the latest. Further, from the middle of June 1726 to the end of the year Montesquieu was absent from Paris and could not have made the traditional visits. He was likewise absent from Paris during the only other elections (of the Bishop of Langres and of Saint-Aignan) of 1725 and 1726. The story of his frustrated election in either of those years must then be disbelieved. At the most Fontenelle may have hoped for his election in succession to La Force, and prematurely written a speech of welcome.

believed for which evidence can be shown, the story is simple, and evidence is sufficiently abundant in the correspondence of Bouhier and his friends, and the official records of the Academy.

On 26 October a vacancy was created by the death of Madame de Lambert's friend Sacy. Bouhier, who in his seclusion at Dijon was the recipient of confidences from the most diverse correspondents, was told by the Marquise that Montesquieu's election was expected. She wishes that Bouhier were in Paris to vote for him, but we shall at least have the consolation, she admits that Sacy will be adequately praised.[1]

The author of the *Lettres persanes*, however, was in the embarrassing position of having poked fun at the Academy, and if he were to disavow this work, he would be without any literary standing. This was explained to Bouhier by his friend Matthieu Marais, himself most anxious to join the immortals.[2]

Bouhier none the less expects Montesquieu's election, for he speculates on what he will say about Sacy in his *discours de réception*.[3] On 1 December, writing again to Marais, Bouhier says that he thinks Montesquieu's election assured, unless the Cardinal-Minister intervenes. Indeed, he adds, a man deserves some favour who does for the Academy what in time past men did for the Gospel, leaves wife, children, occupation, and home.[4]

On 11 December the Academy met to elect a new member. Only eighteen members were present, this being less than a quorum. One of their number opposed the suspension of the standing order which fixed the quorum, and the election was therefore postponed until 20 December.[5] After the meeting of 11 December the learned but two-faced D'Olivet, one of the Academicians who had been present, wrote to the absent Bouhier giving him a more detailed account of the proceedings than is afforded by the official record. The *faction Lambertine* was so well organized, he declares, that there was no other candidate

[1] Mme de Lambert to Bouhier, 17 November 1727 (Bibliothèque V. Cousin, MS. 2, no. 83).

[2] Marais to Bouhier, 24 November 1727 (B.N., MSS. fr. 24415, f. 297; published in Marais, *Journal*, III, p. 501).

[3] Bouhier to Marais, 24 November 1727 (B.N., MSS. fr. 25541, f. 172).

[4] Bouhier to Marais, 24 November 1727 (B.N., MSS. fr. 25541, f. 174; published in E. de Broglie, *Les Portefeuilles du président Bouhier*, Paris, 1896, p. 174).

[5] *Registres de l'Académie française*, Paris, 1895, 3 vols., II, p. 239.

than the Gascon President; but a new circumstance (which had been foreseen by Bouhier) arose at the last moment: it was learnt that the Cardinal was displeased by the *Lettres persanes*, and that if Montesquieu were elected the King would probably refuse his approval. Fleury had not come himself to the Academy, of which he was a member, to make this announcement but had caused it to be known that in his view the choice of Montesquieu would be disapproved by all right-thinking men. It was the twenty-second *Lettre persane*,[1] says D'Olivet, which had given offence: this is where King and Pope are described as two magicians. D'Olivet finally congratulates himself on having so far disguised his real feeling as to have been invited to dine with the supporters of Montesquieu by their leader the Abbé Mongault.[2]

This account is substantially supported by Marais, who not being an academician had not been present. He tells Bouhier that Montesquieu had refused to disavow the *Lettres persanes*:

> le pauvre n'a pu désavouer ses enfants, quoique anonymes; ils lui tendaient leurs petits bras persans, et il leur a sacrifié l'Académie française.

Marais thinks that someone else will have to be found for the vacant seat.[3]

According to Montesquieu, it was the Jesuit Tournemine who drew Fleury's attention to the heterodox ideas expressed in the *Lettres persanes*, and stirred up in the Cardinal's mind opposition to the election of Montesquieu.[4] Fleury thereupon, if D'Alembert's account is reliable, as seems likely,[5] informed the Academy that he had not read the *Lettres persanes* but that trustworthy persons had warned him of the poison contained in the work,

[1] *L.P.* 24 in the modern critical editions.

[2] D'Olivet to Bouhier, 11 December 1727 (B.N., MSS. fr. 24417, f. 82; published in Ch.-L. Livet, *Histoire de l'Académie française par Pellisson et d'Olivet*, Paris, 1858, II, pp. 412–13.

[3] Marais to Bouhier, 17 December 1727 (B.N., MSS. fr. 24415, f. 237; published in Marais, *Journal*, III, p. 505 and by Broglie, *Portefeuilles*, p. 175).

[4] *Pensée* 472 (Bkn. 1737); and cf. Guasco, *Lettres familières*, (1768), XL (Nagel III, p. 1343, n.d.).

[5] D'Alembert's account (Nagel I, A, pp. vii–viii) is quoted by François Richer, editor of the 1758 edition of the *Œuvres de Montesquieu*, with the comment, 'M. de Secondat a certifié la vérité de son récit' (*Année littéraire*, 1776, VI, p. 50).

and that the King would never assent to the election of its author.

After the meeting on 11 December Montesquieu lost no time in going to see Fleury. His only recorded previous contact with the Cardinal was a letter of congratulation which he sent him on his receiving the red hat.[1] What passed between them now is only imperfectly known; but D'Alembert claims that, the President refusing either to avow or disavow the *Lettres persanes*, and saying that he ought to be judged only after the work had been read and not on the basis of a delation, Fleury did in fact read the book and smiled on its author. In any event, on Tuesday, 16 December, Fleury wrote to the Maréchal d'Estrées, *directeur* of the Academy, saying that after Montesquieu's explanation he was no longer opposed to his election.[2]

On the following Saturday, the Academy met and elected Montesquieu.[3] The election was not unanimous, but many of his previous opponents rallied to support him out of sympathy, finding it better, says D'Olivet (whose own thoughts were confided only to his guardian angel) to imperil the honour of the society, than to agree to 'la flétrissure de ce fou.'[4] All the intrigue against him, says Madame de Lambert on the other hand, has been to the shame of humanity;[5] but D'Estrées, the *directeur*, was praised by D'Alembert years later for having behaved with great virtue and dignity.[6]

Montesquieu took his seat on 24 January 1728, and his *discours de réception* was a masterpiece of eloquence and of verbal finesse. To praise Sacy was not a difficult task and he discharged it admirably; to make the customary eulogy of Richelieu, whom he execrated, was less easy but not less effectively done. There is a faint undertone of ambiguity in his words as he tells the Academicians:

Vous nous étonnez toujours quand vous célébrez ce grand ministre qui tira du chaos les règles de la monarchie; qui apprit à la France le secret de ses forces, à l'Espagne celui de sa faiblesse, ôta à l'Allemagne

[1] Montesquieu to Fleury, *s.d.* (Nagel III, p. 863).

[2] D'Olivet to Bouhier, 20 December 1727 (B.N., MSS. fr. 24417, f. 84; published in Livet, *Histoire*, II, p. 413.

[3] *Registres*, II, p. 239.

[4] D'Olivet to Bouhier, loc. cit.

[5] Mme de Lambert to Bouhier, 8 January 1728 (B.N., MSS. fr. 22412, f. 255; published in Broglie, 'Les Mardis').

[6] *Eloge* (Nagel I, A, p. ix).

ses chaînes, lui en donna de nouvelles, brisa tour à tour toutes les puissances, et destina, pour ainsi dire, Louis le Grand aux grandes choses qu'il fit depuis.[1]

The *directeur*, now Mallet, who is remembered today for this episode alone, had to receive the new member. He had shown his speech in advance to several members, and although one of them, Valincourt, had thought it likely to antagonize Montesquieu, he delivered it unchanged. His ostensible words of praise Montesquieu took for insults, and resented.[2] He refused to allow his speech to be printed along with Mallet's, and some modification had to be made by the *directeur* for the printed record.[3] Even the modified text, indeed, mocks the anonymity of the *Lettres persanes* and the audacities which they contain, and instructs the new academician not to think it his sole duty to criticize others.[4]

After his reception Montesquieu attended two sessions; he found D'Olivet reading his history of the Academy; but he refrained from opening his mouth.[5]

A provincial visitor to Paris wrote early in March to a Bordelais friend of the President, saying that he thought Montesquieu likely to remain in Paris, especially after his election to the Academy.[6] He was wrong. Montesquieu had achieved his aim in the metropolis, and he departed from Paris in the month of April. Three years were to elapse before he returned.

[1] Nagel I, A, p. liv; Pléiade I, p. 63.

[2] Valincourt to Bouhier, 28 January 1728 (B.N., MSS. fr. 24420, ff. 441–2).

[3] D'Olivet to Bouhier, 20 April 1728 (B.N., MSS. fr. 24417, f. 88; published in Livet, *Histoire*, II, p. 416).

[4] *Pièces concernant les ouvrages et la vie de M. le Président de Montesquieu*, Geneva, 1756, pp. 102–6; *Registres*, II, p. 241, n. 1.

[5] D'Olivet to Bouhier, loc. cit.

[6] Lafond (of Nantes) to Sarrau de Boynet, 24 March 1728 (Bx, MS. 828, XX no. 14).

V

TRAVELS IN ITALY, 1728–9

I. ART AND ARCHAEOLOGY

MONTESQUIEU left Paris on 5 April 1728[1] in the company of the first Earl Waldegrave. He had not been to La Brède or seen his wife since January of the previous year, and was not to do so again until May 1731. Older than most men who made the Grand Tour in the eighteenth century, he had advantages which they had not, for he did not have to rely in social intercourse solely on his birth and inherited rank. He had a name which was now well known, and his status as a member of the French Academy enabled him easily to enter the most celebrated of intellectual circles. Waldegrave, moreover, was a useful travelling companion. Amenable in that he was gay and light-hearted, he was also the nephew of the Duke of Berwick, whose prestige stood high in the courts of Europe; but unlike his uncle he had accepted the Hanoverian Settlement, and he was proceeding to Vienna as George II's ambassador.

They travelled through Ratisbon and sustained an accident to their carriage which necessitated a long ride on horseback[2] and involved a delayed arrival at Vienna, for though they had expected to be no more than a fortnight en route,[3] they did not reach their destination until 26 April.[4]

While at Vienna the President began to keep an account of his travels, in varying degrees of detail, and the entire account, with the exception of his stay in England, is extant and has been published. Since he never completely revised it for publication, though he was entertaining this project towards the end of his life, it has the advantages and disadvantages of the private document. It is not well written, but it is sincere and at times outspoken, and it has the great merit of revealing clearly what

[1] Secondat, *Mémoire*, p. 399; Waldegrave and Walpole to Newcastle, 30 March 1728 (B.M., Add. MSS. 32755, ff. 42 sq.).

[2] Bulkeley to Montesquieu, 5 May 1728.

[3] Waldegrave and Walpole to Newcastle, letter cited.

[4] D. B. Horn, *British Diplomatic Representatives, 1689–1789*, London (Camden Society, Third Series, XLVI), 1932, p. 35.

most interested its author. It is one of the earliest of the multitudinous travel diaries of the eighteenth century, Montesquieu preceding the Burgundian Président de Brosses by a decade, and if one excludes the specialized *Diarium Italicum* of Montfaucon it is the first travel account since the *Journal de voyage* of Montaigne to be written by a Frenchman of literary eminence.

At Vienna Montesquieu was presented to the Emperor, and several times met Prince Eugene (with whom he discussed Jansenism)[1] and Marshal Stahremberg, who was known to Berwick. He met, and lengthily enumerates, the entire body of diplomats accredited to the Imperial Court, and became at this time fired with the ambition of becoming an ambassador. He wrote about this to Fleury, to Berwick, to the Duc de Richelieu, who was then French Ambassador in Vienna, but absent on leave, and even to his false friend the Abbé d'Olivet. But although Fleury replied favourably in principle, no action was taken.

From Vienna Montesquieu made a diversion of an unusual and enterprising nature. Indulging the scientific interests which had led him, in 1719, to envisage writing a geological history of the earth, he undertook an expedition which lasted for almost a month to see the mines of Hungary. Visiting first the copper mines of the Chemnitz area, he was particularly interested by a fountain which apparently had the property of converting iron into copper, and carried away with him a bottle of the water from this fountain in order to have it analysed in Venice. He penetrated as far as Königsberg, 200 miles beyond Vienna and little more than eighty short of Cracow, where an English functionary called Potters displayed to him a steam pump, on which he made ample notes, and regaled him largely with Tokay wine. On his return from Italy he broke his journey to inspect the Hartz mines. Again he made detailed notes of what he saw, and finally prepared some papers for the Academy of Bordeaux.

Regaining Vienna on 26 June, he rejected an invitation which reached him from Berwick's son the Duke of Liria, Spanish Ambassador in Russia, who proposed that Montesquieu should visit Moscow, proceed thence to Constantinople and then by sea to Venice. He went instead, not (as has sometimes been claimed) to Belgrade,[2] but directly through Gratz and Laibach to Venice.

[1] Secondat, *Mémoire*, pp. 399–400.
[2] Vian, p. 115.

Here begins the most fruitful and stimulating part of his travels.

Montesquieu's route led him from Venice to Milan, thence through Turin to Genoa. From Genoa, after a brief exploration of La Spezia and Portovenere, he went through Pisa to Florence, where he spent six weeks. Then proceeding south through Siena and Montefiascone he reached Rome, where he stayed from 19 January to 18 April 1729. He journeyed south again to spend a fortnight in Naples. Returning, he tarried for almost two months in Rome, before going north-east through the Marches to Ancona. He gave a week to Bologna, made a shorter halt at Modena and another at Parma, and crossing his outward path at Verona on 30 July, left Italy by the Brenner. His original intention of visiting Switzerland, which he maintained as late as his stay in Modena, he abandoned.[1]

He travelled with dignity if not in state. He was armed with influential letters of introduction, one of which, from Alary to Luigi Gualtieri, later to become Cardinal and in 1754 nuncio in Paris, has survived.[2] He relied extensively on French diplomatic representatives abroad. He did not, however, on that account, escape all embarrassment. Leblond, the French chargé d'affaires in Milan, suspected Montesquieu of having some sinister motive in his travels and reported in that sense to his government.[3] In Venice, moreover, a strange story lingered for some years about a *contretemps* of which he was the victim. It is claimed that friends warned him of the probability that on his departure from Venice the police, under instructions from the administration, would search his luggage, confiscate the many and notoriously outspoken notes which he had made while in that city, and perhaps arrest him. When in due course he left Venice by boat, he was perturbed to see a number of gondolas following

[1] Secondat (*Mémoire*, p. 401) and the biographers who follow him, notably D'Alembert and Maupertuis, are incorrect in saying that Montesquieu visited Switzerland.

[2] Its wording is most eulogistic: 'C'est un homme fort aimable et dont le commerce peut être aussi utile qu'agréable. Il a non seulement beaucoup de savoir mais un esprit vif et enjoué qui le rendait pendant qu'il était ici les délices de toutes les bonnes compagnies' (Alary to Gualtieri, 9 May 1729, B.M. Add. MSS. 20670, ff. 73–7).

[3] See Mlle F. Weil, 'Promenades dans Rome en 1729 avec Montesquieu' (*Technique, art, science*, 1958), citing documents in the Ministère des Affaires étrangères. The Ministry replied to Leblond telling him that his doubts were unfounded.

him, and fearing a perquisition, flung all the papers in his possession into the lagoon.[1]

It would be curious to take in turn each of the places visited by Montesquieu and compare his comments on it with those of other travellers of the age and to observe where they agree and where disagree; to compare, for example, De Brosses's statement about Genoa on departing from it, that the only pleasure that city affords is the joy one has on leaving it,[2] with Montesquieu's lament over the inhospitable nature of the Genoese, his assertion, made perhaps from the standpoint of a winegrower, that Genoa is the Narbonne of Italy, and his abominable verses beginning:

Adieu, Gênes détestable,
Adieu, séjour de Plutus,
Si le ciel m'est favorable,
Je ne vous reverrai plus.

But it is more useful to consider the various influences to which Montesquieu was subjected in Italy, and the social groups in which he moved, and first to mention the remarkable effect which Italy exerted on his aesthetic interests.

He had already written some part of what is now known as the *Essai sur le goût* before he had crossed the Alps. The doctrine

[1] The first account of this episode is given by Grosley in a letter to an unknown correspondent, dated from Venice on 4 August 1758, but published only in his *Œuvres inédites*, Paris, 1812–13, III, p. 418. A more detailed account appears in the same author's *Observations sur l'Italie et sur les Italiens*, London, 1774, II, pp. 68–69. According to a variant of this story, Montesquieu, while in Venice, was visited by a stranger who warned him that he had incurred suspicion on account of the freedom of his comments on politics and that his lodgings were about to be searched. The President, afraid for his life, burned all his manuscripts, only to learn afterwards that the whole episode was a practical joke perpetrated by Chesterfield as a result of a conversation with Montesquieu. The earliest authority for this story is the Florentine Gatti, who reported it to Diderot (Diderot to Sophie Volland, 5 September 1762, in Diderot, *Correspondance*, ed. G. Roth, IV, Paris, 1958, pp. 136–40). It is also related in the *Mémoires* of Pierre-Victor de Besenval (Paris, 1805, I, pp. 187–90), possibly on the authority (though he does not claim this) of his father, who appears to have met Montesquieu in Florence (Nagel II, p. 1086; Pléiade I, p. 654). The variant is clearly false. Montesquieu's first act on meeting Chesterfield at The Hague, thirteen months after leaving Venice, was to present him a letter of introduction from Waldegrave; and it is clear from Chesterfield's correspondence that he did not leave his post at The Hague during the whole period of Montesquieu's stay in Italy. Grosley's account, however, is likely to have some basis of fact, and Grosley was a scrupulous scholar.

[2] C. de Brosses, *Lettres familières*, ed. Y. Bézard, Paris, 1931, I, p. 79.

contained in this fragment seems to have been a simple materialistic subjectivism, developed abstractly without reference to works of art. Now, he made a very serious attempt to educate himself in the fine arts, beginning in Vienna under the guidance of an elusive individual known as the Chevalier Jacob. All that is disclosed about this man is his enthusiasm for painting and for the fair sex. Not even his nationality is revealed. But it was he who gave Montesquieu his first grounding in painting, informing him both about the history and the technique of that art. Montesquieu made notes from what Jacob had told him, and these are still preserved in the *Spicilège*.[1] Jacob accompanied the President as far as Venice.

The architectural splendour of Venice did not make on Montesquieu the powerful impression which it made on other travellers, in spite of its being the first Italian city he saw. Much more space is taken up in his correspondence with references to the celebrated courtesans, of whom he soon tired, and in his journal with descriptions of dredging machines, and the only even moderately long account of any work of art deals with the treasure of Saint Mark's. It is not until he arrives in Florence that his artistic interest is fully aroused. Here he praises the Cathedral and Santa Maria Novella, in spite of their being Gothic edifices, and he describes Giotto's campanile as the best Gothic in Europe. Unlike other visitors, he is unenthusiastic about the Medici chapel then being added to the church of San Lorenzo. But he writes an entire work about the artistic treasures of Florence. He did not rapidly pass through the galleries he visited. He examined them in great detail, and in the company of experts, and he has left notes which amount to a *catalogue raisonné* of all Florence's artistic possessions. He used Misson's guide-book, Addison's *Remarks on several places in Italy*, and *Les Délices de l'Italie*, which he stigmatizes as 'mon mauvais livre'. He was conducted round the Uffizi by one Bianchi, and received guidance at other times from the younger Piemontini. Statuary above all captivates him: he gave to the study of it day after day of his time, and the whole of his mind.

Few cities gave Montesquieu more pleasure than Rome. He

[1] *Spicilège* 461 (MS., pp. 413–20). Waldegrave's MS. *Journal of his Embassy to Germany* [*sic*], *1727–8*, now at Chewton, makes two references to his meeting Jacob in Paris in 1727 and 1728.

told a friend later that there were few places to which he would more readily have retired.[1] He devoted himself to a thorough exploration of the city, now with a French sculptor, both Bouchardon and Adam of Nancy being mentioned in his journal, now accompanied by one Prideaux, possibly the son of the English scholar Humphrey Prideaux.[2] His tastes in Rome are conventional. His enthusiasm is unending for Raphael, whose School of Athens above all wins his commendation. Fidelity to nature, freedom from all mannerism, and perfect management of light and shade, are the merits he discerns in Raphael. Likewise he admires Michelangelo. He praises the proportions of Saint Peter's, saying, as others have since him, that it appears smaller than it is. In the Sistine Chapel, though he reproaches the painter with errors of perspective, he is overcome with the majesty and strength of the achievement. He departs from the conventional traveller's judgement, however, in disapproving of the steps of the Trinità de' Monti, and in saying not a word about the style of the Castel Sant'Angelo.

The most striking fact about the President's interests in Rome is the absence of any close attention to the remains of the ancient world. He displays no serious archaeological enthusiasm at all. There are passing references to the Arch of Constantine, to the Forum and the Capitol; there is a rather more detailed discussion of precious stones of the ancient world; there are occasional references to statues, but fewer than at Florence, and his interest is exclusively aesthetic; there is a comment on the absence of windows from Roman houses; a word of praise is bestowed on the *Nozze Aldobrandine*; and that is all. There is no realization that the remains of the ancient world have value as historical evidence. He comments cynically that there is nothing to lose by excavation, for even if you find only bricks, they will pay you for your trouble. Finally, meeting Cardinal Alessandro Albani and seeing his collections, he remarks, 'Le cardinal Albani a des inscriptions qui marquent certaines époques de Rome', and says no more. This lack of concern for archaeology is surprising in a man who five years later was to publish a work on Roman history, and throws an interesting light on his historical method.

[1] Duclos, *Œuvres diverses*, Paris, 1802, IV, p. 91.
[2] V. Degrange, *Catalogue d'autographes*, no. 54, 1952.

II. THE CHURCH

Pietro-Francesco Orsini had been a good Dominican and a conscientious bishop, and he had not sought elevation to the Papal throne. To one of the cardinals in the Conclave of 1724, reports Montesquieu, he had said as he tried to escape through the window, 'I am incapable. I know nothing except how to be a friar. I shall govern badly.'[1] He became Pope nevertheless, with the title of Benedict XIII, and his reluctance was shown to be justified. He was a bad administrator. He did not, reports another French traveller, even read the dispatches from his nuncios, describing them as 'faiseurs de gazettes'.[2] His prestige, low already, was reduced further by riots which occurred in Rome in January 1729, the agricultural population of the Papal States having been brought to the verge of starvation by inability to work owing to heavy rains.[3] The natural gloom of the Pope communicated itself to the town: 'sous Benoît XIII,' laments Montesquieu, 'Rome aussi triste que sainte.' He does not seem to have been received in audience.[4] Benedict XIII had little to commend him to Montesquieu, who respected neither monastic devotion nor political ineptitude. He remarks that Benedict is both despised and hated, because all his wealth and his solicitude go to his former diocese of Benevento, and because he is governed in all things by his creature, the execrable Cardinal Coscia. When, a year later, the Pope dies, Montesquieu writes with joy to a clerical friend that Rome is now delivered from the base tyranny of Benevento. Give us now, he exclaims, a Pope with a

[1] 'Sono incapace. Non so che qualche fraterie. Io governerò male.' (Nagel III, p. 1178; Pléiade I, p. 746).

[2] Silhouette, *Voyage de France, d'Espagne, de Portugal et d'Italie*, Paris, 1770, 4 vols., I, p. 252.

[3] *Daily Post Boy*, 31 January, 1729.

[4] A story is told of Montesquieu's being received by the Pope and being authorized by him, as a mark of especial favour, to abstain from fasting for the rest of his life. The next day an official brought the written dispensation and demanded a large fee. The economical spirit of Montesquieu revolted. He handed back the document, saying, 'The Pope is an honest man; his word is enough for me and I hope it will be enough for God.' This anecdote, which appears in the Plassan edition of Montesquieu (Paris, 1796, IV, p. 487), is told there in connexion with Lambertini (Benedict XIV). Vian (pp. 119–20), aware that Montesquieu never met the later Pope, transfers it to Benedict XIII. Stories of this kind abound about Lambertini, but not about Benedict XIII of whom they would be implausible, and this anecdote must be adjudged false.

sword like Saint Paul, not a rosary like Saint Dominic or a beggar's bag like Saint Francis. Let infallibility be used, not to refute Quesnel, but to frustrate the Emperor![1]

There was gloom, too, in the Sacred College. Ten years later De Brosses says that few cardinals are exempt from moroseness. There were in their number, nevertheless, some men of geniality and of distinction. The Biblioteca Angelica possesses a manuscript, bearing no indication of authorship, which gives a frank and often malicious account of the characters of those cardinals who were resident in Rome in 1728.[2] Coscia is violently denounced, and the writer lingers with evident delight over his account of the humble origins of this now unpopular favourite. Alberoni, then living in Rome in retirement from politics, is frowned on likewise. Imperiali is described as having been a great favourite of Clement XI, and a candidate for the Papal throne in each of the two preceding conclaves. Lorenzo Corsini said to be extremely popular with his brother cardinals—a fact attested in 1730 by his election to the pontificate—but to intervene little in politics during the present reign. He is praised for spending not more than a single month each year at Frascati. The dissolute Ottoboni (whom Montesquieu credits with sixty or seventy bastards) is said to have reformed his ways, either genuinely, or through hypocrisy, in order to please Benedict XIII; and he is mentioned in a *mot* attributed to the scandal-loving Lambertini, later to mount the throne as Benedict XIV. Five things, said Lambertini, I do not believe: the sanctity of the Pope, the faith of the King of England,[3] the poverty of Coscia, the conversion of Ottoboni, and (referring to the Vatican's prosecutor in criminal causes) the devotion of Fiorelli in saying Mass. Little is said of Annibale Albani, save that he was not greatly concerned with the government of the Church; his brother Alessandro, it is remarked, is much less interested in politics than in collecting antiques, from dealing in which he has acquired a considerable fortune. Bentivoglio is able and highly esteemed, but tends to alienate affection because of his rebarbative nature and his partiality. Polignac finally receives an elogium. His

[1] Montesquieu to Cerati, 1 March, 1730.

[2] *Brevi notizie delle azioni e costumi degli Eminentissimi Cardinali viventi in Roma . . . sotto il pontificato di Benedetto XIII* (Biblioteca Angelica, MS. 2192).

[3] The Pretender James Edward.

humanity and his affability are highly praised, as is his devotion to the interests of the French Court, whose ambassador he was in Rome. All these cardinals, except Lambertini who was away from Rome during Montesquieu's visit, are referred to by the President. Apart also from Coscia and Ottoboni, he was personally acquainted with them all. Alessandro Albani, to whom he came with a letter from the Marquis de Breil, Sardinian Minister in Vienna, he found amiable and intelligent, but little esteemed in Rome. He reports that he has sold 25,000 crowns' worth of statues to the King of Poland. He had a long talk with Alberoni about Spain, and found him a brusque man with few topics of conversation. Imperiali he rated very highly as a man of sense and parts, and not seeming more than sixty, though he was almost eighty years of age. He felt affection for Lorenzo Corsini and saw him frequently, for, in spite of his great age, he lived an active social life in Rome. His salon was one of the main centres of intelligent conversation, and his reputation stood high in the learned world. It was to him that Vico dedicated his *Scienza nuova*. Montesquieu knew both him and others of his family, and in the *Voyages* he enumerates the reasons for which Corsini will not become Pope. Here he was mistaken, because, though almost blind, Corsini ascended the Papal throne in 1730 as Clement XII.

Of all the *porporati*, however, it was Polignac whom Montesquieu loved most. Not knowing him before his visit to Rome, he was presented to him by a letter from Bonneval.[1] The President was a frequent visitor to his palace and came to know him well. The Cardinal de Bernis has given a memorable portrait of Polignac. Noble in bearing, graceful in conversation, a connoisseur of the arts and a protector of artists, intelligent, well-informed, amiable and benevolent, so learned that Bernis consulted him as if he were a dictionary, an excellent Latinist, he only just fell short of being a great man; but he lacked fibre and resolution.[2] He maintained an almost royal table,[3] and the galleries of his

[1] Bonneval to Montesquieu, 2 October 1728.

[2] Cardinal de Bernis, *Mémoires et lettres*, ed. F. Masson, Paris, 1878, I, pp. 61–67.

[3] When he remarks (Nagel II, p. 1100; Pléiade I, p. 668) that no cardinal spends more than 2,000 *livres* annually on his table, Montesquieu means cardinals *in Curia*, and not ambassadors who happen to be cardinals. The tradition of hospitality in the French Embassy in Rome continued. De Brosses

palace were well stocked with the rarest antiques. Montesquieu spent much time inspecting his exhibits, and the Cardinal accompanied him on various expeditions within the city and in its environs. But it was from his conversation that Montesquieu profited most. The topics discussed, on all of which Polignac had clear and intelligent things to say, ranged from theology to the recent history of France. He was full of information about the arcana of diplomacy. On the secret history of *Unigenitus*, on court life under Louis XIV, on the intrigues of Roman conclaves, the Cardinal gave Montesquieu information which is recorded in one or other of his notebooks. On weighty philosophical problems Polignac held forth with great ease. 'Monseigneur,' Montesquieu said to him, 'vous ne faites pas des systèmes, vous dites des systèmes.'[1] When the first canto of Polignac's poem, the *Anti-Lucretius*, not published until after his death, was read privately in Rome on 4 June 1729, Montesquieu was present. He was filled with admiration for what he calls an immortal work in which, for a second time, Descartes triumphs over Lucretius.[2] Ten years later, everyone in Rome asked De Brosses for news of Polignac, and expressed the hope that he would come to Rome for the impending conclave.[3] Montesquieu, a week after meeting him for the first time, writes that he is one of the most likeable men he has ever met, and is the idol of Rome.[4]

Montesquieu did not confine his ecclesiastical acquaintance to cardinals. But he did not see many Jesuits.[5] He was, however, prepared to see anyone from whom he could obtain information, and was particularly anxious to inform himself about China, continuing the process of instruction which he had begun in 1713 with Hoange. Present in Rome was Fouquet, a French Jesuit from Burgundy, who had spent thirty years in China as a missionary and was now living in socially active retirement in

(op. cit., II, pp. 316–19) gives an account of a single meal given in 1739 by Saint-Aignan who was then ambassador, which cost 12,000 *livres*, not counting losses of plate.

[1] *Pensée* 2149 (Bkn. 1349).

[2] *Pensée* 1308 (Bkn. 938).

[3] De Brosses, op. cit., II, pp. 38–39.

[4] Montesquieu to Berthelot de Duchy, 28 January 1729.

[5] He is wrong when many years later he tells Guasco that he only met one Jesuit in Rome, Vitry, who often came to dine at Polignac's table (Montesquieu to Guasco, 9 April 1754). He forgets that Fouquet was a Jesuit.

Rome, with the title of Bishop of Eleutheropolis.[1] Montesquieu saw much of him, liked him, and laid under abundant contribution Fouquet's insatiable love of talk.[2] Many conversations are minuted in Montesquieu's notebooks, and the President learnt a great deal from them about the manners, religion, and government of the Chinese as well as of the size and rate of reproduction of their population.[3] It was probably Fouquet who put Montesquieu in touch with Mattia Ripa, another returned missionary, who was seeking to establish a college for the Chinese in Naples. With the support of Benedict XIII, and in spite of the opposition of the Viceroy of Naples, this project was being pursued, and Ripa had already a few Chinese disciples in Naples.[4] Montesquieu regarded this project as the only possible way of causing the Chinese missions to succeed.

In the second half of the eighteenth century there was an active and organized Jansenist movement in Rome,[5] which differed in several important respects from the French Jansenist movement of the eighteenth century. Less outspoken than the French, since few of its members ventured openly to attack the Bull *Unigenitus*, less concerned than the French with the jurisdictional aspect of Jansenism, terms such as Gallicanism and Ultramontanism being incapable of having meaning in Rome, the Italian Jansenists, who had influential supporters in the Sacred College, were less hostile than most of the French to the progress

[1] The Vatican Library contains the papers of Fouquet (MSS. Borg. lat. 565–7), which throw an extremely interesting light on eighteenth-century China. They are worthy of detailed study, and Fouquet's diary of life in China is well worth publication. See on Fouquet A. H. Rowbottom, 'China in the *Esprit des lois*: Montesquieu and Mgr Fouquet' (*Comparative literature*, 1950), and H. Bernard-Maître, 'Un ami romain du président de Brosses: Jean-Nicholas Fouquet' (*Mémoires de l'Académie de Dijon*, 1947–53). It may be noted that Fouquet's nephew was at Juilly with Montesquieu (*Dossier manuscrit des pensions*).

[2] De Brosses (op. cit., II, pp. 262–3) also attests the garrulousness of Fouquet ('J'ai appris de lui toute la Chine complète, excepté ce que je voulais savoir').

[3] He also obtained from Fouquet a benefice for his secretary Duval (Montesquieu to Cerati, 21 December 1729 and 1 March 1730).

[4] Four, according to Montesquieu, but five, according to the *Biografia degli uomini illustri del Regno di Napoli*, which gives their names, a mixture of Italian and Chinese, such as Giambattista Ku.

[5] See A. C. Jemolo, *Il Giansenismo in Italia prima della Rivoluzione*, Bari, 1927, and (a detailed treatment from the orthodox standpoint) E. Dammig, *Il Movimento giansenista a Roma nella seconda metà del secolo XVIII*, Vatican City, 1945.

of ideas and to the Enlightenment. Its three principal leaders, towards the middle of the century, were Cardinal Passionei, Bottari, and Foggini. Passionei, not yet a cardinal at the time of Montesquieu's visit, was absent from Italy, being Nuncio in Switzerland. Bottari (who like Passionei enters Montesquieu's history at a later stage, when *L'Esprit des lois* is being examined by the Congregation of the Index) the President, rather surprisingly, did not meet during his Italian travels. Foggini was too young then to have been known to him. The three principal lieutenants of these three leaders were Niccolini, Cerati and Martini. The last of these, a canon, was known to Montesquieu at Florence, though probably not intimately. Niccolini and Cerati, however, were in different case. Antonio Niccolini, of a wealthy Florentine family, was close to Montesquieu's heart. In a list which he gives of men met in Rome, arranged in order of his affection for them, Niccolini comes first.[1] They corresponded afterwards for many years, and Montesquieu's last letter to Niccolini, written a few weeks before his death, ends with the subscription, 'Mon cher abbé, je vous aimerai jusqu'à la mort.' Cerati was an intimate friend of Niccolini, and in the end became even more closely attached than he to Montesquieu; for Cerati visited France, saw much of Montesquieu in Paris, and attained such intimacy with him that he was permitted to read parts of *L'Esprit des lois* while it was being written. These two excellent clerics, Niccolini and Cerati, approached Jean-Baptiste de Secondat ten years after his father's death, asking if they might contribute to the cost of a bust of Montesquieu, to be presented to the Academy of Bordeaux.[2] Their affection for the President extended not only beyond the grave, but what is more, beyond the immediate sorrow of bereavement.

If to the fact of these friendships, contracted in Rome, is added Montesquieu's acquaintance, already mentioned, with the Corsini family, to which Niccolini was allied by the marriage of his sister, and Cerati and Bottari by close friendship, and which later was regarded as a powerful supporter of the Jansenist cause, it is seen that the President was very close to the Roman Jansenist movement in its embryonic stage; a fact significant both in the history of Jansenism and in the history of Montesquieu.

[1] Nagel II, p. 1191; Pléiade I, p. 759.
[2] Secondat to Guasco, 25 March 1765 (Nagel III, pp. 1553–4).

III. PERSONAL ENCOUNTERS

In the social intercourse of Italian society Montesquieu gave as well as received. A French monk writes from Rome in 1729, 'Monsieur de Montesquieu de Bordeaux se distingue ici par son brillant. C'est un homme de belles-lettres.'[1] There were indeed many Frenchmen and other non-Italians, lay as well as ecclesiastical, whom Montesquieu met in Italy, sometimes travellers like himself, sometimes permanently domiciled there. He met the Frenchman Silhouette at Parma and very probably in Rome too, for they were there at the same time and knew the same people.[2] Silhouette was interested in things Chinese,[3] he was well thought of by Madame de Lambert,[4] and was an acquaintance of Desmolets.[5] His path was more than once to cross Montesquieu's in later life. In Rome the President stayed for some time—four months has been claimed—in the same hotel as Jacob Vernet, a particular which is recorded by Vernet but not by Montesquieu.[6] The hotel is likely to have been the Monte d'Oro in the Piazza di Spagna, where De Brosses also stayed and which he describes as the only place in Rome where a foreigner can live.[7] Vernet was a Swiss Calvinist minister of middle class extraction, nine years younger than the President, but well acquainted with the intellectual society of Paris. He knew Lelong of the Oratory, Fontenelle, Mairan, and Tournemine, and thus had some claim both to the friendship and to the hostility of Montesquieu. While in Italy he became well informed about the scholarship and literature of the peninsula to an extent which enabled him, on his return to Switzerland, to join the editorial board of the *Bibliothèque italique*, a well-organized and intelligent journal of which Montesquieu eventually possessed a complete run. He was present

[1] Maloet to Montfaucon, 20 April 1729 (B.N., MS. fr. 17710, f. 57).

[2] Silhouette's *Voyage* was published in 1770. It does not contain any reference to Montesquieu.

[3] He published his *Idée générale du gouvernement et de la morale des Chinois* in 1729.

[4] Saint-Hyacinthe to Des Maizeaux, 4 June 1732 (B.M., Add. MSS. 4284, f. 156).

[5] Desmolets to Des Maizeaux, 27 July 1731 (B.M., Add. MSS. 4285, f. 259v).

[6] Saladin (?), *Mémoire historique sur la vie et les ouvrages de M. Jacob Vernet*, Paris, 1790, p. 11.

[7] De Brosses, op. cit., II, p. 12.

with the President at the canonization of John Nepomucene, and this was not, says his biographer, the only occasion they had to discuss the decadence of the Romans. Vernet, it will be seen, played an exceedingly important role later in Montesquieu's life, for it was he who supervised the publication at Geneva of *L'Esprit des lois*. In discharging this duty he shows himself to be a man of vigorous, intelligent, and arbitrary mind.

One of the most curious figures of eighteenth-century Italy was a Jew called Athias.[1] His father an advocate at Salamanca, the son took up residence at Leghorn, married his niece, which involved him in endless discord with his brother who was her father, and began to collect books. He was a student of subjects so diverse as chemistry and Hebrew, and he had many friends in the intellectual world. It was his delight to converse with men of parts who passed through Leghorn (it was here that he met Mattia Ripa returning from China) but he frequently diverted himself by making visits to Florence. Montesquieu, twice in the *Voyages* and once in the *Spicilège*[2] refers to meeting a Livornese Jew at Florence; he describes him as a man of letters, and as the principal Jew of Leghorn. He discussed with him the trade of Portugal and the Inquisition, as well as the population of Leghorn. He gives him the name Dathias, a slight and easily explicable variant from Athias, and there can be no doubt that this is the same man. He may well, it will be seen, have put Montesquieu in touch with important figures in the intellectual life of Naples.

At Venice Montesquieu met two exiles of notoriety and had prolonged conversations with them. These are Bonneval and John Law. The Comte de Bonneval was famous because of his adventurous military exploits, but also, and more especially, because of his eventual conversion to the Moslem faith and his assumption of the title of Pasha. Montesquieu and Bonneval were scarcely separated during the President's stay in Venice.[3] Innumerable conversations are reported in the *Voyages*, the *Pensées* and the *Spicilège*. Bonneval was an unending source of gossip about the military and diplomatic history of the eighteenth century. He was also acutely interested in machinery, and Montesquieu listened to him as readily on the one subject as on

[1] On this figure see F. Nicolini, *Autobiografia di Giambattista Vico*, Milan, 1947, pp. 184–90, 'Un ebreo massone: Giuseppe Athias'.

[2] *Spicilège* 472 (MS. pp. 433–6).

[3] Nagel II, p. 1016; Pléiade I, p. 583.

the other, frequently, however, with sceptical hesitations; for often he appends to the account of something told him by Bonneval the remark 'to be verified'. John Law, likewise in Venice, was nearing the end of his days. This Scotsman who had risen from humble origins to be French Minister of Finance, whose ante-room was filled by night with those noblemen who, unable to speak to him the previous day, hoped for an audience in the morning,[1] was regarded with revulsion by Montesquieu. But this feeling was overcome by his curiosity. He had heard much of Law both at court, during the short time he spent there, and also from his Bordelais friend Melon who had been secretary to the Minister and was an economist in his own right. Montesquieu had a long conversation with the exile; he was presented with a manuscript work on French commerce;[2] and his final comment on the man was that he was more in love with his ideas than with his money. The following year Law died, not in destitution, but leaving 80,000 crowns, a small sum, however, compared with his previous fortune.[3]

Much more important, however, because a centre of intrigue, in the society of exiles in Italy was the Jacobite court. Prince James Edward, usually known as the Chevalier de Saint-George, took up residence in Rome on 9 February 1729, some three weeks after Montesquieu's arrival in that city. He had previously been living at Bologna. The German Keysler, travelling in Rome shortly after the visit of Montesquieu, reports that 'the figure made by the Pretender to the British crown . . . is in every way very mean and unbecoming.' The Roman court had ordered that he should be styled King of England. The Italians, says Keysler, 'sometimes by a kind of jocular civility term him *il Rè di qui*, i.e. "the local king, or king here, *Rex in partibus*"; whereas the rightful possessor is styled *il Rè di qua*, "the king there", i.e. in England, upon the spot.'[4] Montesquieu observed the Pretender at the canonization of John Nepomucene, and remarked:

Ce prince a une bonne physionomie et noble. Il paraît triste, pieux.

[1] *Spicilège* 331 (MS., pp. 293–4).

[2] *Œuvres complètes de Law*, ed. J. Harsin, Paris, 1934, I, pp. xxxix–xliii, and III, pp. 67–261. The manuscript, which had found its way to the library of Chartres, was destroyed during the 1939–45 war.

[3] De Brosses, op. cit., II, pp. 27–28.

[4] J. G. Keysler, *Travels through Germany, Bohemia, Hungary, Switzerland, Italy and Lorraine*, London, 1756–7, II, p. 46.

On dit qu'il est faible et opiniâtre. Je ne le sais pas par moi-même, n'en étant pas connu.[1]

It is surprising that Montesquieu did not seek an audience of the Pretender, which his friendship with Berwick, the Prince's natural brother, would easily have procured for him. It may be that he feared that to have been received at the exiled court would have compromised him later in England; and he was well acquainted with the role in Rome of the mysterious Baron von Stosch who, ostensibly a collector of antiques, was in reality a spy whose function was to report Jacobite activity, and visits received by the Pretender, to the government in London. Montesquieu might have feared that he would be suspected of being an envoy of Berwick. He did not regard himself, however, as debarred from meeting the Pretender's wife, the Princess Sobieska. He was received by her during his second stay in Rome, on 25 June, when she had but recently arrived from Bologna, her husband having already departed to the villa at Albano which the Pope had lent him. Her two sons, Charles Edward and the future Cardinal of York, were also present, and Montesquieu was impressed by them. He lamented the disaffection between the Princess and her husband: they add, he said, to the misfortunes which Providence has given them. The President may also have been acquainted with others of the exiled court. He saw the third Earl of Jersey at the canonization ceremony. Hay, who according to Montesquieu procured the cardinal's hat for Tencin, might well have been mentioned to him by Andrew Michael Ramsay, who was closely connected with the Jacobites and a friend of Hay. He certainly knew the Earl of Dunbar, Hay's father-in-law and the Pretender's adviser. But Montesquieu's familiarity with Jacobite circles in Rome is slight, compared with that, for example, ten years later, of the Président de Brosses, who very frequently dined at the royal table.

Montesquieu circulated much in those native intellectual circles in Italy which, though they included ecclesiastics, were not primarily connected with the Church. His initiation began as soon as he arrived in Italy, for his sponsor in Venice was the erudite and much travelled Antonio Conti, whom he had probably already known in Paris. Conti had a wide range of interests. He had translated Racine's *Athalie* into Italian verse, and had himself

[1] Nagel II, p. 1131; Pléiade I, p. 699.

composed a tragedy on Julius Caesar, which won the high commendation of Vico.[1] He had conversations with Montesquieu about dramatic theory,[2] and also, being himself interested in music, caused his visitor to meet his friend Marcello, whom he was trying to induce to translate Plutarch's treatise on music, but whom the President characterized as *une espèce de fou.* Conti may have spoken to Montesquieu about Lady Mary Wortley Montagu, some of whose verses he translated into Italian; and the President appears to have discussed Conti with his English friends, for he reproduces a couplet written on him:

His fancy and his judgement such,
Each to the other seems too much.[3]

Conti was at the forefront of the intellectual movement in Italy in his day, and had as wide a circle of acquaintance in Italy as in France. It was probably he who procured entry for Montesquieu into the collections of Vallisnieri at Padua, certainly he who made the President known to the learned Countess Clelia Borromeo, the Milanese counterpart of Madame du Châtelet, possibly he, indeed, who introduced Montesquieu to Cerati.

Meeting at Turin the physicist Roma, at Turin likewise seeing again Bernardo Lama whom he had known already in Paris,[4] at Florence meeting Marcello Venuti, who caused him to be admitted to the Etruscan Academy of Cortona,[5] and whose brother Filippo he was later to know very closely at Clairac and at Bordeaux, Montesquieu failed to meet the astronomer Bianchini, who died at Rome while the President was there, and the geometer Manfredi, who was absent from Bologna when Montesquieu passed through. He succeeded, however, in seeing both Maffei and Muratori.

Scipione Maffei of Verona, a polymath like most scholars of his day, was too closely in sympathy with the Jesuits for Montesquieu to have had a continued and affectionate regard for him, and he describes him as the leader of a sect. But he was a man of note, and one of whom Lord Chesterfield said to his son that Verona

[1] Toaldo, *Notizie*, p. 62.
[2] *Spicilège* 464–5 (MS., pp. 429–30).
[3] *Pensée* 595 (Bkn. 1340).
[4] *Spicilège* 365 (MS., pp. 324–5).
[5] Montesquieu to Filippo Venuti, 17 March 1739. Venuti performed the same service for Vernet about the same time. He was also a close friend of Athias.

would be worth going to for him alone.[1] Montesquieu knew several of the works of Maffei. He refers to his work on amphitheatres, and cites his *Istoria diplomatica*.[2] It is likely also that he was acquainted with his treatise *Della scienza chiamata cavalleresca*, which expresses, in its discussion of chivalry, notions relating to honour similar to those contained in *L'Esprit des lois*. Maffei's later work on usury and the debate which it provoked are likely to have occasioned some of the discussion of commerce which occurs in Montesquieu's masterpiece.

Muratori, the librarian of Modena, was seen and admired by Montesquieu. The rigorous erudition of the editor of the *Rerum italicarum scriptores* was a form of scholarship which appealed more to Montesquieu at a later stage in his career. The many merits of his *Considérations sur les Romains* do not include accurate textual study and comparison of authorities. He did not on that account, however, think less of the man. He found him unaffected, charitable and learned, 'enfin . . ., un homme du premier mérite.' Muratori's works are cited in *L'Esprit des lois*, and it is probable that the greater solidity of scholarship and documentation which Montesquieu exhibits in his last books on feudalism are the lesson he has learnt from Muratori.

IV. NAPLES

Already interested in the principles of government and in social problems, Montesquieu sought more reliable information about these than could be afforded by a study of the temporal power of the Pope or the usages of the Pretender's court. In his journey southwards, and during his return to the north alike, he attended closely to the political and social systems he encountered. In Venice he found that virtue and the republican form of government were not inseparable; he observed with surprise the extent of the political power of the Jesuits;[3] he commented disparagingly and memorably on the hollowness of the liberty of the Venetians:

Quant à la liberté, on y jouit d'une liberté que la plupart des honnêtes gens ne veulent pas avoir: aller de plein jour voir les filles de joie; se

[1] Chesterfield to his son, 7 August 1749 (*Letters*, ed. Dobrée, IV, p. 1377).
[2] *Spicilège* 448 (MS., p. 406).
[3] *Pensée* 394 (Bkn. 1328).

marier avec elles; pouvoir ne pas faire ses pâques; être entièrement inconnu et indépendant dans ses actions: voilà la liberté que l'on a.[1]

In Venice and also in Leghorn he set an example followed by the most celebrated nineteenth-century English traveller in Italy, by visiting the galleys, where he found not a single unhappy countenance.[2] In Turin he met Victor-Amedeus II, and was impressed by his remembering a visit paid years before by the Abbé de Montesquieu, his uncle. But this example of enlightened despotism does not attract him. He exclaims that for nothing in the world would he be a subject of one of these little princes; they know all your actions, your income, your every movement. Far better is it to be buried in the obscurity of a large State. In Modena, notwithstanding his esteem for the good sense and good government of the Duke, he makes the remark that poverty and dishonesty on the part of the people go together. The Modenese, oppressed by taxes, will rob you if you try to change money, while the more prosperous inhabitants of Bologna are honest in their dealings.

Such reflections were bound to spring to Montesquieu's mind in Naples. The southern kingdom in the early eighteenth century passed through an interregnum, lasting from 1707 to 1734, between the direct rule of Spain and the Bourbon monarchy. It was now an Austrian possession and the Emperor's sovereignty was exercised by a Viceroy, who during Montesquieu's stay in Naples was Count von Harrach. Though the President, having met him already in Vienna, thought well of Harrach, who was a man of some intellectual calibre (in 1773 he was to be *Lucumone*, or president and protector, of the Academy of Cortona), he observed that all was not well with the government. He did not meet a single German who knew or was known by a single Neapolitan. The Emperor, he notes, in order to maintain his troops, has had

[1] Nagel II, p. 981; Pléiade I, p. 548. Montesquieu, both in the fact of commenting on liberty in Venice, and in the nature of what he says, seems to be following the guide-book of Misson which he is known to have possessed and used: 'Je vous dirai en deux mots ce que c'est que cette liberté. Ne vous ingérez en façon quelconque dans les affaires de l'Etat; ne commettez point de crimes énormes, punissables par la justice, de telle manière que leur trop d'éclat oblige nécessairement à en faire la recherche; et du reste, faites sans aucune réserve tout ce que bon vous semblera, sans appréhender seulement le *qu'en dira-t-on*, voilà la liberté de Venise' (*Voyage d'Italie*, Utrecht, 1722, I, pp. 224–5).

[2] *Pensée* 31 (Bkn. 550).

to impose taxes amounting in all to a million Neapolitan crowns, and the poverty of the people is thus exacerbated. The poorest of the Neapolitans, indeed, are the poorest men on earth. The *lazzi* or *lazzaroni* are almost naked, and they live entirely on grass. They tremble, says the President, citing them to prove that it is the miserable who are most readily afraid, at the smallest whiff of smoke from Vesuvius: 'ils ont la sottise de craindre de devenir malheureux.'[1]

Nothing, however, shows Montesquieu so clearly the abject condition of the people of Naples than their attitude to the miracle of Saint Januarius, which served also to draw a contrast for him between religion in Naples and religion in Rome. The congealed blood of the saint, preserved in a phial in the cathedral, is liquefied on three occasions in each year. Montesquieu was present on the anniversary of the saint's translation, which occurs on the Saturday before the first Sunday of May, in 1729 on 30 April. A failure of the miracle is held to be a portent of disaster, earthquake, plague, or war; and the occurrence in January 1729 of heavy rains, coinciding with the emission of smoke from Vesuvius, while flames were pouring out of the mouth of Etna, engendered fear of natural calamity.[2] The populace inevitably were eagerly awaiting the liquefaction and they were not disappointed. Montesquieu reports that the miracle in fact occurred in his presence, although there were nine heretics present in the church, and he discusses possible explanations at some length both in the account of his travels and in the *Pensées*.[3] He is satisfied that the miracle occurred; he witnessed it again, in fact, when it was repeated in the ensuing week. He is convinced of the good faith of the clergy and of the people. The priests are not deceivers, but he thinks it likely that they are themselves deceived; for the cause of the liquefaction must clearly be the heat of the candles on the altar, and of another candle which is always held in close proximity to the reliquary. He admits that this is but a conjecture, and he does not finally exclude the possibility of a genuine miracle. But he goes immediately to lament the superstitious character of the people, and remarks that 'le peuple de Naples, où tant de gens n'ont rien, est plus peuple qu'un autre.'

[1] *Romains*, ch. xiv (Nagel I, C, pp. 449–50; Pléiade II, p. 147).
[2] *St. James's Evening Post*, 6–8 February 1729.
[3] *Pensée* 836 (Bkn. 2201).

The intellectual life of the élite in Naples in the early eighteenth century had a vigour which few European cities could rival, and Montesquieu came into contact with several aspects of it. One of its foremost figures is Celestino Galiani, uncle of the celebrated raconteur Ferdinando Galiani, a friend of most of the scholars of the peninsula, and associate of the Italian Jansenists, and accused of Jansenism himself. It was at Rome, where he taught ecclesiastical history, that Montesquieu met this future Chaplain-General of the Kingdom of the Two Sicilies, who was to become celebrated as the reformer of the University of Naples. His main impact on Neapolitan society, however, was to be made later.[1] At the time of Montesquieu's visit there were three principal currents of ideas in the Parthenopean capital, associated primarily with the names of Gravina, Giannone, and Vico.

Gian Vincenzo Gravina, who had died in 1718, enjoyed great renown in the eighteenth century. Garat in his memoirs was to place him on the same level as Rousseau and Montesquieu and to pronounce his name with great reverence. He even wrote:

> 'La loi est l'expression de la volonté générale.' Gravina en Italie, Montesquieu en France, avaient suspendu ce lustre à leurs belles pages,[2]

a claim scarcely more true of the Neapolitan than of the Frenchman. Gravina made important contributions both to belles-lettres and to the study of Roman law, and it is likely that Montesquieu was already acquainted with his reputation. The *Bibliothèque française*, a periodical in which the President himself had occasionally published essays, contained in the year 1727 an unsigned letter addressed to Jean-Jacques Bel of Bordeaux, whose friendship with Montesquieu is well known. This letter bears the title *Lettre de M*^xxx^ *à M. Bel, conseiller au Parlement de Bordeaux, en lui envoyant une dissertation latine, de M. Gravina, sur la poétique.* The author, who refers to an earlier article in the same journal, written by Bel in criticism of Dubos, discusses the poetic theories of Gravina, and expresses his regret at having been unable to obtain a copy of his *Ragion poetica*. This letter shows

[1] See F. Nicolini, *Un grande educatore italiano, Celestino Galiani*, Naples, 1951.

[2] Garat, *Mémoires historiques sur la vie de M. Suard . . . et sur le XVIIIe siècle*, Paris, 1820, I, p. 195.

that there was interest in Gravina in Bordeaux; and the subsequent presence of the *Ragion poetica* in Montesquieu's library suggests that he may have taken note of it.

Gravina achieved great distinction as a historian of Roman law. He did not regard Roman law as a subject which could be understood by the scrutiny, however thorough, of texts in the void, but he related the study of law to that of politics and to the history of institutions in a way which few of his contemporaries, perhaps Domat alone, had adopted. His *Origines iuris civilis* was one of the great works of scholarship of the eighteenth century. Eventually translated into French, after the death of Montesquieu, with the significant title *Esprit des lois romaines*, it is a work which Montesquieu studied very seriously. It is more than once specifically cited in *L'Esprit des lois*; there are several references to it in the *Pensées*; and Montesquieu made from it lengthy extracts now lost. In his earliest study of Roman law he does not use Gravina who is not mentioned in the *Collectio juris*, which reflects his legal studies up to the time of the *Lettres persanes*. When it is seen that the Neapolitan fame of Gravina was so great that a century after his death he was described in his native city as 'one of the most sublime geniuses that Nature in her magnificence has ever produced',[1] and when it is noted that in Naples Montesquieu met, in the erudite jurisconsult and Jansenist theologian Costantino Grimaldi, one of Gravina's pupils,[2] and may well have met others, it becomes at least probable that it was his visit to Naples which made the President aware of the legal writings of Gravina, and opened his eyes to a more thorough and imaginative study of Roman law.

The second of the great Neapolitan figures of the age was not dead but was in the early stages of an exile which was to be protracted and to end miserably. Pietro Giannone had published in 1723 the four quarto volumes of his *Istoria civile del regno di Napoli*. Appearing with the approbation of the Viceroy, who at this stage was Cardinal Althan, this history of Naples was dedicated to the Holy Roman Emperor, and it evoked so much enthusiasm from the deputies of the city of Naples, that a very few days after the publication they honoured the author and presented

[1] *Biografia degli uomini illustri del Regno di Napoli*, I, Napoli, s.d. (*c.* 1814).

[2] G. Orloff, *Mémoires historiques, politiques et littéraires sur le royaume de Naples*, Paris, 1821, IV, p. 389.

to him a piece of plate costing 135 *ducats*.[1] But not everywhere did the work receive so favourable a welcome; for Giannone makes an outspoken attack on the interventions of the Church in the government of Naples. Using direct and unequivocal language, he denounces the Popes for engaging in intrigue, for arousing and playing on fear and jealousy among princes. He declares that the wealth of the Church has increased with every calamity which has overtaken the people; while in particular the Jesuits, not content with directing the consciences of the citizens, have sought to rule their homes. This revival of the anti-Papal attitudes of the Ghibellines of the Middle Ages might give pleasure to the Emperor; it could give none to the Pope, to whom Giannone's attack on the political activities of his Court, unwelcome at any time, was doubly so at a moment when new limits to his jurisdiction were being proposed by the Jansenists.

The ecclesiastical attack on Giannone was vigorous. He was accused of a multitude of heretical or unorthodox propositions, ranging from the assertion of the legality of concubinage to the denial of the miracle of Saint Januarius; and when on 1 May 1723 the miracle did not take place his position in the city became dangerous. Montesquieu gives of this situation an account which is in broad agreement with Giannone's, though it was written before Giannone's was published.[2] The monks of Naples informed the people that the failure of the miracle was a result of the impious book which had just seen the light of day, and Giannone was obliged, in order to avoid stoning, first to go into exile and then to flee the country. Meanwhile the Archiepiscopal Vicar, the Bishop of Castellaneta, declared him excommunicate, and his work was placed on the Index of Prohibited Books. The attitude of the civil power, albeit wielded in Naples by a Cardinal, was more sympathetic. It was found necessary to sequestrate all copies of his work, but he received timely notification of this move; and the Viceroy facilitated his flight by providing him with a passport.

Giannone now took refuge with the Emperor and spent several years at Vienna, receiving a pension and being under the especial protection of Prince Eugene. It was during this period that

[1] *Vita di Pietro Giannone* (by himself), in *Opere postume*, Naples, 1770–7, II, p. 24.

[3] *Apologia dell'Istoria civile*, in *Opere postume*, I, pp. 4 sq.

Montesquieu visited Vienna and on several occasions encountered the Prince as well as Garelli, one of the main opponents of the Jesuits at the Imperial Court, and a protector of Giannone. But no evidence suggests that he either met or heard of Giannone at this time. He heard his name mentioned in Naples, possibly by Grimaldi, still a frequent correspondent of the exile, possibly by the new Viceroy, Harrach, himself, who was very well disposed towards the fugitive and who, according to Giannone's own account,[1] has been urged by Prince Eugene to find an adequate situation for him. If it was later that Conti and Prince Trivulzio (known to the President in Milan) knew Giannone, at least Montesquieu may have heard his name from Jacob Vernet, who was not only going to publish extracts from his work in the *Bibliothèque italique*, but also was to become, for a time, Giannone's patron and protector in Switzerland when he had left Austria.

It is not long after the President's return from his travels that he makes a note of the desirability for writing a civil history of France, like that of Giannone for Naples;[2] and a little later writes in the *Spicilège* that he must buy the *Istoria civile*, which he describes as good.[3] He had not then bought it, however, and the date of that observation is about 1738.

His direct and first-hand acquaintance with the book came later; and what seems mainly to have impressed him is not the anti-curialism but the historical method of the author. Giannone says in his introduction that it is not his aim to deafen the reader with the roar of battle and with the noise of armies, which for centuries have made Naples a theatre of war. Still less does he intend to fill his work with descriptions of the natural beauties and the gentle climate of the Kingdom. This civil history, of a kind which he believes new, will treat the government of Naples, its laws and its customs. The book is true to this intention of the author; it is not a mere catalogue of battles, or of monarchs and viceroys. It describes the laws of the land, the health of the people, pestilences and their causes, the erection of new buildings and the cutting of new roads, the condition of the University, the state of jurisprudence. It endeavours, in fine, to consider in

[1] *Vita di Pietro Giannone*, pp. 111–12.
[2] *Pensée* 446 (Bkn. 954).
[3] *Spicilège* 660 (MS., p. 631.)

relation to the history of Naples all those various elements in the life of the community whose relevance to the study of laws was to be so memorably stressed by Montesquieu. It is this fact, primarily, and not Giannone's attitude to the Papacy, which is reponsible for Montesquieu's interest in his work, an interest which will be seen later to be fruitful.[1]

Gravina was dead and Giannone was in exile; the third of the intellectual leaders was living in Naples but his talent was largely unrecognized. It was recognized, however, by his friend Paolo Mattia Doria, who was a vain, repetitive man, jealous of the reputations of the great (he goes so far as to call Newton himself a 'petit-maître à la mode'). He expressed, none the less, some ideas which were far from commonplace in his major work, *La Vita civile*, and between it and the works of Montesquieu there are some close and pregnant similarities. It seems that Montesquieu studied and used this work, and he may even have known it (it was present in Barbot's library) before his travels. It seems likely, too, that the President called on Doria in Naples.[2]

If he did, his interest in Vico[3] may well have been further stimulated. It had been awakened when he was in Venice, as is shown by a sentence which he there wrote in his journal:

> Acheter à Naples: *Principii d'una nova Scienza di Joan-Batista Vico, Napoli.*[4]

Montesquieu was in Venice from 16 August to 14 September 1728. The original edition of the *Scienza nuova*, now known as the *Scienza nuova prima*, appeared at Naples in 1725. The next edition was not published until 1730. Now early in 1728 (on 3 January and 10 March) Antonio Conti wrote to Vico (whom he did not previously know) expressing admiration for his work and supporting very strongly a suggestion which had been made

[1] Another direct reference to Giannone supports this view. Montesquieu suggests (*Pensée* 1690, Bkn. 353) writing the civil history of Algiers, and sketches it in a page. The anecdote of which this history consists relates to an imaginary attempt to introduce banking into the State, and is probably an allegorical satire of John Law. Civil history, for Montesquieu, includes the history of commerce.

[2] See my article, 'Montesquieu et Doria' (*RLC*, 1955).

[3] Legend has been more loquacious than history concerning the relations of Montesquieu and Vico. A definitive assessment of the problem has been made by W. Folkierski, 'Montesquieu et Vico' (*Congrès 1955*).

[4] Nagel II, p. 1008; Pléiade I, p. 575.

by another Venetian, Lodoli,[1] that a new edition should be published in Venice.[2] Vico, an unsystematic correspondent, eventually agreed to this suggestion, and the manuscript corrections which he proposed and which amounted to 300 sheets, reached Venice in October 1729. Montesquieu's visit to Venice came at a time when Conti was in negotiation with Vico, and possibly when he was still awaiting Vico's first reply. It is not unreasonable to assume that it was Conti who urged the President to acquire the *Scienza nuova.*

This, however, was not an easy thing to do in Naples; for the work was out of print and rare, all available copies having been bought up at an early date by the Venetian Resident in Naples, and sent to Venice where great interest in the work had been expressed. It is therefore possible that Montesquieu tried to buy the *Scienza nuova*, failed, and never thought about the book again.[3]

The question which arises now is whether Montesquieu met Vico at Naples. His failure to allude to a meeting in the *Voyages* is inconclusive: he does not refer to meeting either Jacob Vernet or Marcello Venuti, whom he is known, from other sources than the *Voyages*, to have encountered. That Vico's name does not appear in Montesquieu's list of the greatest savants of Italy[4] does not mean that he did not meet him; it means that he did not put him in this category. There were, moreover, other possible links between Montesquieu and Vico. Cardinal Lorenzo Corsini, whose

[1] Montesquieu reports in his *Voyages*: 'A Venise, j'ai vu . . . le père Sodoli, Franciscain, homme de lettres, qui travaille à plusieurs éditions des Pères' (Nagel II, p. 1016; Pléiade I, p. 594). I venture to correct this (against the manuscript, which is in the hand of a secretary of a date more than twenty years later) to Lodoli. Carlo Lodoli (1690–1711) was a Franciscan, a mathematician and man of letters, a close friend of Conti and Maffei, and the constructor of a pneumatic machine which cannot have failed to interest Bonneval (Maffei to Vallisnieri, January 1720, in Maffei, *Epistolario*, ed. C. Garibotto, Milan, 1955, I, p. 333). I can discover no trace of any Venetian called Sodoli.

[2] Vico, *L'Autobiografia, il carteggio, e le poesie varie*, ed. B. Croce and F. Nicolini, Bari, 1929, pp. 63–65.

[3] It has often been asserted that a copy of the *Scienza nuova* is to be found at La Brède. This goes back to the following sentence in a review by E. Bouvy of the first edition of Croce's *Bibliografia vichiana*: 'De fait, s'il faut en croire une personne bien informée, un exemplaire de la première édition de la *Scienza nuova* existerait à la bibliothèque de La Brède' (*Bulletin italien*, Bordeaux, 1904, p. 363). My prolonged searches at La Brède have not found this volume, nor is it mentioned in the catalogue of Montesquieu's library.

[4] Nagel II, p. 1213; Pléiade I, p. 781.

Roman palace Montesquieu has been seen to frequent, was Vico's protector. Both the first edition and later (Corsini then being Pope) the *Scienza nuova seconda* were dedicated to him, and the Cardinal praised the work for the ancient dignity of its language and the solidity of its doctrine.[1] Vitry, the Jesuit whom the President met at Polignac's table, corresponded with Vico and praised the plan and the learning of his work.[2] Celestino Galiani was a correspondent of Vico and received from him a copy of the *Scienza nuova*. The missionary Ripa knew Vico[3] and the Jew Athias had advance knowledge of the publication of the work, and communicated his information to Muratori.[4] Finally, even to the small abode of Vico, a stone's throw from the Church of the Gesù Nuovo which Montesquieu admired, there penetrated the influence and prestige of the House of Stuart. For Vico had been appointed to his chair through the influence of Rostaino, Duke of Popoli, a former subordinate of Berwick in Spain; and more significantly, Rostaino's niece and sister-in-law, Ippolita, notwithstanding her rank, used frequently to visit Vico in his own humble house, was godmother to one of his daughters, and was for many years his protectress; and her family, Cantelmo-Stuart, claimed descent from the ancient kings of Scotland, had had this claim ratified by Charles II of England in 1683, and were to entertain the Chevalier de Saint-George when he visited Naples in 1731.[5] So august a patronage might well have reconciled Montesquieu to visiting Vico in his house, and might even have led him there.

It is possible, then, that Montesquieu met Vico; but it is an exaggeration to say, as Croce has said, that it is almost certain.[6]

[1] Corsini to Vico, 8 December 1725 (*Autobiografia*, etc., pp. 192–3).
[2] Vitry to Vico, 5 January 1726 (ibid., p. 204).
[3] *Autobiografia*, ed. F. Nicolini, Milan, 1947, p. 188.
[4] Ibid., p. 190. [5] Ibid., pp. 170–4.
[6] *Bibliografia vichiana*, Naples, 1947, I, p. 292.

VI

TRAVELS IN ENGLAND, 1729–31

I. ROYAL AND DUCAL FIGURES

ON the last day of July, in 1729, Montesquieu left Trent, and, travelling through the night without halting, reached Innsbruck in bitterly cold weather on 1 August. He tarried for a fortnight in Munich, suffered in Augsburg both from a fever and from physicians who had been selected for their religious opinions rather than their professional skill ('Let my doctor be a Turk', he protested, 'provided he is a good doctor'), proceeded rapidly through the Rhineland, turned eastwards and arrived at Hanover, an outpost of English civilization, on 14 September.[1] He lingered in that area until 8 October, when he began a rapid journey (four days and four nights without leaving his post-chaise) to Utrecht. On 15 October, he arrived by canal at Amsterdam, proceeded thence to The Hague, and on 31 October departed for England. After a voyage made depressing by hail and torrential rain,[2] he arrived in London on 3 November.[3] The most important period of his life began.

It is also one of the least known periods of his life. If there existed an account of Montesquieu's stay in England comparable with his Italian journal, a far more vivid light would be thrown both on his social life and on the processes of his mind. The names are known of over a hundred individuals whom he met in Italy; in his much longer stay in England it is reasonable to believe that he knew a greater number; but the names of those with whom his acquaintance is attested scarcely exceed a score. His Italian journal is an important historical source, on which Pastor, for example, extensively drew in his *History of the Popes*. An English journal, did it exist, would be even more interesting.

The unhappy truth is that such a journal was in fact written

[1] Montesquieu's account gives the date 24 September, which the context shows to be clearly erroneous (Nagel II, p. 1272; Pléiade I, p. 844), and which I amend on the basis of travelling time.

[2] J. Huxham, *Observationes de aere*, 2nd edition, London, 1752, p. 36.

[3] In Old Style, still in force in Great Britain, the dates of arrival and departure are 20 and 23 October. All English dates in this chapter are given in Old Style.

by Montesquieu. In 1818, Montesquieu's grandson Joseph-Cyrille (the son of his daughter Denise) dispatched to his cousin Charles-Louis de Montesquieu, son of Jean-Baptiste de Secondat and then living at Bridge Hill near Canterbury, a vast collection of manuscripts. The catalogue of these survives, and one item listed is described thus:

Carton contenant:

Un *Voyage en Italie et dans quelques parties de l'Allemagne, Voyage en Angleterre* mis au net, prêt à imprimer, pouvant former un vol. in-octavo.[1]

Charles-Louis died at Canterbury in July 1824. His will, drawn up on 4 February 1822, contains the following clause:

I desire that all my manuscripts which shall be found after my decease may be carefully packed up and sent to Prosper de Montesquieu of Bordeaux . . . if then alive, but if he shall be dead, then that [they] be burned immediately.[2]

Prosper (or Charles-Louis-Prosper) was the son of Joseph-Cyrille. He was alive when his cousin died at Canterbury, and in fact survived until 1871. To the catalogue of 1818 is appended a note in the hand of Prosper:

Tous les manuscrits (*deleted and amended to* une partie de ces manuscrits) ont été brûlés par mon oncle à très peu d'exception. Je n'ai rapporté de Londres que quatre volumes reliés . . ., deux cartons ou portefeuilles, l'un intitulé *Voyages*, contenant divers matériaux . . .[3]

This surviving portfolio cannot be other than the manuscript of the *Voyages*, published in 1894–6, sold in 1939, and now in the possession of M. Robert Schuman. The wording of the two lists does not make it flatly impossible that the dossier which came back to France contained also the manuscript account of the travels in England; but it is exceedingly improbable, and it must be held well-nigh certain that Montesquieu's account of his travels in England was burned, in England, by his grandson.

Nor are compensating sources other than exiguous. Fifteen pages of *Notes sur l'Angleterre*, first published in the Lefèvre edition of 1818 with the remark 'Il est inutile de dire comment le

[1] Nagel III, p. 1575.
[2] Principal Probate Registry, Somerset House.
[3] Nagel III, p. 1581, corrected from the original manuscript at La Brède.

morceau suivant s'est trouvé en notre possession' are interesting but fragmentary. There have survived but five letters written by Montesquieu while in England, and only one addressed to him. English sources, too, are uncommunicative. The letters of Pope and Chesterfield, both well edited, show no sign of Montesquieu's stay in England. The unpublished Sloane and Des Maizeaux collections contain little of direct relevance. The memoirs of Lord Hervey are interrupted for the years in question. The records, published and unpublished, of the families of Churchill, Montagu, and Richmond, afford no information. The newspapers of the day maintain an almost complete silence.[1]

It is not to be wondered at that Montesquieu visited England. In the *Lettres persanes* he had shown himself already interested in the English conception of liberty. Usbek alludes to the English view that unlimited power is illegitimate, and Rica explains that in England liberty has been born from the flames of discord and sedition.[2] Already Montesquieu has read Cudworth and Clarendon.[3] He has been acquainted with English diplomatic representatives in Paris: Robinson, secretary of embassy,[4] probably Horatio Walpole, who attended the Entresol, certainly Waldegrave. Berwick he had known since 1716, Bolingbroke in exile he had met and perhaps known well. On a humbler level, he had known the British wine merchants of Bordeaux, he had been the patron of the Irish poet Michael Clancy, of the peripatetic scientist Sully. He was a colleague at the French Academy of the Abbé Dubos, of whom, on the strength of his *Intérêts de l'Angleterre mal entendus*, a lampoonist was to write,

> Anglais, tenez-vous en repos,
> On vous donne l'abbé Dubos;
> Mieux que vous il sait vos affaires.[5]

Of the English language Montesquieu was not wholly ignorant.

[1] The most useful study is J. Churton Collins, *Voltaire, Montesquieu, and Rousseau in England*, London, 1908. In spite of several inaccuracies and shortcomings (some of them surprising: for example, his bewilderment before discrepancies in dating which are readily explained by the difference between Old and New Style), this book is still valuable.

[2] *L.P.* 104, 136.

[3] Nagel III, p. 44; Pléiade I, p. 87; Bulkeley to Montesquieu, 22 October 1723.

[4] Montesquieu to D'Olivet, 10 May 1728.

[5] B.N., MS., fr. 12694, p. 496.

It is related by Diderot that Montesquieu liked to tell of a visit he paid to Blenheim, in the course of which the Duke of Marlborough, after listening to Montesquieu's English for over an hour, begged him not to speak French, since he, the Duke, could not understand it.[1] But this story is unhappily apocryphal, since there was no Duke of Marlborough when Montesquieu visited England, the great Duke having died in 1722 and the title having, by special remainder, passed to his eldest daughter.

While in Rome the President had taken lessons in English from an Irishman.[2] Later, he bought, as well as a useful guide-book entitled *British Curiosities in Art and Nature*, a number of works dealing with the English language: Philips, *Compendious Way of Teaching Ancient and Modern Languages*, Bailey, *Introduction to the English Tongue*, Watts, *Art of Reading and Writing English*, Wallis's English grammar, and Boyer's dictionary. The result of his labours was that he became able to read English, as proved by several passages transcribed and commented on in the *Spicilège*, and at least to understand the language when spoken.

In Italy Montesquieu had met a number of Englishmen, both travellers and Jacobite exiles; but his broad acquaintance with the English began at Hanover. Here he met again his old friend Waldegrave, by whom he was presented to George II, then in residence in his minor kingdom. He was invited to dine at the royal table and was impressed by the monarch's courteous interest in his travels. He was amiably received by Townshend, then Secretary of State and in attendance on the king. When he reached The Hague he presented to the Ambassador, Lord Chesterfield, a letter of introduction from Waldegrave, and was invited to travel to London in Chesterfield's yacht.

The Earl and his guest arrived, as has been seen, on 23 October, O.S. About the same time Bolingbroke returned to England from Aix-la-Chapelle, and Hervey from Italy. The almost simultaneous arrival of three figures so prominent in English society augured well for the social life of the capital. The return of Chesterfield especially was welcomed by the Whigs, and the *Whitehall Evening Post* of 11–13 November 1729 greets him with eulogistic verses:

[1] Diderot to Sophie Volland, 23 September 1762 (Diderot, *Correspondance*, ed. Roth, IV, pp. 161–2).

[2] Nagel II, p. 1110; Pléiade I, p. 679.

The Muse, My Lord, that sheltered by your name
First dares to wander in pursuit of fame . . .,
Adds to the general joy her grateful strain,
And hails you safe to Britain's shore again.

The Tories, on the other hand, prepared what may be a delicate compliment from Montesquieu; for it is perhaps not unreasonable so to interpret a critique of Walpole contained in Bolingbroke's *The Craftsman* of 18 October, in the form of a Persian letter, in which Usbek deplores to Rustan the evils of 'Robinocracy'.

Montesquieu had deserved a compliment; for if one of Spence's *Anecdotes* is to be believed, he had declared shortly before crossing the Channel, 'There are no men of true sense born anywhere but in England'.[1]

The President in due course was presented at Court,[2] and was less impressed by George II than when he had been received at Hanover:

Je regarde le roi d'Angleterre comme un homme qui a une belle femme, cent domestiques, de beaux équipages, une bonne table. On le croit heureux. Tout cela est au dehors. Quand tout le monde est retiré, que la porte est fermée, il faut qu'il se querelle avec sa femme, avec ses domestiques, qu'il jure contre son maître d'hôtel; il n'est plus si heureux.[3]

He thought better of the Prince of Wales, and appears at one time to have thought of dedicating *L'Esprit des lois* to him.[4] The Prince asked Montesquieu to perform for him a literary service of a different kind. The story is told by Montesquieu himself in his preface to a manuscript volume:

Lorsque j'étais en Angleterre, Monseigneur le prince de Galles me chargea de lui faire faire un recueil des meilleurs chansons françaises. Je fis faire celui-ci; mais quand je vis les honnêtes gens de France et ce qu'il y avait de plus respectable tournés en ridicule, je sentis de l'éloignement à faire connaître notre nation par un si mauvais côté. Je n'eus pas le courage de l'envoyer et le gardai pour le mettre dans ma bibliothèque. On ne le doit communiquer qu'avec précaution. Il est vrai que

[1] London, 1820, ed. S. W. Singer, p. 330.

[2] Montesquieu's claim (Nagel III, p. 284, Pléiade I, p. 875) to have been presented on 5 October 1730 (N.S.) in the company of Chesterfield cannot be founded. Chesterfield returned to Holland on 6 August 1730 and remained there until after Montesquieu's departure from England.

[3] Nagel III, p. 287, Pléiade I, pp. 878–9.

[4] *Pensée* 1860 (Bkn. 186).

c'est l'ouvrage de la joie et de la gaieté française, et de cet esprit particulier à elle et que toute autre ne saurait attraper, et qu'on ne peut guère prendre à la rigueur. Ce qui choquerait ailleurs la pureté des mœurs ou la religion même, on ne le doit regarder que comme un délire agréable de notre nation, que le plaisir de chanter console de ses malheurs ou de ses chagrins. Elle s'est réservé la liberté de la table et ne connaît point de loi qui y régisse ses plaisirs.

This anthology of songs was in fact made by Montesquieu. It is a large folio volume, and it contains, transcribed in the hand, sometimes of Montesquieu, but more often of the Abbé Duval, a large number of songs of which very many are of a dubious character. The President, deeming, however mistakenly, that the Prince would frown on so free a collection, forebore to send it; but his grandson presented it in 1818 to the Prince Regent and since that day it has been kept in the Royal Library at Windsor.[1]

It was different topics which he discussed with the Queen, for whom he had a great regard; and indeed Caroline of Anspach, patroness of science and letters, and admirer of such exiled Frenchmen as Desaguliers and Le Courayer, had some title to his esteem. 'La grandeur de votre esprit,' he said to her, 'est si connue dans l'Europe qu'il semble qu'il ne soit plus permis de le louer.'[2]

He did not confine himself, in his conversations with the Queen, to the compliments of a courtier. The French Ambassador in London, the Comte de Broglie, in reply to an inquiry from Paris which was probably inspired by Montesquieu's renewed request to be given a diplomatic appointment, gave in one of his dispatches[3] a description of Montesquieu at Court. The Queen had wished to see the author of the *Lettres persanes*, and their first conversations, says the Ambassador, turned on that work. But the Queen, observing that he was willing to discuss any theme, led him on to expatiate on the French Court and government. On these two subjects he became very audacious, giving

[1] It is with the gracious permission of Her Majesty the Queen that I publish Montesquieu's prefatory note from the volume. I am much indebted to the Royal Librarian, Mr. R. Mackworth-Young, and to his predecessor Sir Owen Morshead, for having drawn my attention to this hitherto unknown manuscript.

[2] *Pensée* 762 (Bkn. 57).

[3] The dispatch is dated 31 October 1730. The relevant portion has been published by F. B[aldensperger], 'Un jugement diplomatique inédit sur Montesquieu en Angleterre' (*RLC*, 1929).

extravagant praise to England and disparaging France. At the Embassy too he was loquacious, and Broglie deemed it expedient to take him to one side and advise him to listen much and say little. Montesquieu did not heed this warning, and his Gascon temperament caused him to say much that the Ambassador would have preferred unsaid.

Conversational daring was not an obstacle to success in society; and Montesquieu was assisted also in entering the houses of the great by his close friendship with the Duke of Berwick. Arabella Churchill, now Mrs. Godfrey, who was Berwick's mother, was still alive when the President arrived in England. Her sister-in-law was no less a person than Sarah, Dowager Duchess of Marlborough, who, like her daughter the *suo jure* duchess, seems to have been known to Montesquieu, certainly by reputation, probably also in person.[1] Nor were they the only figures of ducal rank known to the President. He was affectionately attached to the two noblemen who were known to their friends as *magnifico* and *chiarissimo*,[2] their Graces of Richmond and of Montagu. The second Duke of Montagu had married the daughter of the great Marlborough. He was a patron of learning, a lover of animals, a devotee of Gothic architecture, and a protector of strange and unusual persons. The author of the *Lettres persanes* could not but appeal to one whose correspondence included letters in Arabic and in Chinese, and who had purchased the liberty of an African slave bearing the remarkable name Job the son of Solomon the son of Abraham.[3] Montagu, though in the circumstances of the time he was a Fellow of the Royal Society, was mainly interested in practical jokes. 'All his talents', said the Duchess of Marlborough in 1740, 'lie in things only natural in boys of fifteen years old, and he is about two and fifty: to get people into his garden and wet them with squirts, and to invite people to his country houses and put things into their beds to make them itch, and twenty such pretty fancies like these.'[4]

Montesquieu—who described Montagu as his friend and

[1] *Spicilège* 625 (MS., p. 595); Lady Hervey to Montesquieu, 18 August 1733, and Montesquieu to Lady Hervey, 28 September 1733.

[2] Sir John Chardin to 3rd Duke of Marlborough, 1 May 1735 (*H.M.C.* 45 (1), pp. 385–6).

[3] Letters are preserved in the Duke of Buccleuch's archives at Boughton House.

[4] *The Opinions of Sarah, Duchess-Dowager of Marlborough*, s.l., 1788, p. 58.

protector in England[1]—none the less fell victim to such a prank. More than twenty years later he regaled an English visitor with an account of the Duke:

> You are too young, I suppose, to have known the Duke of Montagu: that was one of the most extraordinary characters I ever met with; endowed with the most excellent sense, his singularity knew no bounds. Only think! at my first acquaintance with him, having invited me to his country seat, before I had leisure to get into any sort of intimacy, he practised on me that whimsical trick which, undoubtedly, you have either experienced, or heard of; under the idea of playing the play of an introduction of ambassadors, he soused me over head and ears into a tub of cold water. I thought it odd, to be sure, but a traveller, as you well know, must take the world as it goes, and, indeed, his great goodness to me, and his incomparable understanding, far overpaid me for all the inconveniences of my ducking. Liberty, however, (added the now venerable political theorist) is the glorious cause! that it is, which gives human nature fair play, and allows every singularity to show itself, and which, for one less agreeable oddity it may bring to light, gives to the world ten thousand great and useful examples.[2]

The second Duke of Richmond had already close connexions with France. His grandmother (the mother of the first Duke, who was a natural son of Charles II) was Louise-Renée de Penancoet de Kéroualle, Duchess of Portsmouth. She survived until 1734, living in France where she was a notable figure in society. The second Duke had intellectual aspirations. He was known to Réaumur; he was admitted in 1728 to honorary membership of the Académie des Sciences;[3] he was a patron of Abraham Trembley;[4] he took his scientific responsibilities as a Fellow of the Royal Society quite seriously.[5] He was, however, renowned for stupidity; but in spite of this, and although it was later reported to Montesquieu that he was reduced almost to bestiality

[1] *Pensée* 2206 (Bkn. 1354).

[2] F. Hardy, *Memoirs of the political and private Life of James Caulfield, Earl of Charlemont*, London, 1810, p. 34.

[3] Réaumur to Bignon, 5 September 1728 (B.N. MS. fr. 22232, f. 270).

[4] The claim made by Trembley's biographer (J. Trembley, *Mémoire historique sur la vie et les écrits de M. Abraham Trembley*, Neuchâtel and Geneva, 1787, p. 55), that Trembley met Montesquieu in England seems inconsistent with such dates of Trembley's travels as are known.

[5] He assiduously collected information for submission to the Royal Society about an earthquake experienced in Sussex (Richmond to Sloane, 27 October 1734, B.M. Sloane MSS. 4053, f. 301).

by his indulgence in the pleasures of the table,[1] the President regarded the time he spent in his company and in that of Montagu as the happiest hours of his life.[2]

II. POLITICAL SOCIETY

Montesquieu found himself moving not only in ducal and Court society, but also in the political circles of the day.

Waldegrave he had known for some time, but could not meet in England, since on ceasing to be Ambassador in Vienna, the Earl had at once been appointed to Paris. Chesterfield, arriving at the same time as Montesquieu, resumed his functions at The Hague in August 1730. His friend and biographer alludes in the following terms to his relations with Montesquieu:

> The author of the *Persian Letters* spent two years in this country, the best part of which were taken up in studying that admirable constitution he was so fond of, and has so well described. He could not derive his informations from better authority than Lord Chesterfield. It is said that Montesquieu, in mixed companies, did not appear equal to the idea conceived of him; but he is universally allowed to have been most amiable, sprightly, and universal, in select societies. Such a man could not fail to please; and having once pleased, soon to become the friend of Lord Chesterfield. We find accordingly that they kept up a regular correspondence, which only ended with Montesquieu's life.[3]

Though this correspondence is not extant, there is evidence that the friendship between the Englishman and the Frenchman was continued; and it is even probable that Chesterfield had his share with Lyttelton in composing an imitation of the *Lettres persanes*, first published in 1735, under the title *Letters from a Persian in England to his friend at Ispahan.*[4]

[1] It was in part for this reason that he (or his wife on his behalf) refused nomination as Ambassador in Paris in 1749 (Bulkeley to Montesquieu, 17 March 1749). His brother-in-law the second Earl of Albemarle (whose mother Montesquieu had met at The Hague in October 1729; Nagel II, p. 1299; Pléiade I, p. 873) was then appointed and was a frequent host to Montesquieu.

[2] Montesquieu to Folkes, 10 November 1742.

[3] Maty, *Memoirs of Lord Chesterfield*, in Chesterfield, *Miscellaneous Works*, London, 1777, I, p. 42.

[4] Lord Hervey to Henry Fox, 13 January 1735 (published in Earl of Ilchester, *Lord Hervey and his Friends*, London, 1950, p. 217).

Waldegrave and Chesterfield, though relatively aloof at this moment from party politics since they were ambassadors, were both Whigs. So was Townshend, whom Montesquieu had met at Hanover, but who left office in May 1730 and retired to his East Anglian estate. With the exception of Hervey (to whom however Montesquieu was less close than to Lady Hervey), the President's acquaintances who were politically active belonged either to the Tories or to the dissident Whigs. He knew Carteret, after his return from Ireland and his defection from the Ministerial party;[1] he knew Pulteney, assisted thereto conceivably by Pulteney's acquaintance with the Abbé Conti,[2] and heard from him stories about the great Duke of Marlborough.[3] Carteret and Pulteney, in time to come, when they had become Earl Granville and Earl of Bath, were to cite Montesquieu in the House of Lords, as a respected authority on Parliamentary usage.[4]

With the great anti-Minister Bolingbroke, the power behind the opposition to Walpole, Montesquieu was already acquainted, and it was through his eyes that Montesquieu saw English politics. 'J'ai connu milord Bolingbroke, et je l'ai déconnu,' he wrote in the *Pensées*;[5] and to Warburton he explained how his friendship with Bolingbroke came gradually to an end without either the Englishman or the Frenchman noticing it: 'sans qu'aucun de nous deux s'en aperçût, nous nous séparâmes pour jamais.'[6] It is not possible to determine the date of the estrangement of the two, and it is certainly not unlikely that it occurred during Montesquieu's stay in England. But throughout that stay he appeared to have read Bolingbroke's journal *The Craftsman.* This Tory periodical was not without renown in France. Marais, who was not an Anglophil, discussed it in his correspondence with Bouhier;[7] extracts from it were translated into French; manuscript

[1] Montesquieu to Domville, 22 July 1749.

[2] Antonio Conti to Des Maizeaux, 2 May 1721 (B.M., MS. Sloane 4282, ff. 262–3).

[3] *Pensée* 593 (Bkn. 1121).

[4] Hume to Montesquieu, 10 April 1749; Mme de Tencin to Montesquieu, 7 June 1749.

[5] *Pensée* 2126 (Bkn. 1351).

[6] Montesquieu to Warburton, 4 July 1752 (*Autographes de Mariemont,* ed. M.-J. Durry, Paris, 1955, II, pp. 499–500).

[7] Marais to Bouhier, 4 September 1732 (B.N., MS. fr. 24414, f. 194).

commentaries and translations were not unknown.[1] Extracts published in the Utrecht press had aroused the ire of Chesterfield, who took steps to prevent a recurrence.[2] In Montesquieu's *Notes sur l'Angleterre* it is made abundantly clear that the President was well aware of the controversial nature of *The Craftsman.* He points out there that it is written by Bolingbroke and Pulteney, and that three advocates read each copy before publication, to guard against breaches of the law.[3] The *Spicilège* contains nine different references to *The Craftsman*,[4] sufficiently spread over Montesquieu's stay in England to make it reasonably clear that he was a regular reader of the journal. The role of *The Craftsman* in the development of Montesquieu's political thought was considerable. It was here that he could read of the ancient spirit of liberty which had governed the development of English history, of the analogies between the history of Rome and that of England which were so often evoked by English politicians, of the invasions which an allegedly dictatorial and corrupt partisan government could make into the prescriptive rights of the people, as guaranteed by the Act of Settlement, of the relevance of Machiavelli's *Discorsi* to the problems of the eighteenth century, of patriotism, enlightened government, of the interests of foreign Courts, and above all, of the separation of the powers.[5] If in *The Craftsman* there were to be found partisan pronouncements dressed up as grave patriotic maxims, jejune inconsistencies, sophisticated slogans, and unfounded lessons of mock history, there were none the less significant and fertile aphorisms which produced effects which were sometimes wholly disproportionate to their veracity. Nor was *The Craftsman* the sole British journal which fell before the visitor's eyes, for there are other extracts, sometimes copied, sometimes cut out, from other newspapers.

[1] The Collection Le Paige possesses a long manuscript commentary on *The Craftsman* and a translation of part of the *Dissertation on Parties*.

[2] Chesterfield to Townshend, 11 January 1729, N.S. (*Letters*, ed. Dobrée, II, p. 85).

[3] Nagel III, p. 285; Pléiade I, p. 876.

[4] 31 January 1729/30; 7 and 28 February 1729/30; 9 May 1730; 13 June (5 September) 1730; 31 October (5 December) 1730; 21 November (19 December) 1730; 28 November (1 August) 1730; 9 January (23 January) 1730/1. These dates are in New Style, and the dates given in parenthesis are those of the reprint of 1731 in which some of them were changed. Montesquieu's references are to the original issues.

[5] See below, pp. 298–301.

Montesquieu's contact with English politics was not limited to the reading of journals and to social intercourse with politicians. Debates at Westminster attracted him, and in his *Notes sur l'Angleterre* he gives an account of two debates in the Commons at one of which he was certainly, at the other probably, present. Sources of information about early Parliamentary debates are not numerous, since reporting them was an infringement of privilege, and Cobbett's *Parliamentary History* is still the main authority. The publication, however, beginning in 1920, of the diary of the first Earl of Egmont,[1] making available a new and rich source of information about Parliamentary activities in the reign of George II, permits clear identification of the Commons debates which Montesquieu describes.

The first of these occurred on 28 January 1729–30. The subject under discussion was the maintenance of a standing army of 17,000 men. The Opposition's main speaker was the unrepentant Tory William Shippen, whose notorious honesty inspired Pope to write the couplet,

> I love to pour out all myself, as plain
> As downright Shippen or as old Montaigne.[2]

He it was, too, according to Voltaire,[3] who began a speech in the Commons with the words, 'The majesty of the people of England would be wounded.' It was a scarcely less remarkable speech which Montesquieu reports in the debate on the army. Only a tyrant or a usurper—bold words to use in the second decade of the Hanoverians—needed to rely on troops to maintain his power. The House, shocked by these words, was compelled by Shippen to hear them again, and Members, fearing a stormy session, called for a division in order to end the discussion. This brief account, which Montesquieu gives in his *Notes sur l'Angleterre*,[4] agrees with Egmont's diary where Shippen is reported as saying, 'that he hoped the German constitution of ruling by an army was not to be introduced here, and that in England a King who should propose to govern by an army was a tyrant.'[5]

[1] *H.M.C.* 63. [2] *Imitations of Horace*, II, i, ll. 51–2.

[3] *Œuvres*, ed. Moland, XXII, p. 102 (*Lettres philosophiques*, ed. G. Lanson, Paris, 1937, I, p. 88).

[4] Nagel III, p. 288, Pléiade I, p. 879.

[5] *H.M.C.* 63 (I), p. 11. A corroborative account is given by Charles Howard in a letter to Lord Carlisle, of 3 February 1729/30: 'Mr Shippen, in his speech, made use of some expressions so very flagrant and undecent, that I took the

The second debate reported by Montesquieu occurred in the Commons on 27 February 1729-30. The occasion was the action of the French Government in re-fortifying the port of Dunkirk in defiance of the Treaty of Utrecht. The discussion was vigorous:

Je n'ai jamais vu un si grand feu. La séance dura depuis une heure après midi jusqu'à trois heures après minuit. Là, les Français furent bien mal menés; je remarquai jusqu'où va l'affreuse jalousie qui est entre les deux nations. M. Walpole attaqua Bolingbroke de la façon la plus cruelle, et disait qu'il avait mené toute cette intrigue.

Bolingbroke, says Montesquieu, was defended by Wyndham; and he goes on to report part of Walpole's speech. The Minister told the story of a peasant who, finding a man hanging from a tree but still alive, cut him down, took him home, and tended him. The next day the peasant found that his cutlery had been stolen. The lesson, which Walpole applied to Bolingbroke's return from exile, was that justice should never be opposed: the malefactor should be taken back where he came from.[1]

Montesquieu's reporting was accurate. The official records confirm that the debate lasted until three o'clock in the morning of the next day.[2] A Member of Parliament writing to his father says that the debate, although lasting until three, was the most worth hearing of any since he entered the Commons.[3] The account given by Egmont is more detailed (though it does not report Walpole's vivid illustration), and shows Montesquieu's veracity:

We sat from twelve to near three o'clock in the morning. The debates were warm on both sides . . . Sir Robert Walpole hinted that Lord Bolingbroke was at the bottom of this inquiry concerning Dunkirk . . . He spoke so sharply against that Lord that Sir William Wyndham took up his defence.[4]

These two debates were famous, and it may well not have been

words down; he said he hoped he should never see these kingdoms so Germanized as to become military . . .; force and violence are the resort of usurpers and tyrants, whose only security is a standing army'. (*H.M.C.* 42, pp. 66–67).

[1] Nagel III, p. 289; Pléiade I, p. 881.

[2] *Journals of the House of Commons*, XXI, London, 1803, p. 469.

[3] Charles Howard to Lord Carlisle, [28] February 1729/30 (*H.M.C.*, 42, p. 68).

[4] *H.M.C.*, 63, I, pp. 71–74.

known in advance that they were going to be. Montesquieu's accounts show his interest in Parliamentary activity, and suggest that he may well have been a frequent attender at least during the session of 1730, which lasted from January to May. They suggest too that his command of the language had become efficient.

Another reference which Montesquieu makes to Parliamentary debates is to the discussion of the Bribery in Elections Bill of 1729.[1] He relates that Townshend, anxious to oppose the Bill for the Government, thought that the Lords, rather than incur, as in previous years, public opprobium for rejecting it, might be well advised to pass amendments of so fierce a nature that the Commons themselves would turn down the Bill. Amendments were accordingly brought forward and passed by the Lords, including one which raised the penalty for bribery from 50[2] to 500 pounds. The Commons, unwilling to be caught in the trap laid by the Upper House, none the less passed the Bill, and a reluctant monarch, with more than reluctant ministers, gave his assent. So, says Montesquieu, this Bill is miraculous, for it has passed against the wishes of King, Lords, and Commons, and the most corrupt of Parliaments has done more than any other to ensure public liberty.[3]

It was in fact on 6 May 1729 that the Lords' amendments were passed, the next day that they were accepted by the commons, and on 14 May that the amended Bill received the Royal Assent.[4] The discussions in their entirety took place before Montesquieu's arrival in England, and his information is second-hand. It is, none the less, detailed and intelligent, and relates that which, otherwise, is in part unknown.[5]

[1] Churton Collins wrongly identifies this Bill as the Pension Bill debated in 1730 and 1731.

[2] Montesquieu erroneously says that the original fine was ten pounds (see *Journals of the House of Commons*, XXI, p. 363).

[3] Nagel III, pp. 289–90; Pléiade I, p. 881.

[4] *Journals of the House of Lords*, XXIII, pp. 419, 423, and 437.

[5] It should be added that Montesquieu knew Admiral Forbes, later Earl of Granard, who in 1729 was nominated governor of the Leeward Islands, a loyal, upright man, a good conversationalist, and than whom 'few men had considered more, or wrote more, upon legislation, politics, political arithmetic, trade and population, manufactures, agriculture, military and naval affairs, voyages and travels' (J. Forbes, *Memoirs of the Earls of Granard*, London, 1868, p. 161; *Spicilège* 518, MS. pp. 482–3).

III. FRENCHMEN IN LONDON

London at this time boasted an active, vigorous, and intelligent community of Frenchmen. Friends of returned Jacobites, the intellectually curious, and the merely ambitious, mingled with Protestant refugees, and in their society differences of rank seem to have counted for little and differences of religion for less. Of the highest station was the Duchesse de La Force, widow of the former protector of the Academy of Bordeaux of whom, disgraced and dead, Montesquieu had in 1726 pronounced a consummately tactful éloge. The Duchess had taken up residence in England, and died in her house in St. James's Place shortly after Montesquieu's return to France.[1] Whether he met her and condoled with her on her relatively impoverished exile is not known.

Humbler, but more influential (though both of them were to end their days in necessitous circumstances) were Des Maizeaux and Desaguliers, both sons of Huguenot ministers, both men of learning, both enjoying the dignity of F.R.S.

Desaguliers, who was a native of La Rochelle, had been educated at Christ Church and was a D.C.L. of Oxford. Though in the end it was to be said of him that he died 'without a guinea and without a grave',[2] he was a protégé of Queen Caroline and chaplain (for he had taken Anglican orders) to Frederick Prince of Wales.[3] An exponent, both by practical demonstration and in less than indifferent verses, of Newton's natural philosophy, he was to be elected in 1742 corresponding member of the Academy of Bordeaux,[4] in whose proceedings, in the same year, he published his prize-winning *Dissertation sur l'électricité des corps*, consisting of a rigorously objective description of thirty different experiments.

Pierre Des Maizeaux was the biographer of Boileau and of Saint-Evremond, the author of a memoir on Toland, the editor of the celebrated *Recueil de diverses pièces* of 1720, in whose two volumes essays by Leibniz (including his correspondence with

[1] *Monthly Chronicle*, May 1731, p. 95.

[2] James Cawthorn, *The Vanity of Human Enjoyments* (1749), in A. Chalmers, *English Poets*, London, 1810, XIV, p. 255.

[3] See Montesquieu to Richmond, 2 July 1735 (in my 'Montesquieu's Correspondence: additions and corrections,' *FS*, 1958).

[4] P. Barrière, *L'Académie de Bordeaux*, p. 68.

Clarke) and Newton were flanked by discussions of Malebranche and Shaftesbury and by a French translation of Anthony Collins, whose close friend Des Maizeaux was. But significant as was Des Maizeaux's contribution to the progress of thought as a result of this volume, it was surpassed by the importance of his association with Pierre Bayle. He had been an intimate personal acquaintance of Bayle. He had edited Bayle's correspondence in 1717 and his *Œuvres diverses* in 1727; he had written a life of Bayle and was to publish it in an edition of the *Dictionnaire historique et critique* in 1730; he was busy preparing an English translation of the dictionary, which appeared finally at London in five folio volumes, beginning in 1734. The extensive correspondence of Des Maizeaux[1] survives to this day in the British Museum and throws a vivid light on international relations in the eighteenth century. It contains no letter exchanged between Montesquieu and the exile; but the width and nature of Des Maizeaux's acquaintance is such—including both Desmolets[2] and Antonio Conti[3]—that there can be no reasonable doubt that they knew each other.

Nor can Montesquieu have failed to know Père Le Courayer. Not a Protestant as were Des Maizeaux and Desaguliers, but a Catholic priest who never claimed to be anything else, he had opposed the Bull *Unigenitus* because of his belief in freedom of conscience, although he did not accept the Jansenist theses condemned in it. In 1723 he published his *Dissertation sur la validité des ordinations anglicanes*, which won him greater favour in England than in France. He found it prudent to leave France, where his work had been condemned, among others by Montesquieu's friend, Mongin, Bishop of Bazas and member of the Academy, in a *mandement* of 1728.[4] An Oxford D.D., the friendship of Lord Percival, and the patronage of Queen Caroline were his reward.[5] The open-minded Desmolets, sympathizing no doubt, as the Oratorians were wont to do, with an appellant from the Bull, praised him to Des Maizeaux, saying that it was impossible to know him without loving him.[7] Nor could Montesquieu,

[1] See J. H. Broome, 'Pierre Desmaizeaux, journaliste' (*RLC*, 1955).

[2] Desmolets to Des Maizeaux, 21 June 1729 (B.M., Add. MSS. 4285, f. 258).

[3] *Recueil de diverses pièces*, I, p. lxxxi.

[4] *Recueil des ordonnances, mandements, et lettres pastorales des archevêques de Bordeaux*, ed. F.-F.-A. Donnet, Bordeaux, 1848, I, pp. 222–5.

[5] See *Diary of first Earl of Egmont, H.M.C.* 63, *passim.*

[7] Desmolets to Des Maizeaux, as cited.

already interested in Fra Paolo Sarpi's *History of the Council of Trent* which he had asked Desmolets to procure for him,[1] think ill of the learned priest who was about to translate it into French.[2]

Another Huguenot refugee, intelligent, industrious, and well connected, was Pierre Coste, a native of Uzès. Like Des Maizeaux, Coste had known Bayle; he had known Locke and with the author's assistance had translated several of Locke's works into French.[3] His translation of the *Essay concerning Human Understanding* in particular was famous. It contained important interpretative notes which future editors even of the English text have used. It was the version quoted by Voltaire and possessed by Montesquieu. Finding in Montaigne a precursor of Locke, he proceeded to publish in 1724 at London the first French text of the *Essais* to appear since their condemnation by the Congregation of the Index in 1676, and the first to be made in accordance with rigorous critical principles.[4] It was in this edition, on splendid paper, and with an imposing list of subscribers who include many members of the Royal Family, Lady Mary Wortley Montagu, Muratori, and the Comte de Caylus who bought twelve copies, that the *philosophes* of the eighteenth century read their great predecessor.

Montesquieu knew Coste. He reports with relish an account given by Coste of a theological treatise *De simplicitate Dei*, of which the first section is headed *De Deo uno et trino*.[5] He mocks him gently when he writes in the *Pensées*:

> J'ai un honnête homme de mes amis qui a fait de belles notes sur Montaigne. Je suis sûr qu'il croit avoir fait les *Essais*. Lorsque je le loue devant lui, il prend un air modeste, et me fait une petite révérence, et rougit un peu.[6]

Montesquieu's raillery was however good-humoured and superficial. The editor of Montaigne and the friend of Shaftesbury could not fail to find favour with one who regarded those writers,

[1] Montesquieu to Desmolets, s.d. (Nagel III, p. 889).

[2] Le Courayer's translation appeared at London in 1736.

[3] See my article 'Renseignements inédits sur Locke, Coste, et Bouhier' (*RLC*, 1953).

[4] See M. Dréano, *La Renommée de Montaigne en France au XVIIIe siècle*, Angers, 1952, pp. 85–89.

[5] *Pensée* 1108 (Bkn. 2170).

[6] *Pensée* 1441 (Bkn. 946), and cf. *Pensée* 1231 (Bkn. 945).

with Plato and Malebranche, as the four greatest poets of humanity.[1] The President, years later, executed commissions for Coste in the book-selling world of Paris.[2]

A more capricious figure was Saint-Hyacinthe. A soldier of fortune whom gossips declared to be a son of Bossuet, he had left his native France (whither none the less he from time to time returned) and he had embraced Protestantism. He was an occasional writer, pamphleteer, journalist, and literary hack, but a hack of a high level. The translator of part of *Robinson Crusoe*, the critic, and therefore the enemy, of Voltaire, the author of a curious volume of *Entretiens des lesquels on traite des entreprises de l'Espagne*[3] full of unshaped but stimulating political ideas, he had various claims to the affection of Montesquieu. He was, moreover, a correspondent and a confidant of Madame de Lambert,[4] and a friend of Montesquieu's friend Melon, with whom he stayed in Paris.[5] That he was a friend of Des Maizeaux goes without saying, and in the circumstances of that surprising age it cannot be held odd that he was an acquaintance of Lady Hervey[6] and of Lord Percival,[7] a Fellow of the Royal Society, and a friend of Scipione Maffei.[8] He thought well of Montesquieu and sought to pay him compliments. He presented to him, on publication, his *Letters giving an account of several Conversations upon important and entertaining subjects*,[9] and the La Brède copy bears an *ex dono scriptoris* inscription. In 1732, moreover, when Saint-Hyacinthe published a new edition of his best-known book, the fanciful, elegant, and delightfully satirical *Chef d'œuvre d'un inconnu*, he added to it a new work with the title *Déification de l'incomparable docteur Aristarchus Masso*. Here he gives an apocalyptic view of Parnassus, with all the world's great literary figures crowding on to the slopes of the mountain. A Persian called Sadi comes forward and engages the writer in conversation:

Pourriez-vous me dire certainement, me demanda-t-il, qui est

[1] *Pensée* 1092 (Bkn. 2095). [2] Montesquieu to Folkes, 13 July 1739.

[3] The Hague, 1719, 2 vols.

[4] See Mme de Lambert, *Œuvres*, Lausanne, 1748, pp. 422–4.

[5] Saint-Hyacinthe to Des Maizeaux, 4 June 1732 (B.M., Add. MSS. 4284, f. 153).

[6] Lady Hervey to Montesquieu, 18 August 1733.

[7] *H.M.C.* 63 (I), pp. 34, 76, 90.

[8] Saint-Hyacinthe to Des Maizeaux, 1 April 1732 (B.M., MS. cited, f. 153).

[9] London, 1731, 2 vols.

l'auteur de ces lettres? me montrant un livre intitulé *Lettres persanes*.

Oui, sage et éloquent Sadi, répondis-je, on le nomme le président de Montesquieu.

Ce livre, reprit Sadi, est un des plus agréables livres que j'aie jamais lus. Nous admirons qu'un Français ait pu si bien exprimer nos mœurs, nos manières, qu'il ait pu penser et écrire comme nous aurions fait nous-mêmes; mais nous ne sommes pas moins étonnés de la liberté qui y règne, par rapport à des coutumes et à des opinions reçues dans votre pays . . . Je vous prie à votre retour en France de faire mille et mille compliments de ma part à cet ingénieux auteur, dont je n'oublierai jamais le nom.[1]

This is perhaps the first time that Montesquieu's name, *en toutes lettres*, appeared in print as the author of the *Lettres persanes*.[2]

IV. THE ROYAL SOCIETY

Saint-Hyacinthe paid to Montesquieu a more solid compliment than this early in 1730, in association with Dr. Teissier.

George-Louis Teissier, or Tessier, came of a family well known in French Protestant circles, and originating from the Cevennes. George-Louis himself was a native of the Kingdom of Hanover and had taken his doctor's degree at Leyden in 1710.[3] In March 1715–16 he was appointed physician to the Royal Household, five years later was elected to a Fellowship of the Royal College of Physicians, and in 1725 to the Royal Society. He was acquainted with Percival, Bolingbroke, and Pope.[4] He

[1] The Hague, 1732, II, pp. 473–5.

[2] Financial circles in London included several Frenchmen or men of recent French origin. Montesquieu alludes, in a letter to Cerati of 21 December 1729, to the *chevalier Lambert* as being his own banker. This would appear to be Sir John Lambert, second baronet, whose father was a Huguenot born on the Ile de Ré. Also living in London was Richard Cantillon whose *Essai sur la nature du commerce en général* throws light on Montesquieu's economic thought. Himself of Irish origin, he had lived for some time in Paris and had made his fortune. His wife was a step-daughter of Charlotte de Bulkeley, Viscountess Clare, who was sister to the Duchess of Berwick and to Montesquieu's friend François de Bulkeley. Cantillon met his end sensationally in 1734, being murdered by his French cook. His widow later married Bulkeley, notwithstanding their relationship. She was known to Montesquieu (Montesquieu to Bulkeley, 18 July 1736), and it is more than likely that Cantillon was also.

[3] On the title page of his thesis, *De substantia corticosa ac medullosa cerebri*, he is described as *Luneburgo-Zellensis*.

[4] Pope to Hugh Bethel, 21–23 May 1742 (*Correspondence*, ed. G. Sherburn, Oxford, 1956, IV, pp. 395–6).

died in 1742, but for a long time after his death there were doctors of his name at the French hospital in London.[1]

It was this doctor, of whom so little scattered information has survived, though he was celebrated in his day, who on 12 February 1729–30, proposed Montesquieu for membership of the Royal Society. The proposal was supported by Saint-Hyacinthe and by Sir Hans Sloane, and two weeks later, on 26 February, Montesquieu was elected by ballot, signed his name, and was admitted to the Society.[2]

Thus, before either of his serious works was published, Montesquieu was a member of the Academy of Bordeaux, the French Academy, the Academy of Cortona, and the Royal Society.

In the learned company of the Royal Society, he by no means found himself isolated.[3] The Dukes of Richmond and Montagu were members. The eighth Earl of Pembroke, so old that Locke's *Human Understanding* had been dedicated to him, had preceded Newton as President. He was famous both at home and abroad[4] as a connoisseur of antiques; and if his collections contained some pieces 'with only very fine names, to which (wrote Hervey) I believe his Lordship stood sole godfather,'[5] they were none the less exceedingly rich. Desmolets had already drawn Montesquieu's attention to them,[6] and the President used the information thus obtained in his essay *De la manière gothique*.[7] He knew Pembroke, and consigned to paper several of the Earl's judgements on literary questions,[8] and many years later was to be visited by his grandson in France.[9]

Woolhouse, the oculist whom Montesquieu had known in Paris years before, was now in London. He had been a Fellow of the Royal Society since 1721. Saint-Hyacinthe was not an aloof or

[1] Haag, *La France protestante*, IX, Paris, 1859, p. 352.

[2] Manuscript *Journal* of the Royal Society, February 1728/30; Montesquieu to Cerati, 1 March 1729/30.

[3] There is firm evidence of his acquaintance with fourteen members, either before or after his election, and his acquaintance with many more cannot reasonably be placed in doubt.

[4] He was known to Antonio Conti (Conti, *Prose e poesie*, II, p. 37).

[5] Lord Hervey to the Prince of Wales, 6 November 1731 (Earl of Ilchester, *Lord Hervey and his Friends*, p. 107).

[6] *Spicilège* 185 (MS., p. 141; *recueil* Desmolets).

[7] Nagel III, p. 277, Pléiade I, p. 967.

[8] *Pensées* 529 (Bkn. 1681); *Spicilège* 526 and 628 (MS., pp. 487 and 597).

[9] Montesquieu to Guasco, 3 November 1754.

unserious Fellow. On 5 February 1729/30 he read a paper 'a new kind of plants called Oxydores' to the Society.[1] With Nathan Hickman, if a very probable identification can be accepted, Montesquieu discussed the Naples liquefaction, and the Englishman gave as rigorously scientific an explanation of the miracle as one would expect from a Fellow of the Royal Society.[2] Alexander Stuart, physician to the Queen, was a serious physiologist, and was later admitted to the Academy of Bordeaux.[3] Sir Hans Sloane, successor to Newton as President of the Royal Society, was a man of renown. The intimacy of Montesquieu's acquaintance with him the evidence does not disclose. He had been as foreign member of the Académie des Sciences since 1708. This title, and the office of President of the Royal Society, involved him in extensive correspondence in more than one language with the *savants* of Europe, not least with the Society's honorary members. Among these was Montesquieu's friend and adviser the Jesuit Castel, who, already in contact with Sloane in 1728,[4] was engaged a year later in translating the *Philosophical Transactions* into French.[5] Shortly after his own election Montesquieu appears to have sought information about the chances of the nomination of Castel; for the Jesuit in the spring of that year writes thus to Sir Hans:

> Monsieur le président de Montesquieu, qui vient d'être associé [à votre auguste et royale société] m'a fait savoir que vous m'aviez fait même l'honneur de m'y proposer.[6]

Castel's ambition was in fact gratified and he became F.R.S.

Through the Royal Society Montesquieu made the acquaintance of Martin Folkes, who had been Sloane's rival for the presidency in 1727, and eventually succeeded him in that office. Folkes was a controversial figure. Stukeley, himself a Fellow, commented on him in the following terms:

> He has a great deal of learning, philosophy, astronomy: but knows nothing of natural history. In matters of religion an errant infidel and

[1] Manuscript *Journal*, February 1729/30.
[2] *Pensée* 836 (Bkn. 2201).
[3] Barrière, *L'Académie de Bordeaux*, pp. 44 and 130; *Recueil des dissertations couronnées par l'Académie de Bordeaux*, V, Bordeaux, 1737–9; Montesquieu to Sarraut de Boynet, 22 May 1737.
[4] Castel to Sloane, 5 December 1728 (B.M., Sloane MSS. 4050).
[5] Castel to Sloane, 24 May 1730 (B.M., Sloane MSS. 4051, f. 33).
[6] Castel to Sloane, 12 April 1730 (B.M., MS. cited, ff. 15–16).

loud scoffer. Professes himself a godfather to all monkeys, believes nothing of a future state, of the Scriptures, of revelation.[1]

Such was the hostility between two parties in the Royal Society. Montesquieu's own preference between the irreconcilable clerical archaeologist and independent *esprit fort* is made sufficiently clear by his judgement on Folkes:

> Si on m'avait demandé quels défauts il avait dans le cœur et dans l'esprit, j'aurais été embarrassé de répondre.[2]

It is not surprising that no letter, quotation, or allusion links Montesquieu and Stukeley.

Among other Fellows known to Montesquieu were John Conduitt and Thomas Hill. Conduitt was married to a niece of Newton and had succeeded his illustrious uncle as Master of the Mint. His greatest concern was over the fame of Newton, whose papers he had inherited. He supplied information to Fontenelle for the éloge in the Académie des Sciences which became famous; but he was dissatisfied with Fontenelle's use of the material, doubtless finding it hard to forgive the Frenchman's unshaken enthusiasm for Descartes. Hill likewise was an official at the Mint, holding the title of King's Clerk and Clerk of the Papers.[3] He was a close associate of the Duke of Richmond, to whose son he was appointed tutor. He travelled with the Duke, accompanying him on his expedition to France in 1728.[4] A friend of Folkes, he was acutely interested in the affairs of the Royal Society, and in 1735, introduced by Montesquieu, he conveyed to Fontenelle the news of his election as a foreign member.[5]

The international connexions of the Royal Society were further strengthened during Montesquieu's stay in England by the election as a foreign member of a Scot, but a Scot as thoroughly French as a Scot could be. This was Andrew Michael Ramsay, known already to Montesquieu as a member of the Entresol. Fresh from the composition of the *Voyages de Cyrus*, first published in 1727, Ramsay brought out in 1730 the fourth edition in

[1] Stukeley's Commonplace Book (cited by S. Piggott, *William Stukeley, an Eighteenth-Century Antiquary*, Oxford, 1950, p. 143).

[2] *Pensée* 2124 (Bkn. 1355).

[3] Chamberlayne, *Magnae Britanniae notitia*, London, 1728, part II, p. 142.

[4] See Earl of March, *A Duke and his Friends*, London, 1911, 2 vols., *passim*.

[5] Hill to Conduitt, 12 March 1735 (*H.M.C.*, 8th Report, part I, p. 63).

English, with a list of subscribers which included no less than four cardinals (Alberoni, Fleury, Polignac, and Rohan), twenty-seven dukes and duchesses, a multitude of lesser peers, several diplomats, the Comte d'Argenson, Madame de Lambert, Carteret, and Sir Robert Walpole. Ramsay had achieved election to the Royal Society just before Montesquieu—he was elected on 11 December 1729 and admitted a week later[1]—and on 10 April 1730 he received a distinction which Montesquieu never enjoyed: he was on that day (by no means without controversy) admitted D.C.L. of Oxford *honoris causa*.[2] To be almost simultaneously honoured by the vigorously politically conscious and divided Royal Society,[3] and by the Tory and even Jacobite University, largely dominated by Robert Shippen, recently Vice-Chancellor and brother of the opposition Member of Parliament, was no mean feat.

V. FREEMASONRY

The paradoxical Ramsay, among many attributes not usually found in a single individual, was a freemason. Nor was he the only member of that society whom Montesquieu knew. Masonic rolls of 1723, listing the members of the Horn Tavern Lodge at Westminster, include Waldegrave and Nathan Hickman.[4] Two years later the Lodge meeting at the Bedford Head Tavern at Covent Garden shows among its members one Hewer Edgley Hewer,[5] a Fellow of the Royal Society along with Montesquieu, to whom he appears to have given Colley Cibber's adaptation of *Le Cid*.[6] Among the most significant pioneers of freemasonry in England was Desaguliers, who was Grand Master in 1719–20

[1] Manuscript *Journal*, December 1729.

[2] Thomas Hearne, *Remarks and Collections*, ed. H. E. Salter, Oxford, 1915, X, p. 264.

[3] Cf. Hearne's *ex parte* judgement: "The affairs of the Royal Society are now in such an unsettled state, occasioned by parties, that learning is not regarded among them, but party and private interest sway all, so that things are deplorable. . . . This Society is now as much tinged with party principles as any public body, and Whig and Tory are terms better known than the naturalist, mathematician, or antiquary" (ibid., pp. 402–3).

[4] *Quatuor Coronatorum Antigrapha*, X, Margate, 1913, p. 6.

[5] Ibid., p. 27.

[6] Montesquieu's copy (London, 1719), still at La Brède, shows Hewer's bookplate.

and on three subsequent occasions Deputy Grand Master. In the third decade of the century the interest of the nobility in freemasonry increased and both the Duke of Montagu and the Duke of Richmond served as Grand Masters, Richmond being also for several years Master of the Horn Lodge.[1]

It is not surprising, in view of these prominent names, that the following paragraph is to be read in *The British Journal* on Saturday, 16 May 1730:

> We hear that on Tuesday night last [12 May 1730], at a Lodge held at the Horn Tavern in Westminster, when the Duke of Norfolk, Grand Master, Nathaniel Blackerby, Esq., Deputy Grand Master, and other grand officers, as also the Duke of Richmond, Master of the Lodge, Marquis of Beaumont, Lord Mordaunt, Marquis de Quesne, and several other persons of distinction were present; the following foreign noblemen, Francis-Louis de Gouffier, Charles-Louis President de Montsquier [*sic*], Francis Comte de Sade; as also John Campfield, Esq., William Cowper of Golden Square, Esq., and Captain John Mercer, were admitted members of the Ancient and Honourable Society of Free Masons.[2]

Some of the individuals here mentioned can be identified and others not. The eighth Duke of Norfolk was not a prominent figure in national life. Blackerby appears to have been a treasurer of charitable and philanthropic organizations. He was treasurer of the freemasons' own charity,[3] and also of the commissioners for building fifty new churches.[4] The Marquisate of Bowmont (which should be so spelled) is the courtesy title of the heir to the Scottish Dukedom of Roxburghe. The person here referred to is the son of the first Duke, who succeeded his father in 1740/1. In January 1729/30 he was created Baron Ker in the peerage of the United Kingdom, and took his seat in the Lords as an anti-Walpole Whig. Lord Mordaunt, a young man just down from Balliol, became fourth Earl of Peterborough in 1735. The Marquis

[1] D. Knoop and G. P. Jones, *The Genesis of Freemasonry*, Manchester, 1947, pp. 173–6. This is the most useful guide to early freemasonry, along with B. Faÿ, *La Franc-maçonnerie et la révolution intellectuelle du XVIIIe siècle*, Paris, 1935.

[2] This is the only reference to Montesquieu which I have discovered in the English press during the whole of his stay in England, with the exception of the attribution to him, in an advertisement of its English translation, of his friend Melon's *Mahmoud le Gasnévide* (*Weekly Medley*, 29 November 1729).

[3] Knoop and Jones, op. cit., p. 201.

[4] Chamberlayne, op. cit., part II, p. 162.

Du Quesne (not De Quesne) is Gabriel, grandson of the famous admiral Du Quesne. He lived in exile in England as a Protestant; he had served the British Government in Jamaica, and was now in London, where he was a member of the Society for the Propagation of the Gospel.[1] He married an Englishwoman, sister of the Whig M.P. for Wigan, and his son took Anglican orders.[2] The three British commoners defy identification, though it is likely that William Cowper was related to, and perhaps son of, an older man of the same name who had been secretary to Grand Lodge in 1723–4.[3]

Of the two French noblemen admitted freemasons along with Montesquieu, one was connected with families well known to him. François-Louis de Gouffier, Marquis de Thois, was first cousin to the first Duke of Richmond, his mother (whose first husband was the seventh Earl of Pembroke) being sister to the Duchess of Portsmouth. François, Comte de Sade, on the other hand, was a diplomat who sometimes undertook secret missions. His son, Donatien-Alphonse-François, born ten years later, was the infamous marquis.

The importance of freemasonry in the development of the Enlightenment has been both asserted and denied. It has not yet been definitely assessed. It is interesting to see Montesquieu, at this early stage of his career, associated with the movement. It is not the last time that it will be mentioned in the narrative of his life.

VI. LITERARY CIRCLES

Dr. John Arbuthnot was a freemason, his name being shown on the roll of the Bedford Head Tavern Lodge in 1725:[4] he was a Fellow of the Royal Society; he was in correspondence with Sloane; he was physician to the Queen; he was well known to Bolingbroke, Chesterfield, Pulteney, the Duchess of Marlborough, Lady Hervey. He had a brother who lived in Paris; he knew D'Olivet.[5] He is mentioned in the *Spicilège*[6] and cited in *L'Esprit*

[1] Ibid., p. 247.
[2] Haag, *La France protestante*, 2nd ed., V, Paris, 1886, col. 962.
[3] Knoop and Jones, op. cit., p. 168.
[4] *Quatuor Coronatorum Antigrapha*, X, p. 27.
[5] D. Olivet to Bouhier, 2 December 1735 (B.N., MSS. fr. 24417, f.140).
[6] *Spicilège* 781 (MS., pp. 790–1).

des lois.[1] In the convivial society of those days, it is most unlikely that Montesquieu and he never met, and if they did meet, the fact is important, both on account of the probable influence on Montesquieu's mature thought of Arbuthnot's *Essay concerning the Effects of Air on Human Bodies*, and on account of the Doctor's friendship with Pope.

Pope was indeed the most celebrated figure in the literary society of London. Addison had been dead for ten years, Steele for a few weeks, when Montesquieu came to England. Newton had died in 1727 and in the same year Swift had departed to Ireland, whence he was never more to return. The age of Johnson, Garrick, and Horace Walpole had not yet come. Pope was at the height of his fame.

Lady Hervey was well known to the President and corresponded with him subsequently. Though she conveyed, and he reciprocated, the best wishes of Lord Hervey, both Montesquieu's personal interest and his political sympathy were much more with his wife than with the husband, Pope's Sporus, 'the pure white curd of asses' milk'. She was closely connected with the Duchess of Marlborough, and with the Duke and Duchess of Richmond, and she interested herself benevolently in Saint-Hyacinthe.[2]

Two other friends of Pope whom passing mention shows to have known Montesquieu are Cleland and Hooke.

William Cleland, father of the scurrilous author of the *Memoirs of a Coxcomb*, had Jacobite loyalties.[3] He lent his name to the preface to the *Dunciad*. He was familiar with the Dowager Duchess of Marlborough, with Chesterfield, and with Arbuthnot. Known to Montesquieu, he is twice quoted in the *Spicilège*, once in the expression of a simple, cynical, Mandeville-like moral sentiment,[4] once in a comment on Machiavelli. He appears to have taught Montesquieu not to be deceived into regarding Machiavelli as no more than the apostle of all political wickedness:

> Machiavel n'a parlé des princes que comme Samuel en a parlé, sans les approuver. Il était grand républicain.[5]

[1] *Lois*, XVI, 4.

[2] Lady Hervey to Montesquieu, 18 August 1733; Montesquieu to Lady Hervey, 28 September 1733.

[3] See R. Carruthers, *Life of Pope*, London, 1757, pp. 257–63.

[4] *Spicilège* 601 (MS., p. 554).

[5] *Spicilège* 529 (MS., p. 487).

He may thus have led Montesquieu to his more mature view of the Florentine Secretary.

With Nathaniel Hooke Montesquieu had various points of encounter. He was a member of a Jacobite family, his uncle having been created Baron Hooke of Hooke by the Chevalier de Saint-George. He was well known to Bolingbroke; he was the hired apologist of the Dowager Duchess of Marlborough, being recommended to her in that capacity by Chesterfield.[1] It was he who induced Pope, on his death-bed, to receive the last rites of the Roman Catholic Church.[2] He was an admirer of Fénelon and a friend of Ramsay. He translated into French the Chevalier's *Vie de Fénelon* and also his very successful *Voyages de Cyrus*. Montesquieu, not surprisingly, knew him in England;[3] that their acquaintance may not have been fruitless is hinted at by the fact that Hooke, like Montesquieu, and at about the same time, wrote a Roman history, and by a brief anecdote reported by Spence:

> Mr. Hooke used to say that there were three reasons why a man would choose to live in England: liberty, liberty, liberty![4]

There is no direct evidence that Montesquieu knew Pope. He refers four times to him in the *Pensées*, he possessed the 1736 edition of his works, the *Essay on Criticism*, both in French and English, and Du Resnel's translation of the *Essay on Man*. An edition in nine octavo volumes listed in the Paris post mortem inventory[5] is presumably Warburton's, which was presented by the author.[6] He was certainly interested in Pope and his works, and the social relationships of Montesquieu's English friends were such that he can hardly have failed to meet him. But the absence of any trace of an encounter suggests that neither was greatly influenced, nor perhaps greatly impressed, by the other.

Pope's enemy, Lady Mary Wortley Montagu (for she had quarrelled with Pope before Montesquieu's visit) is now known to

[1] Maty, op. cit., I, pp. 115–16. [2] Spence, *Anecdotes*, pp. 321–2.

[3] Bulkeley to Montesquieu, 5 May 1749. Hooke's son, it is disclosed here, was an enthusiastic admirer of Montesquieu's works. He was a Doctor of the Sorbonne, and had the unhappy task of serving as chairman of examiners of the notorious thesis of the Abbé de Prades, which was responsible for the first suppression, in 1752, of the *Encyclopédie* of Diderot and D'Alembert.

[4] Spence, op. cit., p. 342.

[5] *Catalogue de la bibliothèque de Montesquieu*, ed. L. Desgraves, Geneva and Lille, 1954, p. 242.

[6] Montesquieu to Charles Yorke, 4 December 1753.

have been acquainted with the President.[1] She had commented favourably on the verisimilitude of the local colour in the *Lettres persanes*, as she was qualified to do;[2] she was later to express great admiration for Montesquieu;[3] she had many friends in common with him, the most interesting and the one who was closest to each being the Abbé Conti. The President possessed, or at least had sight of, and analysed in his notebook, a manuscript copy of her essay *Sur la maxime de Monsieur de La Rochefoucauld, qu'il y a mariages commodes, mais point de délicieux*, a theme on which Lady Mary was admirably qualified to write.[4] There has recently come to light a letter addressed to her by the President,[5] which makes it possible to reconstruct an episode of whose kind there were perhaps many in Montesquieu's life in England, but which is the only one to be recorded.

Two French children, professional dancers, a brother and sister named Sallé, had visited London in 1717. They had performed in public at the theatre in Lincoln's Inn Fields, for a week, before very considerable audiences.[6] The sister visited London again in the winter of 1730–1, and brought recommendations to Montesquieu from Madame de Lambert and from Fontenelle, of which the second survives.[7] Fontenelle explains to the President that Mademoiselle Sallé is poor and in need of assistance, and warns him that she is virtuous; he asks Montesquieu to interest himself in her behalf, and perhaps even to ask the Queen to take pity on her.

Montesquieu was not idle in response to this request. He organized a benefit performance of *Les Fourberies de Scapin* at the Theatre Royal in Lincoln's Inn Fields. It was envisaged in the first place for Monday, 23 March 1731, but in fact was postponed

[1] R. Halsband, *The Life of Lady Mary Wortley Montagu*, Oxford, 1956, gives a very valuable picture of Lary Mary, particularly in relation to her foreign acquaintances.

[2] See above, p. 33.

[3] Caldwell to Montesquieu, 26 May 1746 (*FS*, 1958).

[4] *Spicilège* 576 (MS., p. 533). Lady Mary's essay, now published, is to be found in her *Letters and Works*, London, 1861, II, pp. 421–8.

[5] Halsband, op. cit., p. 234. I have published the letter (which is dated 11 March 1730/1), with the kind permission of its owner the Earl of Harrowby, in my article last cited.

[6] J. Nichols, *Literary Anecdotes of the Eighteenth Century*, II, London, 1812, p. 63.

[7] Fontenelle to Montesquieu, November 1730.

and occurred on Thursday of the same week.[1] Montesquieu begged Lady Mary to be present, using the patronage of Fontenelle, Madame de Lambert, and Lady Stafford as arguments. In fact the play was a great success. The King and Queen, and many persons of quality, were present, and the price of seats in the pit was increased from three to five shillings. Montesquieu's initiative was abundantly successful. He displayed in England the same genial benevolence which characterized his actions in France.

[1] See E. Dacier, *Une danseuse de l'Opéra sous Louis XV. Mlle Sallé* (1707–56), Paris, 1909, pp. 65–69.

VII

LES ROMAINS, 1731–4

I. *LA MONARCHIE UNIVERSELLE*

AFTER his return from England, Montesquieu made a brief visit to Paris and (on 21 May 1731) attended the Academy. The end of June found him in the south-west again, and he remained there until the spring of 1733. He had left a number of literary tasks unfinished, and to some of these he returned. Between 1731 and 1733, so far as the evidence of manuscripts reveals, he was concerned with the collection of new material and the transcription of old material on the most varied themes, fitting it into what must have been an amorphous framework. Cross references and marginal notes in the *Pensées* disclose that this framework was sometimes simply called *Journal* or *Bibliothèque*, sometimes *Journal espagnol* or *Bibliothèque espagnole*; sometimes it was known as *Le Prince*, sometimes as *Les Princes*, once as *Journal de livres peu connus*. The form of this work appears to have been envisaged as a collection of opinion put into the mouth of an imaginary person called Zamega. There is no direct survival of the work, but the *Pensées* contain many traces of its contents. It included some of the material originally destined for the *Traité des devoirs*; it probably included also the *Considérations sur les richesses de l'Espagne*. Material from it was used in the *Considérations sur les Romains*, in *Arsace et Isménie*, and in *L'Esprit des lois*. At times its publication seems to have been envisaged, at times it was used simply as a storehouse for disconnected thoughts. It is a mystery in the literary activity of Montesquieu.

The Spanish bias shown in some of the titles given to this collection illustrates a continuous interest of Montesquieu. Spain had occupied him already in the *Lettres persanes*, where the seventy-eighth letter contains an amusing account of Spanish character and usages. The inhabitants of the peninsula are described as proud and grave, showing their gravity mainly by wearing spectacles and moustaches. They are polite—the Inquisition never burns a Jew without apologizing to him—and sometimes they are intelligent. But their literature is devoid of sense and wit. You would say on visiting one of their libraries, writes

Rica, that it had been written and assembled by a secret enemy of human reason. Only one of their books is good: 'celui qui a fait voir le ridicule de tous les autres.'

Montesquieu's interest in Spain went beyond this derisive curiosity about the Iberian character and literature. He followed closely Spanish foreign policy and the diplomatic relations of Spain and France. This caused him to be greatly preoccupied with the theme of universal monarchy.

The union, in the sixteenth century, of vast dominions in the hands first of Charles V and then of his son Philip II of Spain had caused the threat of universal monarchy under the Spanish ruling house to seem a real one. The marriage, in 1660, of Louis XIV to his cousin the Infanta Maria Theresa of Spain, revived the danger of universal monarchy, this time under the French King, whose ambition readily exploited dynastic opportunities. Had Montesquieu been ignorant of European history, he could have learned of these developments from the pages of J.-F. Bernard's *Réflexions morales, satiriques et comiques*, which are thought to have inspired the *Lettres persanes*. Here it is a critical Persian philosopher who is made to assert:

> Depuis le grand empereur des Allemands, nommé Charles-Quint, [les Chrétiens] n'ont cessé, tantôt les uns, et tantôt les autres, d'aspirer à la monarchie universelle.[1]

There had been many echoes of this political theme in the world of literature. Campanella showed his loyalty to the ruling house of Naples by defending the Spaniards against their critics, in his much discussed *De monarchia Hispanica* (Amsterdam, 1640), where he suggested the best means of bringing Spanish territorial ambitions to fruition. In 1667 the advocate Bilain expounded the arguments in favour of Louis XIV's pretensions in his *Traité des droits de la Reine très chrétienne*, and in the same year the vigorous diplomat and pamphleteer Baron Lisola sought to refute these arguments and squarely to raise against Louis XIV the charge of aspiring to establish universal monarchy, in his *Bouclier d'Etat et de justice*. All three of these books were possessed by Montesquieu, and another, *La Monarchia universale del rè Luigi XIV*, published in Italian in 1689 and at once translated into French, was by an author, the extraordinary Gregorio

[1] Cologne, 1711, p. 224.

Leti, cited elsewhere by Montesquieu,[1] who could read detailed reviews of this work in at least two of the journals which he owned and read.[2]

The President was able also to witness, from close quarters, political events of his own day which stimulated his interest in this same theme. The year 1715 saw a change in the relative positions of France and Spain. No longer did a King of France control his neighbour through a Madame des Ursins. Instead, the King of France was an infant who might not survive, and the King of Spain was his uncle who was prevented from being next in order of succession to the French throne only by a renunciation which might not be irrevocable. Spanish policy was shaped by the indomitable Alberoni, who was anxious to revive the greatness of Spain, and who encouraged Philip V to claim the regency of France on the strength of being more closely related to the infant King than was the actual Regent Orléans. The conspiracy to overthrow Orléans, organized by the Spanish ambassador,[3] was unsuccessful. France declared war on Spain, the command being given to the Duke of Berwick. The fall of Alberoni made reconciliation with Spain possible. It was delayed, however, by the death of Orléans, for his successor, Bourbon, at the instigation of Madame de Prie, abandoned the projected marriage of Louis XV to the Infanta of Spain, and it was left to Fleury, in the Treaty of Seville of 1729, to restore amity.

Montesquieu had followed these events. Bourbon, Madame de Prie, Berwick, and the Abbé de Livry,[4] the envoy who announced to the Spanish court the abandonment of the proposed marriage, were all known to him. In Italy he had encountered Alberoni, living in exile in Rome, and the Cardinal had fought over again with Montesquieu his old battles.[5] In England he had doubtless learned to see diplomatic history from yet another angle. Nor did the specific problem of universal monarchy fail to present itself, hinted at always by the motto of the city of Bordeaux: *Lilia sola regunt lunam, undam, castra, leonem.* Doria, whom the President probably met at Naples, has left manuscripts in which

[1] *Lois*, VII, 11.

[2] *Histoire des ouvrages des savants*, 1689, and *Bibliothèque universelle*, 1688.

[3] This conspiracy is referred to in *L.P.* 126.

[4] Duc de Liria to Montesquieu, 26 March 1725.

[5] Nagel II, pp. 1125–7; Pléiade I, pp. 694–5; *Spicilège* 690 (MS., pp. 658–9).

he accuses both Peter the Great and even Fleury of cherishing the ambition of establishing universal monarchy.[1] It is probable that it was in England that he first read a curious treatise on Spanish politics, written in Italian by a Scotsman and published in Edinburgh. This was the *Discorso delle cose di Spagna* of Andrew Fletcher,[2] a Scottish writer of advanced views who had been a pupil of Gilbert Burnet and who is most celebrated as the first enunciator of the often misquoted opinion, 'if a man were permitted to make all the ballads, he need not care who should make the laws of a nation.' Fletcher's aim is to warn neighbouring princes of Spain's ambition to establish universal monarchy, and to explain meanwhile the reasons for Spanish decadence. It was later that Montesquieu acquired Fletcher's works which are still to be found at La Brède;[3] but it is most probable that he first heard of them during his stay in England. Acquaintance with this *Discorso*, added to an interest in Campanella revived either in Italy or in England (where many manuscript copies of the *De monarchia Hispanica* were to be found in country houses)[4] may well have occasioned Montesquieu's next work.

This was a small treatise entitled *Réflexions sur la monarchie universelle en Europe*. Printed in 1734, it was at once withdrawn from circulation, and only one copy, now at La Brède, and bearing autograph corrections, is known to exist. Its 44 pages constitute the first published work of Montesquieu to deal with a political theme. The argument of the work is simple. The creation of a universal monarchy, never hitherto practicable, is now more difficult than in the past, because of changes in the methods of war and in the relationship between military and economic power. Mankind has on several occasions been on the verge of being forced into a universal monarchy, the instigators of which were in turn Charlemagne, the Normans, the Papacy, the Tartars, the Turks, the Emperor Charles V and his successors in Spain,[5]

[1] Naples, Biblioteca nazionale, MS. Branc. V. D. 3. [1], ff. 81–82 and 20.

[2] Included in his *Political Works*, first edition, Edinburgh, 1698, and reprinted in 1732 and 1737.

[3] The La Brède copy is Edinburgh, 1737, the catalogue entry being inaccurate.

[4] See L. Firpo, *Ricerche Campanelliane*, Florence, 1947, pp. 287–93.

[5] The explanation of the economic weakness of Spain is taken from the *Considérations sur les richesses de l'Espagne*, which is largely incorporated in this work.

and finally, at least in the opinion of his enemies, Louis XIV. Each of these attempts to institute universal monarchy failed for a specific reason, and these reasons are enumerated. Europe can now be regarded as a single whole or 'une grande république' consisting of mutually dependent powers. The treatise closes with a discussion of the true definition of the strength of a State.

This slim volume contains already several of the ideas which will later reappear in *L'Esprit des lois* and are now held typical of Montesquieu: the classification of nations into northern and southern with varying characteristics, climate being the cause of the differentiation; the distinction between government based on laws and arbitrary government; the unnatural character of unlimited and despotic power; the praise of liberty; the insistence that the wealth of a country must be based on productivity and that precious metal is no more than a symbol; the political importance of feudalism; and finally—the only one of these ideas to be expressed otherwise than in passing or developed on any scale—the dependence of the nature of a government on the extent of the territory governed.

The treatise was withdrawn from circulation, simply (according to the annotation on the manuscript of the *Considérations sur les richesses de l'Espagne*)[1] for 'des raisons'. Marginal notes on the printed volume are more specific: because it was printed from a bad copy, says one, while another admits the fear that certain passages might be wrongly interpreted,[2] the references to Louis XIV being no doubt the passages in question.

The importance of the *Monarchie universelle* is extrinsic. It shows, more clearly than anything else, and more precisely since its date is known with greater reliability than can be derived from the study of handwriting, the presence in Montesquieu's mind, in 1734, of many ideas which are to come to fruition in *L'Esprit des lois*.

One further specific allusion veils a mystery not yet resolved. Paragraph XXIII reads thus:

> Dans la dernière guerre de Louis XIV que nos armées et celles de nos ennemis étaient en Espagne éloignées de leurs pays, il pensa arriver des choses presque inouïes parmi nous, les deux chefs d'accord entre eux furent sur le point de jouer tous les monarques de l'Europe et de

[1] Nagel III, p. 140, n.f.; Pléiade II, p. 1477.

[2] Nagel III, pp. 361 and 363; Pléiade II, p. 1479.

les déconcerter par la grandeur de leur audace et la singularité de leurs entreprises.

What vast project was thus conceived by Marlborough and Berwick? In 1708 Marlborough made private and clandestine overtures to Berwick with a view to ending hostilities. They were rejected by Louis XIV, though Berwick was favourably inclined. Peace was not signed, the correspondence was destroyed, and the mystery has remained impenetrable.[1] Has Montesquieu, who was in Berwick's confidence, read too much into a chance word? Or had the two generals concerted a grand design to ensure lasting peace?

Let it be added that during the years 1731–4 there came from the pen of Montesquieu another work which was to exceed in influence anything else which he wrote. This was the famous discussion of the English constitution in which the doctrine of the separation of the powers is enunciated. Begun doubtless in England, nourished by conversations with statesmen, by attendance at Parliamentary debate, by reading the journals of the day, Montesquieu's description of the English constitution was finished in 1734.[2] The President abandoned his intention of publishing it forthwith. He kept it, frequently revised and modified it,[3] and published it eventually in 1748 as the sixth chapter of Book XI of *L'Esprit des lois*.

II. PREPARATION AND PUBLICATION

Voltaire remarks on the delight of the English in making comparison between the history of Rome and that of their own country.[4] Speeches in the House of Commons and articles in journals attest the truth of this assertion. *The Craftsman* especially presented to its readers many analogies between Roman and

[1] See on these negotiations the *Mémoires du maréchal de Berwick, écrits par lui-même*, Paris, 1780, II, pp. 51–53; Sir Charles Petrie, *The Marshal Duke of Berwick*, London, 1953, pp. 232–4; and especially Sir Winston Churchill, *Marlborough, his Life and Times*, London, 1947, II, pp. 495–504.

[2] Secondat, *Mémoire*, p. 401.

[3] The manuscript shows no fewer than five different hands indicating corrections spread over perhaps fourteen years.

[4] *Œuvres*, ed. Moland, XXII, p. 102 (*Lettres philosophiques*, ed. Lanson, I, p. 88).

English history. Montesquieu's fascination with the English constitution did not mean that England was to be his exclusive concern in writing from now on. The first fragment preserved from his pen as a child is his *Historia Romana*, an exercise at the College of Juilly. The first communication which he read to the Academy of Bordeaux was the essay entitled *La Politique des Romains dans la religion.* He had read Cicero with enthusiasm. He had written his *Dialogue de Sylla et d'Eucrate*. He had, above all, been to Rome, and had been filled with enthusiasm for the eternal city. 'Rome *antica e moderna* m'a toujours enchanté,' he was later to write enviously to a friend fortunate enough to be living in the eternal city.[1] He had known Nathaniel Hooke in England, while Hooke was engaged in the huge task of translating into English the many quartos of the Roman history of Catrou and Rouillé,[2] with which Montesquieu's writing on Rome was later to be favourably compared.[3] He had read Bolingbroke's 'several strictures on the Roman affairs' in *The Craftsman* which Pope was to describe as 'something like what Montesquieu published afterwards'.[4] *The Craftsman* also, as well as his conversations with Cleland, had rekindled his interest in Machiavelli.[5] Well acquainted with some of the works of the Florentine secretary in 1716, he had subsequently neglected him, regarding him simply as the advocate of unscrupulous methods in politics. In England, however, and probably in Italy also, he had been reminded that Machiavelli was the author of the *Discorsi* as well as of the *Prince*, and that something of value could be learnt from his pages.

Shortly after the President's return from England, he inscribed a list of books in the *Spicilège* under the rubric, 'livres originaux que j'ai à lire'.[6] This reading programme is varied. It includes the Bible, Calvin and Luther, *Hudibras*, Bacon, Clarke and Lucretius. It includes also Machiavelli, and in preparation for reading him in the original text, Montesquieu, who already possessed French translations, acquired an Italian edition of 1729.[7]

[1] Montesquieu to Solar, 7 March 1749. [2] J. Spence, *Anecdotes*, pp. 342–3.
[3] Le Nain to Montesquieu, 28 November 1748. [4] Spence, op. cit., p. 169.
[5] *Craftsman*, 13 and 27 June 1730 (original issue); *Spicilège* 529 (MS., p. 487).
[6] *Spicilège* 561 (MS., p. 521).
[7] On the influence of Machiavelli, see E. Levi-Malvano, *Montesquieu e Machiavelli*, Paris, 1912, and A. Bertière, 'Montesquieu, lecteur de Machiavel' (*Congrès 1955*).

The same page of the *Spicilège* contains a list of books on the later Roman Empire which Montesquieu says he has already read. It is a severe list: Jornandes, Procopius, Agathias, Paulus Diaconus, Flavius Blondus. But it represents only a fraction of all the reading which Montesquieu undertook in his study of Rome. It was his practice to make extracts or synopses of books which he had read, and the accident of mention in the *Pensées* or elsewhere discloses that he had made extracts from Herodotus, Strabo, Pomponius Mela, Ammianus Marcellinus, Constantine Porphyrogenitus, Plutarch, Procopius, Cassiodorus, Justinus, Polybius, Philostrates, Lilius Giraldus, Aulus Gellius, and Livy. Nor can this list be regarded as complete. Sallust, Suetonius, and above all Tacitus, were well known to Montesquieu, and he was acquainted with many of the obscurer Byzantine authors.

Almost the whole of his energy was devoted to the study of these authorities. For two years—*quantum mutatus ab illo*—he did not leave the solitude of La Brède. He no longer had judicial functions to discharge. Social intercourse was reduced to a minimum and even correspondence seems barely to have occupied him. His sole distraction was the care of his estates. He was working in silence at his first serious work, and unless credence is given to the unauthenticated legend that he was assisted by a runaway Benedictine of Saint-Maur,[1] he was working well-nigh alone.[2]

In the early summer of 1733 Montesquieu came to Paris, where on May 2nd he attended the Academy, being so little known that in the minutes he was given the rank of duke. He now made arrangements for the publication of his new work, and prudently decided to follow the precedent of the *Lettres persanes* by publishing in Holland, the Dutch Ambassador in Paris, Van Hoey,[3] acting as intermediary. It is in the autumn of 1733 that he announces the pending publication in a letter to Lady Hervey, whom he asks to read the book when it appears, and to tell him her judgement of it. He is capable, he tells her, of writing either a bad book or a good one.[4]

There was serious risk, however, that the book, whether good

[1] Vian, op. cit., p. 146, citing the unreliable Bernadau.

[2] There are no traces in the surviving manuscripts of the hand of any secretary between 1731 and 1733.

[3] L.-B. Castel, *L'Homme moral*, p. 184.

[4] Montesquieu to Lady Hervey, 28 September 1733.

or bad, would provoke the hostility of the government. Jansenist controversy, exacerbated by the activities of the convulsionaries, made the authorities more than ordinarily sensitive to the expression of any unorthodox opinion. Voltaire's *Lettres philosophiques* had already appeared in English translation in August 1733, and at least two French editions were known to be in process of being printed. Voltaire himself was apprehensive, and remarked that circumstances had changed since the time of the *Lettres persanes*, which had carried their author to the Academy.[1] Nor was his anxiety unfounded, for the *Lettres philosophiques* having been published, the storm burst on Voltaire, while Montesquieu's work was still being printed. Before the middle of April the government had already acted against the *Lettres philosophiques*, on 3 May a *lettre de cachet* was issued against Voltaire, and on 10 June the Parlement of Paris proscribed the book and caused it to be publicly burnt in the courtyard of the Palais de Justice.[2] Voltaire meanwhile took flight, and the vivacious Abbé Le Blanc described to Bouhier in the seclusion of Dijon the enormous sensation caused in Paris, and the danger to which Voltaire was exposed:

> On prétend que la duchesse d'Aiguillon, la duchesse celle-ci, et la duchesse celle-là travaillent à faire sa paix.[3]

It was no part of Montesquieu's intention to be the subject of controversy on this scale. A brush with authority would promote neither his literary nor his diplomatic ambitions. He therefore decided, at the proof stage, to submit the work to a censor of his own choice, and selected for this purpose the Jesuit Louis-Bertrand Castel, professor at the Collège Louis-le-Grand, and former tutor of the President's son. Castel was expected to deal mainly with religious, moral, and philosophical corrections, and in addition he undertook the routine typographical correction of

[1] Voltaire to Cideville, 26 July 1733 (*Voltaire's Correspondence*, ed. Besterman, no. 615; *Œuvres*, ed. Moland, XXXIII, p. 365).

[2] Le Blanc to Bouhier, 15 April 1734 (*Voltaire's Correspondence*, ed. Besterman, no. 698; H. Monod-Cassidy, *Un voyageur-philosophe au XVIIIe siècle*, Cambridge (Mass.), 1941, pp. 200–4); *lettre de cachet*, Maurepas to La Briffe, *Voltaire's Correspondence*, no. 710; arrêt de la cour du Parlement, facsimile, ibid., III, pp. 267–8).

[3] Le Blanc to Bouhier, 3 June 1734 (B.N., MSS. fr. 24412, f. 440v; Monod-Cassidy, op. cit., pp. 209–11).

the proofs. On points of substance, he made many suggestions to Montesquieu, doing so with skill and tact, but also (as was his wont) with great prolixity. The President, according to Castel's own account, welcomed these corrections and encouraged the Jesuit to speak his mind.[1]

At the beginning of June the book is on sale, but copies are exceedingly rare. The reason for this is that the authorities are hostile, and are exerting pressure on Montesquieu to produce a Paris edition, with royal privilege, and therefore with some modifications of the text.[2] Castel, capable and officious, assists Montesquieu again. Madame de Tencin also concerns herself with it. This famous figure of Parisian society is now for the first time seen to appear in Montesquieu's life. She protests against his absent-mindedness and his failure to look after his own interests in relation to the censorship department.[3] In spite of these difficulties, the Paris edition came out in July.[4] Montesquieu presented it to his colleagues of the French Academy,[5] and dispatched three copies to London for the Royal Society.[6]

The work when published was received by the reviewers with no more than moderate approval. The *Bibliothèque raisonnée* begins a twenty-page abstract by attributing it to the author of the *Lettres persanes*, and praises it for learning, wit, and penetration.[7] A long extract in the *Journal littéraire* of The Hague declares it worthy of its author, and says it can be read with pleasure.[8] The *Journal de Verdun* gives little comment, but devotes six pages to an extract dealing with Justinian.[9] The *Bibliothèque française*, which eight years earlier had published extracts from the *Traité des devoirs*, simply announces the work, and while complaining of lack of continuity and occasional obscurity, concedes that it has vigour and originality.[10] The *Journal des savants*, on the other

[1] Castel, op. cit., pp. 184–5.

[2] Le Blanc to Bouhier, 3 June 1734, as cited.

[3] Mme de Tencin to Montesquieu, May 1734, and Montesquieu to Mme de Tencin, May 1734 (Nagel III, pp. 968–9).

[4] Le Blanc to Bouhier, 20 July 1734 (B.N., MSS. fr. 24412, f. 445; Monod-Cassidy, op. cit., pp. 211–13).

[5] *Registres de l'Académie française, sub die* 30 August.

[6] Montesquieu to [Sloane?], 4 August, 1734.

[7] 1735, pp. 288–311.

[8] 1734, pp. 156–65.

[9] *Suite de la clef*, September 1734, pp. 163–8.

[10] 1734, pp. 365–6.

hand, makes no more than the barest of announcements, and it is not until 1748 that the work is noticed at length.[1]

This is not a very enthusiastic reception, and private individuals are similarly lukewarm. Le Blanc thinks the book inferior to the *Lettres persanes*.[2] Lord Hervey writes of it and its author:

> I like it; though he has three faults that I hate. He is sometimes obscure, sometimes contradicts himself, and sometimes, in order to say things which nobody ever said before him, says things which nobody will ever say after him.[3]

The German Bielfeld, though himself approving the work (which he was later to translate) and enjoying the acquaintance of its author, reports than when it appeared it was unpopular in Paris and was described as *la décadence de Montesquieu*.[4]

It is the correspondence of Bouhier and Marais which shows in the clearest way the reactions of two intelligent and well-informed men. Bouhier, having received an inquiry from the scholar and nobleman Caumont,[5] living in Avignon, addresses himself to Marais for information, and forgetting what Le Blanc has already told him, asks the title and subject of Montesquieu's new book, which he understands to be inferior to the *Lettres persanes*.[6] Marais at first contents himself with a second-hand judgement, saying that Montesquieu has ill used the Roman people whom he depicts as knaves and rascals.[7] Bouhier will not accept this *a priori* condemnation, orders Marais to read the book, and says that he himself has sometimes thought that the masters of the universe were no more honest than anyone else.[8] Marais reads the book and is delighted to find his prejudice confirmed. When reading of the Romans' conquests he was afraid and almost cried out for help. This is the real decadence of literature, he declares;

[1] Paris edition, 1734, p. 780; 1748, pp. 555–61.

[2] Le Blanc to Bouhier, 20 July 1734 (as cited).

[3] Hervey to Henry Fox, 15 August 1734 (Earl of Ilchester, *Lord Hervey and his Friends*, p. 203).

[4] Bielfeld to Lamprecht, 15 August 1741 (Bielfeld, *Lettres familières et autres*, The Hague, 1763, II, pp. 28–35).

[5] Caumont to Bouhier, 16 July 1734 (B.N., MSS. fr. 24410, f. 77).

[6] Bouhier to Marais, 31 July 1734 (B.N., MSS. fr. 25542, f. 237).

[7] Marais to Bouhier, 5 August 1734 (B.N., MSS. fr. 24414, ff. 348–9).

[8] Bouhier to Marais, 10 August 1734 (B.N., MSS. fr. 25542, f. 288).

no previous historian has written in this way: it is a Persian style.[1] Bouhier tentatively defends Montesquieu's disparagement of the virtue of the Romans, and says he could have cited a letter of Mithridates, quoted by Sallust, where the Romans are described as *latrones gentium.*[2]

Yes, says Marais, Montesquieu could have cited the letter had he known it. But he cites no authorities: his book is like the blind man in the *Lettres persanes* who acts as a guide through the streets of Paris.[3]

Bouhier, having at last received the book, concedes that Montesquieu has studied Roman history with some care. But he finds the work fragile and superficial, and is surprised that the President's friends did not warn him. A fortnight later, having read it through, he allows it to have some merits, and reproaches it with many obscurities and foretells that it will annoy many people, notably (for what is said about episcopal jurisdiction) the Jansenists.[4]

The correspondence closes when Marais pronounces the verdict, 'Véritablement, ce n'est pas un livre',[5] a judgement curiously like that written by Voltaire to his friend Thieriot:

> This book is full of hints, is less a book than an ingenious *table des matières* writ in an odd style.[6]

III. MONTESQUIEU AND THE HISTORICAL TRADITION

If Marais and Voltaire had declared that Montesquieu's book was not a history of Rome, they would have been on safer ground than in asserting that it was not a book. In judging the work its title must be remembered: *Considérations sur les causes de la grandeur des Romains et de leur décadence.* Inspired perhaps in his choice of title by Marsollier's *Histoire du ministère du cardinal Ximenès, où*

[1] Marais to Bouhier, 12 August 1734 (B.N., MSS. fr. 24414, f. 352).
[2] Bouhier to Marais, 19 August 1734 (B.N., MSS. fr. 25542, f. 240).
[3] Marais to Bouhier, 22 August 1734 (B.N., MSS. fr. 24414, f. 350).
[4] Bouhier to Marais, 26 August and 6 September 1734 (B.N., MSS. fr. 25542, ff. 242 and 244).
[5] Marais to Bouhier, 17 September 1734 (B.N., MSS. fr. 24414, f. 312).
[6] Voltaire to Thieriot, ? November 1734 (*Voltaire's Correspondence*, ed. Besterman, no. 780; *Œuvres*, ed. Moland, XXXIII, p. 466).

l'on voit l'origine de la grandeur de la monarchie d'Espagne, les causes de sa décadence . . ., which he possessed in the edition of 1693 and to which his researches on Spanish decadence may well have sent him, Montesquieu was engaged not in historical narration but in the study of historical causation, and such straight narrative as the book contains is simply the framework and the basis for his observation on causation.[1]

If indeed the *Considérations* are judged as a work of straightforward historical scholarship, they are found wanting. It has been shown by Camille Jullian that in each chapter Montesquieu chooses arbitrarily a single authority, or sometimes two, whom he follows without question. In the first chapter he follows Dionysius of Halicarnassus, neglecting Livy; in the second chapter he leans on Vegetius and Frontinus; in the next ten chapters his authority is usually either Appian or Polybius, with an occasional borrowing from Florus or Sallust.[2] He does not compare different texts, he seldom examines the reliability of the author followed, he sometimes exaggerates and magnifies his evidence. A method of this sort, derisory by standards of the present day, was already far from adequate in Montesquieu's own age. The most thorough and scrupulous examination and combination of authorities had been made in the two monumental histories of Lenain de Tillemont, of whom Gibbon was to say that his 'inimitable accuracy almost assumes the character of genius'.[3]

Nor, if the President's handling of texts is imperfect, does he compensate for this with masterly treatment of archaeological evidence. Historians had begun to rely on archaeology. Montesquieu was a contemporary of Montfaucon, and a friend of others,

[1] Much is owed in the ensuing discussion to Camille Jullian's edition of the *Considérations*, to two articles by A. Momigliano, 'La Formazione della moderna storiografia sull'Impero romano' (*Rivista storica italiana*, 1936) and 'Ancient History and the Antiquarian' (*Journal of the Warburg and Courtauld Institutes*, 1950), both reprinted in his *Contributo alla storia degli studi classici*, Rome, 1955, and to G. Giarrizzo, *Edward Gibbon e la cultura europea del settecento*, Naples, 1954.

[2] Greek authors he read usually in French translation, Latin authors in the original, and he possessed the best editions of most of them. His most skilful handling of texts is in chapter XVI when he discusses the pay of the Roman soldiers; but this is an addition not found before the 1748 edition of the *Considérations*.

[3] *Memoirs of the Life of Edward Gibbon*, ed. G. B. Hill, London, 1900, p. 182.

like Fréret and Boze, who in a smaller but still thorough way advanced archaeological science. In Rome he had been interested in other things than classical antiquities, and in the *Considérations* does not seem to envisage the possibility that statues, vases, and inscriptions may be relevant to his task. He uses archaeological evidence but once, and that occasion was unfortunate. In chapter XI he alludes to an inscription to be found near Cesena, and which he himself had seen during his travels.[1] It gives the text of a decree of the Senate calling down the wrath of the gods and of the State on any military commander who should cross the river Rubicon accompanied by his troops. But the inscription was a fabrication of a later age, and already in Montesquieu's day its authenticity was doubted by the most serious scholars.[2]

Montesquieu had moved in the society of Maffei at Verona and of Muratori at Modena. None the less, his historical method, strictly so called, and as illustrated in the *Considérations*, is of no great value and might well have exposed him to greater censure than he got. But it was not the essential part of his work and was no more than incidental to his main preoccupations. In order to understand these it is necessary to understand the treatment in his day of some of the main problems of historiography.

The first of these is the relationship between secular and ecclesiastical history. Bodin, in his *Methodus ad facilem historiarum cognitionem* of 1566, had sought to set secular history free from the control of scriptural and patristic authority by insisting on the division of history into three parts, human, natural, and divine, of which the first, so far as Bodin was concerned, mattered more than the other two. This scission effected the laicization of history and in particular facilitated the study of the history of the Roman Empire separately from that of the early Church. The same principle was followed by many in the seventeenth century, notably by Bossuet and Tillemont. Bossuet's *Discours sur l'histoire universelle* is divided into three parts. The first is simply a chronological introduction, but in the other two, entitled *La Suite de la religion* and *Les Empires*, Bossuet effects the division urged by Bodin, but effects it for other reasons. He

[1] Nagel II, p. 1201; Pléiade I, p. 769.

[2] 'Merito prudentissimus quisque marmor hoc pro adulterino ac longe posteriori demum saeculo . . . conficto habet' (Cluverius, *Italia antiqua*, Lugd. Bat., 1624, I, p. 297).

is concerned not to emancipate secular history but to preserve religious history from contamination and from rational investigation. His justification can be found in the pages of Saint Augustine, whose memorable distinction between the City of God and the earthly city is not less relevant than his insistence, emphasized after him by Jansenius and (in the *Logique de Port-Royal*) by Arnauld and Nicole, on the different fields of operation of authority and faith.

Nor is it surprising that Tillemont, educated at Port-Royal and having strong Jansenist sympathies, should maintain the same division between lay and ecclesiastical history. He had not indeed always thought to do so. He insists that there is a strong relationship between sacred and profane history, and that the one cannot be understood without the other. 'Il devait donner,' writes his biographer, 'en un seul corps l'histoire des empereurs et celle de l'Eglise: ses amis lui conseillèrent alors de les séparer.'[1] He obeyed them, and cutting his book in two, began publication of two separate ponderous works.[2]

An historian cannot doubt, however, that Tillemont's original intention was the right one. The secular and the religious histories of the first six centuries of the Christian era cannot be properly understood in isolation. From the point of view of the principles of the Enlightenment, what was necessary was that both sacred and profane history should be rationally and freely studied, the historian being at liberty to question any authority and to regard no tradition as sacrosanct. The scission urged by Bodin was useful, since it emancipated part of the field. The task remaining for eighteenth-century historians was the emancipation of the whole field, the introduction of scientific historical principles into ecclesiastical as well as lay history, and the dispassionate examination of Christianity.

It might have been expected that the author of the *Lettres persanes* would have selected this task as his own. But the *Considérations*, daring as they are in many respects, maintain with regard to Christianity a memorable silence. Even when dealing with the lives and policies of Diocletian, Constantine, and Julian,

[1] Tronchay, *Vie de M. Lenain de Tillemont*, Cologne, 1711, p. 19.

[2] *Histoire des empereurs et des autres princes qui ont régné pendant les six premiers siècles de l'Eglise*, Paris, 1690–1738, 6 vols., and *Mémoires pour servir à l'histoire ecclésiastique des six premiers siècles*, Paris, 1693–1712, 16 vols.

Montesquieu forbears to mention Christianity. It is true that elsewhere in the book he reports in dispassionate terms a much simplified and largely notional debate on Christianity between Symmacus on the one hand and Orosius, Salvianus, and Saint Augustine on the other. He refers to the effect on criminal law of Christianity and more particularly of heresies within Christianity. He alludes to the cowardliness which bigotry can induce. He discusses at some length disputes on images and monastic interventions in politics. He disparages the crusades. But these references are all either simply incidental or allusions to abuses and to special and limited manifestations of Christianity. A writer in the vanguard of the Enlightenment, treating in 1734 the reasons for the decline of the Roman Empire, might have been expected boldly to list Christianity among them, perhaps even to give it pride of place. Montesquieu's past activity would lead one to expect this of him. In his discourse to the Bordeaux Academy he had treated religion as an important factor in Roman history under the kings and in the early days of the republic. In the *Lettres persanes*, particularly in his discussion of the causes of depopulation, he treated religion as an important factor in the development of societies, and included Christianity itself in his investigation. In the *Considérations*, he does not move on, but retreats, from this position. The Abbé Raynal, spokesman of the most doctrinaire of the *philosophes*, reproves him for this reticence;[1] and the examination of Christianity in relation to Rome is left to the incisiveness and prejudice of Gibbon half a century later.

Montesquieu's silence, it is true, is in some measure occasioned by his belief that Christianity was not a historical phenomenon of great importance. Many people, he asserts in the *Pensées*, have interpreted too literally what the Fathers have said, and believes that the main preoccupation of the Emperors was the extirpation of Christianity. This is quite wrong, says Montesquieu; the Emperors scarcely thought of Christianity: 'c'était la moindre de leurs affaires.'[2] If the mention of Christianity in the *Considérations* is meagre, the explanation in part lies in the author's attempt to see events in what he felt to be true historical perspective.

But that cannot have been his determining reason. He was still

[1] *Histoire philosophique et politique des deux Indes*, The Hague, 1776, I, p. 8.
[2] *Pensée* 1562 (Bkn. 2166).

a very recent academician, anxious to build for himself a reputation as a serious writer and to live down the *Lettres persanes*. He was perhaps still ambitious to impress authority favourably with his own suitability for a diplomatic appointment. He had been cautious enough to submit the *Considérations* for correction to Castel, a Jesuit, and to accept Castel's recommendations.[1] He had agreed to the publication of lengthy extracts in the *Mémoires de Trévoux*, even at the cost of submission to yet another Jesuit censor. He wished his book to be suitable to appear in Paris with royal approbation and privilege. These are both signs which indicate and reasons which explain Montesquieu's motive in his abstention from serious treatment of Christianity: his anxiety to provoke no hostile criticism.

This timidity has led him into his acceptance of the separation of sacred and profane history: an acceptance which at times becomes explicit. He appends a footnote to a hostile comment on Constantine:

> Dans ce qu'on dit de Constantin on ne choque point les auteurs ecclésiastiques, qui déclarent qu'ils n'entendent parler que des actions de ce prince qui ont du rapport à la piété, et non de celles qui en ont au gouvernement de l'Etat.[2]

In another place he goes so far as to cite the *De civitate Dei*:

> Saint Augustin fit voir que la Cité du Ciel était différente de cette Cité de la Terre, où les anciens Romains, pour quelques vertus humaines, avaient reçu des récompenses aussi vaines que ces vertus.[3]

Nor, as the separation of sacred and profane was not the only doctrine of the Saint, is it the only trace of Augustinianism to be found in the *Considérations*.[4]

The teaching of Saint Augustine which most influenced Bossuet in his *Discours sur l'histoire universelle* was that of providentialism in history.[5] Augustine had insisted that human kingdoms were

[1] Castel to Montesquieu, March 1734 (Nagel III, p. 960).

[2] *Romains*, ch. XVII (Nagel I, C, p. 476; Pléiade II, p. 168, n.a.).

[3] *Romains*, ch. XIX (Nagel I, C, pp. 487–8; Pléiade II, p. 177).

[4] Montesquieu (who had already cited the work in his *Dissertation sur la politique des Romains dans la religion*) possessed a fifteenth-century manuscript, on vellum, of the *De civitate Dei*.

[5] See G. Hardy, *Le 'De civitate Dei' source principale du 'Discours sur l'histoire universelle'*, Paris, 1913.

established by providence, and that the greatness of the Roman Empire was so to be explained.[1] Bossuet maintained that the great empires of the earth had worked to the glory of God and the prosperity of his religion. It is God, he said, who forms kingdoms to give them to whom he will, and who makes kings serve his ends. Montesquieu had already used this phraseology in his *Eloge de la sincérité*;[2] he returns to it in the *Considérations*. Writing of the establishment of Christianity, he alludes to the secret paths which God chooses and which he alone knows;[3] twice he uses the phrase 'God permitted', once insignificantly, but once in relation to the misfortunes which overtook Christianity:

> Dieu permit que sa religion cessât en tant de lieux d'être dominante, non pas qu'il l'eût abandonnée, mais parce que, qu'elle soit dans la gloire ou dans l'humiliation extérieure, elle est toujours également propre à produire son effet naturel, qui est de sanctifier.[4]

Add to these a passage from the *Pensées*, roughly contemporary with the *Considérations*, ending with the assertion:

> Si l'établissement du Christianisme chez les Romains n'était que dans l'ordre des choses de ce monde, il serait, en ce genre, l'événement le plus singulier qui fût jamais arrivé.[5]

It is seen that Montesquieu pays at least formal tribute to the providentialist school. But the examples show that he limits the role of providence to the history of religion; there is no trace of providentialism applied to secular history. And when it is seen that the second passage is followed at once by a quotation with seeming approval of Pascal's claim that sickness is the Christian's true state; that the third passage, though doubtless intended for the *Considérations*, was not in fact included and was relegated to the *Pensées*, and that it comes at the end of a lengthily developed argument of the type *credo quia absurdum*, it must be asked whether the ostensible providentialism of these isolated passages is sincere or whether it is an ironical literary device of the type

[1] *De civitate Dei*, V, 1.
[2] Nagel III, p. 66; Pléiade I, p. 105.
[3] *Romains*, ch. XVI (Nagel I, C, p. 463; Pléiade II, p. 158).
[4] *Romains*, ch. XXII (Nagel I, C, p. 509; Pléiade II, p. 194).
[5] *Pensée* 969 (Bkn. 2148).

which Diderot and his collaborators were later to make famous in the *Encyclopédie*.[1]

IV. PHILOSOPHICAL HISTORY

A sporadic and insincere acceptance of providentialism is far from being a definition of Montesquieu's explanation of the rise and fall of Rome. When he finally sums up his contentions, it is in these terms:

> Rome s'était agrandie parce qu'elle n'avait eu que des guerres successives, chaque nation, par un bonheur inconcevable, ne l'attaquant que quand l'autre avait été ruinée. Rome fut détruite parce que toutes les nations l'attaquèrent à la fois et pénétrèrent partout.[2]

But this summary, with its stress on good fortune, although his own, does not do justice to his arguments. It would indeed have been surprising if it did. For though the Abbé Vertot's Roman history, which the President possessed, is insignificant, and possesses no more philosophy than what is contained in the title, Campanella's work on the Spanish monarchy was packed with ideas, and Montesquieu needed to read no more than the first page of his copy to find a complete framework for his researches:

> In the acquiring and managing of every dominion and principality, there usually concur three causes: that is to say, *God*, *prudence*, and *occasion*: all which, being joining together, are called by the name of *fate*; which is nothing else but a concurrence of all the causes working by virtue of the first. And hence also is *fortune* sprung.[3]

Montesquieu's observations on causes have something in common with the ideas of Campanella.

The greatness of the Republic, says Montesquieu, was based

[1] Disparagement of Montesquieu from the methodological point of view should not obscure the fact that he shows sound judgement on many points of detail. In his acceptance of the authenticity of Procopius, in his praise for Florus, in his appreciation of the significance of the office of censor, and in his attitude to the fortifications of Justinian, he was specifically approved by Gibbon.

[2] *Romains*, ch. XIX (Nagel I, C, pp. 493–4; Pléiade II, p. 182).

[3] T. Campanella, *A Discourse touching the Spanish Monarchy*, London, 1654, p. 1, and *De monarchia Hispanica*, Amsterdam, 1640 (possessed by Montesquieu) p. 3.

on its success in wars of conquest and on its skilful assimilation of conquered peoples. War was natural to the Republic. The institution of annual consulships made each holder of the office eager to distinguish himself, and to do so rapidly. The consuls were continually proposing wars to the senate, and the senate was glad to accept this mode of distracting the people's attention from its complaints. Since all the citizens, as well as all the soldiers, received directly or indirectly a share of the booty, wars were popular, and the nation, constantly belligerent, was destined either to defeat or to a great increase in size and power. The military organization of the Romans, which Montesquieu examines in detail, was sound; the opponents were weak, whether for political, economic, or military reasons, and when vanquished, they were treated by the Romans with great wisdom, with generosity or with brutality as each case deserved. Montesquieu devotes the whole of his sixth chapter to the treatment of subject peoples. Meanwhile within the walls of the city conditions were such as to promote the greatness of Rome. The spirit of liberty was the soul which gave life to the State: an implicit attack on Bossuet who had seen excessive love of liberty as the prime cause of the decline of Rome, and an echo of Bolingbroke who had asserted that:

> in the greatest revolution of the greatest government of the world, losing the spirit of liberty was the cause and losing liberty was the effect.[1]

The divisions among the people of Rome, far from being dangerous and prejudicial to the life of the State, were healthy and vigorous and made the State flourish.[2] The republican constitution contains a carefully contrived system of checks and balances, so that any abuse of power could be at once arrested. The heart of Rome behind the armies was strong and the Republic therefore prospered.

The reasons for the decline of the Republic—and for Montesquieu the Principate and the Empire are themselves stages in the decline of Rome—are his next concern. The growth of Epicureanism, the vaulting ambition of Caesar and of Pompey, the abandonment of the Republican division of political authority,

[1] Bossuet, *Discours sur l'histoire universelle*, III, vii (Paris, 1681, p. 551); *Craftsman*, 27 June 1730.

[2] Cf. Machiavelli, *Discorsi*, I, iv.

are all factors which helped to procure the decline of Rome. But there is another cause, more important than these because necessary and irresistible. This is the size which the Republic had attained. It was too large for effective control to be exercised over armies, too large for the people to remain unanimous in their love of liberty and hatred of tyranny, too large for dissension to be healthy since dissension now took the form of civil war, too large for the original laws of the State still to be appropriate. Hence Rome was bound to decline, and if the Republic had not been brought to an end by Caesar and Pompey it would have been brought to an end by others:

> Si César et Pompée avait pensé comme Caton, d'autres auraient pensé comme firent César et Pompée; et la république, destinée à périr, aurait été entraînée au précipice par une autre main.[1]

The decline of Rome was then inevitable on account of its growth; and its growth had been the cause of its greatness:

> Elle perdit sa liberté parce qu'elle acheva trop tôt son ouvrage.[2]

Under the Empire the process of decline was accelerated. The causes were numerous: there were immediate causes, such as the partition of the Empire after the transfer of the seat of government to Constantinople, the introduction of Asiatic pomp and softness at the emperors' courts, the infiltration of monks into politics, the greater strength of potential invaders, and the success of invasion. But there were more fundamental causes than these, which it was impossible to resist. The spirit of the Roman people had become corrupt, a necessary consequence of the rapidity of change from Republic to Empire. The extent of the Empire's territory was too great. The emperors' authority was inevitably tyrannous, because, as a general law, 'il n'y a point d'autorité plus absolue que celle du prince qui succède à la république.'[3]

The destinies of the Roman State were then governed by a multitude of causes. Of these causes some were necessary and others were accidental. By means of what formula does Montesquieu link them together?

He has first recourse to what he calls the *esprit général*. Already

[1] *Romains*, ch. XI (Nagel I, C, p. 427; Pléiade II, p. 129).
[2] *Romains*, ch. IX (Nagel I, C, p. 416; Pléiade II, p. 120).
[3] *Romains*, ch. XV (Nagel I, C, p. 454; Pléiade II, p. 150).

in his early fragment *De la politique*, which was part of the *Traité des devoirs*, he had expressed the notion of a common character to be found in any society, which is the result of countless separate causes, and which controls the operations of the State.[1] He brings this notion forward again in the *Considérations*. The tyranny of the emperors resulted from the *esprit général* of the people; the *esprit général*, closely akin to the manners and morals of the people (hence the great importance of the censors in Roman society), is equal in power to the laws. After these assertions comes the clearest statement:

> Il y a dans chaque nation un esprit général sur lequel la puissance même est fondée: quand elle choque cet esprit, elle se choque elle-même, et elle s'arrête nécessairement.[2]

It is not until he prepares Book XIX of *L'Esprit des lois* that Montesquieu analytically defines what he means by *esprit général*; but the notion is present in his thought at an early date.

The existence of underlying and predetermined causes of political developments (whether embodied or not in the *esprit général*) limits the freedom of action of the statesman. Hence, says Montesquieu, the mistakes which statesmen make are not always free.[3] Thus the Roman Republic, once it had disappeared, could never be restored: the causes which had destroyed it still remained.[4] The question then arises: what of free will? are every historical process and event to be regarded as predetermined at every stage? Montesquieu indicates the nature of his answer when he says:

> La république devant nécessairement périr, il n'était plus question que de savoir comment et par qui elle devait être abattue.[5]

He expresses this picturesquely when he likens the internal discords of Rome to the fires of a volcano, which emerge as soon as some piece of matter provokes an increase in their fermentation.[6] He makes a distinction between the cause of an event and its occasion. The cause is outside human control, the occasion

[1] Nagel III, pp. 168–9; Pléiade I, p. 114 (cited above, p. 75).
[2] *Romains*, ch. XXII (Nagel I, C, p. 519; Pléiade II, p. 203).
[3] *Romains*, ch. XVIII (Nagel I, C, p. 481; Pléiade II, p. 172).
[4] *Romains*, ch. XII (Nagel I, C, p. 431; Pléiade II, p. 132).
[5] *Romains*, ch. XI (Nagel I, C, p. 421; Pléiade II, p. 124).
[6] *Romains*, ch. VIII (Nagel I, C, p. 404; Pléiade II, p. 111).

depends on man's activity; the lack of an occasion may postpone the operation of a cause, but it cannot prevent it for all time. Had Caesar and Pompey not been ambitious men, it has been seen,[1] other ambitious men would have come forward to destroy the Republic. Had Charles XII not been defeated at Pultava, writes Montesquieu,[2] maintaining this argument in *L'Esprit des lois*, he would have been defeated elsewhere:

> Les accidents de la fortune se réparent aisément; on ne peut pas parer à des événements qui naissent continuellement de la nature des choses.

This distinction between occasion and cause, which many will regard as the most significant element in Montesquieu's philosophy of history, is found in other writers than Montesquieu. It is found in Vico.[3] It is found in Vico's friend Paolo Mattia Doria, and the passage in the *Considérations* which more than any other defines and clarifies Montesquieu's doctrine on causation is directly inspired by *La Vita civile* of Doria:

> Ce n'est pas la fortune qui domine le monde . . . Il y a des causes générales, soit morales, soit physiques, qui agissent dans chaque monarchie, l'élèvent, la maintiennent, ou la précipitent; tous les accidents sont soumis à ces causes . . . en un mot, l'allure principale entraîne avec elle tous les accidents particuliers.[4]

The central doctrine of the *Considérations* may well come to Montesquieu from this little known Neapolitan philosopher. To say this is not to disparage Montesquieu: the *Considérations* are a far greater book than *La Vita civile*; nor does one disparage Montesquieu in remarking that what he has done in his work on the Romans is to solve for the historian the problem of determinism as it had been solved for the metaphysician by Malebranche.

[1] See above, p. 166. [2] *Lois*, X, 13.

[3] *Scienza nuova prima*, I, xii (ed. F. Nicolini, Bari, 1931, p. 31). The same idea is more succinctly expressed in *Il Diritto universale*, ch. xlvi: 'Utilitas occasio, honestas est caussa iuris et societatis humanae' (ed. F. Nicolini, Bari, 1936, I, p. 54).

[4] *Romains*, ch. XVIII (Nagel I, C, p. 482; Pléiade II, p. 173). The passage from Doria runs thus: 'Le cose che accadono in questo mondo, così fisiche come morali, sono cagionate dal quasi infinito combinamento delle cose . . . Di più questa infinita variazione degli umani accidenti sta soggetta a certe regole generali, alle quali tutti i particolari stanno soggetti' (*La Vita civile*, Augsburg, 1710, pp. 131–2; Naples, 1729, pp. 124–5). The 1710 edition was possessed by Barbot. See on this subject my article 'Montesquieu et Doria' (*RLC*, 1955).

The distinction between the First Cause and occasional causes which was made by the author of *De la recherche de la vérité* has been carried into history by Montesquieu.

There remain to be said two other things in praise of the *Considérations*.

The first is that Montesquieu, true to the nascent conception of the philosophical historian, adorns his work with reflections and observations which refer to many things other than his immediate subject matter. He makes remarks about Louis XIV, about John Law, about the Jacobites, about the *lazzaroni* of Naples. He makes some remarks which involve him in trouble and compel him to modify his printed text. This is the case when he praises suicide, and when he says that the Spaniards (like Turks) show that there exist nations fit to possess uselessly a great empire. The separation of the powers is shown as a good arrangement in government. Liberty (praised in the same year by Voltaire in the *Lettres philosophiques*) is shown as a desirable end in society: this was new language for the French to hear. Finally, Montesquieu makes a categorical denial of the legality of despotism which is simultaneously a rejection of the concept of sovereignty in political theory, a rejection which serves more than does anything else to differentiate his ideas from those eventually expressed by Rousseau:

> C'est une erreur de croire qu'il y ait dans le monde une autorité humaine à tous les égards despotique; il n'y en a jamais eu, et il n'y en aura jamais: le pouvoir le plus immense est toujours borné par quelque coin.[1]

The other thing which must be said about the *Considérations* is that in no other work, with the exception of the *Défense de l'Esprit des lois*, does the President handle the French language with such consummate skill. His language is chaste and economical: the more impressive, then, is the occasional figure of rhetoric, the rapid antithesis, the crystalline epigram. The Stoics, ignorant of Christianity, are like 'ces plantes que la terre fait naître dans des lieux que le soleil n'a jamais vus'. Of the harshness of Brutus prepared for the nation's sake to slay his father, Montesquieu declares, putting more meaning into six words than any other writer can, 'la vertu semblait s'oublier pour se surpasser elle-même'. If men take their own lives, there is 'un instinct naturel

[1] *Romains*, ch. XXII (Nagel I, C, p. 519; Pléiade II, p. 202).

et obscur, qui fait que nous nous aimons plus que notre vie même'. Rarely, but with engaging informality, the President discards the impersonality of his writing and lets his heart appear. Then he is able to define the fruits of Octavius's reign as 'l'ordre, c'est-à-dire une servitude durable'. He is able, in the last paragraph of the book, to write, 'Je n'ai pas le courage de parler des misères qui suivirent.'

The *Considérations* are a great landmark in Montesquieu's life and in the history of letters. They have also great intrinsic merit.

VIII

PARIS, 1734–48

I. THE RETURN TO PARIS

THREE years of foreign travel and two years of rustic retirement had not destroyed Montesquieu's taste for the society of the metropolis. Between the spring of 1733, when he began his first stay of length in Paris since his return from England, and the publication of *L'Esprit des lois* in 1748, he spent rather more time in Paris than in the south-west, and would have spent still more time there had he not been impoverished by the War of the Austrian Succession. Since 1728 both Paris and the President had changed. Montesquieu had talked with Prince Eugene, with the Queen of England, and (before he became Pope) with Clement XII. He was accepted in intellectual circles. He was a Fellow of the Royal Society. And he was no longer the man of a single book. The society in which he was to move in Paris was different from the society he had known before. The Entresol had been suppressed, Madame de Lambert was dead, the revels of Bellébat had ended. The Berthelot family enters Montesquieu's life no more, and there is no evidence of his seeing the Matignons again, save for a four day visit which he paid to the Comte de Matignon at La Rochelle in 1734.

The Court from time to time still claimed him, his sponsor being now Mademoiselle de Charolais, sister to Mademoiselle de Clermont who mysteriously passed through his life in the 20's. He still occasionally visited Chantilly.[1] Faithful through the years was Bulkeley who, as befitted a persistent courtier, kept his friend informed about the rumours and intrigues of Versailles. Montesquieu's friendship with Bulkeley and with Bulkeley's nephew François de Fitz-James, Bishop of Soissons, was unaffected by the death of Berwick, who was killed in action in 1734. The Fitz-James family, proposing to publish the memoirs which Berwick had left, asked Montesquieu to write an introduction for them. He did so with no great haste. His éloge of Berwick was found among his papers after his death, and was published in 1778. It

[1] Montesquieu to Richmond, 2 July 1735 (*FS*, 1958).

gives an admiring and decorous picture of the Marshal, and though unfinished is written with polish and distinction.

Montesquieu had two new interests in Paris. The first of these was the Academy. Though not so faithful an attender as Fontenelle or Alary, whenever he found himself in Paris he was careful to appear three or four times. On 1 April 1739 he was elected *directeur* for the ensuing quarter and was at once more regular in attendance, being present at fourteen sessions in three months. In all he attended 111 sessions.[1] Membership of the Academy inevitably meant acquaintance with almost all the literati of the day. Fontenelle and Hénault were old friends; they were joined by Marivaux, Moncrif, Bussy-Rabutin, who was Bishop of Luçon but whose great merit was that he reproduced better than any one else the tone of *la vieille cour*,[2] and others. Montesquieu was present in 1743 when his friend Mairan was elected; he was influential in procuring the election at the same time of Maupertuis,[3] who reciprocated five years later by causing Montesquieu to be elected to the Academy of Berlin.[4] On one occasion the President supported the candidature of Trublet, saying 'Je donne ma voix à Monsieur l'abbé Trublet, aimé et estimé de Monsieur de Fontenelle', but without success.[5] On 22 September 1746, when Duclos was elected, Montesquieu for the first time coincided with Voltaire. Membership of the Academy infallibly brought its members the acquaintance of aspirants to that honour. Trublet was one of these, and the amiably garrulous Le Blanc another. Le Blanc, as befitted an Anglophile, was a great admirer of Montesquieu, dined with him several times and once at the British Embassy,[6] defended him against denigrators such as Silhouette,[7] and for a time lived with his friend Melon.[8]

Montesquieu's other new interest in Paris was freemasonry, with which he had become associated in London.

[1] *Registres de l'Académie française*, III.

[2] Hénault, *Mémoires*, p. 360.

[3] Maupertuis, *Eloge de Montesquieu*, Berlin, 1755, p. 48.

[4] Montesquieu to Formey, 3 June 1747.

[5] J. Jacquart, *L'Abbé Trublet*, Paris, 1926, p. 336, citing D'Alembert. Trublet was finally elected in 1761.

[6] Le Blanc to Bouhier, 16 August 1733, March 1734, and 3 June 1734 (B.N., MSS. fr. 24412, ff. 426v, 432, and 440v; Monod-Cassidy, op. cit., pp. 183, 199, and 210).

[7] Le Blanc to Bouhier, 17 June 1738 (B.N., MSS. fr. 24412, f. 516; Monod-Cassidy, pp. 301–2).

[8] Le Blanc to Bouhier, 16 August 1733 (as cited).

The Whitehall Evening Post for 5–7 September 1734 contains the following notice:

We hear from Paris that a lodge of free and accepted masons was lately held there, at Her Grace the Duchess of Portsmouth's house, where His Grace the Duke of Richmond, assisted by the Earl of Waldegrave, President Montesqueir [*sic*], Brigadier Churchill, Edward Young Esq., Register of the Most Honourable Order of the Bath, and Walter Strickland Esq., admitted several persons of distinction into that most ancient and honourable society, among whom were the Marquis de Brancas, General Skelton, and the President's son.

A year later the same journal, in its number for 18–20 September, prints a longer paragraph:

They write from Paris, that His Grace the Duke of Richmond and the Rev. Dr. Desaguliers (formerly Grand Masters of the Ancient and Honourable Society of Free and Accepted Masons, and now authorized by the present Grand Master under his hand and seal and the seal of the order) having called a lodge at the Hôtel Bussy in the Rue Bussy, His Excellency the Earl of Waldegrave, His Majesty's Ambassador to the French King; the Right Hon. the President Montesquiou [*sic*]; the Marquis Lomaria [viz. Locmaria]; Lord Dursley, son to the Earl of Berkeley; the Hon. Mr. Fitz-Williams; Messrs Knight, father and son; Dr. Hickman; and several other persons, both French and English, were present; and the following noblemen and gentlemen were admitted into the order, viz. His Grace the Duke of Kingston; the Right Hon. the Count of S. Florentin, Secretary of State to His Most Christian Majesty; the Right Hon. the Lord Chewton, son to the Earl of Waldegrave; Mr. Pelham; Mr. Herbert; Mr. Arminger; Mr. Cotton; and Mr. Clement; after which the new brethren gave a most elegant entertainment to all the company.

Freemasonry had already been introduced into France from England. A lodge was established by Lord Derwentwater about 1725, and in less than ten years there were five or six hundred freemasons in all in Paris.[1] This list of those present at these two gatherings shows close family relationships between many of the members, and official relationships between others.[2]

[1] *Encyclopédie, Supplément,* Paris and Amsterdam, 1777, III, p. 134.

[2] The Duchess of Portsmouth had been mistress of Charles II and the second Duke of Richmond was her grandson, while Lord Dursley was her great-grandson. Gouffier (admitted a freemason with Montesquieu in 1730) was her nephew, while Gouffier's mother, her sister, was widow of the seventh Earl of Pembroke. The Mr. Herbert alluded to is probably a brother of the ninth Earl

Montesquieu's enthusiasm is shown by his introduction of his son, then aged no more than eighteen, and by a letter written by him to the Duke of Richmond:

Soit le bien arrivé le docteur Desaguliers, la première colonne de la maçonnerie. Je ne doute pas que sur cette nouvelle tout ce qui reste encore à recevoir en France de gens de mérite ne se fasse maçon.[1]

Freemasonry meanwhile was spreading to the provinces, a lodge being established at Bordeaux in 1732 by English merchants. This caused some preoccupation to the Government. Boucher, intendant of Bordeaux, in a letter to Fleury on 2 April 1737, denounced Montesquieu as being a freemason, and reported that he had provisionally forbidden him to associate with the society. Fleury replied, approving this step and commending Boucher's diligence, and asking him particularly to point out to Montesquieu the displeasure which this society caused to the King.[2] The following year Clement XII issued the Bull *In eminenti apostolatus specula* in which freemasonry was categorically condemned and anyone encouraging, harbouring, joining, or inducing others to join the freemasons was pronounced excommunicate *ipso facto*.[3]

There is no subsequent mention of Montesquieu's association, and though it may have had some bearing on his subsequent friendships—with Lord Morton for example—it played no great part in his life.

With foreign visitors in general, Montesquieu now associated on a larger scale than before his travels. The diplomatic corps he knew extensively: Waldegrave, Schaub, and Albemarle, British Ambassadors; two Danish envoys, Schulenberg and Bernstorff, representatives of the Netherlands, Turkey, Genoa, Portugal, and Russia are all mentioned either in his correspondence or in his notebooks. The Sardinian envoy was Solar, commander of the Order of Malta and an old friend whom he had

of Pembroke, who married a Fitz-William, one of whose brothers is here referred to. Waldegrave was Berwick's nephew, and Brigadier Churchill was his cousin, being a bastard of Charles Churchill, brother to Marlborough. On the French side Locmaria's stepfather was a son of Mme de Lambert, and in 1736 his cousin married the daughter of the Marquis de Brancas.

[1] Montesquieu to Richmond, 2 July 1735 (*FS*, 1958).

[2] *Arch. hist. Gironde*, XXVI.

[3] The Bull was issued on 28 April 1738 (*Bullarium*, XXIV, Turin, 1872, pp. 366–7).

known—and initially despised—at Vienna. Many private visitors from abroad came to see him, armed with introductions from the friends he had made during his travels, and sometimes those friends themselves, to his great joy, came to revive their acquaintance and to drink to his health. Visitors from England were particularly numerous. Martin Folkes, successor to Sloane as President of the Royal Society, visiting Paris in 1739, met all the men of science in Paris. Montesquieu (who had abandoned a projected visit to England the year before)[1] was overjoyed to see him, introduced him to Polignac, now living in Paris, and extracted from him a promise to send his son for a year to Bordeaux, where Montesquieu would be his mentor and ensure that he would be a *libertin* only as far as a *galant homme* ought to be.[2] Hervey's eldest son met the President in Paris in 1740. Sir Andrew Mitchell, later British envoy in Berlin, visited Paris in February 1735, and enjoyed for some time the society of Montesquieu,[3] who alludes to him with great regard in his correspondence. Another visitor about the same time was Richmond's friend and protégé Thomas Hill, seeking an introduction to Fontenelle.[4] A little later there arrived the celebrated Sir Francis Dashwood, later to become Lord Le Despencer and a Minister of the Crown, but now notorious for his lack of morals and his blasphemous proclivities. Montesquieu gives him a letter of introduction to the learned and genial Abbé Niccolini,[5] not knowing, or deeming it irrelevant, that Dashwood on a previous visit to Italy had been the perpetrator of a scandalous scene in the Sistine Chapel, where on Good Friday, in the dimly lighted chapel, disguised and cracking a horsewhip, he had been taken for the devil. After this episode, he was obliged hastily to leave the Papal States.[6]

[1] Montesquieu to Folkes, 19 August 1738.

[2] Montesquieu to Folkes, 14 February 1741.

[3] A. Bisset, *Memoirs and Papers of Sir Andrew Mitchell, K.B.*, London, 1850, p. 6.

[4] Thomas Hill to John Conduitt, 12 March 1735 (H.M.C., 8th Report (i), p. 63.

[5] Montesquieu to Niccolini, 4 October 1739.

[6] Horace Walpole, *Memoirs of the Reign of King George III*, ed. G. F. R. Barker, London and New York, 1894, I, p. 136, n.1. During this ill-omened visit to Rome, Dashwood had in fact, unknown to Montesquieu, made the acquaintance of Niccolini, who subsequently remembered their meeting with surprising cordiality, and refers to it specifically in two letters, for knowledge of which I am indebted to Miss B. Kemp of St. Hugh's College (Niccolini to Dashwood, 21 November 1762 and 13 May 1763, Bodl., MS. dd. Dashwood Bucks. c. 46).

Foreign visitors from remoter parts included Stanislas Konarski, the leading figure in the Polish Enlightenment, and one who, even before his death, was to be described as *clarissimum Poloniae lumen.*[1] His friendship with Fontenelle, and his great admiration for the *Considérations sur les Romains*, make it likely that he encountered Montesquieu.[2] Likewise from the east came Stephen Evodius Assemani, titular Archbishop of Apamea in Syria, full of information about the Church in China and in Ethiopia,[3] and from the less remote east the Moldavian Prince Antiochus Cantemir.[4] Son of Demetrius Cantemir, whose history of the Ottoman Empire enjoyed a great renown, he was himself a man of letters of no mean quality. He translated into Russian the *Lettres persanes*, Fontenelle's *Entretiens sur la pluralité des mondes*, and Algarotti's *Il Newtonianismo per le dame*, wrote satires himself, and began to compile a Russian–French dictionary. Introduced doubtless by common friends, who included the oculist Gendron (for Cantemir suffered with his eyes), Maupertuis, and the Duchesse d'Aiguillon, Montesquieu knew Cantemir, but respected him more than he liked him,[5] repelled perhaps by his cold personality and his admiration for Bossuet.[6] Much of Montesquieu's information about Russia may have been derived from conversations with Cantemir, perhaps even the opinion that you must flay a Muscovite alive to make him feel.[7]

Another foreign visitor was Scipione Maffei, who arrived in Paris from Dijon, where he had been staying with Bouhier, on 23 January 1732. He was accompanied by the learned Séguier of Nîmes. Montesquieu, who had already met Maffei at Verona,

[1] I. D. A. Jamoski, *Excerptum Polonicae litteraturae*, Bratislava, 1764, I, p. 80.

[2] J. Fabre, *Stanislas-Auguste Poniatowski et l'Europe des lumières*, Paris, 1952, pp. 63 and 66.

[3] *Spicilège* 643 (MS., pp. 607–8). Perhaps Montesquieu's identification is wrong and it was Evodius's uncle, Joseph Simon Assemani, Archbishop of Tyre, whom he met. The uncle's dates and movements are more compatible with the information given by Montesquieu. See E. Tisserant, 'Notes pour servir à la biographie d'Etienne Evode Assémani' (*Oriens christianus*, 1932).

[4] See M. Ehrhard, *Le Prince Cantemir à Paris (1738–44)*, Paris, 1938.

[5] He wrote to a close friend of Cantemir after the Prince's death, 'Vous trouverez partout des amis pour remplacer celui que vous avez perdu; mais la Russie ne remplacera pas si facilement un ambassadeur du mérite du prince Cantemir' (Montesquieu to Guasco, 1 August 1744).

[6] 'M. de Meaux était, disait-il, son héros' (Guasco, *Vie du prince Antiochus Cantemir*, prefaced to *Satires du prince Cantemir*, London, 1750, p. xcv).

[7] *Lois*, XIV, 2.

displays no great affection towards him, although he was ordinarily amiably disposed towards Italians. Maffei moved in the circles of Fontenelle, Boze, Mairan, and Maupertuis, but lived more in the salon of Madame de Verteillac,[1] which was not frequented by Montesquieu, and was perhaps too highly esteemed by Voltaire for the President to think well of him. Nor was his theological outlook congenial, for while in Paris he flung himself gratuitously into the Jansenist controversy, and became an outspoken advocate of the Bull *Unigenitus*: an attitude which might have been forgiven in a cleric and a Frenchman, but in a layman and an Italian evoked hostile comment even from his friends.[2] His works, however, were not unknown to Montesquieu, and may in some places have influenced *L'Esprit des lois*. The only certain trace of their encounters in Paris is a comment made by Séguier in his travel diary, where he lists the literary figures of Paris:

M. le président de Montesquieu, qui est d'un esprit vif et enjoué, et qui est l'auteur des *Lettres persanes* et de la *Décadence de la grandeur des Romains* [*sic*].[3]

Séguier, however, like most of those who met Montesquieu, gives no example of this vivacious wit.

Another Italian visitor, and doubtless more welcome than Maffei, was the excellent Cerati. This learned and universally beloved ecclesiastic, now raised to the dignity of Monsignor, arrived in France in the summer of 1742 and stayed there, with an interruption for a visit to England, until the autumn of 1744. He enjoyed a wide circle of acquaintance: Mairan, Trudaine, Falconet, Réaumur, Fontenelle, and Voltaire himself, not to mention a large number of clerics, prominent in whose number were the Jansenists Mésenguy and Fitz-James, Bishop of Soissons.[4] Among all his friends there were few, and perhaps none, whom he loved more than Montesquieu.

The President, writing to Folkes, says that Cerati and he often drink Folkes's health; Cerati he describes as a good, worthy, and excellent man, and praises him for having abandoned theology

[1] See Maffei, *Epistolario*, Milan, 1955, I, p. 634, and G. Boissier, 'Un savant d'autrefois' (*Revue des deux mondes*, 1 April 1871), p. 457.

[2] Notably Lévesque de Burigny and La Bastie (Boissier, loc. cit., p. 459).

[3] Nîmes, Bibliothèque Séguier, MS. 129, f. 45.

[4] A. Cerati, *Elogio di Mgr G. Cerati*, Parma, 1778, p. 33.

for natural science:[1] an unfounded compliment, but one which explains in part why Montesquieu was willing to discuss with Cerati the work he was writing, a mark of confidence and esteem vouchsafed to very few. And when this work is completed, he says, what better could he do than sail along the Languedoc canal and onwards to Pisa, and ask Cerati for *une bonne soupe*?[2]

Another bond than common intellectual interests linked the two. The Italian suffered from the same malady of the eyes as Montesquieu, and his journey to France was largely inspired by the need for resting them.[3] Montesquieu without doubt discussed with Cerati their common ailment; he introduced him to Gendron, the best oculist in France, whose great joy was to give alms to the poor and to those persecuted for their Jansenism.[4] Cerati did not think less well of him on that account.

Some years later, when Cerati visited Naples, he called on the not yet famous Galiani, who singled out for mention in his diary two characteristics of his learned visitor: that he esteemed greatly the Président de Montesquieu, and that he never mixed water with his wine.[5]

II. THE GREAT SALONS

The intellectual salons of Paris were Montesquieu's delight from 1733 onwards. They had at that time a new importance in the social life of Paris. The drawing-rooms of the seventeenth century were based on rank and station. Madame de Lambert, departing from the old exclusiveness, had invited men of letters as well as the nobility; but she had deemed it prudent to invite them on different days. After her death, those who sought to succeed her organized their drawing-rooms differently. Rank and blood did not automatically procure invitations, while wit and intelligence did; and if princes and dukes were not excluded, they were cultivated more and more for their intellectual merits. Family relationships become less important in the course of the

[1] Montesquieu to Folkes, 21 January 1743.

[2] Montesquieu to Cerati, 19 April 1746 (*FS*, 1958).

[3] Cerati to Bottari, 8 April 1740 (Rome, Biblioteca Corsiniana, MS. 1589, f. 144).

[4] Guasco, *Lettres familières*, XXVI (Nagel III, p. 1115).

[5] Naples, Biblioteca della Società napoletana di storia patria, MS. XXXI, c. 22, f. 149v.

century, and common literary interests become more important.

Montesquieu's own social outlook changed in the same way and at the same time. Willing from his earliest days, thanks to the Academy of Bordeaux, to choose friends of humbler rank than his own, he becomes in the course of his life less and less disposed to mix with the *noblesse d'épée* unless birth and wit are combined. He is found therefore in most of the salons of the Paris of his day, whether the hostesses were of humble or of noble birth. None of them gave him more pleasure than that of the Hôtel Brancas, situated in the Rue du Cherche-Midi not far from the Rue Saint-Dominique where Montesquieu had now taken a house. The two families which provided the nucleus of the society were those of Brancas and Beauvau.

The Marquis de Brancas, head of one branch of the family, Marshal of France, twice ambassador in Madrid, was already known to Montesquieu in 1725.[1] He was a worthy man, but slow and dull, and Montesquieu cites him in the *Pensées* as an example of the rule that children do not, intellectually, resemble their parents.[2] For his son, the Comte de Forcalquier, well known to Montesquieu from about 1740, was a man of parts. He was perennially ill; a bitter female tongue mocked him as an *éternel mourant*;[3] but he bore his trials with fortitude and died in 1753 at the age of forty-three. His sister Marie-Thérèse, by her first marriage Comtesse de Rochefort, was a famous figure in her day. Her cousin's wife, the Duchesse de Brancas, was scarcely less so.

The distinction of the Beauvau family had carried its head, the Prince de Craon, to the office of Governor of the Grand Duchy of Tuscany, and a tribute was paid both to his rank and his intellect when he was elected in 1739 *lucumone* of the Academy of Cortona.[4] Montesquieu, to his regret, did not meet him in Italy, but he knew him subsequently, and was an admiring friend of his son the Prince de Beauvau, a soldier, later a Marshal of France, who had a reputation for probity, valour and wit.[5] Montesquieu saw in him the stuff of greatness,[6] and the Prince had a

[1] Montesquieu to Brancas, 22 May 1725. A member of the Brancas family was at Juilly with Montesquieu.

[2] *Pensée* 1426 (Bkn. 1176).

[3] Mme d'Aiguillon to Montesquieu, 1 November 1751.

[4] Cortona, MS. 433.

[5] Hénault, *Mémoires*, p. 230.

[6] Montesquieu to Cerati, 28 March 1748.

deep regard for Montesquieu: coming to Bordeaux as military commander ten years after the President's death, he presented a marble bust of him to the Academy.[1] Closer still to Montesquieu's affections was Beauvau's sister, Princesse de Lixin by her first marriage, Marquise, then Duchesse, de Mirepoix, by her second. The President sang her praises in verses less than mediocre,[2] and if contemporary opinion can be relied on, he was her accepted lover.[3] With her husband, none the less, he maintained very amiable relations.

There were other nobles of high rank in the Brancas salon, among them the Duc de Nivernais, the Duchesse d'Aiguillon, an important figure in Montesquieu's life, the Duchesse de Luxembourg, descended from Colbert, and the Duchesse de Boufflers. This lady, who later became the second wife of the Duc de Luxembourg, was celebrated in verses by Montesquieu, but she won renown from posterity as the protectress of Rousseau. The most interesting figures in the salon, however, were not those of the highest rank. Although both Forcalquier and his brother Céreste were reputed to be *dévots*,[4] Helvétius and Duclos were popular in the house, Duclos at one time living there.[5] This noisy, outspoken, licentious writer, a loyal friend and an inimitable raconteur, later to become the chief of staff of the *philosophes* in their struggles, had perhaps known Montesquieu as early as 1726 when Montesquieu was simply the author of the *Lettres persanes* and Duclos was a quite unknown frequenter of the Café Procope and friend of Fréret and La Motte.[6] The genial, wealthy Helvétius was not to reach the height of his fame until the publication of *De l'esprit* in 1758, but Montesquieu

[1] Secondat to Guasco, s.d. (Nagel III, pp. 1554–5).

[2] The poem begins:

La beauté que je chante ignore ses appas;
Mortels qui la voyez, dites-lui qu'elle est belle,
Naïve, simple, naturelle,
Et timide sans embarras.

(Nagel I, C, p. 608; Pléiade II, p. 1469).

[3] Bulkeley to Montesquieu, 21 January 1749; Mme de Tencin to Montesquieu, 20 May 1749; Solar to Montesquieu, 27 August 1749. It was in the company of Mme de Mirepoix that Montesquieu travelled in 1747 to the exiled Polish court at Lunéville, where her sister was the royal favourite.

[4] Mme de Tencin to Richelieu, 12 June 1744 (*Correspondance du cardinal de Tencin et de Mme de Tencin avec le duc de Richelieu*, s.l., 1790, p. 343).

[5] *Fiche de police* (B.N., MSS, n.a.f. 10771, f. 161).

[6] P. Meister, *Charles Duclos (1704–72)*, Geneva, 1956, p. 13.

recognized his merit already, saying 'Je ne sais si Helvétius connaît sa supériorité; mais pour moi, je sens que c'est un homme au-dessus des autres.'[1] Also present was the sensual Abbé de Bernis, unregenerate and thought of not as one who would attain the purple, but as a haunter of the *coulisses* of the Opera. When he was twenty, he writes in his memoirs, he used to dine with Fontenelle, Montesquieu, Mairan, Maupertuis, and Crébillon, and he was struck with the modesty and simplicity of Montesquieu.[2] It was the Brancas salon which launched him on his career and carried him through the portals of the Academy.[3] Hénault likewise was one of the company, learned, gay, a courtier, and a close friend of the Comte d'Argenson. He had frequented the society of Bellébat in the days of the Regency. The Entresol had met in his house. He had sold his legal office at the same time as Montesquieu, in order to devote himself to social and intellectual pursuits. Accompanying Hénault was his faithful friend the Marquise Du Deffand. Of a recent and modest noble family, abandoned by her husband, she possessed a little house in the Rue de Beaune, and her talent and generosity procured for her a wide circle of friends and correspondents, of whom Horace Walpole is the best known.

The performance of short comedies was the characteristic occupation of the Brancas salon. Montesquieu speaks with admiration of the *badineries charmantes* of Forcalquier, and of the gargantuan suppers,[4] and Hénault tempts him to Paris with an account of the pleasures that await him:

> une actrice admirable, *dulce ridentem, dulce loquentem*, des comédies que du temps de Térence on aurait attribuées à Scipion et à Laelius, et des ballets qui sont dignes de tout le reste.[5]

Nor were the conversations inferior. Sometimes serious, sometimes conducted for effect, they touched on topics of all kinds, now dealing with gossip, now with works of literature, now with social problems. The Duchesse de Brancas reports one such

[1] Saint-Lambert, memoir on Helvétius, prefaced to *Le Bonheur*, London, 1772, p. xviii.

[2] Bernis, *Mémoires et lettres*, ed. Masson, I, pp. 34–35 and 94. Bernis was born in 1715. Montesquieu made extracts from his works.

[3] Hénault, *Mémoires*, pp. 214–15.

[4] Montesquieu to Duclos, 15 August 1748.

[5] Hénault to Montesquieu, 4 November 1748.

conversation, brilliant and vivacious, on the reasons for the differences between the society of Paris and that of Versailles, and shows Madame d'Aiguillon and Montesquieu making common cause against Madame du Châtelet and Voltaire.[1] Hénault, writing to Madame Du Deffand, describes a more modest gathering, when Montesquieu, he, and a few others were taking supper with Madame de Mirepoix:

Notre souper fut fort gai: nous raisonnâmes beaucoup, nous causâmes, pas une épigramme, point d'escrime, un souper assez bon; ensuite nous jouâmes au piquet.[2]

The nature of the social intercourse in the salons depended mainly on the character of those who frequented them, and particularly on the character of the great ladies. Madame de Tencin, Madame de Mirepoix, Madame Du Deffand, the Duchesse d'Aiguillon, the Duchesse de Chaulnes, Madame Dupré de Saint-Maur, Madame Dupin, Madame Geoffrin: these were renowned figures in their day, and Montesquieu knew them all and knew most of them well. They were distinctive figures, though time has blurred the traits of the characters. Some of them were charming, some were harsh and grasping; some were learned, some were ignorant, some were wealthy and others poor. Horace Walpole, in a letter which deserves to be remembered, succeeded in evoking the individual personality of these ladies, and in setting them in their social background:

Madame Geoffrin . . . is an extraordinary woman, with more common sense than I almost ever met with. Great quickness in discovering characters, penetration in going to the bottom of them, and a pencil that never fails in a likeness—seldom a favourable one. . . . She has little taste and less knowledge. . . . She is an epitome of empire, subsisting by rewards and punishments.

Her great enemy, Madame Du Deffand, was for a short time mistress of the Regent, is now [in 1766] very old and stone blind, but retains all her vivacity, wit, memory, judgement, passions, and agreeableness. . . . In a dispute, into which she easily falls, she is very warm and scarce ever in the wrong: her judgement on every subject is as just as possible, on every point of conduct as wrong as possible: for she is all love and hatred. . . .

[1] Duchesse de Brancas, *Mémoires*, ed. E. Asse, Paris, 1890, pp. 17–21.

[2] Hénault to Mme Du Deffand, 17 July [1742] (Mme Du Deffand, *Correspondance complète*, ed. Lescure, I, p. 67).

Madame de Mirepoix's understanding is excellent of the useful kind, and can be so when she pleases of the agreeable kind. She has read, but seldom shows it, and has perfect taste. . . . She is false, artful, and insinuating beyond measure when it is her interest, but indolent and a coward. . . .

Madame de Rochefort is different from all the rest. Her understanding is just and delicate, with a finesse of wit that is the result of reflection. Her manner is soft and feminine, and though a *savante*, without any declared pretentions. She is the *decent* friend of Monsieur de Nivernais.[1]

Of the great ladies not mentioned here by Walpole, the Duchesse d'Aiguillon is the most celebrated. Aiguillon is close to Clairac and not far from the village of Montesquieu, and Madame d'Aiguillon was well known in the society of the south-west. Herself a Crussol, descended from the first peers of France, the Ducs d'Uzès, she was married to a Richelieu, whose elevation to the rank of duke was her achievement. She was of greater intellectual power than most women of fashion in her day. Chesterfield instructs his son to seek her acquaintance, saying that 'her house is the resort of one set of *les beaux esprits*'.[2] She was one of the few women who borrowed books from the Bibliothèque du Roi.[3] She was a friend of Maupertuis, and sought to understand his scientific works. She knew several languages. She had been a close friend of the minister Maurepas before his disgrace, and the note made on her by the police for their files says that Maurepas used to sup with her every day.[4] She is commemorated—unless it be Madame Geoffrin—under the name Cydalise in Palissot's comedy *Les Philosophes*. Montesquieu's attitude to the Duchess is not shown as a friendly one in the comments which survive. He regrets that she likes her enemies more than she likes her friends, that she has the pride of a pedant and all the faults of a lackey, that she was more given to lying than any other woman in France.[5] But hostility in his private journal did not exclude, and may even have facilitated, amity in

[1] H. Walpole to Gray, 25 January 1766 (Walpole, *Correspondence*, ed. Mrs. Paget Toynbee, Oxford, 1903–5, VI, pp. 404–7; Gray, *Correspondence*, ed. Paget Toynbee and L. Whibley, Oxford, 1935, III, pp. 912–15).

[2] Chesterfield to his son, 30 June 1751, O.S. (*Letters*, ed. Dobrée, IV, p. 1763).

[3] B.N., *Registre des prêts* (MS.); she borrowed one by one the five volumes of a Byzantine history in 1741.

[4] *Fiche de police* (B.N., MSS. n.a.f. 10781, f. 6).

[5] *Pensées* 1394, 1370, 1393 (Bkn. 1372, 1370, 1371).

personal relations. In spite of having a lawsuit with her,[1] Montesquieu virtually lived in her house when he was in Paris,[2] and she was present when he died.

Probably through his acquaintance with Madame d'Aiguillon, Montesquieu entered the agreeable and unusual circle of the Comte de Maurepas.

Maurepas, whose family connexions were of the highest,[3] succeeded his father as Secretary of State in 1725, and won a name for himself as a patron of science. Disgraced in 1749, as a result of the machinations of Madame de Pompadour, he withdrew into involuntary retirement in the country, to emerge twenty-five years later, at the summons of Louis XVI, to resume his office. During the two decades preceding his fall, he was the centre of a gay society, known as the *Académie de Ces Messieurs*, of which the other most prominent members were Moncrif, Nivelle de La Chaussée, Duclos, Crébillon fils, the Comte de Caylus, and Montesquieu. Caylus was a close friend of Antonio Conti, and of the sculptor Bouchardon who had conducted Montesquieu round the galleries of Rome, and he had an appreciable reputation as an archaeologist. Others belonging from time to time to this group were the Marquis d'Argenson, the frivolous Abbé Voisenon, Pont-de-Veyle, faithful companion to Madame Du Deffand, Collé, Vadé, at one stage (it appears) D'Alembert and even Voltaire.[4] This group of *dilettanti* produced some volumes of facetious verses and tales in prose. The *Recueil de Ces Messieurs*, attributed to Caylus but probably a joint production, appearing in 1745, contains miscellaneous pieces which seek to recapture some of the spirit of the *Lettres persanes*. There is a Spanish tale called *Liradi*, and some Turkish reflections on the Christian notion of love. Yet more interesting are the *Etrennes de la Saint-Jean*, published for the first time in 1742, and subsequently reprinted in the works of Caylus. A member of

[1] Guasco, *Lettres familières*, XXXIX (Nagel III, p. 1425).

[2] Ibid., LIV (Nagel III, p. 1526).

[3] Both by descent and marriage he belonged to the Phélypeaux family. His wife was sister to the Comte de Saint-Florentin, and sister-in-law to the late Comte de Plélo, who had been an active member of the Entresol, and whose daughter, in 1740, married a son of Mme d'Aiguillon. His sister was married to the Duc de Nivernais.

[4] See *Précis historique de la vie de Voisenon*, in Voisenon *Œuvres*, Paris, 1781, I, p. xii, and (s.v. Vadé) his *Anecdotes littéraires* (*Œuvres*, IV, pp. 73–74).

the Brancas family affirms[1] on the authority of Caylus that Maurepas, Caylus and Montesquieu were responsible for this volume, and nothing in the contents excludes the possibility of Montesquieu's participation. There is a dialogue on marriage, in question form; there is a short story entitled *Le Prince-Bel-Esprit et la Reine Toute-Belle*, and there is an entertaining and frivolous *Lettre persane d'un monsieur de Paris à un gentilhomme turc de ses amis*. Though Montesquieu may have discussed politics with Maurepas and Italian art with Caylus, it seems likely that these trivial and facetious pieces were the delight of his leisure, and whiled away an occasional half hour in the house of Madame d'Aiguillon.

Two other ladies of society are interesting for special reasons, Madame Dupin and Madame Dupré de Saint-Maur because they connect, or could have connected, Montesquieu with Rousseau and with Diderot. Dupré de Saint-Maur was an academician who wrote a work on currency which Montesquieu may well have used, and which was on the shelves of his library. His son was later to become intendant of Bordeaux. His wife had a firm place in Montesquieu's affections. He gives her the perhaps meagre praise that he prefers her to Madame d'Aiguillon,[2] but affirms, according to Guasco, that she was equally fitted to be one's mistress, one's wife or one's friend.[3] She was an active member of a social group based on Trudaine, who was a friend of Helvétius and Mairan, a member of the Académie des Sciences and *intendant des finances*. They met in Paris at Trudaine's house in the Marais, and in the country at Montigny. Here Montesquieu met the Chevalier de Jaucourt, the most faithful of all Diderot's allies in the *Encyclopédie*, and the archaeologist Sainte-Palaye, who had been Joseph de Secondat's contemporary at Juilly.[4] Montesquieu's friend the scientist Réaumur was in the habit of meeting Madame Dupré de Saint-Maur. On one famous occasion he was about to supervise an operation for cataract on a girl blind from birth, hoping to be able to give her the power of sight. The blind girl's first moment of vision was clearly going to

[1] *Lettres de L. B. Lauraguais à Mme* xxx, Paris, an X, p. 242.

[2] Montesquieu to Guasco, 4 October 1752.

[3] Guasco, *Lettres familières*, XLII (Nagel III, p. 1440).

[4] A. Cerati, *Elogio*, p. 87 (which suggests also that Falconet was of this circle); Juilly, *Dossier manuscrit des pensions*, p. 188. More than one member of the Trudaine family was at Juilly simultaneously with Montesquieu.

be of vital importance to all those philosophers who contended that ideas proceed from the senses, and many of them, Diderot being in their number, were invited to be present. The operation was performed. The girl saw. But soon suspicious circumstances made it clear that she had already seen before, and it was at length disclosed that the genuine operation had already been performed secretly for the delectation of Madame Dupré de Saint-Maur. Diderot, angry at this deceit, wrote his *Lettre sur les aveugles*, and in the first paragraph accused Réaumur of having deliberately rebutted intelligent observers, preferring as his audience 'quelques yeux sans conséquence'.[1] On reading this description of herself, Madame Dupré, proud of her scientific powers, is said to have had her revenge by procuring the imprisonment of Diderot in the fortress of Vincennes, where he remained for three months.[2] Whether this account of Diderot's incarceration be the true one or not,[3] the episode cannot have endeared Diderot to Madame Dupré, and it shows that Montesquieu was the close friend of Diderot's declared enemy.

In the case of Madame Dupin, investigation of her family connexions is profitless, since her parents were unmarried, and her prominence in eighteenth-century society is therefore in itself an indication of the changing social outlook. Her husband was a tax-farmer, with all that that implies of wealth and influence, She had many correspondents and many guests.[4] Most favoured of all was the Abbé de Saint-Pierre, much admired by Montesquieu who had known him in the salon of Madame de Lambert and at the Entresol. Voltaire and D'Olivet, neither of them a friend of Montesquieu, were of her acquaintance; but she cultivated also Mairan, Fontenelle, Marivaux, Bernis, Sallier, and Buffon among the men, and among the women Madame de Mirepoix, Lady Hervey, Madame de Tencin and the Comtesse de Forcalquier. Montesquieu was her correspondent, her guest, and her purveyor of wine, none of which relationships, however, prevented her and her husband from behaving with great foolishness on the publication of *L'Esprit des lois*. What is most interesting

[1] Diderot, *Œuvres complètes*, ed. Assézat and Tourneux, Paris, 1875–6, I, p. 279.

[2] *Mémoires* [*sur*] *Diderot par Mme de Vandeul sa fille* (ibid., I, pp. xlii-xliii).

[3] It has been placed in doubt, after J. Pommier and F. Venturi, by R. Niklaus, in his critical edition of the *Lettre sur les aveugles* (Geneva and Lille, 1951), p. xi.

[4] See G. de Villeneuve-Guibert, *Le Portefeuille de Mme Dupin*, Paris, 1884.

about Madame Dupin is that her secretary was Jean-Jacques Rousseau. Although slow to recognize the full extent of Rousseau's merits, she did not exclude him from her table, and it is quite likely that Montesquieu met him in her house. Rousseau, in any case, knew Duclos, Mairan and Alary; he dined from time to time with Boze, he knew Montesquieu's protégé Deleyre, and was linked by a common interest in music with Père Castel and with De Gascq, an amateur of the violin who held a presidency in the Parlement of Bordeaux. He knew the Piedmontese family of Solar, having been an aspiring lover of the daughter of the Marquis de Breil, who was a close friend of Montesquieu.[1] None of these relationships, however, seems to have procured for Rousseau the acquaintance of Montesquieu. The President, who would not have found Rousseau a man after his own heart, may indeed have met him, but no word betrays that fact; and though he once read his name in the letter from Hénault,[2] he seems to have lived in an almost complete and perhaps voluntary unawareness of the future author of *Du contrat social*.[3]

From so many names famous in the chronicles of the social life of Paris between 1730 and 1750, one deserves to be singled out for especial mention. It is that of Madame de Tencin.[4] She came from a family of no great antiquity or rank. In her youth she was imprisoned in a convent, from which she escaped memorably if uncanonically, for she used the experience to write a novel of real merit.[5] Known now as the unfrocked nun, she devoted herself to a career of love-making, beginning with Matthew Prior during his diplomatic residence in Paris, and not stopping short, according to contemporary rumour, of her brother

[1] See Rousseau, *Confessions*, pp. 93–96 and 291–4.

[2] Hénault to Montesquieu, 13 February 1752.

[3] Contrary evidence is afforded by a letter from Caperonnier de Gauffecourt to Rousseau, of 9 December 1764, where a postscript contains the words: 'M. le président de Montesquieu m'a dit bien des fois qu'il n'y a que vous de capable de travailler sur l'*Esprit des lois*' (Rousseau, *Correspondance générale*, ed. Dufour and Plan, XII, Paris, 1929, p. 134). The veracity of this statement, however, cannot be regarded as certain. There is no reason to believe that Montesquieu and Gauffecourt were acquainted, and Rousseau's already published works are unlikely to have given Montesquieu the opinion attributed to him.

[4] See P.-M. Masson, *Madame de Tencin*, Paris, 3rd edition, 1910.

[5] This was the *Mémoires du comte de Comminges* (1735). Montesquieu claimed that he and Fontenelle alone knew that she was the author (Guasco, *Lettres familières*, VIII; Nagel III, p. 1027).

the Archbishop of Embrun. She was a well-known figure in the society of the Regency and the years immediately following. The result of one of her *amours* was the birth of a son, whom she abandoned, but who was later to attain eminence under the name D'Alembert. In 1726 a cast-off lover called La Fresnais committed suicide, endeavouring to throw the guilt on Madame de Tencin. She was imprisoned in the Bastille under an accusation of murder, and much activity was required on the part of her friends to procure her release. Having regained her freedom, she resolved to seek fame of another sort. Leaving her scandalous past behind her, she decided to become a patroness of literature. She was assisted in this by the rank of her brother, who in spite of the mediocrity of his mind and his great ignorance—he is reported to have believed that Paraguay was on the Coromandel coast[1]—became cardinal and minister. But she relied mainly on her own charm and talent. She was insuperably loyal to her friends, even after their death. D'Olivet had chanced to speak ill of La Motte in an address to the Academy in 1738; Madame de Tencin, meeting him a few days later 'jeta feu et flamme' against him.[2] Réaumur, when she died, had for a time to abandon his work through grief; her sole desire, he says, was to give pleasure to her friends.[3] She won for herself a position of such distinction in French life that the learned and virtuous Benedict XIV himself was glad to correspond with her and spoke of her in terms of great regard.

Her means did not permit entertainment on the scale of Madame Geoffrin. Her company was select, and the most frequent guests at her table were known as the Seven Sages. They were Fontenelle, Mairan, Marivaux, Duclos, Mirabaud, Boze, and Astruc. The first two of these were friends of Montesquieu of old standing. Marivaux, Duclos and Mirabaud were his colleagues in the Academy. Boze was an archaeologist who was more than once in touch with the President about elections to the Académie des Inscriptions.[4] Astruc, finally, the son of a Protestant minister of Montpellier, and a doctor, was the closest to the

[1] Hénault, *Mémoires*, p. 287.

[2] D'Olivet to Bouhier, 12 March 1738 (B.N., MSS. fr. 24417, f. 203).

[3] Réaumur to Trembley, 10 January 1750 (*Correspondance inédite entre Réaumur et Abraham Trembley*, ed. M. Trembley, Geneva, 1943, p. 333).

[4] Boze to Filippo Venuti, 10 March 1743 (Cortona, MS. 497, f. 72v); Montesquieu to Guasco, 1 March 1747.

affections of Madame de Tencin, and succeeded in becoming her sole heir. Montesquieu had a different opinion of him. Astruc, he declares, has never said anything, he has only repeated; Astruc is continually trying to tell things he does not know to those who do; 'Astruc vous ennuie et vous offense'.[1]

It was not Astruc, however, who set the tone in Madame de Tencin's salon. Marmontel describes an evening in her house in terms which enable one to appreciate Talleyrand's famous lament over the passing of the society of the *ancien régime*.[2] Marmontel had gone there, in 1749, to read his new tragedy. Present were Montesquieu, Fontenelle, Mairan, Marivaux, Helvétius, Astruc, and others unnamed; and among them sat Madame de Tencin, whose *bonhomie* and natural simplicity made one think she was an ordinary housewife and not the mistress of so illustrious a gathering. Marmontel read his play, and the discussion began. Marivaux was anxious to display *finesse* and sagacity; Montesquieu, more calmly, waited for the ball to come to him, but was prepared for it when it did; Mairan likewise awaited his opportunity; Astruc did not deign to wait; Fontenelle alone, having entered his tenth decade, allowed opportunity to come without seeking it; Helvétius was collecting a harvest so that he might sow himself another day. This was the society in which Montesquieu lived in Paris: graceful, polished, artificial, and very seriously devoted to conversation. It was in this society that Montesquieu handed to Madame de Tencin a letter from Chesterfield, written in French, which was read to the assembled company. Thereupon Fontenelle cried, 'This *milord* is mocking us, by writing French more correctly than we do ourselves.' The resultant murmurs of discontent were quelled by the hostess, who recalled the charm of Chesterfield's conversation. 'Let him come back then', said the guests,' and we will forgive him for having more wit than ourselves.'[3]

Madame de Tencin's correspondence with Montesquieu shows her in no very different light. Playful and vivacious, reproaching him for beginning his letters with 'un grand Madame' while she begins her own with the phrase 'mon petit Romain', light and

[1] *Pensées* 979, 1243, 1647 (Bkn. 942, 943, 944).

[2] Marmontel, *Mémoires*, ed. M. Tourneux, Paris, 1891, I, pp. 232–4.

[3] Mme de Tencin to Chesterfield, 22 October 1742 (Chesterfield, *Letters*, ed. Dobrée, II, p. 519).

charming in tone: these qualities she certainly showed; and the professions of friendship and affection go beyond the ordinary stylistic flourishes of the day. But she possessed also a solid realism and business sense. She gave him advice and assistance in the publication of the *Considérations*; she was the first person in Paris to receive a copy of *L'Esprit des lois*, and she saw its first Paris edition through the press capably and efficiently. She was a reliable and altruistic friend of Montesquieu.

III. GUASCO

Far from altruistic, and of very dubious reliability, was a strange and controversial character whose acquaintance Montesquieu made in 1738 or very soon after, and who was to become his closest friend: the Abbé de Guasco.[1]

Ottaviano di Guasco was born in 1712 at Bricherasio, a small Piedmontese village near Pinerolo. His father was intendant of Piedmont and belonged to the lesser nobility. The son, beginning his education at Asti and at Turin, interested himself particularly in theology and Hebrew, and although suspected of favouring the ideas of the *philosophes*, took orders. In 1738 he left Piedmont to come to Paris, partly as a result of the hostility towards his family of the Marchese d'Ormea, partly in order to obtain treatment for his eyes, which caused him great trouble and involved him for a few months in total blindness.

In Paris he enjoyed great and rapid social success. This was brought about partly by his learning, which could not be placed in doubt, partly by the protection of influential friends, partly because of his language, which was a strange mixture of French and Italian, and which was accompanied by an expressive pantomime. One of his letters gives an example of the songs he from time to time sang:

[1] On Guasco, see his own notes to the *Lettres familières*; B.-J. Dacier, 'Eloge de M. l'abbé de Guasco' (*Histoire de l'Académie royale des inscriptions et belles-lettres*, XLV, Paris, 1793); L. C. Bollea, *Storia di Bricherasio*, Turin, 1928, I, pp. 600–8; Renato Zanelli, 'Ottaviano Guasco di Bricherasio' (*Informatore pinerolese*, 29 September and 6 October 1945); and my own 'L'Abbé de Guasco, ami et traducteur de Montesquieu' (*Actes de l'Académie nationale des sciences, belles-lettres et arts de Bordeaux*, 1958).

A la santad de la mio mestresse,
Begam encora qualche guttuts;
A cho ch'un tal puli figliù
Remplit de tendresso;
Moi se la conneissias, hélas,
Beuvias lu vierre tut ras![1]

Physically, he was of unusual aspect: his complexion was pale but his eyes were edged with red. His character and occupations were dubious. The police regarded him as having more than one profession, and he was widely reputed to be a spy.[2] His own brothers, in their correspondence, refer to him as an animal and as an unclean parasite.[3] Galiani refused to become a member of the Académie des Inscriptions since it would have meant associating with Guasco.[4]

This man found his way to the heart of Montesquieu. Chesterfield describes him as Montesquieu's complaisant,[5] Galiani as Montesquieu's *hétéroclyte d'affection.*[6] Grimm says that many great men stand in need of *pauvres diables* to follow them around, and that Montesquieu was always accompanied by Guasco, *un plat et ennuyeux personnage*, boring, tedious, and indiscreet.[7]

It was his ailing eyes which first attracted Montesquieu's sympathy, and their friendship rapidly became close. He frequently stayed at La Brède. He was well thought of by Madame de Montesquieu. He was introduced by the President to the Academy of Bordeaux. He was endowed by him with a hundred acres of uncultivated land near Martillac.[8] His candidature for the Académie des Inscriptions was pressed by Montesquieu.[9]

He was intimate with Prince Cantemir. His satires, written in

[1] Guasco to Venuti, 20 September 1747 (Cortona, MS. 497, ff. 133–4). I can do no more than reproduce exactly the very improbable spelling.

[2] *Fiche de police*, 1 September 1750 (B.N., MSS. n.a.f. 10782, f. 50).

[3] 'Un vero animale . . ., cacciato da molte case come un parassito sporchissimo' (cited by R. Zanelli, loc. cit.).

[4] Galiani to Mme d'Epinay, 11 August 1770 (*Correspondance*, ed. Perey and Maugras, Paris, 1881, I, p. 231).

[5] Chesterfield to his son, 19 November 1750 (*Letters*, ed. Dobrée, IV, p. 1622).

[6] Galiani to Mme d'Epinay, 28 June 1770 (*La Signora d'Epinay e l'abate Galiani, Lettere inedite*, ed. F. Nicolini, Bari, 1929, p. 66).

[7] *Correspondance littéraire*, VII, Paris, 1879, p. 391.

[8] Guasco, *Lettres familières*, XLVII (Nagel III, p. 1504).

[9] Montesquieu to Guasco, 1 March 1747.

Russian, he translated into French with the Prince's assistance, at the request of the Duchesse d'Aiguillon;[1] and when the Chancellor imposed deletions from the text, Montesquieu interested himself and informed Guasco.[2] He was a friend of Chesterfield who, though attributing to him 'more knowledge than parts', urged his son to seek his acquaintance and to use it.[3] When in England in 1750, he was accepted in high society and lived much in the houses of the great.[4] In Rome he was at least once the guest of Cardinal Passionei at Frascati.[5] In France he was received wherever Montesquieu was received. He frequented the house of Madame Geoffrin, and in fact was once forcibly ejected from it: an ignominy which he avenged in 1767, when publishing Montesquieu's *Lettres familières*, by including some letters—which not impossibly he had forged—in which Montesquieu expressed very unflattering opinions about that celebrated hostess.[6] He was a favourite in the society of Trudaine at Montigny, and of life here he himself gives an interesting description. He had no occupation save to write in the morning, to eat a great deal at lunch, to walk, ride, or drive, with many others, after lunch, to read Anson's *Voyage round the World* in the evening, and (at the President's request) to compose Italian verses.[7]

This strange figure evoked no moderate sentiments; he was hated or beloved. Of his learning, however, there can be no doubt: it is sufficiently attested by the two volumes of *Dissertations historiques, politiques, et littéraires* (Tournay, 1756) and by his very handsome *De l'usage des statues des anciens* (Brussels, 1768), as well as by the various manuscripts preserved, many unpublished to this day, in the library of the city of Verona. That Montesquieu saw merit in him was his greatest merit, and for that, indeed, he was so well known, that when blindness descended on him an English poet was impelled to write:

[1] Montesquieu to Guasco, 1 March 1747.

[2] 'Già mi ha scritto Montesquieu della castrazione fatta dal Cancelliere al Cantemir' (Guasco to Venuti, 12 February 1749, Cortona, MS. 572, ff. 16–17).

[3] Chesterfield to his son, 4 February 1751 (*Letters*, ed. Dobrée, IV, p. 1675).

[4] Guasco to Venuti, 18 May 1750 (Modena, Biblioteca estense, Autografoteca Campori, Guasco, no. 157).

[5] Guasco to Venuti, 22 December 1753 (Modena, as before, no. 222).

[6] Grimm, *Correspondance littéraire*, VII, pp. 389–93; P. de Ségur, *Le Royaume de la rue Saint-Honoré*, Paris, 1897, p. 295.

[7] Guasco to Venuti, 17 October 1749 (Cortona, MS. 572, f. 18).

Alas! while fame expects the volume penned
By high-souled Montesquieu's attractive friend,
Calamity, that strikes ambition mute,
Obstructs the writer in his dear pursuit!
His injured eyes in cruel quiet close
And sink from glorious toil to dark repose.[1]

Meanwhile he enjoyed life and gave the President counsel which was by no means invariably foolish.

[1] William Hayley, *An Essay on Sculpture*, London, 1800, pp. 148–9.

IX

LIFE IN GUYENNE, 1734–55

I. HOME AND FAMILY

THE road between Paris and Bordeaux was frequently travelled by Montesquieu, who was not afraid of long journeys. It was only after long and serious thought that he rejected the idea of visiting Maupertuis in Berlin in 1747,[1] and Cerati in Pisa about the same time;[2] he seriously thought of visiting England in 1739.[3] The journey between the metropolis and La Brède did not dismay him. If it was enlivened in one direction by the thought of the gaiety and brilliance of Parisian society and of old friends about to be seen again, in the other the traveller was sustained by the anticipated calm and tranquillity of the country, by the sense of proprietorship which his estate gave him, by the thought of the devoted and beloved peasants he was going to see again, by the contact with his library's thousands of volumes which he was about to resume, and perhaps even by the thought of living again with the quietly efficient and patient Madame de Montesquieu. Between the beginning of 1733 and the end of 1748 he made the journey at least seven times in each direction.

He had a choice of three principal routes when travelling to the south-west. To the east, he could go through Périgueux to Libourne, and spend the last night on his own property at Raymond; to the west, he could come through Saintes (as he doubtless did when he had visited Matignon in his command at La Rochelle)[4] and sail upstream from Blaye to Bordeaux or even to Beautiran, the river port which was nearest to La Brède and stood on his own land; or he could follow a route lying between the two and more direct than either, through Poitiers and Angoulême, crossing the Dordogne at Saint-André de Cubzac and meeting the Garonne at Bordeaux itself.

It is not hard to imagine the feelings of Montesquieu as he draws near to his home. Around him, from whatever direction

[1] Montesquieu to Maupertuis, June 1747.
[2] Montesquieu to Cerati, 31 March, 1747.
[3] Montesquieu to Folkes, 19 August 1738.
[4] Montesquieu to Bulkeley, 24 October 1734.

Château de La Brède

he approaches, extend his own vineyards, dusty green in colour, rich, if the year is good, with promise of riches for himself. He crosses the unpredictable Garonne, powerful and rapid or sluggish and mud-girt according to the weather: if the river is full, his property may have suffered.[1] He passes the junction at La Prade, taking the road which eventually enters the Landes and joins the highway to Bayonne. After little more than a mile he has reached the village of La Brède. In its romanesque church his father lies buried. Far to the left is Saint-Morillon, to the right lies Martillac, both of them his own property. He passes the miller's house, where he spent the first three years of his life and learned the sing-song Gascon accent which he hears now on all hands. He leaves the village behind him and advances further in the direction of Saucats along the now deserted road. After less than a mile he reaches a gate on the right. It is opened for him, and his carriage bears him through a belt of trees which screen the buildings from the road. He enters the open parkland, and before him, slightly to the right, stands the castle. He sometimes affects to despise it as a Gothic edifice,[2] but he is impressed by the charm of the memories it harbours, which are expressed in the inscriptions over the two drawbridges: *O rus, quando te aspiciam?* and *Deliciae domini.*

It was at La Brède that he was most happy. He used to enter the houses of the peasants, to talk to them about their children, to settle their disputes, and to seal the agreement with a glass of wine.[3] He talked to them in their own patois,[4] and found among them, he used to say, many a Solon and a Demosthenes.[5] Wandering through his grounds with a white cotton cap on his head and a vine-prop on his shoulder, he was sometimes taken for a peasant by visitors who, addressing him as *tu*, asked him the way to the château;[6] and English visitors, seeing him jump over a fence rather than open the gate, were surprised at the carefree

[1] A flood had some years before carried away an island which the President owned in the upper reaches of the Garonne (Montesquieu to La Vrillière, 22 November 1723).

[2] Montesquieu to Guasco, 1 August 1744 and 4 October 1752.

[3] M. de Lapouyade, 'Impressions d'une Allemande à Bordeaux en 1785' (*RHBx*, 1911, pp. 255–6).

[4] Latapie, in Baurein, *Variétés bordeloises*, III, I.II.

[5] J.-B. d'A. Devienne, *Histoire de la ville de Bordeaux*, Bordeaux, 1771, p. 504.

[6] Garat, *Mémoires historiques sur la vie de M. Suard*, I, pp. 102–3.

demeanour of a reputedly grave philosopher.[1] The life of the fields was indeed his delight.

> O fortunatos nimium, sua si bona norint,
> Agricolas,

he exclaimed once to Abraham Trembley who was visiting him at La Brède, adding that he had often thought of carving these words on the front of his house.[2] Nor were the pleasures of society and conversation absent from his life in the country. Almost every day he visited the village of La Brède. At Eyquem he met Madame Gaussen, pious, gay, and sociable, at La Sauque, in the direction of Beautiran, he visited the intelligent Madame Dorly, at L'Estivette, a small property near the castle, he found the Latapie family, and especially Madame Duguats, whose wit and learning so attracted him that he called her the Madame de Tencin of La Brède.[3] The society of these ladies, not otherwise known to posterity, was the delight of Montesquieu during his country walks.

In the castle itself he was surrounded with familiar objects. On the left, on entering, stands the salon, not luxuriously furnished and boasting no notable works of art.[4] Beyond it is the bedroom, with the secretary's room adjacent: this is where he writes and meditates. A broad spiral staircase leads to Madame de Montesquieu's room and to the library. This is the castle's most distinctive feature. Two doors at the far end lead to the chapel and to the square sitting-room; they are inscribed respectively *In hoc signo vinces* and *Assidue veniebat*. The strange frescoes about the fireplace speak of an earlier age, and it is a simple creed which is taught by the painted maxims in archaic language:

> TON DIEV SVRTOVT AIME D'AMOVR EXTREME
> ET TON PROCHAIN AINSI COMME TOI MEME.

> AV MAGISTRAT REN HVMBLE OBEISSANCE
> IL HA DE DIEV C'EST HONNEVR ET PVISSACE.

[1] Hardy, *Memoirs of Charlemont*, p. 33.

[2] Trembley to Bonnet, 18 November 1752 (Charles Bonnet, *Mémoires autobiographiques*, ed. R. Savioz, Paris, 1948, p. 141).

[3] F. de P. Latapie to the inhabitants of La Brède, 1 June 1823 (reproduced in facsimile, s.d.).

[4] The post-mortem inventory is published in J.-M. Eylaud, *Montesquieu chez es notaires de La Brède*, Bordeaux, 1956.

The shelves of the library contain rare and banal volumes alike: but the rare volumes are rare indeed. Among them are works which have belonged to Malebranche and others which have been in the library of Montaigne. There are incunabula and manuscripts, as well as the most recent works of scholarship and learned journals.

La Brède was now the undoubted headquarters of the Montesquieu family, and the President was the accepted head of the family. His sisters Marie and Thérèse, both nuns, were away from home, and both of them received modest subventions from the President. About Thérèse more information has survived than about her sister. At the age of five she had been placed in the hands of nuns; twelve years later she took perpetual vows, and in due course became superior of the convent of Notre Dame at Agen. Zealous, saintly to the point that her colleagues regarded her as one of the elect, efficient as an administrator of her house, she was so widely respected that when she died at the age of eighty-one her successor dispatched a letter in praise of her virtues to all the superiors of the order.[1]

The President's brother was an ecclesiastic of sincere devotion. He was also a great pluralist. After his nomination in 1743 to the abbacy of Nizor near Toulouse,[2] his full clerical style was 'doyen du chapitre de Saint-Seurin, abbé de Faize, abbé de Nizor, prieur de La Chaussade en Périgord et de Gourlambeau en Agenais.'[3] Montesquieu visited him for a month in 1752 at Nizor, where he was involved in litigation.[4] When in Bordeaux, though he seems to have retained a *pied-à-terre* in the Rue Neuve near the Parlement,[5] the President ordinarily stayed in his brother's house at Saint-Seurin, marked to this day by a plaque.

Seldom absent from La Brède, unless to inspect other properties of the family, was Madame de Montesquieu. She had never been handsome,[6] she was often irascible,[7] she remained a practising Protestant,[8] which may well have occasioned social and even

[1] This letter was privately reprinted in the nineteenth century.

[2] Duc de Luynes, *Mémoires*, Paris, 1860–5, IV, p. 418.

[3] J.-A. Garde, *Histoire de Lussac*, p. 102.

[4] F. Sacase, 'Montesquieu à l'abbaye de Nizor' (*Recueil de l'Académie des jeux floraux*, Toulouse, 1867).

[5] J.-M. Eylaud, op. cit., pp. 53–54.

[6] Hardy, op. cit., p. 34.

[7] See above, p. 79.

[8] Hardy, loc. cit.

legal embarrassment to her husband. But she was a faithful custodian of the estates, and whenever Montesquieu left the south-west, he effected a plenary delegation of powers to her.[1]

Montesquieu's second child was the first to marry. This was his elder daughter Marie-Catherine, who in the domestic chapel of the Château de La Brède was married by her uncle to Vincent de Guichanères, Seigneur d'Armajan.[2] The bridegroom was a modest country gentleman whose father had been known to Montesquieu,[3] and who took his title from a small property in the Sauternes area near Preignac. This conventional alliance was celebrated without pomp,[4] and economically endowed by Montesquieu to the extent of no more than 10,000 *livres*.[5]

The President's son, Jean-Baptiste, after the completion of his education, found himself advancing in his career more rapidly than most men. In 1734, when no more than eighteen years of age, he was admitted advocate, and was elected to the Academy of Bordeaux. Two years later, he was elected *directeur* of the Academy, and became, by his father's purchase, counsellor of the Parlement of Bordeaux.[6] Jean-Baptiste was an amiable savant and a man of parts, whose fame would have been greater had he been the son of a nobody. He is, in his own right, well worthy of study, and the archives of La Brède are rich in documents illustrating his career.

It was desirable that he, as Montesquieu's only son, should contract a worthy and profitable marriage alliance. Accordingly, after a contract signed on 24 August, and a betrothal ceremony celebrated on 27 August 1740, Jean-Baptiste married Marie-Catherine-Thérèse de Mons on 30 August 1740, in the church of Saint Christoly at Bordeaux, the ceremony being performed by the bridegroom's uncle Joseph de Montesquieu, with the assistance of an Irish priest called O'Sullivan. The marriage contract made the most careful dispositions for the future. The bridegroom's parents undertook to settle on him 300,000 *livres* of which 90,000 *livres* were to be provided by his mother, while the bride's parents endowed their daughter with the same amount.

[1] Eylaud, op. cit., *passim*.
[2] *Extrait d'état civil* (at La Brède).
[3] Fr.-R. Guichanères d'Armajan to Montesquieu, 3 January 1719.
[4] Montesquieu to Godefroy de Secondat, 24 January 1745.
[5] Montesquieu's will (Nagel, III, p. 1574).
[6] J. Delpit, *Le Fils de Montesquieu*, Bordeaux, 1888, pp. 31–33.

Meanwhile Montesquieu promised to pay his son an annual income of 6,000 *livres*, while the Seigneur de Mons undertook to provide a home, food, servants, and an annual payment of 2,000 *livres*.[1] The newly married pair enjoyed then an income of 8,000 *livres* in addition to a complete domestic establishment, and in addition also to Jean-Baptiste's stipend of 375 *livres*.[2] They could look forward to much greater affluence when they eventually inherited 600,000 *livres* in all from their parents.

After four and a half years Jean-Baptiste's marriage remained sterile, and Montesquieu began to worry about the future of his family and name. There remained still unmarried his younger daughter Marie-Josèphe-Denise, usually known as Denise, much loved by her father, sensible and intelligent beyond her years, and occasionally acting as his secretary.[3] An English visitor finds her 'a sprightly, affable, good-humoured girl, rather plain, but at the same time pleasing',[4] of which qualities the plainness rather than any other is attested by the demure portrait which remains at La Brède.

In relation to her, Montesquieu, late in 1744, made an indirect approach through his brother Joseph to his third cousin Godefroy de Secondat, who lived at Agen, suggesting, in order to maintain the fortunes of their declining family, that he, Godefroy, should marry Denise.[5] Godefroy agreed to this proposal, and the President sent him a memorandum explaining how simply and unelaborately the marriage should take place, and subsequently dispatched his agent Latapie, who was entrusted with the financial details. It was envisaged at first that the marriage should be celebrated in the seclusion of the village of Montesquieu, but later Clairac was thought a more suitable place. No ostentatious clothing was provided; no servant was to accompany Denise. No wedding presents were to be given. On 25 March 1745, with Joseph de Secondat celebrating, Marie and Godefroy were married at Clairac.[6] The contract, signed a fortnight before, provided for a settlement on Denise of 70,000 *livres*, of which Madame de Montesquieu was to pay 60,000 *livres*, a third in

[1] Ibid., pp. 35–37. [2] Arch. dép. Gironde, C 4066–7.

[3] See my article, 'Les Secrétaires de Montesquieu' (Nagel II, pp. xlii–xliii).

[4] Hardy, op. cit., p. 34.

[5] Montesquieu to Godefroy de Secondat, 28 December 1744.

[6] *Extrait d'état civil* (at La Brède). The often accepted date of 25 May is inaccurate.

the form of a house at Preignac, the rest to be received by Denise, without interest, only after her parents' death. The President's own share, of no more than 10,000 *livres*, was to be paid in the form of an annual contribution of 500 *livres* charged to the estate of the barony of Montesquieu. The bridegroom was to endow his bride with 5,000 *livres*. These arrangements, if not generous, were at least clear; but the marriage seems to have been more than most a simple business transaction, inspired by Montesquieu's desire inexpensively to ensure his posterity. Almost a hundred years later, Stendhal discovered the story still current at La Brède of Denise's reluctant compliance with her father's insistence.[1]

Montesquieu's precautions proved in the end to be not unfounded. Jean-Baptiste's wife gave birth in 1749 to a son, who however died without issue in 1824. The family's name was perpetuated by the offspring of Denise and Godefroy. From them are descended the present Baron de Montesquieu and the Comtesse de Chabannes, proprietor of La Brède.

II. LANDS AND FORTUNE

The arms of Secondat de Montesquieu are 'azure, two escallops in chief or and in base a crescent argent'[2] and the punning motto is *Fortuna virtutem secundat*. The full legal style of Montesquieu, as revealed by numerous documents, runs as follows:

> Haut et puissant seigneur messire Charles-Louis de Secondat de Montesquieu, chevalier baron de Montesquieu, La Brède, Martillac et Saint-Morillon de La Brède, seigneur de Raymond et autres places, ancien président à mortier au Parlement de Bordeaux, l'un des quarante de l'Académie française.

To these can be added the lordship of Goulart, near Montesquieu (a barony according to one description),[3] and two lordships inherited from his uncle, those of Castelnouben near Agen and of Talence on the southern fringe of Bordeaux.[4] He is also, on

[1] Stendhal, *Voyage dans le midi*, Sceaux, 1956, pp. 76–77.

[2] For this translation of the French blazon 'D'azur à deux coquilles d'or en chef et un croissant d'argent en pointe' I am indebted to Mr. Colin Cole, Portcullis Pursuivant of Arms.

[3] Eylaud, op. cit., plate 6.

[4] *Arch. hist. Gironde*, X, p. 268.

one occasion, probably inaccurately, described as Baron of Saucats.[1]

His land included some of the richest wine-producing territory of France. Francisque Michel, in the last century, published the text of a memorandum, written in 1730, descriptive of the wine production of the Bordeaux area. Here it is explained that there were at that time five main growths: Graves, Palu, Entre-deux-mers, Langon, Barsac, and Preignac. The best of the red Graves was in a class of its own,[2] selling sometimes—and mainly to English customers—for as much as 1,500 *livres* a cask. With this exception, it was the best wines only which fetched as much as 200 *livres* a cask, and in this category fell the white Graves, of which La Brède is a species, and the sweeter Preignac, where Madame de Montesquieu held property. More modest was the white wine of Entre-deux-mers, used mainly for the production of brandy, and not selling for more than 90 *livres* a cask.[3] These were the main wines of Gascony; but Montesquieu's best wine, a red Graves, highly prized until the vineyard fell into decay in this century, was the red wine coming from the humble and isolated property of Rochemorin, lying between Martillac, of which it was a dependency, and Léognan, and approached only by the poorest of poor roads.

Montesquieu was proud of his property and sought to increase its value.

> Je n'ai point aimé à faire ma fortune par le moyen de la cour; j'ai songé à la faire en faisant valoir mes terres, et à tenir ma fortune immédiatement de la main des Dieux.[4]

Leaving on one side an unsuccessful attempt to raise the barony of Montesquieu to a marquisate,[5] the President was continually occupied with the ordinary activities of a landowner: litigation about islands in the Garonne near Montesquieu, legal action to procure the removal of a weathervane erected without permission, the granting of leave to construct a dove-cote to the parish priest

[1] Eylaud, op. cit., p. 87.

[2] The term Graves was of wider extension in the eighteenth century, and included what is now known as Médoc.

[3] F. Michel, *Histoire du commerce et de la navigation à Bordeaux*, Bordeaux, 1870, II, pp. 126–9.

[4] *Pensée* 973 (Bkn. 5).

[5] Redon des Fosses to Montesquieu, 15 December 1731.

of Bequin, two miles north-east of Montesquieu.[1] He was constantly buying and exchanging, and occasionally selling land. The notarial archives of La Brède alone list forty-one purchases, twenty exchanges, and six sales of land effected by Montesquieu.[2]

He was vigorous in the maintenance of his feudal rights and privileges. In 1746 he appealed successfully to the government against Bordeaux representatives of the Treasury, who were concerning themselves with the maintenance of roads within the area of his own jurisdiction at La Brède.[3] He was relentless in his pursuit of poachers, describing them as bipeds against whom traps should be laid, since they did a hundred times more damage than foxes and badgers.[4] When the inhabitants of Saucats were slow to perform their *corvée* of repairing the road near La Brède, he asked the authorities to send an archer, not to do harm to them, but to intimidate them a little.[5] He was most rigorous in the collection of debts, and was very ready to distrain in order to recover tiny sums. In January 1746 he threatened a perquisition against the wife of a stonemason and a cobbler, for a mere 35 *livres*. In 1753 he distrained to recover debts of 8, 5, and 7 *deniers*, with other very modest debts in kind.[6]

Finally, he engaged in a law-suit against the municipality of Bordeaux, in relation to the boundary separating Martillac from Léognan to the west. This litigation, begun as early as 1726, occupied him for many years, and involved the production of memorandum after memorandum. Sometimes the documents in question were printed. One of these, bearing the date 1741, shows that Montesquieu did not delegate the direction of his affairs to others, since the sentences are clearly his own. He believed that whatever had to be written should be written well. The memorandum ends with these words:

Monsieur de Montesquieu a ses dénombrements, ses assises, ses baux à fief, qui parlent tous pour lui. Contre qui porte-t-il ces titres? Contre des parties qui ont avoué, par leur commissaire, les principales

[1] *Arch. hist. Gironde*, XXIV, pp. 273–4, 272, and 280.

[2] Eylaud, op. cit., p. 98. [3] Arch. dép. Gironde, cat. série C, t. IV, p. 33.

[4] Montesquieu to Barbot, 8 March 1752; and cf. J. Barennes, 'Montesquieu et le braconnage à La Brède' (*RHBx*, 1912).

[5] Montesquieu to Tourny, 9 September 1754.

[6] The *denier* was one 240th part of a *livre*. Eight *deniers*, therefore, at the eighteenth-century rate of exchange, corresponded approximately to one-third of a penny. The indebtedness in kind might be evaluated, in the cases in question, at about 5 *livres*. Eylaud, op. cit., pp. 85–94, gives these and other examples.

inductions qu'il en a faites. Qui sont ces parties? Des gens qui, par leurs titres anciens et nouveaux, n'ont aucun intérêt à la chose; qui sont encore mieux combattus par leurs propres titres que par ceux de Monsieur de Montesquieu . . . Quelle réponse à tout cela? qu'un air de confiance que prend le syndic chaque fois qu'il est abattu,

> *Duris et ilex tonsa bipennibus . . .*
> *Per damna, per caedes, ab ipso*
> *Ducit opes animumque ferro.*[1]

One cannot be displeased that such a controversialist won 1,100 acres, albeit of waste land.[2]

In a few sentences of advice written for his grandson, Montesquieu asserts that 'la fortune est un état, et non pas un bien';[3] and undoubtedly he believed that the ownership of land imposed on him fixed and clear obligations. He saw it as his duty to be rigorous in exacting that to which he was legally entitled. It was also his duty to succour his tenants and labourers when they fell into distress.

Such an occasion arose near the middle of the century. In 1748, Bordeaux was smitten by famine. The Archbishop d'Audibert de Lussan issued a *mandement* in which he explained that wars and famines were God's instruments for punishing the iniquities of peoples.[4] He also organized material assistance for the poor. The President meanwhile, learning that distress was great at Montesquieu, departed thither post-haste, assembled the clergy from the four surrounding parishes, appointed them distributors of grain which he supplied free of charge from his granaries, and returned to La Brède before his tenants learned of his generosity.[5] If the detail of this story is open to question,[6] there is still no reason to deny it any basis in fact.

A similar act of *bienfaisance* is attested by a document in Montesquieu's own hand bearing the date 26 December 1752.[7] This is a certificate in which the President testifies that in 1709 a child of approximately two years of age was left at the gate of

[1] Arch. dép. Gironde, C 914.
[2] Guasco, *Lettres familières*, XLVII (Nagel III, p. 1504).
[3] *Pensée* 2170 (Bkn. 72).
[4] F.-F.-A. Donnet, *Recueil des ordonnances*, I, pp. 296–300.
[5] Bernadau, *Tableau de Bordeaux*, Bordeaux, 1810, pp. 206–7.
[6] Bernadau is inaccurate, for example, in assigning to this episode the date December 1750. Montesquieu was then in Paris.
[7] Bx, MS. 1969.

the house of his uncle the Président de Montesquieu. The uncle, and later Montesquieu himself, brought up the child. When he came of age he went out, learned a trade, and built up a small fortune. Now he wishes to marry, has no birth certificate, and Montesquieu gives him this document instead.

In addition to La Brède and to the property at and near Montesquieu, the President held land in Entre-deux-mers. The road running eastwards from Bordeaux to Brane passes through two villages called Baron and Saint-Quentin de Baron, traversing a countryside which is pleasantly undulating, fertile, and well wooded, and displays many varied shades of green. Between these two villages stands the farm of Raymond or Ramonet, built by a Du Bernet, and coming into the Secondat family by marriage at the same time as the *présidence à mortier*. The house is attractive, large, and spruce, but unpretentious, and to this day Montesquieu's bedroom is pointed out, simple and unornate like a peasant's chamber. Here he was able to live a comfortable and quiet country life. His farming activities here were on a large scale, and he augmented them by the purchase in 1751 of the fief of Bisqueytan in the parish of Saint-Quentin.[1] Thereafter he enjoyed the title of Seigneur de Bisqueytan. Twelve different *métairies* depended from Raymond or Bisqueytan, and when he died there were in all at Raymond 458 *barriques* or hogsheads of wine: the produce of none but a very large vineyard.[2]

Very little is known of Montesquieu's establishment at Raymond, and not much more about the household at La Brède. Montesquieu had the reputation of being kind to servants, and when once seen to scold them, remarked apologetically that they were clocks which it was occasionally necessary to wind up.[3] One only of the indoor servants retains his identity. This is a valet-de-chambre called Mansancal, a name found occasionally mentioned in the notarial archives of La Brède,[4] an exceedingly comical and picturesque individual, if the portrait still kept in the bedroom of the château is to be trusted. The foreman labourer, fluent in his Gascon speech, was one Guillaume

[1] Montesquieu to Denise de Secondat, 30 December 1750; to Latapie, 16 December 1750, 17 January and 15 February 1751; Eylaud, op. cit., pp. 80–82.

[2] Eylaud, op. cit., pp. 170–1.

[3] Chaudon and Delandine, *Nouveau Dictionnaire historique*, Caen and Lyons, 1789, VI, pp. 309–10.

[4] Eylaud, op. cit., pp. 66 and 87.

Grenier, known as L'Eveillé.[1] The names of two gamekeepers have been recorded, Jean Billau and Jean Bosser, of a coachman, Annet Godofre, and of two stewards, Jean Argeau and Charles Couloumié.[2] Montesquieu's father had brought to La Brède in 1680 a friend or subordinate called Pierre Latapie, who died, aged about eighty in 1739.[3] His son, likewise Pierre, became the President's intimate adviser, and eventually acquired the status of judge of La Brède, a title which he had at least from 1743 onwards and probably earlier. It was his duty to administer seignorial justice under Montesquieu, but he acted also as the President's general financial and legal counsellor and agent, and many letters were exchanged between them. Montesquieu combined in his missives clear and unambiguous instructions with polished and affectionate language expressing many compliments and concern for Latapie's family.

Latapie's son, François de Paule Latapie, lived from 1739 to 1823.[4] Brought up at La Brède, he was the close friend and travelling companion of Jean-Baptiste de Secondat. A savant of some distinction, he was successively professor of botany and of Greek. In the year of his death he founded a prize, awarded annually to this day, to be given to the maiden of the village of La Brède most recommendable for her moral conduct, her filial piety, and her respect for duty. As the author of the chapter on La Brède in Baurein's *Variétés bordeloises*, he is one of the earliest and most direct authorities on the life of Montesquieu. To this day a tradition among the servants at the château insists that he served as secretary to the President, and Stendhal, writing in 1838, reports the same belief.[5] Latapie's date of birth suggests that his efficacy as secretary to Montesquieu was limited, and his handwriting (which in its mature form is well enough known) is not among those identified in the manuscripts which survive. But there is no reason to place in doubt his claim to have been a frequent companion of the President in his strolls through the

[1] Montesquieu to Guasco, 1746 (Nagel III, p. 1076), and 16 March 1752 cf. Eylaud, op. cit., p. 66 and plate 2.

[2] Eylaud, op. cit., pp. 65–70.

[3] *Extrait d'état civil* (at La Brède).

[4] There seems no reason to support Bernadau's claim (Vian, p. 301) that the young Latapie was an illegitimate son of Montesquieu.

[5] Stendhal, op. cit., p. 77.

fields and to the villages in the neighbourhood of La Brède.[1]

The extent of Montesquieu's estate and number and apparent dignity of his stewards and administrators suggest that he was a man of considerable fortune. He did not, however, regard himself as being rich, and he was not lavish in his expenditure, as his arrangements for the wedding of Denise show clearly. He had the reputation of being parsimonious. The unreliable Soulavie reports that when in Paris, the President never ate in his own house, and that his carriage was drawn by two broken-down coach horses.[2] The Duc de Luynes makes a similar report.[3] English visitors to La Brède were surprised at the plainness of his table.[4] He was not prompt in the discharge of all his obligations. The archives of La Brède contain two letters to Montesquieu from the Dominicans of Saintes, written in 1734, requesting payment of a small rent charge owed to them by him. They complain that payments are long overdue and that they have had no reply to their requests. The sum involved is a mere 25 *livres*.

Like other proprietors of the Bordeaux area, he was very dependent on the sale of his wine, and the War of the Austrian Succession, lasting from 1740 to 1748, hit all of them severely. An English traveller described their plight to a friend:

> The nobility of Bordeaux have suffered more by the war than the merchants as they have no fund of ready money and live by the sale of their wines. They were most of them in the country during my stay there and had ordered bushes to be set up at their doors to have their wine sold by retail.[5]

Montesquieu was completely cut off from his English market and was obliged to live at La Brède for the whole of the period of three years from September 1743 to September 1746, his longest stay in the country since the publication of the *Lettres persanes*. In the spring of 1743 he had borrowed some 7,000 *livres*.[6] When in 1748 news of peace came Réaumur, writing to Cerati, said that

[1] Latapie to the inhabitants of the commune of La Brède, 1 June 1823 (reprinted in facsimile, s.d.).

[2] Soulavie, *Pièces historiques sur les règnes de Louis XIV, Louis XV et Louis XVI*, Paris, 1809, II, p. 328.

[3] *Mémoires*, XIV, pp. 36–39.

[4] Hardy, op. cit., p. 35.

[5] Caldwell to Henry Belasys, s.d. (but about 1746) (John Rylands Library, Bagshawe Muniments B 3/7/1, f. 8).

[6] Chabot to Montesquieu, 12 April 1744.

this would mean a considerable increase in income for Montesquieu.[1]

The President had already received a considerable gain as a result of the death, in August 1747, of D'Albessard, who had been the purchaser, in 1726, of a life-interest in his legal office. Montesquieu offered the Presidency now to his son—a financially altruistic move. But Jean-Baptiste was not interested, and indeed intimated that he would like to divest himself of the counsellorship in the Parlement which his father had ceded to him. Montesquieu debated for a time about the best course of action, and considered resuming the *mortier* himself.[2] Bulkeley, misinformed, wrote to congratulate him on having done so, a decision which he regarded as admirable.[3] But Montesquieu decided not to tie himself more closely to Bordeaux, and the office was sold outright.[4] It was bought by Le Berthon, who was *premier président* of the Parlement, and wished to surrender this new office to his son. He undertook to pay 130,000 *livres* within eight years. At the same time the counsellorship was sold for 40,000 *livres*.[5]

It has been claimed that Montesquieu's income at the end of his life was 60,000 *livres*,[6] the equivalent of £2,400 at the eighteenth-century rate of exchange. This figure, if it were accurate, would certainly represent a comfortable income. It was fifty times Diderot's stipend as editor of the *Encyclopédie*. But for a landed proprietor with several houses to maintain it does not indicate great affluence. There were several landowners in France with incomes of half a million *livres*. Voltaire, dying in 1778, enjoyed at the end of his life an income of not less than 200,000 *livres*.[7]

It is, however, possible to calculate with approximate accuracy the income and capital of Montesquieu at two different moments in his career. In a letter to Madame de Lambert, dated 1 December 1726, he declares that his income is now 29,000 *livres*, a figure which, if it errs, does so on the side of generosity, since he is boasting of his independence. This was written after the first

[1] Réaumur to Cerati, 29 May 1748 (Charavay Catalogue, November 1957, no. 271; facsimile).

[2] Montesquieu to Guasco, 28 March 1748.

[3] Bulkeley to Montesquieu, 14 August 1748.

[4] A reason for the sale of the office suggested in the *Memoirs of Charlemont* was Montesquieu's disagreement with the intendant Tourny. See below, pp. 214–17.

[5] *Arch. hist. Gironde*, LV, pp. 138–43.

[6] Soulavie, loc. cit.

[7] L. Nicolardot, *Ménage et finances de Voltaire*, Paris, 1854, p. 62, suggests 206,000 *livres*; J. Donvez, *De quoi vivait Voltaire?*, Paris, 1949, p. 175, proposes 231,000 *livres*.

sale of his office, for which he received an annual payment of 5,200 *livres*. If this sum is deducted, the difference of 23,800 *livres* may be taken as a high estimate of his income from real property. It has been calculated that revenue from agricultural land in France at this time was 4 per cent. of the price.[1] On the basis of this proportion, an income of 23,800 *livres* represents a capital value, likewise generously computed, of 595,000 *livres*.

There exists at La Brède a treaty between Jean-Baptiste Secondat and his sister Denise, dated 18 March 1756, which deals with the apportionment between them of their inheritance, and contains the valuation of Montesquieu's estate at the time of his death. The gross figure is 654,563 *livres*, divided into movable belongings valued at 124,563 *livres*, and real estate of 530,000 *livres*. The proceeds from the sale of the Presidency (which had been completed by 22 July 1754)[2] in part were devoted to the purchase of Bisqueytan and in part are represented by a portion of the movable estate. The revenue likely to result from real property of 530,000 *livres* in 1755 (when the ratio was falling and in general for wine-producing land was 3·6 per cent.)[3] is 19,000 *livres*. These figures cannot be regarded as rigorously exact, since they are based on approximations; and it would be surprising if Montesquieu's landed income declined during his lifetime, the trend between 1726 and 1755 being to increase. But bearing in mind the statement made by his son, that in spite of heavy expenses caused by his travels, his social life, the care for his eyes and the publication of his works, Montesquieu handed on to his children the modest inheritance he had received from his fathers,[4] it can fairly confidently be asserted that Montesquieu's real property was worth about half a million *livres*, and that his income from it was of the order of 20,000 or 25,000 *livres*. This fortune permitted him to live with dignity but not with display.

III. BORDEAUX

Bordeaux, being a great administrative and commercial centre, received numerous visitors. Helvétius, who maintained an apartment in the town,[5] was led thither from time to time by his duties

[1] G. d'Avenel, *Histoire économique de la propriété*, Paris, 1895–1912, II, pp. 4–5.
[2] Eylaud, op. cit., p. 109.
[3] D'Avenel, loc. cit.
[4] Secondat, *Mémoire*, p. 402.
[5] Helvétius to Montesquieu, 26 August 1748.

as a tax farmer, and used these opportunities both to make contact with Montesquieu[1] and also (if his first biographer is to be believed) to stir up the citizens of Bordeaux to resist the extortionate taxes which it was his duty to impose:[2] an act of independence of which the owner of La Brède, Rochemorin, and Raymond cannot have disapproved.

The Marquis de Mirabeau, not yet the author of *L'Ami des hommes*, likewise visited Bordeaux. Vauvenargues wrote to him expressing envy at his proximity to Montesquieu and at his being able to enjoy the conversation of a man who wrote so well.[3] Mirabeau may then have valued the President's opinions. More than thirty years later he was to say to Gustavus III of Sweden, who mentioned the author of *L'Esprit des lois*:

> Montesquieu! les rêveries surannées de cet homme ne sont plus estimées que dans quelques cours du nord.[4]

It was in the curiously cosmopolitan society of Bordeaux that Montesquieu found a link with the philosophers of eighteenth-century Scotland. Joseph Black, eventually professor of chemistry at Edinburgh University, was born at Bordeaux, where his father was a wine-merchant, in 1728. Adam Ferguson writes:

> While Mr. Black, the father, lived at Bordeaux, the great Montesquieu, being President of the Parliament or Court of Justice in that province, honoured Mr. Black with a friendship and intimacy, of which his descendants are justly proud. They preserve letters, or scraps of correspondence, that passed between the President Montesquieu and their ancestor, as they would titles of honour descending in their race. On a paper wrapped round a bundle of such letters, the following note is found in the handwriting of Joseph Black: 'My father was honoured with President Montesquieu's friendship on account of his good character and virtues. . . .' No words, added to those used by his son, to delineate the father's character, can improve it; and nothing more is wanting to account for the regard with which he was honoured by the President Montesquieu. This illustrious personage, together with a great simplicity of heart in himself, had a glowing sense of modest merit in others, and a partiality also for the manners and institutions of

[1] Mme de Tencin to Montesquieu, 2 December 1748; Trudaine to Montesquieu, 18 January 1749.

[2] Saint-Lambert, memoir prefaced to Helvétius, *Le Bonheur*, London, 1772.

[3] Vauvenargues to Mirabeau, 24 December 1738 (Vauvenargues, *Œuvres posthumes*, ed. D.-L. Gilbert, Paris, 1857, p. 109).

[4] Michaud, *Biographie universelle*, s.v. Mirabeau.

the British nations, which he thought singularly happy, and in respect of which he willingly listened to any important details. On being acquainted with Black's intention of leaving Bordeaux, he wrote to him a letter, in which, with other expressions of kindness, are the following: 'je ne me fais point à l'idée de vous voir quitter Bordeaux. Je perds le plaisir de vous voir souvent et de m'oublier avec vous'.[1]

When the son, in 1754, took his degree in medicine, he sent some copies of his thesis, *De humano acido a cibis orto*, to his father, who presented a copy to the President.[2] John Black had married a daughter of Robert Gordon (likewise a wine-merchant in Bordeaux), who was related to the family of Adam Ferguson, and Ferguson himself was later to marry Black's granddaughter. Thus the author of *An Essay on the History of Civil Society*, greatly influenced by Montesquieu's doctrines, finds a link with the author of *L'Esprit des lois* on the banks of the Garonne. If the correspondence between Montesquieu and Black could be rediscovered—it has hitherto eluded all pursuit—much might be learned about the intellectual relations of France and Scotland. That the two men found other things to discuss than Graves and Sauternes, is suggested by the list of subscribers to James Simon's *Essay towards an historical account of Irish coins*, published at Dublin in 1749. Named along with Barbot and Folkes are 'John Black, merchant, Bordeaux' and 'Hon. Charles de Secondat de Montesquiou, President of the Parliament of Guyenne', as well as Jean-Baptiste de Secondat.

Such friendships as this, however, were not the centre of Montesquieu's social life in Bordeaux, nor was even his attendance, frequent though it may have been, at the salon of Madame Duplessy, the gayest, most learned, and most sparkling of the hostesses of Bordeaux.[3] His strongest loyalty was still to the Academy of Bordeaux, unweakened by his membership of the older and more famous body in Paris. Soon after his return from his travels he read papers on the fountains of Hungary, the mines

[1] Adam Ferguson, 'Minutes of the Life and Character of Joseph Black, M.D.' (*Transactions of the Royal Society of Edinburgh*, V (1805), pt. III, pp. 101–17). The various plagiarisms of this article, by Robison and Brougham, resulted, when used by Villemain (*Journal des savants*, 1855), in the assertion that Montesquieu's acquaintance was with *Mrs.* Black, whom Vian (p. 23) promoted to *milady*.

[2] J. Robison, preface to Joseph Black, *Lectures on the elements of Chemistry*, Edinburgh, 1803, I, p. xxviii.

[3] Grellet-Dumazeau, op. cit., *passim*.

of Germany, and on the nature of sound. Another paper was read for him in his absence on the sobriety of the inhabitants of Rome, on 15 November 1732, and yet another, not extant, was communicated by him with the title *Formation et progrès des idées.* In 1739 he read two further papers on scientific subjects; one of them dealt with respiration and the other with the temperature of mineral waters. Even after the publication of *L'Esprit des lois* he did not disdain to present a paper on the nature of different languages. He had already twice held the office of director (in 1718 and 1726) and was nominated again for the years 1735 and 1748, on the second of these occasions being succeeded by his son. In 1736, doubtless at the instigation of Montesquieu, Polignac was elected protector of the Academy, and he was thanked by a deputation consisting of Melon, Montesquieu, Mairan, Secondat, and two others. Montesquieu appears to have acted as intermediary between the Academy and the Cardinal.

Not long after the publication of the *Romains*, Montesquieu revived his scientific interests. He thought of rewriting and revising the papers which he had previously read to the Academy; he engaged in experiments again himself, consulting Mairan about the relative magnification of different microscopes.[1] He had made in England a set of instruments which he presented to the Academy.[2] But sometimes his scientific occupations were less serious. It is Stendhal who heard in Bordeaux the story of Montesquieu's conversation with three or four colleagues in the hall of the Academy, where a vase of carnations stood by a window through which the sun was streaming. Inconspicuously, he turned the vase round; and a little later exclaimed, 'Gentlemen, how can science explain the fact that the shaded side of this vase is hot while the side turned to the sun is cold?' He avowed his practical joke only when it became clear that the pride of his colleagues was becoming far too engaged in the learned discussion which had begun.[3]

Elections to the Academy occupied him seriously. He approached Silva, court physician, and Bordelais by birth, about becoming a member.[4] He resisted a proposal to elect Castel,

[1] Montesquieu to Mairan, 27 June 1737.

[2] *Arch. hist. Gironde*, III, p. 208.

[3] Stendhal, op. cit., pp. 75–76.

[4] R. Céleste, 'Le Bordelais J.-B. Silva, médecin du roi Louis XV' (*Revue philomathique de Bordeaux et du Sud-ouest*, 1910).

saying that two Jesuits were already enough.[1] In 1741 he suggested that Martin Folkes should be elected, and two years later the Englishman became an associate member,[2] and in 1745 he was followed by Guasco. The year following, in Montesquieu's absence, Voltaire received the same honour. He was later to mock the Academy of Bordeaux in *Candide*. No comment by Montesquieu on his election is recorded; but earlier, on the possibility of Voltaire's election to the Académie française, he had written words which he might well have applied to the younger body:

> Il serait honteux pour l'Académie que Voltaire en fût; il lui sera quelque jour honteux qu'il n'en ait pas été.[3]

A joint démarche on the part of Montesquieu and Melon in 1736 resulted in an election big with consequence for the Academy: the author of the *Lettres persanes* and the author of *Mahmoud le Gasnévide* joined in support of the author of an obscure and fanciful *Lettre d'un rat calotin*. This was Jean-Jacques Bel, Montesquieu's contemporary at Juilly, a counsellor in the Parlement, a man of letters well known even in Paris, vigorous and independent to the point of criticizing La Motte and even Fontenelle, though both of them were much admired by Montesquieu.[4] Of his correspondence with the President only one letter in each direction survives, but these are more than enough to make the disappearance of the rest deplorable. He acted as literary adviser to Montesquieu on more than one occasion, and the President showed deference for his judgement. In his youth Bel had aspired to form a rival body to the Academy of Bordeaux, with less specially scientific interests. From 1713 to 1719 he had assembled a group of friends each Thursday in his father's house. One of them would read a paper on a literary, aesthetic, or moral topic; discussion followed; and then two others were appointed to examine the paper and produce for the following week a written report on it and on the discussion it had provoked.[5] Perhaps it

[1] Montesquieu to Barbot, 23 November and 20 December 1741.

[2] Montesquieu to Folkes, 14 February 1741 (not 1744 as in Gebelin–Morize edition).

[3] *Pensée* 896 (Bkn. 925).

[4] See P. Courteault, 'Le Conseiller au Parlement de Guienne Jean-Jacques Bel' (*Trésors de la Bibliothèque municipale de Bordeaux*, Paris, 1936).

[5] E. Féret, *Statistique générale du département de la Gironde*, III (i), *Biographie*, Bordeaux and Paris, 1889, s.v. Bel.

was as a result of this rivalry that his election to the Academy was delayed until he was forty-three years old. It was then, however, a particularly significant election on account of his having become deeply involved in the municipal politics of Bordeaux.

Claude Boucher, himself the son of a high functionary, after being intendant of Auvergne became in 1720 intendant of Guyenne. He did not wait long before producing ambitious and not unenlightened plans for the urban development of Bordeaux. He was particularly anxious to clear a portion of the quais from the Rue du Chapeau Rouge to the Cour des Aides, and to construct there a block of buildings which would add greatly to the dignity of the town.[1] These plans incurred great hostility, partly on account of the unpopularity in certain quarters of their proponent. Boucher, it has been seen,[2] had had conflict with Montesquieu about the further planting of vines in Guyenne, and had received the President's witty complaints with ill humour. He had denounced Montesquieu to the Government as a freemason.[3] It is not surprising that the President formed the hostile opinion of him which is expressed in the *Pensées*:

> Je disais de l'intendant Boucher: 'Je veux bien que l'on donne la toute-puissance aux intendants; mais, si l'on en fait des Dieux, il faut, au moins, les choisir parmi les hommes non pas parmi les bêtes.[4]

Montesquieu's dislike for Boucher was shared by his colleagues and former colleagues of the Parlement. They decided to oppose his plan, and Bel was appointed to convey their protest to the Government. He indited a memorandum in which perhaps he erred by exaggerating his case, which was based on legal, commercial, military, and aesthetic grounds. Boucher was a good controversialist. His reply to the military argument, that the new construction would limit the firing range of the fort of Bordeaux, the Château-Trompette, was to produce a certificate from the head and deputy engineers of the fort declaring that the proposed construction would in no way affect the firing range, and that the only impediment to the complete efficiency of the fort was in fact Bel's own house, the Hôtel de l'Esplanade.[5] Several detailed plans were now produced for the proposed square, one of them actually involving the demolition of Bel's house. The Parlement

[1] See P. Courteault, *La Place royale de Bordeaux,* Paris and Bordeaux, 1923.
[2] See above, p. 82. [3] See above, p. 174.
[4] *Pensée* 1353 (Bkn. 1872). [5] Courteault, op. cit., pp. 48–49.

meanwhile was distressed at the proposal to construct a new customs house in the new Place Royale; for the present office was lodged in a building owned by D'Albessard, the wealthy purchaser of Montesquieu's presidency; and D'Albessard derived from it an annual rent of 4,000 *livres*, and would be unlikely to let it so lucratively again. D'Albessard and Bel were both defeated in the contest (though Bel's house was not in fact demolished) and Bordeaux gained that fine hemicycle now known as the Place de la Bourse.

Bel's election to the Academy in 1738 was thus a reward for his services, an expression of confidence and solidarity, and a hostile gesture against the intendant.

Not long after his election Bel fell ill, and on 16 August 1738 died at the age of forty-five. When his will was opened, it was found that he had left his controversial house, his library, and his scientific instruments, to the Academy of Bordeaux, imposing the condition that the books should be accessible to the public on three days in each week. This was the beginning of the municipal library of Bordeaux, one of the finest of French provincial libraries, perhaps the richest of them all.[1]

The acquisition of Bel's house seemed perhaps to be the turning-point in the fortunes of the Academy. It had already had more than its share of ill luck. The collapse of the currency under Law had hit it severely. Its first protector, the Duc de La Force, had fallen into disgrace; his successor, Morville, had had a similar fate. Various attempts to obtain dignified or even adequate premises had failed, and the Academy contented itself perforce with modest accommodation in the Hôtel de Ville. Now it had a palatial home. Bel's house, of modern construction, was of fine design and of dominant position. The acquisition of both house and library placed the Academy in an unprecedentedly strong position. The condition of public accessibility of the books was not onerous, as there was now a paid librarian, and it gave the Academy a place of enhanced importance in the life of the town.

Boucher retired as intendant of Guyenne in 1743, and his place was taken by the Marquis de Tourny, who was a man of parts.[2] He arrived in Bordeaux in July. The following January,

[1] R. Céleste, *Histoire de la bibliothèque de la ville de Bordeaux*, Bordeaux, 1892.

[2] M. Lhéritier, *Tourny*, Paris, 1920, 2 vols., is a serious and well-documented study.

on Montesquieu's proposition,[1] he was elected a member of the Academy—an honour which Boucher had never in all his twenty-three years received—and the following year was elected *directeur*.

Tourny did not allow his membership of the Academy to deflect him from what he considered his duty to Bordeaux. He wrote to the Comte d'Argenson, Minister for War, deploring the absence of promenades from Bordeaux, and proposing the construction of an avenue, which would be created by enlarging the Esplanade of the Château-Trompette.[2] He at first met with resistance in Paris, but eventually his plans were approved in principle by the minister.[3] It was a question of cutting back ill-aligned property belonging to the Dominicans; but this raised the problem of the exceedingly prominent house of Bel, now belonging to the Academy, which was set at an oblique angle to the road, and presented a serious difficulty to any town planner. Tourny's proposal was to conceal the house by a southward prolongation of the façade wall of the Dominicans' property, the land on which this would be done belonging to the municipality. The compensation proposed to the Academy was the opening of a new road, inevitably a very minor one, which would give them a new façade in an inconspicuous place.

The discussions seemed almost interminable, since the Academy itself was by no means united, Tourny having supporters among the members, and some of them being particularly influential: Caupos, D'Albessard, De Gascq, and Le Berthon the Premier Président.[4] The anti-intendant party included Barbot, Lavie, and Jean-Baptiste de Secondat. Montesquieu's own relations with Tourny had not, hitherto, been unamiable, at least by contrast with his attitude to Boucher. He corresponded affably and even jocularly with him.[5] He lent him a carriage when the intendant had to organize a grandiose reception for two visiting Spanish princesses.[6] When, isolated at La Brède, he wished to see a criticism of himself which had appeared in the *Mémoires de Trévoux*, it was from Tourny, through Barbot, that he borrowed

[1] Bx, MS. 1699 (2).

[2] A thorough and definitive treatment of the resultant controversy is given by X. Védère, *Les Allées de Tourny*, Bordeaux, 1929 (also printed in *RHBx*, 1929–31).

[3] Védère, op. cit., p. 122.

[4] Lhéritier, op. cit., II, p. 368.

[5] Montesquieu to Tourny, 3 August 1745.

[6] Lhéritier, op. cit., I, p. 259.

a copy.[1] His lawsuit with the *jurats* of Bordeaux made it expedient that he should remain on good terms with Tourny, for, as he pointed out to Guasco, intendants carry more weight than an ex-President.[2] He found himself now, however, driven more and more into opposition to Tourny.

The *jurats* of Bordeaux, who were on Tourny's side, proposed to sell for building two strips of ground on the Esplanade front of the Academy's premises. The Government authorized this step, to the dismay of the Academy, who appointed a commissioner to investigate the whole situation. He discharged his task brilliantly, for he produced evidence that the land in question belonged, not to the municipality, but to the king.

This claim was represented to Tourny. He rejected it. The Academy retorted by giving Montesquieu full powers to conduct its affairs in Paris. The struggle now became vigorous. Within less than a month Montesquieu, taking full advantage of his friendship with Trudaine, who was Intendant des Finances, obtained for the Academy, from the king, a lease of the land in question at a purely nominal rent.

The *jurats* meanwhile, anxious to establish a *fait accompli*, had sold the land, and building operations were initiated. The Government ordered Tourny to end them. He did not comply, appealing on legal grounds against the royal concession. Memorandum followed memorandum on each side, and the contest was protracted until the early months of 1751, when a tripartite conference was held in Paris, attended by Trudaine, Tourny, and Montesquieu, and arrived at a settlement. The terms involved a nominal cession by the Academy to the *jurats* of the land in question, on condition that no building of any kind should be erected and that the land which had already been excavated should be filled in. The Academy, for its part, agreed to the opening of a new street on its flank, and ceded the land required for this purpose at a price of 8,000 *livres*. These terms involved only minimal concessions by the Academy and substantial ones by the town, and Tourny did not conceal the fact that he had been compelled to yield to Trudaine's desire to give pleasure to his friend in a matter which to him was largely indifferent.

Montesquieu's success, however, was not final. The *jurats*

[1] Barbot to Montesquieu, 7 April 1749.

[2] Montesquieu to Guasco, 20 February 1747.

rejected the compromise, and the question was re-opened. Fifteen months later, Montesquieu again appeared victorious. He wrote to Guasco:

C'est une terrible chose de plaider contre un intendant, mais c'est une chose bien douce que de gagner un procès contre un intendant.[1]

Even now, however, his joy was unfounded. The quarrel was still further drawn out. It ended only after his death and after the death of Tourny, and it ended as a victory for Tourny. The President had viewed the whole affair with great seriousness, regarding the activities of Tourny as arbitrary and offensive to private interests. Once he was involved in the struggle, it became a trial of strength between Tourny and himself. His civic disagreement with the intendant may indeed have inspired his refusal to resume his presidency.[2]

Bordeaux, however, as a result of the intendant's policy, gained for herself one of France's noblest streets, the Allées de Tourny.

IV. CLAIRAC

Seventy miles up-stream from Bordeaux stand the village and castle of Aiguillon at the junction of the Lot and the Garonne. A few miles further up the Garonne lies Port-Sainte-Marie, the river port serving the village of Montesquieu, while at a similar distance up the Lot is Clairac. This area was well known to the President, and its society played an important part in his life. He had relatives at Agen who also owned the barony of Montagnac three miles to the south-east of Montesquieu; and, if he only rarely visited the property from which he took his name, he frequently stayed at Clairac where his wife's family, Lartigue, was prominent.

Clairac is set in a most attractive countryside of small hills and dales, well watered by the Lot. It is now a tranquil and undisturbed town, with many old buildings, which for the most part are ill preserved. But not even the medieval house which

[1] Montesquieu to Guasco, 8 August 1752.

[2] Hardy, *Memoirs of Charlemont*, p. 35. Hardy's account, though not true in every detail, is likely to have been based in its generalities on Montesquieu's conversations.

bears the newly painted legend, not only that Montesquieu stayed in it, but also that Japhet, son of Noah, died there in the year 2907 B.C., convinces the visitor that in the past Clairac was a town of real significance and the centre of a vigorous intellectual life.

This, none the less, is true. In the eighteenth century Clairac was even a cosmopolitan centre. The main reason for this is quite specific. Clairac, though a largely protestant town, was the seat of a mitred abbot whose duties included that of proselytization. Henry IV, as a proof of the completeness of his conversion to catholicism, bestowed this abbacy on the Chapter of Saint John Lateran, as a result of which there was a direct link between Clairac and Rome. In 1738 Filippo Venuti was nominated to represent the Chapter at Clairac.

The Venuti family[1] belonged to Cortona in Southern Tuscany. It was a noble family, and several of its members had intellectual achievements to their credit. Ridolfino Venuti was an archaeologist of repute and the author of two works on Rome which Piranesi illustrated. Marcello was the most celebrated: he organized the excavations at Herculaneum. Filippo, their brother, who joined them in founding at Cortona the Accademia Etrusca, was a canon of Saint John Lateran, but not much liking life in the ecclesiastical capital (he wrote to a friend that he found nothing but lies in the mouths of the priests of Rome)[2] was pleased when his Chapter nominated him to look after its interests at Clairac. He arrived at his destination on 5 August 1738. He found Clairac a rich city of commerce, productive of an exceedingly sweet wine, predominantly protestant, there being only one thousand Roman Catholics among its fifteen thousand inhabitants, and having in its vicinity, to his great joy, Roman remains within his own jurisdiction.[3]

Not long after his arrival in Clairac he made the acquaintance of Montesquieu, who was delighted to know the brother of the Marcello Venuti who, meeting him in 1729 in Florence, had

[1] See T. Venuti de Dominicis, *I Venuti*, Rome, 1889; G. Mancini, 'Contributo dei Cortonesi alla coltura italiana' (*Archivio storico italiano*, 1921, and separately, Florence, 1922); H. Weinert, 'Filippo de' Venuti' (*Archivio storico italiano*, 1954).

[2] Mancini, op. cit., p. 138.

[3] Florence, Biblioteca Marucelliana, MS. A. CXCVII, 8 (*Diario del viaggio del Sig. Canonico Filippo Venuti*), ff. 232–3.

introduced him to the Academy of Cortona.[1] Montesquieu now repaid his debt to the family, for on 17 March 1739 Venuti was elected to the Academy of Bordeaux. His academic career from this moment on was more successful than his progress in the Church. For some of his brethren in the Chapter which had appointed him turned against him and sought to terminate his appointment, partly because the remittances which he made to Rome from the revenues of the abbey were deemed inadequate,[2] partly because his relations with the protestants of Clairac were too amiable.[3] Montesquieu came to his rescue. He appealed to Madame de Tencin, asking her to intervene with her brother the Cardinal; he enlisted the support of the Duchesse d'Aiguillon, who exercised great influence over Maurepas. Then he devised another plan. This was to make Venuti librarian of the Academy of Bordeaux. The Academy, since the death of Bel, had an extensive library of which the titular custodian was Barbot. The librarian had a modest stipend of 800 *livres*, but he was housed in addition. Montesquieu sounded Venuti about his willingness to accept this office. Barbot and Sarrau were consulted and agreed. Barbot then resigned the title of librarian, and the commissioners appointed by the Academy, jointly with Bel's executor, appointed Venuti to the post. The Abbé did not relinquish all ecclesiastical functions, and at a later stage was still involved in difficulties which led Montesquieu to intervene with Nivernais; but he was able to devote himself primarily to scholarship and literature and his fame grew. He translated into Italian *Le Temple de Gnide* and, by way of contrast, Louis Racine's poem, *La Religion*, as well as Lefranc de Pompignan's *Didon*. He composed a eulogistic and fantastic poem, *Il Trionfo letterario della Francia*. He read many papers to the Academy of Bordeaux. In 1754 several of these were collected together by Jean-Baptiste de Secondat, then perpetual secretary, and published at the Academy's expense under the title *Dissertations sur les anciens monuments de la ville de Bordeaux*. Secondat, in his foreword, praises the author's grace and the amenity of his wit, and the Academy's official

[1] Montesquieu to Venuti, 17 March 1739. The accusation made by M. Gebelin (*RHBx*, 1913, p. 71) that Venuti presented to Montesquieu one of his brother's books, passing it off as his own, seems to me unsubstantiated. Filippo Venuti had already published works of his own to his credit.

[2] Guasco, *Lettres familières*, VI (Nagel III, p. 1018).

[3] Montesquieu to Barbot, 9 July 1742.

imprimatur commends his learning, judgement, and taste. Montesquieu's prediction, that this man might become one of the most celebrated in Europe,[1] was not wholly unfounded.

In 1750 Cerati wrote to his friend Bottari to ask whether Venuti was suitable, in point of devotion and piety, for ecclesiastical preferment; in point of learning he knew him to be well qualified, and he was known to be highly esteemed by Benedict XIV.[2] The result of the inquiry was satisfactory. When Venuti left France, it was to receive promotion in the Church, for he became Provost of Leghorn.

He had formed in France a great circle of devoted friends and correspondents. Letters still preserved at Cortona show him to be in contact with Bimard de La Bastie, Baron von Stosch, Bon of Montpellier, Desmolets, Lefranc de Pompignan, and with Maurepas himself, who wrote to announce Venuti's election to the Académie des Inscriptions.[3] Guasco became an intimate ally; and the two most faithful correspondents were Madame de Pontac and the Chevalier de Vivens.

The Pontac family was one of great dignity. It was reputedly allied to the house of Bourbon.[4] One branch was descended from the Président de Thou, and was recently linked by marriage to the family of the Duchesse d'Aiguillon. Another branch was related to Montesquieu's own family and a portrait of Anne de Pontac, who married Pierre de Secondat in 1600, hangs still at La Brède. The family had often held legal offices, including that of *premier président* of the Parlement of Bordeaux. Many of their estates were contiguous to Montesquieu's: they possessed the titles of marquis of La Prade, baron of Beautiran, and lord of Bisqueytan. The Comtesse de Pontac, sometimes known as the Comtesse de Belhade, was a celebrated figure in the south-west. Guasco stayed with her and wrote verses to her. Montesquieu, if writing to anyone near her, did not fail to salute *la charmante comtesse*. She was a close friend of Venuti, and his neighbour in Bordeaux, for she occupied an apartment in the Academy's house where the librarian also lived. Her letters to Venuti, filled for the most part with domestic gossip, are most frequently

[1] Montesquieu to Barbot, 9 July 1742.

[2] Cerati to Bottari, 23 March 1750 (Rome, Biblioteca Corsiniana, MS. 1589, f. 233).

[3] Cortona, MS. 497, ff. 66–67.

[4] O'Gilvy, op. cit., II, p. 353.

dated from Sauviac, plausibly identifiable as a property near Bazas, where a celebrated Pontac had been bishop in the sixteenth century, and she affected to dislike Bordeaux: 'le séjour de Bordeaux me fait d'avance une frayeur mortelle', she wrote on the eve of a summer visit.[1] She was a widow, and had a son who was a friend of the Marquis de Paulmy,[2] D'Argenson's son, and a daughter whom Guasco found attractive. She herself contracted a marriage in 1752 which Montesquieu regarded as deplorable: she married for the sake of money, and possibly married an American.[3]

François de Vivens—a most engaging figure—was her friend, perhaps also her kinsman.[4] He was the close friend of Venuti. He seems to have been related to Madame de Montesquieu,[5] and was more closely related to the Chevalier de Jaucourt. His family had been Huguenot, and had renounced Protestantism only after the Revocation of the Edict of Nantes. Vivens himself, born in 1697, after his education at the Collège de Guyenne, spent six years in England. On his return he stayed for some time in Paris, where he became the friend of Mairan, and then settled on his property, devoting himself to agriculture and to scientific study. Becoming an academician of Bordeaux in 1742, he was at the centre of the intellectual life of the region. In his country house there assembled what has been known as the Cénacle de Clairac: Montesquieu, Jean-Baptiste de Secondat, Guasco, and Venuti are to be found there.

Montesquieu was often at Clairac. He maintained the most friendly relations with Vivens. When the Chevalier penned an amiable Persian letter to the President, he probably referred to Clairac when he wrote:

J'ai des terres à Chiraz, lumière de l'occident. Toi qui connais notre

[1] Mme de Pontac to Venuti, 2 July 1747 (Cortona, MS. 497, f. 125).

[2] Mme de Pontac to Venuti, 3 March 1747 (ibid., ff. 116–17).

[3] Montesquieu to Guasco, 16 March 1752 (and Guasco's note).

[4] Mme de Pontac's maiden name was De Barry, which was the name also of a property owned by Vivens one mile north-east of Clairac. On Vivens, see Saint-Amans, *Notice biographique sur M. de Vivens*, Agen, 1829, and R.-L. Larnaudie, 'L'Invention du paratonnerre à Clairac' (*Revue des amis du Musée de peinture de Bordeaux*, 1953–4).

[5] According to documents preserved at La Brède, both the maternal grandmother and a paternal uncle of Mme de Montesquieu were called Labat de Vivens.

pays mieux que nous-mêmes, tu n'ignores pas que Chiraz est l'endroit de la Perse où l'on recueille les vins les plus exquis.[1]

Montesquieu and Vivens, with Secondat, seem to have conducted scientific experiments, and to have been particularly interested in the flight of birds. This was an old preoccupation of Montesquieu, who soon after the *Lettres persanes* had written in the *Pensées* a few pages of scientific if *a priori* notes on the subject, ending with the suggestion that he should read Borelli, *De motu animalium*, which he in fact acquired a few years later.[2] The description of their experiments was committed to paper by Secondat, writing (it has been claimed) under his father's dictation. The conclusions which Vivens drew from them are contained in various places in his works, but especially in an essay entitled *Du vol des oiseaux* published for the first time in 1935.[3] His finding is that the body of a bird is filled with an elastic substance whose nature is centrifugal, so that it is naturally impelled, without effort of its own, to rise in the air at a right angle to the ground. This extraordinary theory, whose proponent regarded it (such are the vicissitudes of terms) as Cartesian, cannot have commended itself to Montesquieu, at least to Montesquieu *bien conseillé*; nor did the piety of kinship lead Jaucourt, though he corresponded with Vivens on this topic, to incorporate his ideas in the article *Oiseaux* of the *Encyclopédie*.

Vivens, Montesquieu and his son, and the two Italians, were not the sole members of the Cénacle de Clairac. There came *savants* from the busy and picturesque town of Nérac fifteen miles to the south. Brescon was a doctor in practice at Mézin,

[1] Nagel III, p. 1544. [2] *Pensée* 79 (Bkn. 758).

[3] J. Duhem has dealt with this question in five places: 'Fragments inédits du chevalier de Vivens et de Montesquieu sur une nouvelle théorie du vol des oiseaux' (*Révolution française*, 1936); *Histoire des idées aéronautiques avant Montgolfier*, Paris, 1943, pp. 316–17, 347; *Musée aéronautique avant Montgolfier*, Paris, 1944, pp. 166–8; 'Une théorie inédite de la locomotion aérienne' (*Mercure de France*, 1 November 1935); 'Du vol des oiseaux, par Vivens et Montesquieu' (ibid., 15 November 1936). Duhem has had unpublished documents in his possession, and has published facsimiles of some pages. But after admitting in the first article in the *Mercure de France* that there is proof of Montesquieu's share in the experiments, but none of his share in the resultant essay, he should not have published this essay above Montesquieu's name. A serious and scholarly publication of the documents in question (which it is a merit to have discovered and evaluated) is much to be desired. It may be noted that Montesquieu's attitude to Vivens's *Essai sur les principes de la physique* was very reserved (Montesquieu to Vivens, 12 July 1746).

who beguiled his leisure moments with the composition of verses which (as well as his scientific essays) he submitted to Montesquieu. Raulin of Nérac wrote and published extensively. When his *Observations de médecine* appeared in 1754, the foreword explained that Montesquieu had seen the work and had encouraged publication. His *Dissertation sur les ingrédients de l'air* contained in the same volume had likewise been submitted to Montesquieu, who alludes to it in the *Pensées*.[1] The manuscript remains in the library of Bordeaux.[2] Jacques de Romas was Nérac's most famous son.[3] Born in 1713, he was a magistrate at Nérac, a landowner, but above all an experimental scientist. Working in close association with the three Dutilh brothers of the same town, with Vivens, and with Secondat, he devoted himself to the study of electricity. In particular he used a kite connected to a metal bar as a lightning conductor, in order to examine the electrical discharges produced during a thunderstorm. It was Vivens who invented the name *brontomètre* for this apparatus. The experiments, according to some accounts, were conducted in the presence of Montesquieu; but it is possible that he was confused with his son.[4] In either case, however, they were reported to him,[5] and it was in his province and with his encouragement that some of the eighteenth century's most significant advances in the study of electricity were made.

The fame of scientific activity at Nérac attracted thither in 1746 no less a person than Lady Mary Wortley Montagu;[6] but neither the talent of Romas, nor the discovery that Raulin was a disciple of her friend Dr. Arbuthnot, kept her there. For great minds and conquerors alike, *Unus non sufficit orbis*, said the wandering Sir James Caldwell, writing of Lady Mary, but with himself doubtless in mind.[7] This half-mad Irishman, armed with letters of introduction from Montesquieu whose goodwill he captured, toured the whole province, dining with Venuti at

[1] *Pensée* 2091 (Bkn. 731). [2] Bx MS. 828, vol. 103, no. V.

[3] See P. Courteault's *Notice* prefaced to Romas, *Œuvres inédites*, ed. J. Bergonié, Bordeaux, 1911.

[4] Bernadau, op. cit., p. 203. Confusion between Montesquieu and his son was not unknown in their lifetime. The *Bibliothèque raisonnée* of 1747 gives a long and thorough account of Secondat's scientific experiments, attributing them all to the President.

[5] Courteault, op. cit., p. 33. [6] Courteault, op. cit., p. 2.

[7] Caldwell to Montesquieu, July–August 1746 (*FS*, 1958).

Agen, meeting Duclos and Forcalquier on holiday in the Pyrenees, being imprisoned as a spy at Toulouse because he wandered suspiciously on bird-chasing expeditions, and finally endeavouring to induce Guasco to accompany him on an expedition to Egypt.[1] Not less than men of science, eccentrics also haunted the provinces as well as the metropolis.

[1] See R. Halsband, 'Lady Mary Wortley Montagu as a friend of continental writers' (*Bulletin of the John Rylands Library*, 1956), as well as Caldwell's letters to Montesquieu, in Nagel III and *FS*, 1958.

X

PREPARATION OF *L'ESPRIT DES LOIS*, 1734–48

I. ISOLATED VENTURES

MADAME GEOFFRIN'S daughter met Montesquieu during a visit which he paid to the exiled Polish court at Lunéville in 1747. She found him exhausted and unable to discuss the most banal topics. On the eve of his departure she is said to have addressed him, in the presence of the entire court, in these terms:

> Président, je vous suis bien obligée; car vous avez paru si sot, et par comparaison m'avez si fort donné l'air d'avoir de l'esprit, que, si je voulais établir que c'est moi qui ai fait les *Lettres persanes*, tout le monde ici le croirait plutôt que de les croire de vous.[1]

Her words throw light on what differentiates the President from most of his companions in the social life of the age. For them the *conversazione* and the dinner were the focus of life. Literature interested them, certainly, but it was the literature of the epigram, the satirical characterization, the short story and the casual dramatic exercise, the literature of social intercourse. Montesquieu, it is true, practised literature of this sort, and made to it more valuable contributions than the comedies of the Brancas salon and the facetious trivialities of the *Recueil de Ces Messieurs*. At some date unknown, but not later than 1738, he wrote his *Histoire véritable*, which did not see the light of day until the late nineteenth century. Its alternative title, *Le Métempsychosiste*, discloses its theme. It is the autobiographical account of the transmigrations of a soul, which occupies in turn the bodies of a dog, a wolf, an ox, an elephant, of many different men and women, and of a eunuch. Trivial though the work is, and bearing no stamp of genius, it is still amusing, in places exceedingly amusing. It is skilfully written, the cleverest part of it being perhaps the incarnation in the eunuch. It had a certain circulation in manuscript, being submitted by Montesquieu to his Bordeaux friend Jean-Jacques Bel. It may be asked whether it was seen also by the

[1] Marquis de Ségur, *Le Royaume de la rue Saint-Honoré*, pp. 141–2.

President's Parisian friend, the academician Moncrif, who himself, in 1749, read an opera on the same theme to the Academy in the presence of Montesquieu.[1]

Arsace et Isménie is a work of higher quality. Shortly before September 1742, Montesquieu was staying in the Palace of Madrid with Mademoiselle de Charolais, sister of the Duc de Bourbon. She ordered the President to write a novel.[2] Working perhaps with some haste, and drawing on the old fragments collected together before his travels under the title *Le Prince*, he wrote *Arsace et Isménie* (or as it was at one time called *Arsame*). He submitted it to the judgement of Madame de Mirepoix, who made four or five valued criticisms, and then to Barbot. The President never saw fit to publish it, and it was only in 1783, in a volume of *Œuvres posthumes*, that it came to light. Its merit is uneven. The conclusion, especially the pages excised from the 1783 edition, is weak and contains some jejune political maxims. But the earlier part of the work (and the entire story fills fewer than 50 octavo pages) compels the reader's attention, and evokes his sympathy for the unhappy lovers. It is a tale of the east, of the artificial and stylized east from which Montesquieu scarcely advances even in *L'Esprit des lois*, of a society where violence is spontaneous and passion is indomitable. Arsace performs great exploits of love and arms when he is but seventeen years old; both he and Isménie, and even the eunuch Aspar, have distinct personalities. The narrative powers of Montesquieu are shown to be considerable, and his style possesses succinct individuality. The description of an eastern palace consists of six lines of real distinction, leading to the sentence, 'tout ce qui inanimé est riant, et tout ce qui a de la vie est sombre'. The treatment of passion is that of Prévost rather than that of Marivaux, and the talent displayed is not inferior to that of Prévost.

Arsace et Isménie and the *Histoire véritable* are the most lasting of Montesquieu's ephemeral productions. But at the same time he had more serious preoccupations. He was actively engaged on a history of France. Great fragments of his writing on this subject appear in the *Pensées*, where they occupy 70 pages of the second volume.[3] His account begins with the Merovingians and

[1] Montesquieu to Trudaine, 25 September 1749 (*FS*, 1958).

[2] Montesquieu to Barbot, 8 September 1742.

[3] *Pensées* 1302, 1306 (Bkn. 595, 596).

proceeds through the Middle Ages, where he gives particular attention to Louis XI,[1] to his own times. There are interesting personal judgements in these pages: he stigmatizes Richelieu and Louvois as the two worst citizens France has ever had, adding that he could name a third (undoubtedly Law) but would spare him in his disgrace. There are epigrams in the President's most characteristic style: Henry IV, he says, was converted and regarded nothing as more sacred than his crown; the Pope has power only through the ostentation of power. But in spite of these merits, the fragments of the history of France are undistinguished, because they are but fragments and lack all sustained argument.

In his desire to document himself about the times of Louis XIV and the succeeding Regency, he left Paris where he was staying in the August of 1734 to pay a visit to the Duc de Saint-Simon, then living in retirement in Normandy. Saint-Simon was occupied in writing his account of the times through which he had lived, and Montesquieu heard from him anecdotes about Madame de Montespan and Madame de Maintenon which were eventually published, in the nineteenth century, in the Duke's *Mémoires*, but which Montesquieu meanwhile copied down into the *Spicilège*.[2] This process of informing himself about recent history he had begun in Rome in his conversations with Polignac; he continued it now also in conversations with Schaub, formerly British Ambassador in Paris, who revisited Paris in 1736.[3] His intention to write a historical work was at one moment fixed and serious. He regarded himself—and said so in the *Pensées*—as being in an admirable position for writing a history of recent times. Adequately wealthy to be independent, he had never been involved in public affairs, but had known many who were. He had travelled. He had legal experience.[4] But this project was never realized, perhaps because he became increasingly dissatisfied with that form of historical writing which consists simply of narration of events in the life of courts and monarchs. A wider and broader notion of history developed in his mind during these years, and arose in large measure from the example of Giannone, before the

[1] He even wrote, it appears, a history of Louis XI, which the carelessness of a secretary destroyed (Guasco, *Lettres familières*, XXIV; Nagel III, p. 1097).

[2] *Spicilège* 570, 657 (MS., pp. 529–30, 617–29).

[3] *Spicilège* 772 (MS., pp. 775–9).

[4] *Pensée* 1183 (Bkn. 539).

reputation of whose *Istoria civile* he inclines, saying that a civil history of France ought to be written.[1]

To write the history of France was an ambitious aim; but the President had still a vaster project in his mind, of which the history of France might be merely a part.

II. THE DECISION

His son relates that after the publication of the *Considérations sur les Romains* Montesquieu rested for two or three months. He had for some years cherished the notion of writing a grandiose work of political and legal theory. He had already in his drawers much material which had been collected in the past and which he could use in such a work, which perhaps he had assembled with such a work in mind. Earliest among these were the fragments of the *Traité des devoirs*, never published and perhaps never completed, but replete with relevant material and largely inspired by Pufendorf, who again, in a work on law, might well be his guide. The *Considérations sur les richesses de l'Espagne* contained ideas on economic theory which he would wish to incorporate. The *Réflexions sur la monarchie universelle* had already been set up in type but had never been published, and useful material would be found there. But most important of all was the essay on the constitution of England, which contained ideas new to the French and yet worth expressing. A public whose interest in England was being stimulated by many writers, notably by Voltaire whose *Lettres philosophiques* appeared in 1734, might well see in this essay the most valuable part of the whole work.

Montesquieu had then already begun to prepare his great work, and had material ready. His friends put pressure on him, and he was himself in any case desirous of fame. In 1734, probably late in the year, he made the final decision and bent his energies to the task.

This was the turning point of his life. That such a decision should be made by Montesquieu is perhaps not surprising. That

[1] *Pensée* 446 (Bkn. 954). It is hard to believe that the historical fragments of the *Pensées* constituted the attempt to write such a history. They contain no trace either of the anticurialism of Giannone, or of his comprehensive conception of social and institutional history.

it should have been carried through to its infinitely laborious conclusion is very remarkable indeed. Montesquieu as he was known to the public in 1734 was the author of indifferent papers to a provincial academy, of the *Lettres persanes*, a scintillating satire certainly, but easily written and not the result of hard and lengthy toil, of the *Temple de Gnide* and finally of the work on the Romans, brilliant without doubt, and thoughtful, but devoid of sound historical basis. There was nothing in his existing literary publications to foretell what was now about to be composed. A rakish courtier, an *habitué* of fashionable drawing-rooms, an unremembered member of the Entresol, a provincial landowner, a would-be but rejected diplomat, a magistrate who had sold his office, Montesquieu had given no evidence at least to the outer circle of his friends of any capacity to undertake the massive labours which lay ahead of him. His eyesight, moreover, in spite of great care and expert medical advice, was feeble and he was continually menaced by complete blindness. The composition of *L'Esprit des lois* required an immense effort, both physical and intellectual, and the tenacity of purpose and power of organization which it attested are equalled in Montesquieu's age and country only by Diderot's triumphant completion of the *Encyclopédie*.

III. THE MODE OF WORKING

Beyond all doubt the labours were going to be massive. It was not a question of committing to paper ideas which were already present, *a priori*, in his mind. It would be foolish and inaccurate to yield to any of the prejudices which he had castigated in the *Lettres persanes*, and his own preconceived notions, unless tested and verified, were prejudices like any others. '*Ipse dixit*', he writes, 'est toujours une sottise.'[1] No assembly of beliefs, no country, no civilization, not Christendom itself, could be regarded as being by definition the exemplar of what is good. All civilizations must be examined, and analysed with an open mind, and all aspects of these civilizations, religious and scientific as well as legal and political, were to be his concern. Rapid generalization was without value; detailed documentation was necessary. For this purpose he had already available an admirable library. In

[1] *Pensée* 66 (Bkn. 2094).

part inherited, it had been added to at various times by the President himself.[1] There survive some early book bills from Bordeaux booksellers. Desmolets, an expert in all bibliographical matters and librarian of the Paris Oratory, was called on from time to time to help. During Montesquieu's travels, his secretary the Abbé Duval catalogued the library, and it was found to contain over 3,000 works. The president had brought many books back with him from Italy and from England. There were still many gaps on his shelves, although there was no corner of the world whose history was not represented there. But Folkes, now President of the Royal Society, frequently sent books from England, and the President bought fairly extensively in France. These books found their way to La Brède. He had another collection in Paris, of more modest proportions, but about which there is much less information, the post-mortem inventory, which is the only available source, naming but a few of the works. He had friends, notably Barbot, with rich libraries from which they were prepared to lend. The Academy of Bordeaux had a library; and Montesquieu used also to borrow books from the Bibliothèque du Roi.[2] The resources on which the President could draw for his reading were extensive. Much of his work was done in Paris, some of it was doubtless done in Bordeaux where he stayed with his brother the Dean of the Church of Saint-Seurin. Some may have been done at Raymond, some at Clairac, some even at Montesquieu. But the great bulk was undoubtedly undertaken at La Brède itself. The distractions of life in the country were less menacing than those of Paris. At La Brède he had tranquillity and space, and there he had the greatest part of his library. Part of each day was doubtless spent attending to his estates, giving instructions to L'Eveillé, consulting his legal adviser Latapie, inspecting the hedges, the roads, and the *chais*. The rest of the day was devoted to work, either in the library itself, that vast upper room, cool in summer but with difficulty heated in winter (and winter at La Brède might be severe indeed) or in his bedroom

[1] That the greater part was inherited is suggested by the fact that one work in five deals with theology, while the average proportion of theological works in the 500 libraries studied by Daniel Mornet is one in fourteen ('Enseignements des bibliothèques privées (1750–80)' in *RHLF*, 1910).

[2] The borrowers' records at the Bibliothèque du Roi (now the Bibliothèque Nationale) do not go back beyond 1735. The first entry by Montesquieu is on 16 January 1747.

below, where the abrasion of the mantel, caused by the President's feet, is to be seen to this day. From time to time, when in search of complete seclusion, he may have worked in a tiny room, dungeon-like, carved out of the thickness of the wall, and adjacent to his bedroom. Here, the tradition says, he wrote the chapter on the liberty of the citizen.[1] But wherever his work was undertaken, it was his own private task. It was not the subject matter of his conversation. His method was that of the solitary scholar. Few indeed were those who knew what was in hand, fewer still those with whom it was discussed.

Not only was Montesquieu concerned with acquiring information; it was necessary to record and classify it. He did not make cards or *fiches*, as his son was to do, using the back of playing cards for this purpose; he used notebooks. The *Pensées* and the *Spicilège* have already been referred to. The *Spicilège* was a casual notebook which, since it had accompanied Montesquieu on his travels, had become a repository of the most diverse information, notably of extracts and cuttings from English newspapers. But in general its relationship to his serious reading is less than that of the *Pensées*. The *Pensées*, in fact (and about this time Montesquieu began the second volume), were a storage place of material of various kinds which might eventually prove useful. The greatest number of pages are occupied with fragments discarded from previous works and which he might conceivably wish to use again. For the President was loath to destroy anything. Paragraphs rejected from the *Traité des devoirs*, from the *Princes*, from the *Considérations*, appear transcribed in the *Pensées*. Beside them are ideas and reflections which occurred to Montesquieu in the course of his reading and which seemed to him likely to be useful. All these appear in the *Pensées*; and when they have been incorporated in whatever work they were destined for (usually *L'Esprit des lois*), he writes in the margin the single word 'Mis' or sometimes 'Mis dans mes *Lois*,' occasionally drawing a line through the passage in question. Realizing that often an idea becomes clear only when it is committed to paper, he assembled a vast array of thoughts and notions in the *Pensées*. In order to clarify one of his most difficult problems, that of the relationship between physical and moral causes, he wrote his *Essai sur les causes*, gradually put together as his reflections proceeded,

[1] Labat, 'Le Château de La Brède', p. 177.

progressively drawn on for *L'Esprit des lois*, but still added to after he had begun to draw on it. It was a transit camp of ideas.

The *Pensées* and the *Spicilège*, with additions such as the *Essai sur les causes*, were however not adequate, and other volumes were called into use. An English visitor to La Brède reported the presence there, soon after Montesquieu's death, of forty folio volumes of commonplace books,[1] a probable exaggeration both as to number and to size. But there were undoubtedly many volumes, and from references in various places, mainly in the *Pensées*, it is possible to form a picture of these notebooks.

There were volumes with the following titles:

Geographica
Politica
Politica-Historica
Juridica
Mythologica et antiquitates
Anatomica
Historia universalis
Commerce

Each of the first two of these consisted of at least two volumes. One of them, *Anatomica*, if not others, had been begun before the President's travels. Yet other volumes may have existed and probably did; only one volume survives. This is *Geographica tome II*, prepared between 1733 and 1743.[2] It contains analyses of a number of accounts of travels, beginning with Addison's *Remarks on Several Parts of Italy* (which Montesquieu admits he did not finish reading) and including works on which the President was in any case known to have drawn, such as La Loubère on Siam, the travels of Bernier, and the *Lettres édifiantes* of Jesuit missionaries. There are also minutes of conversations between Montesquieu and the Chinese traveller Hoange. The extracts consist of an analysis, in varying degrees of detail, of the works read, with an occasional interspersed comment by Montesquieu himself, this comment being introduced by an asterisk. Six-sevenths of the volume is written in the hands of secretaries, the remaining seventh being in the President's hand.

[1] Hardy, *Memoirs of Charlemont*, I, p. 38.

[2] This manuscript is described in my article 'Montesquieu: two unpublished documents' (*FS*, 1950) and by F. Weil, 'Le Manuscrit des *Geographica* et l'*Esprit des Lois*' (*RHLF*, 1952). Extracts from it are printed in Nagel II.

Secretaries were indeed extensively used by Montesquieu, and from 1715 onwards he does not seem to have been without. Very little is known about their identity.[1] They were numerous, the hands of nineteen being distinguishable in the manuscripts. Some served the President for but a short time, perhaps not more than a few weeks. Some were employed also, either at the same time or later, by the Academy of Bordeaux. The names of some of them are known, but with varying degrees of reliability. His daughter, Denise, boasted that she had been her father's secretary, and there is no reason to think that he did not make occasional use of her, though no traces survive. In the first four years after the publication of the *Considérations*, Montesquieu had but one secretary, possibly a disaffected Benedictine of Saint-Maur.[2] In 1739 and 1740 he had two secretaries. In 1742 he may have had as many as six. At times, no doubt, they acted as amanuenses, copying out anew pages which had become so charged with alterations and corrections as to be well-nigh illegible. Often it was the duty of the secretary to read to Montesquieu when his eyes were tired.[3] At times there was an English-speaking secretary,[4] the last one being an Irishman called Florence Fitzpatrick. But the secretaries do not ever seem to have been précis-writers. The analyses contained in the *Geographica* and elsewhere do not, when in the hand of a secretary, differ at all from the passages in Montesquieu's hand in style or method. Spelling mistakes occasionally indicate that they wrote from dictation: 'Cinq-Mars' appears in the *Pensées* as 'Saint-Mars,' in the manuscript of *L'Esprit des lois* as 'Saint-Marc.' Montesquieu himself read the books he analysed, and he drew up the analyses himself.

Montesquieu had already had for some time the habit of making extracts from the books he had read. In his youth, he had applied this technique on a vast scale in the *Collectio juris*; and at an early stage in his life, certainly before his travels, he had made extracts from Petronius, from the work of Hyde on the Persians, from the Koran, from Chardin, and from some periodicals. Most of these have been lost, but references to them in the *Pensées* make it possible approximately to date them. Later, but

[1] See my article, 'Les secrétaires de Montesquieu,' in Nagel II, pp. xxxv–xliii.

[2] Vian, p. 146.

[3] Montesquieu to Charles Yorke, 6 June 1753.

[4] Ibid. and Montesquieu to Hume, 3 September 1749.

still before 1748, there are to be found references to extracts from Plutarch's *Lives*, from Pufendorf, Algernon Sidney, Polybius, and Aristotle. Extracts from Aulus Gellius, Pomponius Mela and Ammianus Marcellinus were probably made as part of the preparations for the *Romains*. In all more than ninety titles of works analysed are known, either through reference or because the manuscript survived, and it would be surprising if there were not many more. Analyses at second-hand, moreover, were made from the *Journal des savants*, the *Histoire des ouvrages des savants* and the *Bibliothèque universelle*.[1]

What is particularly significant about the books in this way analysed by Montesquieu, with some very few exceptions such as *The Craftsman* from which extracts appear in the *Spicilège*, and bearing in mind that extracts from Aristotle, Plato, and Gravina are lost and cannot enter into immediate consideration, is that they are the sources of his evidence and not the sources of his doctrine. The history of the assembly and co-ordination of Montesquieu's ideas is not reducible to a simple formula: his different fields of investigation need separate study. The volumes of extracts are the instrument of his documentation. They necessitated prolonged and arduous toil; and it is revealing that Montesquieu argues that continued idleness, often placed among the joys of paradise, ought instead to be numbered among the torments of hell.[2] Those who paint a picture of the President, elegant in wig and lace, uninterested in knowledge, an idle dilettante and a cultivated epigrammatist at best, are far from the truth. The quality of his documentation is more open to doubt. Gibbon mockingly says that he has 'used and abused the relations of travellers';[3] Boswell reports a dictum of Dr. Johnson:

> Whenever [Montesquieu] wants to support a strange opinion, he quotes you the practice of Japan or of some other distant country, of which he knows nothing. To support polygamy, he tells you of the island of Formosa, where there are ten women born for one man.[4]

It is true that the President's sources are sometimes selected in a

[1] A list of works analysed by Montesquieu is given below, pp. 411–18.

[2] *Pensée* 1085 (Bkn. 2128).

[3] Gibbon, *Decline and Fall*, ed. J. B. Bury, III, p. 75, n. 11.

[4] Boswell, *The Tour to the Hebrides*, ed. G. B. Hill and L. F. Powell, Oxford, 1950, p. 209.

carefree way, with more thought for the odd than for the representative. But the quality of his information is not to be judged by standards available only to a later age. The letters of missionaries, the accounts of returned travellers, written sometimes in order to impress or to amuse rather than to inform, were the most reliable sources on which anyone could draw for information about the east; and when Montesquieu discusses Europe or the Mediterranean basin, his authorities are more sober. The abnormal and the out-of-the-way, moreover, present a greater challenge to the historian and the philosopher, and a system which aims at completeness must explain them as readily as it explains the commonplace and the well-known.

'Il fallait beaucoup lire, et il fallait faire très peu d'usage de ce qu'on avait lu', the President says to himself.[1] An example of his method of using his sources can be taken from the *Lettres édifiantes*. The *XIe Recueil* of these letters, published at Paris in 1715, gives the text of a letter from Gabriel Marest to Germon, both Jesuits, written from the Illinois village Cascaskias on 9 November 1712. It contains the following sentence, which appears on p. 315:

> Nos sauvages ne sont pas accoutumés à cueillir le fruit aux arbres; ils croyent faire mieux d'abattre les arbres mêmes: ce qui est cause qu'il n'y a presque aucun arbre fruitier aux environs des villages.

In the manuscript *Geographica II* there appears (fl. 317v) in the hand of Montesquieu, an extract, followed by his personal comment:

> Les sauvages, pour cueillir le fruit des arbres, abattent les arbres mêmes, ce qui fait qu'il n'y a que peu d'arbres fruitiers autour du village. C'est l'image des rois despotiques.[2]

The passage appears again in the manuscript of *L'Esprit des lois:* but the page is new and bears only the handwriting of Montesquieu—which means that the text had been so altered and corrected that it had to be rewritten entirely. The manuscript carries the same text as the edition. It is now the thirteenth chapter of Book V:

> Quand les sauvages de la Louisiane veulent avoir du fruit, ils coupent l'arbre au pied, et cueillent le fruit. Voilà le gouvernement despotique.

[1] *Pensée* 1862 (Bkn. 189).
[2] Nagel III, p. 958 (slightly altered).

In this way it can be seen how the text read by Montesquieu is transformed, passing through his notebook, and becomes one of the most famous chapters of *L'Esprit des lois*.[1]

The physical substitution of one page for another is a technique which is several times used in *L'Esprit des lois*. The manuscript as it exists now in the Bibliothèque Nationale consists of three different papers. The earliest is a paper of slightly smaller size than the rest. Apart from subsequent corrections, it is written in a hand which dates from 1739 to 1741. It represents an early draft of the work of which only this modest residue—twenty-four chapters in all—remains. The rest of the manuscript, of slightly larger format, falls into two parts, differentiated by the paper. One paper, finer in texture and with a different watermark which in fact bears the date 1742, is subsequent to the other, and its use indicates in some cases later composition, in other cases later revision: it is often impossible to say which. The study of the paper of the manuscript alone discloses the existence of three different and successive phases of composition. The study of the handwriting complicates the problem and multiplies the phases. The chronological study of the sources expands and enriches the study of the manuscript, and leads to conclusions which, though much more tentative, are also much more abundant, and enable one to see the chronological sequence of *L'Esprit des lois*.

Within each chronological phase, however, even leaving on one side those moving pages where Montesquieu, his eyesight failing, writes in a large, sprawling, and child-like hand,[2] there are fascinating evidences of revision, such as are afforded by very few major authors. Two examples of this may be given. The first is taken from the famous ironical chapter, *De l'esclavage des nègres* (XV, 5). The third sentence of this chapter originally read:

[1] A recent study of the *Geographica* by Mlle F. Weil ('Les *Geographica* et l'*Esprit des lois*', in *RHLF*, 1952) has made some important generalizations about Montesquieu's use of his sources. When the extracts from a book have been made, Montesquieu refers thereafter to them and not to the original, and in some cases his page references, even when published, are to the pages of *Geographica* and not to the pages of the original. He not infrequently modifies the text, in order to improve either grammar or comprehensibility. He rarely uses, in *L'Esprit des lois*, any extracts on which, in *Geographica*, he has not made a personal comment introduced by an asterisk. From time to time he is found to solicit the text, and to generalize from single instances.

[2] Such pages are, for example, pp. 126, 141, and 142 of vol. III of the manuscript (*Lois*, XIII, 12, 16, and 17).

Le sucre serait trop cher, si l'on ne faisait travailler la plante qui le produit par des esclaves, et si on les traitait avec quelque humanité.

The first change was the complete deletion of the sentence. The second change was its complete restoration, a marginal annotation saying that it must not be suppressed. Next, this annotation itself is crossed out, and the whole sentence once more deleted. A further repentance causes it to be marked *bon*. It was now transcribed again, but without the last conditional clause:

Le sucre serait trop cher, si l'on ne faisait travailler la plante qui le produit par des esclaves.

In that form it finds its way into the first edition.

The other example which may usefully be selected shows Montesquieu hesitating for reasons which are not of an exclusively stylistic order. It is the beginning of Book XXV, dealing with laws in relation to religion. The original reading of the first chapter of this book after the title, *Des motifs d'attachement pour une religion*, runs thus:

Les hommes pieux et les athées parlent toujours de religion, l'un parle de ce qu'il aime, l'autre parle de ce qu'il craint. Dans les gouvernements modérés les hommes sont plus attachés à la morale et moins à la religion; dans les pays despotiques ils sont plus attachés à la religion et moins à la morale.

The first revision consists of the insertion, at the beginning of the second sentence, of the weakening phrase, 'On pourrait peut-être dire que', and of the substitution twice of 'déterminés par' for 'attachés à'. The second revision consists of the deletion of the whole of the second sentence, with its bold and 'philosophical' generalization. The third revision, not shown in the manuscript but presented by the first edition, consists of the creation of a new first chapter, with the title *Du sentiment pour la religion*, preceding the old first chapter which now becomes the second, and consisting of a single sentence detached from the following chapter but slightly modified:

L'homme pieux et l'athée parlent toujours de religion; l'un parle de ce qu'il aime, et l'autre de ce qu'il craint.

This method of composition shows, not merely that the surviving manuscript of *L'Esprit des lois* cannot be described as the *premier jet*, but that there never was, and never could have been, a manuscript legitimately so described. When any passage for which material sufficient for this investigation is available is traced back to its starting point, that starting point is found to be something other than and prior to *L'Esprit des lois*. Dictation was the method by which both the original extracts and the revisions were made, and signs of this method are seen in such phrases as 'Voyez, je vous prie'.[1] But the form in which the text of the work survives is not the result of spontaneous dictation. Buffon, disapproving of the concision and the elliptic character of Montesquieu's style, said that there was a physical reason for it. The President, he said, was almost blind, and

> il était si vif que la plupart du temps il oubliait ce qu'il voulait dicter, en sorte qu'il était obligé de se resserrer dans le moindre espace possible.[2]

Buffon is wrong. Montesquieu's finished product was the result of continued and deliberate transference of sentences from one place to another, of intentional polishing, of conscious pursuit of the epigram and the paradox, of the constant suppression of the redundant and of the intermediate link between two ideas, of the rearranging of a sequence of ideas so that the consequence precedes the cause.

Montesquieu claimed that he had spent twenty years of his life writing *L'Esprit des lois*, but that twenty years was far from long enough.[3]

IV. THE SEQUENCE OF COMPOSITION

When the *Considérations sur les Romains* were published in 1734, the chapter on the English constitution was ready.[4] Late in 1734 or early in 1735 the final decision to write *L'Esprit des lois* was made. Montesquieu's correspondence meanwhile is silent and discloses nothing about the progress of the work until late in 1741. It is then to Barbot that Montesquieu writes to say how hard he is working:

> A l'égard de mes *Lois*, j'y travaille huit heures par jour. L'ouvrage est immense, et je crois avoir perdu tout le temps où je travaille à

[1] *Lois*, V, 14; XXI, 9.
[2] Hérault de Séchelles, *Voyage à Montbar*, Paris, an IX, pp. 54–55.
[3] *Pensée* 1920 (Bkn. 202).
[4] Secondat, *Mémoire*, p. 401.

quelque autre chose qu'à cela. Il y aura quatre volumes in-12 en vingt-quatre livres . . . J'en suis extrêmement enthousiasmé; je suis mon premier admirateur; je ne sais si je serai le dernier.[1]

It is early in 1742 that he announces that eighteen books are completed and the other six are roughly prepared.[2]

The eighteen books which were ready were not Books I-XVIII. They appear to have started with Book III, then envisaged (it appears from the manuscript) as the first, and to have included also V, VIII, IX, XI, XIV, XV, XVII, XX, XXI, and XXIV, and some of the intervening books. What fine things he could do now, he exclaims, if only he could use his eyes. When he returns to Bordeaux (he is writing now from Paris), he will allow Barbot a sight of the manuscript. A little later, in an incompletely dated letter, he announces the completion of nineteen books, which he will show to Barbot and his own cousin Loyac when he comes to Bordeaux.[3] In September 1743, he returns to Guyenne; the next mention of the work is in a letter almost a year later to Guasco, to whom he confides that the work is advancing with giant's strides since he has ceased to be dissipated by the dinners of Paris.[4] It is indeed on his return from Paris that, with a new secretary, he begins a systematic revision of the whole work, dealing with style, subject-matter, and arrangement.

On 12 February 1745, in Barbot's house, at ten in the morning, he began to read his work to Barbot, Guasco, and his son Jean-Baptiste. All that is known of this meeting is that Montesquieu showed himself most amenable to suggestions for alterations.[5] It was about this time, and perhaps as a result of this reading, that he embarked on the second revision of the work. Not long after he wrote somewhat despondently to Cerati, 'L'ouvrage recule à cause de son immensité.'[6] Less than a year later he tells the learned Italian that six months' work only remains;[7] by the end of 1746, indeed, Montesquieu having now returned to Paris, the book is written and there remains but the final transcription on which he

[1] Montesquieu to Barbot, 20 December 1741.
[2] Ibid., 2 February 1742. [3] Ibid., 1742 (Nagel III, pp. 1031–2).
[4] Montesquieu to Guasco, 1 August 1744.
[5] Ibid, 10 February 1745, with Guasco's note (*Lettres familières*, XI).
[6] Montesquieu to Cerati, 16 June 1745.
[7] Ibid., 19 April 1746 (*FS*, 1958).

then embarks.[1] It is towards the end of June 1747, that he writes to Maupertuis, 'J'ai, grâce à Dieu, fini les ouvrages que j'avais commencés'; he feels happy as a boy let out of school.[2]

V. THE PUBLICATION

Meanwhile the problem of publication was being studied by Montesquieu, with the assistance of Guasco.[3] The conditions of censorship made it inexpedient to attempt to publish in France; French relations with Holland not being good, the President abandoned the idea which he had had of confiding the work to a Dutch publisher. It was to Switzerland therefore that he turned. Now in the summer of 1747 Pierre Mussard, a Swiss diplomat who was remotely related to Rousseau,[4] was in Paris, charged with the negotiation of treaty between the French and Genevan governments. Here he often saw Montesquieu and was highly thought of by him. Eventually the President asked him if he would accept the task of arranging the publication of *L'Esprit des lois*. Mussard undertook this responsibility with joy and loyally devoted himself to the task, bearing the manuscript with him to Geneva. Here, with venial indiscretion, he showed the work to a friend who was well known to the scientist Bonnet, to whom the chapters dealing with religion were read, and Bonnet's immediate reaction was an earnest of the informed applause which was to come. The scientist says that he felt a whole series of new sensations; he was transported with joy, surprise, and admiration. Here, he says (and he was unaware of the author's identity) was an intellect above the level of mankind; a great revolution in the world of thought was to be brought about.[5]

Mussard found a publisher in Barrillot, whom Rousseau describes as one of the worthiest men he had ever known,[6] and who

[1] The manuscript of the Bibliothèque Nationale represents this stage of the work; the final transcription is lost.

[2] Montesquieu to Maupertuis, late June 1747.

[3] See F. Gebelin, 'La Publication de l'*Esprit des lois*' (*Revue des bibliothèques*, 1924).

[4] Rousseau, *Correspondance générale*, I, p. 347.

[5] C. Bonnet, *Mémoires autobiographiques*, ed. R. Savioz, Paris, 1948, pp. 138–41.

[6] Rousseau, *Confessions*, p. 215.

had just published the *Principes du droit naturel* of Burlamaqui. To supervise the details of publication and to correct the proofs he selected a celebrated professor and minister of the Calvinist Church. This was Jacob Vernet, whom Montesquieu had known in Rome but had lost sight of since; he had been the protector of Giannone, and he combined an intelligent regard for enlightenment with an arbitrary and domineering personality.

The type was now being set up in Geneva and Guasco was at work on an Italian translation.[1] Montesquieu, after a recuperative visit to the Polish Court at Lunéville, prepared a new edition of the *Considérations sur les Romains*. But that was not the end of his labours. Using material assembled many years before, he wrote, or rewrote, Book XXVI on the applicability of laws, where the influence of Domat is most marked, and Book XXIX on the composition of laws. Pressed by Vernet, he embarked on three more books, the most arduous of all to write; Book XXVIII on the development of the civil laws of the Franks, and Books XXX and XXXI on the theory of feudal laws. It is at this time that he is seen from the registers to have borrowed from the Bibliothèque du Roi the *Grand Coutumier*, Brussel on fiefs, Muratori, Congringius, Du Cange on Saint Louis, Bouhier on the *Coutume de Bourgogne*, Loyseau, and Papon, as well as some older works. He tells Cerati that the book on the civil laws of the Franks will be read in three hours but has taken three months to write, and his hair has turned white in the process.[2] Letter after letter from Vernet demands the books on feudal laws. Eventually, in September 1748, they arrive in Geneva, and Vernet, who has now received the entire work, writes to the President that he can say more justly than Ovid [*sic*], *Exegi monumentum*, and that he has given fine lessons to kings and to peoples.[3] Montesquieu, for his part, as the work nears its end, confides to his notebook the reflection that he has built a temple to *ennui* and to patience.[4]

An intention to dedicate the work to the Prince of Wales[5] was abandoned; but the second volume, starting with Book XX, was to open with an *Invocation aux Muses*, a page of lyrical prose in which the author expresses the faith which had sustained him

[1] Montesquieu to Guasco, 17 July 1747.
[2] Montesquieu to Cerati, 28 March 1748.
[3] Vernet to Montesquieu, 11 September 1748.
[4] *Pensée* 1933 (Bkn. 406). [5] *Pensée* 1860 (Bkn. 186).

through his toils, the belief that the graces of literature should adorn the severest of researches. He begs the Muses to enable him to conceal his labours, and to disguise his thoughts as feelings. Vernet would not tolerate this, and Montesquieu's page of rhetoric was excised from *L'Esprit des lois* against his wishes.

A number of other changes were made in the course of printing. A chapter on the government of the Netherlands was excised lest it should inconvenience French foreign policy. A hostile comment on Richelieu was modified; and five criticisms of monarchy were slightly attenuated.[1]

It had become known that Montesquieu was about to publish something. When in the course of 1748 *Les Mœurs*, by Toussaint, was published and then banned, Chesterfield, for one, thought that its author was Montesquieu.[2] The Chevalier de Jaucourt was better informed, for his cousin wrote to him from Geneva on 13 October 1747, saying that a work entitled *L'Esprit des lois* was being printed and that it was attributed to 'un de vos plus beaux esprits'—an attribution, he says, which it will be easy to test when the work has appeared.[3]

Although the town of Geneva had certain privileges regarding the exportation of books into France,[4] difficulties often arose. It was not easy for Jaucourt to receive even the innocuous treatise of Burlamaqui, for in 1747 everything printed at Geneva was suspect in the eyes of the customs officers. Vernet was not slow to point out to Montesquieu that there was at Lyons a Chambre syndicale which was prone to seize anything of interest entering France from Switzerland.[5] But these difficulties could be circumvented. The French resident in Geneva, Lévesque de Champeaux,

[1] Some of these changes were made when the type had already been set up, and in order to effect them it was necessary to use cancels. Fifteen leaves were detached in various places in the work (11 in vol. I and 4 in vol. II) and amended leaves were stuck in to replace them. The still visible stubs of the old leaves excited several generations of scholars. The problem has now been settled by the examination, by P. E. Schazmann and J. Brethe de La Gressaye of copies, to be found in the Bibliothèque de l'Arsenal and at Berne, containing the original and not very different readings. See P. E. Schazmann, 'Première édition et premier tirage de l'*Esprit des lois*' (*Congrès 1955*).

[2] Chesterfield to Mme de Monconseil, 5 September 1748, O.S. (*Lettres*, ed. Dobrée, IV, p. 1213).

[3] Caze to Jaucourt, 13 October 1747 (Bibliothèque V. Cousin, MS. V, no. 24).

[4] E. de Budé, *Vie de Jacob Vernet*, Lausanne, 1893, p. 130.

[5] Vernet to Montesquieu, 4 September 1748, and 4 November 1748.

was approached by Vernet and exerted himself considerably to facilitate the passage of the work into France. He intervened with Pallu, the intendant of Lyons, prevailing on him to act as intermediary and to permit copies of *L'Esprit des lois* destined for Bordeaux to be addressed to him. Both Champeaux and Pallu, by a fortunate coincidence, had been members of the Entresol twenty years before, and were not ill disposed towards the progress of enlightenment. Champeaux undertook to send copies to Madame de Tencin and to the Chancellor of France, D'Aguesseau. Barrillot's son, who had now succeeded his deceased father, prepared to send two or three hundred copies to England, where a considerable sale was expected; the author was to receive himself seventy copies which were to be sent to an address in Holland. These were the preparations for the publication of *L'Esprit des lois*. At the last moment the preface was lost, and then found again. The work appeared towards the end of October 1748. The dialogue of praise and blame was not slow to begin.

XI

MONTESQUIEU'S CONCEPTION OF LAW

I. LEGAL PARADOXES

MONTESQUIEU ends his preface with bold words:

> Si cet ouvrage a du succès, je le devrai beaucoup à la majesté de mon sujet; cependant je ne crois pas avoir totalement manqué de génie. Quand j'ai vu ce que tant de grands hommes en France et en Allemagne[1] ont écrit avant moi, j'ai été dans l'admiration, mais je n'ai point perdu le courage: *et moi aussi je suis peintre*, ai-je dit avec le Corrège.

He was prepared for success. He was disinclined, at this first moment, to compromise. He sought to give a vigorous jerk to the minds of his readers, to dazzle by paradox.

He opens his first chapter, the most metaphysical of the entire work, with a definition of laws. They are 'les rapports nécessaires qui dérivent de la nature des choses'. He proceeds immediately, this assertion made, to declare that God is subject to laws, citing as his evidence a dictum from Plutarch's *Moralia*, that the law is king over all mortals and immortals.

This was a surprising attitude to law, and a surprising definition, to come from the pen of one who had been a celebrated magistrate and who was still known by the title of President. The jurists of the past, whose example he claimed to be following, had given far different definitions. For Grotius, a law was 'a rule of moral actions, obliging us to that which is just and reasonable' or in the original Latin, 'regula actuum moralium, obligans ad id quod rectum est'.[2] For Pufendorf, law is 'une volonté d'un supérieur, par laquelle il impose à ceux qui dépendent de lui d'agir d'une certaine manière qu'il leur prescrit'.[3] For Burlamaqui, law is to be defined basically as 'une règle prescrite par le souverain d'une société à ses sujets'.[4] Hobbes meanwhile had defined law as 'the command of that person, whether man or court, whose precept

[1] It is only in the second edition, published in 1749, that he acknowledged a wider debt by adding here the words *en Angleterre*.

[2] *De jure belli ac pacis*, I, i, IX (Amsterdam, 1712, p. 8).

[3] *Le Droit de la nature et des gens*, tr. Barbeyrac, Amsterdam, 1712, 2 vols., p. 89.

[4] *Principes du droit naturel*, Geneva, 1747, p. 89.

contains in it the reason of obedience';[1] while for Aquinas law was 'regula quaedam et mensura actuum, secundum quam inducitur aliquis ad agendum, vel ab agendo retrahitur'.[2] Nor was this anything other than the normal sense of the word admitted by lexicographers. The 1695 edition of the dictionary of the French Academy knows no other meaning of the word *loi* than: 'constitution écrite qui ordonne ce qu'il faut faire et qui défend ce qu'il ne faut pas faire'.

Montesquieu's use of the word *loi* was totally different and the bewilderment or even the ire of his commentators is not astonishing. The hostile Bonnaire inquires how a relationship, however necessary, can be regarded as a law. A tree, he says, has a relationship with the earth whence it draws its sap; but is it a law that a tree should be planted in the ground?[3] A far more intelligent and more sympathetic commentator exclaims at the beginning of his first chapter, 'Une loi n'est pas un rapport et un rapport n'est pas une loi.'[4] It is certainly clear that Montesquieu's juristic precursors and their disciples are speaking one language, and he is speaking another.

A calm and patient criticism from an admirer is supplied as early as 1751. David Hume describes Montesquieu as an 'author of great genius, as well as extensive learning'; he praises his entire work as 'the best system of political knowledge that, perhaps, has ever yet been communicated to the world', but he is uneasy about the opening chapters, which he thinks incompatible with the rest:

This illustrious writer sets out with a different theory, and supposes all right to be founded on certain *rapports* or relations; which is a system that, in my view, will never reconcile with true philosophy. Father Malebranche, as far as I can learn, was the first that started this abstract theory of morals, which was afterwards adopted by Dr. Clarke and others; and as it excludes all sentiment, and pretends to found everything on reason, it has not wanted followers in this philosophic age.[5]

[1] *De cive* (*English Works*, ed. Sir W. Molesworth, II, London, 1841, p. 183).

[2] *Summa theologica*, I, II, q. xc, art. I.

[3] Bonnaire, *L'Esprit des lois quintessencié*, s.l., 1751, I, p. 28.

[4] Destutt de Tracy, *Commentaire sur l'Esprit des lois de Montesquieu*, Paris, 1819, p. 1.

[5] Hume, *An Enquiry concerning the principles of morals*, London, 1751, pp. 54–55. In later editions Hume added to the names of Malebranche and Clarke that of Cudworth.

Malebranche indeed, whom Montesquieu was very ready to admire, had in his *Traité de morale* expressed the ideas attributed to him by Hume. Although he makes no express definition of a law as a relationship, he comes near to doing so on more than one occasion in the first chapter of this work. An example is afforded by these lines:

> Puisque la vérité et l'ordre sont des rapports de grandeur et de perfection réels, immuables, nécessaires, rapports que renferme la substance du verbe, celui qui voit ces rapports voit ce que Dieu voit, celui qui règle son amour sur ces rapports suit une loi que Dieu aime invinciblement.[1]

Samuel Clarke, insisting on the existence of rigid and ascertainable relationships between things, attributes a normative value to these relationships:

> Il y a donc dans la nature des choses des règles de convenance, et ces règles sont éternelles, nécessaires, et immuables. C'est ainsi qu'en pensent toutes les créatures intelligentes . . . et c'est ici, pour le dire en passant, que je trouve le vrai fondement de la morale.[2]

The likelihood of Clarke's having been used by Montesquieu is increased when it is seen that the Englishman's text contains a vigorous denial of the role of chance in the operations of the world[3] and also an insistence that God is bound by his own laws:

> L'Etre suprême . . . doit toujours agir conformément aux règles les plus sévères de la bonté, de la vérité, de la justice, et des autres perfections morales. C'est une affaire de nécessité, à prendre ce terme, non pas dans le sens des fatalistes pour une nécessité aveugle et absolue, mais pour une nécessité morale.[4]

Montesquieu is thus seen, already, to lean for his legal concepts on writers who were far from being lawyers or even deeply interested in jurisprudence.

[1] Malebranche, *Traité de morale*, pt. I, ch. I, xiv (Paris, 1953, p. 6).

[2] *De l'existence et des attributs de Dieu*, Amsterdam, 1717, p. 175; *Discourse concerning the Being and Attributes of God*, London, 1728, p. 112. I quote from the French translation because (although Montesquieu owned the English edition of 1728) the verbal similarities to Montesquieu are greater in the case of the French text. It has already (p. 71 above) been seen probable that Montesquieu drew on Clarke in his *Traité des devoirs*.

[3] Ibid. p. 4 (French), p. 5 (English).

[4] Ibid., p. 176 (French), p. 113 (English).

II. NATURAL LAW

If in relation to the definition of law Montesquieu is found in general disagreement with the standard juristic authorities of his day, his attitude to the problem of natural law seems at the first glance to be very like theirs. In 1748 the doctrines of the natural law school of jurists were as clear and accessible as they had ever been. Grotius had long before given his celebrated definition of natural law as

> Dictatum rectae rationis, indicans actui alicui, ex eius convenientia aut disconvenientia cum ipsa natura rationali, inesse moralem turpitudinem, aut necessitatem moralem, ac consequenter ab auctore naturae Deo talem actum aut vetari aut praecipi.[1]

The year before the publication of *L'Esprit des lois*, Burlamaqui who though but a compiler was a successful one and a representative figure, had published his manual of natural law at Geneva, and had printed in it the following definition:

> L'on entend par loi naturelle, une loi que Dieu impose à tous les hommes, et qu'ils peuvent découvrir et connaître par les seules lumières de leur raison, en considérant avec attention leur nature et leur état.[2]

Natural law was seen as consisting of *a priori*, God-given precepts rationally discoverable.

More significant in relation to Montesquieu than Burlamaqui and even than Grotius was the last Frenchman to produce a sustained and intelligent exposition of the philosophical basis of law. This was the Jansenist Jean Domat, a friend of Port-Royal, who had attended Pascal on his death-bed. Domat was a magisstrate by profession, and D'Aguesseau as a young man had studied under him. The great monument of his life was his legal treatise, *Les Lois civiles dans leur ordre naturel*,[3] which he himself admired to the point of expressing his surprise that God had used so feeble an agent—'un homme de néant comme moi'—to execute so great a work.[4] The preface to his work possesses the dimensions of a book itself. It has the title *Traité des lois*, and its eleventh and most important chapter is headed *De la nature et de l'esprit des lois*. Perhaps it was here that Montesquieu found

[1] Grotius, op. cit., I, i, X (pp. 9–10).
[2] Burlamaqui, op. cit., p. 142.
[3] Paris, 1689–94.
[4] Sainte-Beuve, *Port-Royal*, Paris, 1908, V, pp. 520–2.

the title for his own work. In any case he possessed Domat's treatise in its first edition, and his copy bears, in this eleventh chapter, frequent underlinings and crosses in the margins.

Laws for Domat are of two kinds: immutable laws, and arbitrary laws. Arbitrary laws are made by men, and are what are more usually called positive laws. Immutable laws, which he occasionally calls natural laws, are made by God. They are justice itself. They are absolute; they govern the past and future alike; they must be studied by the man who seeks to understand law; and they will be found, if studied, to rest on initial principles, which can be discovered by a rational investigation of man's nature and his end. Domat, like other natural law theorists, believes in the anteriority of justice and of natural law to human society and to man-made law.

As early as 1721 Montesquieu had asserted that justice is eternal and is independent of human conventions;[1] in 1725, in the *Traité des devoirs* he had insisted that justice is not dependent on human laws,[2] and that in fact justice is older than human society:

> Si [les hommes] établissent les sociétés, c'est par un principe de justice. Ils l'avaient donc.[3]

In *L'Esprit des lois* he speaks the same language:

> Avant qu'il y eût des lois faites, il y avait des rapports de justice possibles. Dire[4] qu'il n'y a rien de juste ni d'injuste que ce qu'ordonnent ou défendent les lois positives, c'est dire qu'avant qu'on eût tracé de cercle, les rayons n'étaient pas égaux.[5]

There are then for Montesquieu certain principles of justice, or certain laws, older than human society, and on which human society is founded. He is seen to be at one with the theorists of natural law. His language is their language. His opposition to empirical doctrines of natural law is their opposition. His interpretation of Hobbes, and his hostility to Hobbes, are their interpretation and their hostility.

This is not, however, an end of the question. In order to discover what ideas he encloses in the framework of his natural law

[1] *L.P.* 83. [2] Nagel III, p. 160; Pléiade I, p. 109.
[3] *Pensée* 1226 (Bkn. 615).
[4] The manuscript adds here the words, later crossed out, 'avec Hobbes'.
[5] *Lois*, I, 1.

system, it is necessary to examine the second chapter of Book I, and in addition the various isolated references he makes to *loi naturelle, loi de la nature,* and *droit naturel.*[1]

About Montesquieu's investigation of natural law two negative things can first be said. The first is that he is not interested in speculation on the pre-social condition of mankind or the mode of its emergence from that condition into the State. In the *Lettres persanes* he had ridiculed research on the origin of society,[2] and in *L'Esprit des lois* he dismisses the whole question rapidly, displaying only the most meagre, if any, interest either in evidence of the kind afforded by a wild man found in Hanover during the reign of George I, or in the hypothesis of social contract.

Nor is he tempted by the psychological and teleological approach of Domat. For the Jansenist lawyer, echoing the arguments expressed by Pascal in his then unpublished fragment *De l'esprit géométrique,* derives from the two human faculties of *entendement* and *volonté* the first law governing man, that he should seek and love God, and next the second law, that he should unite with and love his fellow men. Montesquieu seems, indeed, expressly to be opposing Domat when he asserts that belief in God, though it may be the most important natural law, is not chronologically the first.

The sum of Montesquieu's natural laws can be divided into two lists:

[1] I have not taken into account here the *Essai touchant les lois naturelles et la distinction du juste et de l'injuste,* which has been recently published (Nagel III, pp. 175–99). The external evidence for attributing it to Montesquieu is flimsy, consisting simply of an annotation on a manuscript copy. The style is feeble and unlike the President's. There are certain resemblances in doctrine. Some of these are to be explained by use of a common source (Pufendorf or Cicero), others as imitations of Montesquieu. The differences in doctrine are to my mind more striking than the likenesses. The prominence of the role of the divinity, the exclusively normative character of the notion of law, the conventional unoriginality of the notion of natural law, are features of the *Essai* which make Montesquieu's authorship of it unlikely. Perhaps more conclusive still is the absence from the *Essai* of those legal notions which were held by Montesquieu both in the *Lettres persanes* and in *L'Esprit des lois,* it being conceded that the *Essai,* if by Montesquieu, was written about 1725. In spite of the able arguments of M. Védère (Nagel III, pp. 175–8) and of M. Dimoff (*RHLF,* 1957), I cannot accept the attribution of the *Essai* to Montesquieu, and am strengthened in my refusal by the support of M. Brethe de La Gressaye. I am inclined to attribute it to a not very intelligent disciple, writing some twenty or thirty years after Montesquieu's death.

[2] *L.P.* 94.

List I

Peace	*Lois*, I, 2
Feeding oneself	do.
Sexual attraction	do.
Life in society	do.
Belief in God	do.
Reproduction at a certain age	*Lois*, XXVI, 3, 14
Attainment of mental maturity at a certain age	*Lois*, XXVI, 3
Freedom and independence by birth	*Pensée* 174 (Bkn. 1935)
Reasonableness	do.
Equality	*Lois*, XV, 7
The fear of death	*rejet* of *Lettres persanes*[1]
Self-preservation	*Lois*, I, 1; X, 3

List II

To defend oneself	*Lois*, VI, 13; X, 2, 3; XXIV, 11
To defend 'la pudeur naturelle'	*Lois*, XXVI, 3
That a woman should not accuse her husband, or a son his father	*Lois*, XXVI, 4
That a son should be grateful to his father for benefits received	*Lois*, XXVI, 5
That parents should educate their children	*Lois*, XXVI, 14
That parents should feed their children	*Lois*, XXVI, 6
That a son should respect his mother and a wife her husband	*Lois*, XXVI, 14
To eschew onanism and homosexuality	*Pensée* 205 (Bkn. 1928)
Negatively, it is not required that children should inherit from their parents	*Lois*, XXVI, 6

Of these two lists the second is much inferior in importance to the first. It consists of injunctions on points of detail, often no more than mentioned in passing. They are for the most part contained in Book XXVI, where Montesquieu's thought is largely nourished by Domat, but where his concern is with a

[1] Pléiade I, p. 1591 (not in Nagel).

subject, highly interesting, it is true, in itself and intelligently handled by him, but peripheral to his main preoccupation. He is treating laws, *dans le rapport qu'elles doivent avoir avec l'ordre des choses sur lesquelles elles statuent*. He is more nearly here a practical lawyer than anywhere else in *L'Esprit des lois*: a fact which makes Book XXVI not less interesting, perhaps, but certainly less characteristic.

A more conclusive reason for the smaller importance of the second list is that the natural laws it contains are simply derived notions based on the initial body of natural laws in the first list. They are wholly contingent on that initial body; they imply the acceptance of it, and they have no independent status themselves. The laws of the first list are in no case laws in which the term has been seen to be used by the jurists. Montesquieu does not say that man has an obligation to feed himself, but that man does in fact feed himself. He does not say that man ought to believe in God, that he ought to be born free, that he ought to be reasonable, but that man does in fact, whether rightly or wrongly, believe in God, that he is in fact born free, that he is in fact reasonable. These laws are not normative. They are descriptive of man's condition. They express no prescriptions, and they are alien to the ordinary conceptions of jurisprudence.[1] They are not natural laws in the sense known to Grotius, Pufendorf, Burlamaqui, or Domat.[2] They are closer to the scientific concept of a law of nature as a law of movement, as used by Descartes,[3] by Montesquieu[4] himself, and made famous by Pope in his epitaph on Newton:

> Nature and Nature's laws lay hid in night;
> God said, Let Newton be; and all was light.

[1] The distinction between the descriptive law of self-preservation and the normative law, that one should defend oneself, illustrates the difference between the two kinds of law: capital punishment for perjury is deplored because it offends the normative law that one should defend oneself (*Lois*, VI, 13); the right of a conqueror is explained as being founded in part on the descriptive law that 'tout tend à la conservation des espèces' (*Lois*, X, 3).

[2] Domat himself uses in one place a descriptive law of nature, when he discusses the conflict between the natural law that a man of mature mind should control his own affairs, and the natural law (the word law being legitimately inferred from the context) that all men do not reach maturity at the same time (ch. XI, §ix, marked in the margin in Montesquieu's copy).

[3] *Les Principes de la philosophie*, II, §37 (Rouen, 1698, pp. 109–10).

[4] *Pensée* 1096 (Bkn. 672).

This scientific concept of a law of nature, though not identical with the notion of law as a relationship, has undoubtedly something in common with it. It attempts to define the relationship between contending opposed forces in the realm of nature, between two different motive powers, or between a motive power and the force of inertia. It attempts to characterize or to define the operations of a part of the material universe or, in Cartesian terms, of extended substance. What Montesquieu attempts to do, on the other hand, by means of his descriptive laws of nature, is systematically to characterize the activities of man in relation to nature, to reduce them to certain simple principles. Having done this, he proceeds in the rest of his book to take these descriptive principles and treat them as normative principles, insisting, albeit often tacitly, that they should constitute the basis of social activity and of positive laws.

Such a procedure was not unknown in moral philosophy. Hume had already observed that in every system of morality there is an imperceptible change from propositions containing *is* and *is not*, to propositions containing *ought* and *ought not*;[1] nor was this tendency least evident in the generation which knew Pope's maxim 'Whatever is, is right'.

In legal and political philosophy, however, it was much rarer. The natural law system which reigned scarcely challenged was based on rational and *a priori* abstractions. Montesquieu sought instead to link it with natural science. This is his first originality, and it won him the enthusiastic approval of one of Europe's most celebrated biologists. Charles Bonnet wrote to say:

> Newton a découvert les lois du monde matériel: vous avez découvert, Monsieur, les lois du monde intellectuel.[2]

And he went on specifically to approve the notion of a law as a relationship, and to say that he had himself worked out the elements of a similar theory and might some day develop it.

Jurists had perhaps less reason for admiration, *teste* Monclar, an eminent magistrate of Provence, honoured by D'Aguesseau with the title of *l'ami du bien*, who wrote:

[1] Hume, *A Treatise of Human Nature*, bk. III, pt. I, sect. 1 (Oxford, 1955, p. 469).

[2] Bonnet to Montesquieu, 14 November 1753.

On trouve dans l'auteur de l'*Esprit des lois* l'homme de génie, le philosophe, l'historien; on n'y trouve point assez le jurisconsulte, nourri des principes du droit public.[1]

The legal theorist of 1748 does not owe a great deal to the former *président à mortier*.[2]

III. ULPIAN AND GRAVINA

Montesquieu was not, however, without precursors. Richard Cumberland, Bishop of Peterborough, had in the first chapter of his *De legibus naturae* of 1672 admonished his readers,

That the whole of moral philosophy and of the laws of nature is ultimately resolved into natural observations known by the experience of all men, or into conclusions of true natural philosophy.[3]

His book, though Montesquieu does not seem to have owned it, was available for him to read in the library of the Academy of Bordeaux, and the eminence and reputation of Cumberland suggest that it is far from impossible that his pages were known to Montesquieu.

Even in Roman law itself the notion of a fixed, natural foundation for man-made law was not unknown.[4] The *Corpus iuris civilis* itself provides a text in support:

Ius naturale est, quod natura omnia animalia docuit: nam ius istud non humani generis proprium, sed omnium animalium, quae in terra, quae in mari nascuntur, avium quoque commune est. Hinc descendit maris atque feminae coniunctio, quam nos matrimonium appellamus, hinc liberorum procreatio, hinc educatio.[5]

[1] Cited, from an unpublished manuscript, by F. Sclopis, 'Recherches historiques et critiques sur l'*Esprit des lois* de Montesquieu' (*Memorie della Reale Accademia delle Scienze di Torino*, 1858; *Scienze morali*, ecc., p. 207).

[2] A comparison between political laws and scientific laws of nature had already been made by Montesquieu in 1721 (*L.P.* 97).

[3] *A Treatise of the Laws of Nature*, London [1727], p. 41. This work became available in 1744 in Barbeyrac's French translation, as well as in the original Latin.

[4] J. de Hoschembar-Lyskowski, '*Naturalis ratio* en droit classique romain' (*Studi in onore di Pietro Bonfante*, Milan, 1930, III, pp. 467–98), gives a thorough examination of 'le calcul juridique basé sur la nature des choses'; he claims that 'la nature des choses' is not a juridical principle as such, but gives several examples of its utilization in Roman law, mainly as a result of Greek influences. The most important of these is Ulpian's passage which I am primarily concerned with here.

[5] *Digest*, I, I, 1.

These words, contained in Ulpian's *Institutes* and thence incorporated in the *Digest*, have puzzled, dismayed, and irritated subsequent commentators, from Cujas who succinctly declares 'ius in bruta non cadit' and Pufendorf who insists that this argument is abusing the term of law, to Pollock who stigmatizes it as 'a conceit borrowed from some forgotten Greek rhetorician',[1] and Jolowicz who, regretting its appearance in the *Institutes*, points out that 'it is an isolated opinion in legal literature, and was never made the basis of any consistent theory.'[2]

The commentators on the *Corpus iuris civilis* read by Montesquieu were not more enthusiastic: Ferrière dismisses Ulpian's passage with the words 'cet instinct des animaux n'est appelé droit qu'improprement',[3] while Mornac's *Observationes* on the *Digest* (Montesquieu's original guide to Roman law) and the President's own notes in his *Collectio juris* are silent on this article.

Ulpian's definition of natural law did not, however, fail to produce a certain echo. It is not unmentioned by Aquinas;[4] it is cited by Azo;[5] it is referred to by Vincent of Beauvais when he distinguishes between descriptive and normative laws, insisting that natural law exists in two modes, *in regulante et mensurante*, and *in regulato et mensurato*.[6]

A significant interest in it is found in early eighteenth-century Naples. Vico, in his early work, published in 1720, *De uno universi iuris principio et fine uno*,[7] identified two parts of natural law: *ius naturale prius*, which is physically caused, and *ius naturale posterius*, of immaterial and rational origin. The second of them is defined as *dominium rationis*, *affectuum aequalitas*, *tutela consilii*, while the first is represented as *tutela sensuum et affectuum libertas*.[8]

[1] Sir H. S. Maine, *Ancient Law*, ed. Sir F. Pollock, London, 1909, p. 76.

[2] H. F. Jolowicz, *Historical Introduction to Roman Law*, Cambridge, 1952, p. 105.

[3] C.-J. de Ferrière, *Institutes*, Paris, 1725, I, p. 26.

[4] *Summa theologica*, I, II, q. xciv, art. 2.

[5] *Select Passages from the Works of Bracton and Azo*, ed. F. W. Maitland, London (*Publications of the Selden Society*, VIII), 1895, p. 82.

[6] *Speculum morale*, Strasbourg, 1476, pt. II, dist. ii.

[7] I quote from F. Nicolini's edition, entitled *Il Diritto universale*, Bari, 1936, 3 vols., I, pp. 76–79).

[8] Vico's individualistic Latin can perhaps be rendered as 'the rule of reason, immunity from passion, under the guidance of the intellect' and 'free rein to the passions, under the guidance of the senses'.

When he asks the question 'Ius naturale quid metaphysicis? quid physicis?' Vico's own response, in relation to natural law of the first kind, is in fact to cite Ulpian's definition, and then to identify this notion with the law of motion as enunciated by physicists: *naturalem motus legem.* He sees it illustrated in the animal kingdom, in sexual union, in procreation, in the education of offspring.

Nor is this pregnant identification of Ulpian's concept of nature's lesson to all animals with the scientist's descriptive laws of motion peculiar to Vico. His predecessor Gian Vincenzo Gravina exhibits this same feature; and whether or not Vico's person or works were known to Montesquieu, the writings of Gravina certainly were. He is cited in *L'Esprit des lois*, and elsewhere, in several places, it is disclosed that the President had made an analysis of at least part of the *Origines iuris civilis.*[1]

The second book of this work, entitled *De iure naturali, gentium, et XII. tabularum,*[2] begins with a chapter in which it is stated that philosophers and jurisconsults have often been confused about natural law, being confronted with the problem of a natural law ordering men to resist natural impulses.[3] They find it repugnant that nature should be condemned by her own laws:

ne honestatis lege per naturam constituta, suis ipsamet legibus natura damnetur.[4]

Such a condemnation would indeed result, should both vice and virtue be founded in nature. His own answer to this problem is elucidated in the second section of this book, entitled *De duplici naturae lege.* The first law of nature governs the whole creation, animals and men alike, and in relation to men both their bodies and their souls. This is the 'common law of nature' or the *lex promiscua.* The second law, called the *lex solius mentis*, has since the fall from grace been in constant conflict with the *lex promiscua*,

[1] *Pensées* 1761, 1763, 1912–13 (Bkn. 209 and 254–6).

[2] The *Origines iuris civilis* was first published in its entirety in 1708. My references are to the Naples edition of 1722.

[3] This problem, often examined in the eighteenth century, is crystallized in a stanza which Pope excised from his *Universal Prayer*:

Can sins of moments claim the rod
Of everlasting fires:
And that offend 'gainst Nature's God
Which Nature's self inspires?

[4] *Origines iuris civilis*, p. 111.

and can prevail over it only with the assistance of God. If the empty terms of the scholastics are to be avoided, *lex promiscua* must be defined, and Gravina, having already described it, and being about to describe it again, in Ulpian's words, as 'that which nature has taught all animals', re-defines it in interesting terms:

That all-pervasive motion, which stimulates and activates all things, constantly and simultaneously producing and destroying different things, and creating one from the destruction of another, and without which all things in existence would lie crowded together in an inert and idle mass.[1]

The scientific laws of nature are thus identified with natural law as understood by Ulpian.

So far as his body is concerned, man is subject to the *lex promiscua*; his mind, naturally, is governed by the *lex solius mentis*. No others of God's creatures are exposed in this way to the conflict of two laws, hence man alone is liable to sin: 'solus homo est culpae capax'. The good man therefore will accept that part only of the *lex promiscua* which is consonant with the dictates of the higher law of the mind: to take food, to beget children, to educate them, and only moderately to indulge the senses. In this way only can the conflict between the two laws of nature be resolved: a banal conclusion, and an anticlimax to an analysis which was astute and intelligent. Like other Cartesians, Gravina illustrates the difficulties attendant upon the harmonizing or synchronizing of thought and extension, however ably he has handled them as analytical hypotheses.

The question which now arises, is how Montesquieu proceeds to isolate and identify his descriptive natural laws. This was an important problem in an age of experimental science, and one presenting difficulties which were to be sensibly evaluated by Rousseau:

Ce n'est pas une légère entreprise de démêler ce qu'il y a d'originaire et d'artificiel dans la nature actuelle de l'homme, et de bien connaître un état qui n'existe plus, qui n'a peut-être point existé, qui

[1] 'Motionem illam ubique pervadentem, omniaque cientem, et agitantem, resque varias assiduo producentem simul, et interimentem, ex interituque unius alteram suscitantem: sine qua otiosa et inertia, constipataque forent universa' (p. 112).

probablement n'existera jamais, et dont il est pourtant nécessaire d'avoir des notions justes, pour bien juger de notre état présent.[1]

In order to ascertain the method of investigation followed by Montesquieu, it is necessary to scrutinize the first two chapters of *L'Esprit des lois*, restoring the primitive text as preserved in the manuscript.

The first chapter of the first book, dealing with laws in relation to different beings, contains a discussion of beasts. We do not know, says Montesquieu, whether they are governed simply by the general laws of motion or by a movement of their own. But their relation to God is in any case no closer than that of any other part of the material world. They have their own natural laws: self-preservation, the preservation of the species. They die, but without fearing death. They preserve themselves in general better than man, and they use their passions less badly.

The following chapter enumerates the first of the natural laws which have been tabulated above in List I. But before this enumeration there had previously existed three paragraphs which are still to be found in the manuscript, though they never found their way into the published text:

Les animaux (et c'est surtout chez eux qu'il faut aller chercher le droit naturel) ne font pas la guerre à ceux de leur espèce, parce que, se sentant égaux, ils n'ont point le désir de s'attaquer. La paix est donc la première loi naturelle.

Je sais bien qu'en disant ceci je contredis de très grands hommes mais je les prie de faire réflexion sur ce sentiment de plaisir que chaque animal trouve à l'approche d'un animal de même espèce que lui. Ils ne sont donc pas en état de guerre et vouloir les mettre dans cet état, c'est vouloir leur faire faire ce que les lions ne font pas.

Que si nous voyons des animaux faire la guerre à ceux de leur espèce, ce n'est que dans des cas particuliers et parce que nous les y instruisons pour notre commodité propre.[2]

If this passage is restored as a link between the first and second chapters of *L'Esprit des lois*, it becomes clear that it is the analogy of animals which is Montesquieu's methodological device for the investigation of natural law. The sentence written in parenthesis, 'c'est surtout chez eux qu'il faut aller chercher le droit naturel',

[1] Rousseau, *Discours sur l'inégalité*, preface, in *Political Writings*, ed. C. E. Vaughan, Cambridge, 1915, I, p. 136.

[2] Nagel III, p. 579; Pléiade II (in part only), p. 996.

shows that he has Ulpian in mind. His awareness of the *Origines iuris civilis*, which he cites twice in the next chapter of *L'Esprit des lois*, makes it exceedingly probable that Gravina is his guide.[1]

Both Gravina and Montesquieu claimed to be Cartesians. Had a Gassendist like La Fontaine urged jurists to seek natural law in the study of animals, there would have been no grounds for surprise. But when a like injunction comes from a Cartesian, believing that animals are but machines without any power of thought, a paradox presents itself. Gravina, however, balanced his *lex promiscua* with his *lex solius mentis*, corresponding to the substances of extension and thought, and if he did not succeed in avoiding some difficulties, at least they were the difficulties inherent in Cartesianism. Montesquieu's case is different.

He had boasted in 1721, when discussing the plant kingdom, that he was a whole-hearted Cartesian because he insisted that plants were governed by the general laws of movement, and not by special laws; and in this respect to be a Cartesian meant much more to be a disciple of Malebranche than to be a disciple of Descartes.[2] An extension of the same problem is seen in the discussion just now alluded to of the laws governing beasts. Malebranche has been thought to be a more thorough-going exponent of the automatism of animals than Descartes[3]—'plus intrépide encore que son maître', said Trublet[4]—and stories were told, notably by Fontenelle, of the ferocity with which the mild and gentle Oratorian Father used to treat dogs, asserting that they could not feel.[5] Montesquieu, early in his life, had declared that all movements of animals and plants can be explained in terms of the movements of liquids in pipes; and many years later he explains animal reactions by the analogy of string instruments.[6] Now in *L'Esprit des lois* his express denial to them of any closer

[1] In 1725 (when still unacquainted, I think, with Gravina) he had already toyed with the notion of animal analogy in relation to natural law (*Pensée* 1266, Bkn. 615). This was bound to predispose him favourably towards Gravina's ideas when he met them. It was the Neapolitan, I would claim, who led him to develop the idea systematically and who drew his attention to Ulpian's 'quod natura omnia animalia docuit'.

[2] See above, p. 25.

[3] L. C. Rosenfield, *From Beast-Machine to Man-Machine*, New York, 1941, pp. 265–9.

[4] Trublet, *Mémoires sur M. de Fontenelle* (in Fontenelle, *Œuvres*, Amsterdam, 1764, XI), p. 137.

[5] Ibid. [6] *Pensées* 76 and 1675 (Bkn. 690 and 551).

connexion with God than the rest of the material world is a reaffirmation of their completely material nature.

It follows from this that the natural laws to be learnt from the study of beasts are comparable in their operations to the laws of the physical universe; that they are in fact simply special manifestations (perhaps the most accessible manifestations) of the laws of the physical universe, and that Montesquieu, in identifying these with 'what nature has taught all animals' is adapting, extending, and rejuvenating, within the limits of Cartesian science, the notion of Ulpian.[1]

How far is Montesquieu, then, to be regarded as a Cartesian? On this point there have been diverse opinions.[2] Lanson, writing in 1896 and expressing views which twenty years later he no longer held in their full rigour, claims that *L'Esprit des lois* is constructed in accordance with Cartesian method and asserts that not a single one of its propositions is based on experimental investigation.[3] Sir Isaiah Berlin, on the other hand, declares:

> For all that Montesquieu speaks of Cartesian methods, he does not, fortunately for himself and for posterity, apply them.[4]

Where is the truth found to lie?

Cartesianism, if its philosophy as a whole be considered, was ill equipped for the making of disciples. Exponents of integral Cartesianism after Descartes were not numerous, and the most celebrated of them, Malebranche, had to perfect and modify

[1] When Montesquieu goes on to add to the laws of nature (as he does, though not in *Lois*, I) reasonableness and the attainment of intellectual maturity at a certain age, as well as belief in God (which in *Lois*, I, he accepts, albeit disparagingly, as a law of nature), the analogy of beasts will of course no longer serve, and it was no doubt the realization of this fact which led him to excise from the final text the statement that it is animals which teach us the law of nature. Those laws of nature which, though still descriptive and not normative, have a moral content, are chronologically later in their development than those ascertained by animal analogy. The rational faculty of man is thus a later growth (an idea re-expressed by Rousseau, op. cit., I, pp. 137–8). Cf. Montesquieu's theory of physical and moral causes, discussed below, pp. 313–19.

[2] A thorough and intelligent discussion on this point is given by C.-J. Beyer, 'Montesquieu et l'esprit cartésien' (*Congrès 1955*).

[3] G. Lanson, 'L'influence de la philosophie cartésienne sur la littérature française' (*Revue de métaphysique et de morale*, 1896, reprinted in his *Etudes d'histoire littéraire*, Paris, 1929).

[4] I. Berlin, 'Montesquieu' (*Proceedings of the British Academy*, XLI, London, 1956), p. 275.

his master's system. Several eighteenth-century writers differentiated between the method of Descartes and his metaphysics, accepting the first and rejecting the second. This was the case with Fontenelle, who also remained an adherent of Cartesian physics, and with Bayle, who also, until almost the end of his life, accepted Cartesian epistemology. Descartes wrote no political or legal treatise, and if Domat applied Descartes's method to the study of law, the result was not greatly different from that already arrived at by Grotius.

Of the eighteenth-century followers of Descartes some were more interested in thought and some in extension. Those who were more interested in extension, and who accepted Descartes's purely mechanical explanation of extension, sometimes wrote and thought as if the universe consisted entirely of extended matter and as if thought and mind did not exist. Their denial of all special intervention of the creator in the workings of the material universe, and their refusal to concede to animals any form of reflection, led them not infrequently into at least the appearance of materialism, although the philosophers of whom they regarded themselves as disciples were Descartes and Malebranche.

This is the case with Montesquieu. The framework of his legal system, with its stress on the eternity of justice, has close terminological resemblances with the deductive systems of Grotius and of Domat, and can legitimately be regarded as having Cartesian affinities. Within this framework are found, as his starting point, natural laws reminiscent of Descartes's descriptive and scientific laws of nature. They are ascertained by the method of animal analogy, which (since beasts are machines) involves an exclusion of any rational element.

To this point Montesquieu remains, though not without inconsistencies, under the banner of Descartes.

But he proceeds to base his moral and political system on these rigid *données* of the physical world, and herein his departure, silent and unadmitted, from Cartesianism is signalized. He has become more of an anti-Cartesian than a Cartesian, and so he must finally be defined. But it is in the name of Descartes and Malebranche that he has moved to their rejection.[1] In the name of

[1] A stimulating and independent discussion of the materialist potentialities of Cartesianism is contained in A. Vartanian, *Diderot and Descartes*, Princeton, 1953.

rationalism, he has moved from a rationally to an empirically based moral system, a journey which an engaging comment in the *Pensées* shows he did not make unwittingly:

A peine eus-je lu quelques ouvrages de jurisprudence, que je la regardai comme un pays où la Raison voulait habiter sans la Philosophie.[1]

IV. SPINOZISM

The opponents of Montesquieu were not slow to raise against him the charge of Spinozism, the first of them being the Jansenist *Nouvelles ecclésiastiques*. Montesquieu was legitimately taken aback by this charge. In his *Traité des devoirs* of 1725 one of his dearest aims had been to refute Spinoza, whose doctrines he held in horror; and one of the most eloquent pages from that treatise appeared on the very threshold of *L'Esprit des lois*:

Ceux qui ont dit qu'une fatalité aveugle a produit tous les effets que nous voyons dans le monde, ont dit une grande absurdité; car quelle plus grande absurdité qu'une fatalité aveugle qui aurait produit des êtres intelligents?[2]

It is impossible to believe that Montesquieu was a deliberate disciple of Spinoza; but he has been, even in the twentieth century,[3] regarded as having embraced Spinoza's views, and the claim must be examined.

It should be noted that in the eighteenth century the word *Spinoziste* was mainly a term of abuse, and often of unthinking abuse. Spinoza was known mainly through an article in Bayle's dictionary, a refutation by Fénelon, and the anonymous *La Vie et l'esprit de Spinoza*, later to change its title to an already famous one, *Traité des trois imposteurs*. Here Moses, Christ, and Mahomet are linked together as the three great deceivers of mankind. Hobbes was often linked with Spinoza; like Spinoza he was more often vilified than read. The word *Spinoziste* is often used to describe indiscriminately both his doctrines and those of the Dutchman. They were popularly regarded as atheists, materialists, and the enemies of all morality.

[1] *Pensée* 1868 (Bkn. 201).
[2] *Lois*, I, 1; and cf. Nagel III, p. 159; Pléiade I, p. 109.
[3] C. Oudin, *Le Spinozisme de Montesquieu*, Paris, 1911; and cf. P. Vernière, *Spinoza et la pensée française*, Paris, 1954, II, pp. 446–66.

Montesquieu was not unacquainted with the works of each. He possessed the *Opera philosophica* of Hobbes in the Amsterdam quarto of 1668,[1] and had two editions of the *De cive* in French. His copy of one of these, the translation of Sorbière, bears the bookplate of the Paris Oratory: the librarian, Desmolets, Montesquieu's close friend, seems to have been kindly rather than conscientious in his functions. Spinoza is not mentioned in the catalogue of La Brède, though a refutation is found there; but the post-mortem inventory of Montesquieu's Paris library mentions the *Tractatus theologico-politicus.*[2] The Academy of Bordeaux possessed several works of Spinoza.[3]

The opposition between Hobbes and Montesquieu has been seen. Hobbes depicts the state of nature as a state of war; Montesquieu insists that the natural condition of men is peaceful. The moral code binding on citizens lay, for Hobbes (or at least for the notional Hobbes of eighteenth-century interpreters) in the fiat of the civil magistrate; for Montesquieu the principles of morality were older than the State itself. Hobbes's view of law was normative, while Montesquieu's was descriptive.

Hobbes, furthermore, differentiates between *ius naturale* and *lex naturalis*. *Ius* establishes liberty to act, *lex* restrains from acting. The state of nature being a state of war,

> the right of nature, which writers commonly call *ius naturale*, is the liberty each man hath, to use his own power, as he will himself, for the preservation of his own nature; that is to say, of his own life; and consequently of doing anything, which in his own judgement, and reason, he shall conceive to be the aptest means thereunto.[4]

The laws of nature, rationally inspired as they are, seek to circumscribe and frustrate this liberty. The first law of nature, 'to seek peace, and follow it', is a direct injunction to resist the natural condition of mankind, and a clear limitation of natural right.

A natural law in opposition to man's natural condition, or an instruction to resist nature made by nature, would be unthinkable

[1] This edition contains Hobbes's own Latin translation of the *Leviathan*. It is noteworthy that this work has not to the present day been translated into French.

[2] *Catalogue de la bibliothèque de Montesquieu*, ed. L. Desgraves, p. 243.

[3] Vernière, op. cit., p. 463.

[4] *Leviathan*, ed. M. Oakeshott, Oxford, 1946, p. 84.

to Montesquieu, and the difference between Hobbes and him is correspondingly enlarged; but it was also unthinkable to Spinoza, who realized the difference between Hobbes and himself in this matter. For, asked by a correspondent how he differed from Hobbes, Spinoza claimed in replying that unlike the Englishman, he had kept *ius naturale* safe and whole.[1] Spinoza and Montesquieu here are at one in their dissent from Hobbes.

About the nature of law in itself, however, they are in disagreement. Montesquieu's laws are relationships, Spinoza's are essentially normative. He concedes that there exist two kinds of law, one made *a necessitate naturae*, the other *ab hominum placito*; but even the first of these is of human institution, and consists of precepts which man can at will reject or accept.[2]

Spinoza's use of the term *ius naturale* raises problems of another nature. By *ius naturale* he understands the rules of the nature of each individual, by which he is caused to be and to act in a certain way.[3] So it is by *ius naturale* that fish swim in water and that the big fish eat the small. Nature has a sovereign right over everything which falls within her power, and the power of nature is the power of God. So too, the right of individuals is limited only by their power. Nor are beasts in any other case. Right and power are coterminous. A wise man has the right to use his wisdom; a fool has the right to use his foolishness. He has the right to do all that his appetite urges. *Ius naturale* is not then governed by reason; its motive forces are desire and power (*cupiditas et potentia*). We are no more under an obligation to live by the law of reason than a cat is under an obligation to live by the law of the lion. We have therefore a right to all things which are or can be brought within our power, and in the exercise of this right we may use all forms of deceit. *Ius naturale* forbids neither violence nor deceit, 'non contentiones, non odia, non iram, non dolos, nec absolute aliquid quod appetitus suadet aversari.' That is the

[1] 'Quantum ad politicam spectat, discrimen inter me et Hobbesium, de quo interrogas, in hoc consistit, quod ego naturale ius semper sartum tectum conservo' (*Opera*, ed. J. Van Vloten and J. P. N. Land, The Hague, 1914, III, p. 172).

[2] "Nihil aliud quam mandatum, quod homines et perficere et negligere possunt . . .; ratio vivendi, quam homo sibi vel aliis ob aliquem finem praescribit' (ibid., II, p. 135).

[3] 'Per ius et institutum naturae nihil aliud intelligo, quam regulas naturae uniuscuiusque individui, secundum quas unumquodque naturaliter determinatum concipimus ad certo modo existendum et operandum' (ibid., II, p. 258).

natural condition of mankind, and it is not very different from the view of Hobbes. Men in the state of nature decide to set up a social organization, and do so by signing a contract; but when the contract is signed (and this is where Spinoza separates himself from Hobbes) it obligates morally only in so far as it can compel. Right and force are still identical after the signing of the contract. Hobbes, on the other hand, promulgates a law of nature which says that the pledged word must be observed. For Spinoza, right reason dictates no subsequent natural law. Within the State there is only positive, man-made law, and the all-pervasive, eternal principle of *ius naturale*, which is not revoked by the contract, the principle that right and force are inseparable. The intellectual ruthlessness of Spinoza knows and seeks no retreat.

He has moved a long way from the position which was to be Montesquieu's. Montesquieu insisted on the existence of primitive reason; it is expressly denied by Spinoza. Montesquieu has announced that justice existed before human societies were established, and is independent of men's conventions. Spinoza says that justice is 'to render to each man what belongs to him *by civil law*'.[1] Even apart from the two major differences which would clearly divide them even if they agreed on all else, that Montesquieu rejects the idea of sovereignty and is not interested in social contract, which are a great part of Spinoza's system, it is clear that the two writers are in disharmony.

But they have one point of singular importance in common. They both believe in the existence of what Spinoza calls *ius naturale* and Montesquieu calls *les lois naturelles*: the basis on which this *ius naturale* rests is not the fiat of a legislator but on the nature of the created universe; it is never abolished but continues to the present day. Modern societies, if they are viable, must conform to it; and thus *ius naturale* becomes vested with a moral and prescriptive character. Here Spinoza and Montesquieu are agreed; to this extent Montesquieu can be termed a Spinozist. It is not a small extent; but it is an accidental similarity, and very far from justifying the description of him as a disciple of Spinoza.

[1] 'Iustitia est animi constantia tribuendi unicuique quod ei ex iure civili competit' (ibid., II, p. 265).

XII

THE THEORY OF GOVERNMENTS

I. THE MORAL ANALYSIS

TRADITION laid down that a political treatise should contain a discussion of the different forms of government, and it was with this general theme that Montesquieu originally intended to begin *L'Esprit des lois*,[1] reserving for use at a later stage his approving description of the English constitution. Meanwhile he needed to document himself. Soon after 1734 he bought two copies of Aristotle's *Politics*. He already possessed two editions in Greek and Latin; he now acquired the French translations of Oresme and of Le Roy.[2] He lists in the *Pensées* several books which he must read for his *système de politique*.[3] They include the *Politics* and also Plato's *Laws*, and when, at a later date, he crosses them out from his list, they have no doubt been read. From Aristotle and Plato he made extracts, both of them lost, but probably both substantial, since the *Pensées* refer to page 103 of the one and page 177 of the other.[4] The references contained in the *Pensées* to these authors are most numerous in the period 1734–8: it is they on whom he relies most in Books II–X of *L'Esprit des lois*. Other sources (notably those analysed in the *Geographica*) can be used in the same way to throw light on the composition of *L'Esprit des lois*. All lead to the same conclusion: the books containing the analysis of governments were largely written during the years 1734–8, and not either before or (in any important measure) after those years.

Before his travels Montesquieu had often reflected on political questions, and had read political authors. He had, perhaps, discussed them at the Entresol, where Plélo had read a paper on monarchical and other forms of government.[5] His interest in the relationship between religion and politics and his acquaintance with Machiavelli are shown as early as 1716 in his *Politique des*

[1] This is disclosed by a displaced title-page for Book III found at f. 73 in vol. I of the Paris manuscript.

[2] *Catalogue*, p. 245, corrected by me.

[3] *Pensée* 907 (Bkn. 80).

[4] *Pensées* 1502, 1766 (Bkn. 1533, 350).

[5] D'Argenson, *Journal et mémoires*, I, p. 98.

Romains dans la religion, the *Lettres persanes* contain many comments on political ideas and institutions, and scattered fragments in the *Pensées* attest the same concern. These early writings are important and valuable for the purpose of tracing the history of Montesquieu's individual ideas, and of his likes and dislikes of different systems of government. But they do not contain any clear-cut and complete analysis or classification of systems of government. This one does not find, so far as surviving evidence shows, before 1734.

Montesquieu claims that each government has its nature, its principle, and its object. His definition of the nature of the different governments is set forth at the beginning of Book II of *L'Esprit des lois*:

> Le gouvernement républicain est celui où le peuple en corps, ou seulement une partie du peuple, a la souveraine puissance; le monarchique, celui où un seul gouverne, mais par des lois fixes et établies; au lieu que, dans le despotique, un seul, sans loi et sans règles, entraîne tout par sa volonté et par ses caprices.

In the next chapter he subdivides the republic into democracy, where the sovereign power is in the hands of the people as a whole, and aristocracy, where it is in the hands of a part of the people.

No major political writer before Montesquieu had founded his work on such an analysis. By far the most widely used classification was a simplification of Aristotle's, and divided governments into monarchy, aristocracy, and democracy, with the occasional addition, after Polybius, of the mixed State.[1] The respects in which Montesquieu's system differs from the classical one are more important than what they have in common. The classical system is based entirely on the location of political power, and on the number of individuals who wield it. Montesquieu is concerned with this aspect, but it is far from being his main interest. He does not make a primary differentiation between aristocracy and democracy, which differ in respect of the location of power; and he separates monarchy and despotism, in which the location of power is identical.

What concerns Montesquieu most is not the location of power but the mode of its exercise. In monarchy the prince chooses to

[1] The distinction between *gouvernement* and *Etat*, of cardinal importance in Rousseau's writings, is not drawn by Montesquieu.

exercise his power in accordance with fixed and established laws. In despotism, he chooses to be guided solely by caprice.[1] The differentiation rests, not on the details of constitutions, but on the policy of those who wield power. It is not enough, therefore, for Montesquieu to study the State at one moment in time; he must consider it in action. He must engage in historical study:

> Il faut éclairer l'histoire par les lois, et les lois par l'histoire.[2]

Thus Montesquieu links together the study of history, of the prudence of princes (or in more modern language, the policy of governments), and of constitutional law.

That a systematic political treatise should be based on such foundations was new. The ideas themselves were not wholly new. Machiavelli had written of republic and monarchy as good States and contrasted them with tyranny which was bad,[3] and Paolo Mattia Doria had produced an analysis closer still to Montesquieu's. This aspiring polymath, having discussed the different forms of government in *La Vita civile* in accordance with the tripartite classical analysis, insists that there are also three modes of life (*forme di vivere*) which are different from the types of government. One of these modes is bad: *la barbara* (or *la pura militare*), while the other two are good: *la civile moderata* (or *la civile economica*) and *la civile pomposa*. He describes the three modes of life in terms close to Montesquieu's definition of the three governments, and it seems likely that the President's line of thought was inspired by the Neapolitan.[4] But whereas Doria clumsily superimposed on the conventional enumeration of governments a classification of societies according to their mode of life, Montesquieu replaces it by such a classification. Originality is the rearrangement of ideas.[5]

[1] A differentiation, exactly similar to Montesquieu's, between despotic and monarchical government, called by those names, is found in Saint-Hyacinthe, *Entretiens dans lesquels on traite des entreprises de l'Espagne*, The Hague, 1719, pp. 212–13.

[2] *Lois*, XXXI, 2. [3] *Discorsi*, I, 10 and 25.

[4] For other examples of Doria's influence, see pp. 257–8 above, and my article 'Montesquieu et Doria' (*RLC*, 1955).

[5] Castel relates that he reproached Montesquieu for having omitted a fourth system of government, *le gouvernement des sauvages*, based on liberty, and claims that Montesquieu, accepting the justice of the reproach, admitted that his own analysis was imperfect (*L'Homme moral*, pp. 187–94). This account may well be true; but Montesquieu is likelier to have yielded to the Jesuit's pertinacity than to his arguments.

To each of his three governments Montesquieu assigns a principle. This is the human passion which activates it. The principle of the republic is virtue, that of monarchy is honour, that of despotism is fear.

Analogies have often been drawn between political governments and moral or intellectual faculties, beginning with Plato, who in the *Republic* describes the characteristic man of aristocracy, of oligarchy, of democracy, and of timocracy, and sees in him devotion respectively to virtue, to gain, to liberty, and to honour. Montesquieu develops this notion further than Plato has done. Virtue, honour, and fear are the human attributes which cause governments to live. They are the moral causes which give them their identity; but they are not simply initial causes: they are continuing causes. Without them governments cannot prosper. When the principle becomes corrupt the government will decline and perish. It is the duty of the legislator to ensure that the principle in his State is vigorous and efficient. If it is disappearing he must revive it.

This sentiment Montesquieu read in the pages of *The Craftsman:*

Those [governments] are the best which, by the natural effect of their original constitutions, are frequently renewed or drawn back . . . to their *first principles.*[1]

But Bolingbroke here is doing no more—as Algernon Sidney, likewise read by Montesquieu, was doing no more when he wrote similar words[2]—than citing Machiavelli. The Florentine Secretary had argued that the only safeguard against corruption and decay of States was that they should be drawn back to their principles:

E cosa più chiara che la luce, che non si rinnuovando questi corpi, non durano. Il modo di rinnuovarli è . . . ridurli verso i principj suoi.[3]

Montesquieu expresses a similar doctrine:

[1] 27 June 1730 (12 September 1730, in 1731 reprint).

[2] 'All human constitutions are subject to corruption, and must perish, unless timely renewed and reduced to their first principles' (*Discourses concerning Government*, London, 1704, p. 103).

[3] *Discorsi*, III, 1. The last phrase, in the translations available to Montesquieu, appears as 'ut ad principia sua revocentur' and 'de les ramener à leurs principes'. A quotation from *Discorsi*, I, 7, which appears in *Lois*, VI, 5, can come only from the Latin text; but Montesquieu could certainly read the Italian text and possessed it, as well as two French translations.

Quand une république est corrompue, on ne peut remédier à aucun des maux qui naissent qu'en ôtant la corruption et en rappelant les principes.[1]

The train of thought which led to the formation of the doctrine of the principles of government seems to have started with Montesquieu's reading of Machiavelli: not his early reading, which inspired the *Politique des Romains dans la religion*, but a later and more thorough study, based on an interest revived during his travels,[2] and fructifying also in the *Considérations sur les Romains*.

II. DESPOTISM

Despotism for Montesquieu is wholly bad.[3] From his earliest to his latest writings he never expresses a contrary view. His hatred of despotism becomes an organized concept, however, only after he has begun, in 1734, to write *L'Esprit des lois*. It was in 1735 that he could read the following evocation of fear as the basis of despotic government:

La plupart des nations d'Asie et d'Afrique ne connaissent point d'autre gouvernement que le despotique. La crainte seule est le fondement de ces empires: l'amour de la patrie et le zèle du bien public sont incompatibles avec la servitude; et cette sorte de gouvernement n'est pas moins contraire aux intérêts de ceux qui commandent que de ceux qui obéissent. Rarement les ministres de ces Etats échappent au ressentiment du prince ou du peuple.[4]

These words were written by Legendre de Saint-Aubin, a magistrate of noble birth who, like Montesquieu, had abandoned legal office in order to devote himself to literary pursuits. His *Traité de l'opinion* is a vast compilation, written to supply the need of the

[1] *Lois*, VIII, 12. [2] See above, pp. 142 and 152.

[3] For a searching study of Montesquieu's conception of despotism, see F. Weil, 'Montesquieu et le despotisme' (*Congrès 1955*), and for an interesting examination of the history of the term, R. Koebner, 'Despot and despotism: vicissitudes of a political term' (*Journal of the Warburg and Courtauld Institutes*, 1951).

[4] Legendre de Saint-Aubin, *Traité de l'opinion, ou mémoires pour servir à l'histoire de l'esprit humain*, second edition, Paris, 1735, V, pp. 75–76 (cited by E. Carcassonne, *Montesquieu et le problème de la constitution française au XVIIIe siècle*, Paris, [1927], p. 52). The second sentence of the passage quoted appears for the first time in the 1735 edition.

non-existent Italian book *Della opinione regina del mondo* desiderated by Pascal.[1] It enjoyed sufficient success to pass through several editions. Montesquieu could find in it many references to his friends Mairan, Castel, and Fontenelle. He could find there a criticism of his own discussion in the *Lettres persanes* of the depopulation of the globe,[2] and its pages contain more than one resemblance to *L'Esprit des lois*.[3] It is by no means impossible that Montesquieu read and analysed at least the chapter *Des différentes sortes de gouvernements*, perhaps incited thereto by Fontenelle who, acting as censor, had read the whole work in 1732 and read the additions for the second edition (which included the significant sentence about fear and despotism) on 4 May 1734,[4] when Montesquieu was in Paris and frequently meeting him.

That despotism is wholly bad is beyond all doubt. A man of sense needs philosophy to endure it, the common people endure it only by force of prejudice: for despotism is destructive by principle.[5] It is corrupt by its very nature[6]—a sentiment which was to be read in the pages of Algernon Sidney: 'All tyrannies have had their beginnings from corruption . . . All governments are subject to corruption and decay, but with this difference, that absolute monarchy is by principle led unto or rooted in it.'[7] It is maintained by violence, bloodshed, and the promotion of ignorance. No new ideas must be permitted among the people; religion, however, may be useful to keep the subjects within their duty, and indeed religion is more influential in despotic States than in others: it is a fear added to fear.[8] Legal penalties are brutally severe, slavery and torture are indigenous. The object of the State is the pleasure of the prince.[9] Despotism is an outrage against human nature.

Where is despotism then to be found? The examples given by Montesquieu are from lands remote either in time or space: Turkey, Persia, Japan, Russia, China. His documentation on

[1] Pascal, *Pensées*, Amsterdam, 1700, p. 156 (ed. Brunschvicg, no. 82).
[2] IV, p. 219.
[3] Most notable is the insistence (V, pp. 6–7) on the distinction between monarchy and despotism, which is claimed to be more fundamental than the differences between monarchy, aristocracy, and democracy.
[4] VI, p. 598. [5] *Pensée* 885 (Bkn. 1823). [6] *Lois*, VIII, 10.
[7] *Discourses concerning Government*, pp. 129 and 131–2. [8] *Lois*, V, 14.
[9] *Lois*, XI, 5.

these States, if dubious in reliability, was extensive in quantity. Travellers' tales provided a seductive, if undependable, array of facts; and Montesquieu was undoubtedly on safer ground in deploring the abominations perpetrated by a sultan and his vizir, leaning on the discipline of Islam, than he could have been if he had named a western Christian monarch and a respected minister.

But a bitter analogy is to be drawn. Why, the President asks in the *Pensées*, are almost all the governments in the world despotic? Not content with asking the question once, he repeats it again and again, and transcribes the passage into *L'Esprit des lois*, where he exclaims that despotism is so evil that one would have expected human nature to revolt against it. But most people are governed by despotism, because any other form of government, any moderate government, necessitates exceedingly careful management and planning, with the most thorough balancing and regulating of political power. Despotism, on the other hand, is uniform and simple. Passions alone are required to establish it, and anyone is good enough for that.[1]

Many of those races which are not already governed by despotism are threatened by it. It is true, writes Montesquieu, that most States in Europe are still governed by *les mœurs*; but if despotism should ever be established there, no *mœurs* or climate would be able to resist.[2] And in the manuscript he adds at this point: 'Qu'on ne regarde pas comme chimériques les changements de cette espèce.' France herself is not exempt from this danger. He has obliquely pointed this out by the quotation from Horace with which the *Réflexions sur la monarchie universelle* are terminated:

Iliacos intra muros peccatur et extra.[3]

France had been governed by Richelieu, of whom he does not hesitate, even in the public pages of *L'Esprit des lois*, to say: 'Quand cet homme n'aurait pas eu le despotisme dans le cœur, il l'aurait eu dans la tête.'[4] Louis XIV is likewise the object of very hostile criticism from the pen of Montesquieu: he feared clever men;[5] he chose bad generals;[6] he identified the State

[1] *Pensées* 831, 892, 918, 934 (Bkn. 1793, 1794, 1795, 633); *Lois*, V, 14 *ad fin.*
[2] *Lois*, VIII, 8. [3] Nagel III, p. 382; Pléiade II, p. 38. [4] *Lois*, V, 10.
[5] *Spicilège*, 452 (MS., p. 408). [6] *Spicilège* 704 (MS., p. 669).

with the capital, the capital with the court, and the court with his person:[1] the sign of a corrupt monarchy which is falling into despotism. The catalogue of the library of La Brède contains in one paragraph, copied out also twice into the *Pensées*, a most mordant and penetrating study of the character of the Roi Soleil:

> Louis XIV, ni pacifique, ni guerrier. Il avait les formes de la justice, de la politique et de la dévotion et l'air d'un grand roi. Doux avec ses domestiques, libéral avec ses courtisans, avide avec ses peuples, inquiet avec ses ennemis, despotique dans sa famille, roi dans sa cour, dur dans les conseils, enfant dans celui de conscience, dupe de tout ce qui joue les princes: les ministres, les femmes, et les dévots; toujours gouvernant et toujours gouverné; malheureux dans ses choix, aimant les sots, souffrant les talents, craignant l'esprit, sérieux dans ses amours et, dans son dernier attachement, faible à faire pitié. Aucune force d'esprit dans ses succès, de la fermeté dans ses revers, du courage dans sa mort. Il aima la gloire et la religion, et on l'empêcha toute sa vie de connaître ni l'une ni l'autre. Il n'aurait eu presque aucun de tous ces défauts, s'il avait été mieux élevé, ou s'il avait eu un peu plus d'esprit.[2]

Nothing could be further removed from the description given in Book XII of *L'Esprit des lois* of the characteristics of a good monarch.[3] Louis XIV was not, in Montesquieu's eyes, a despot although Usbek attributes to him the belief that the Turkish or Persian governments are the best in the world.[4] He was a monarch of the type that causes monarchy to degenerate into despotism. Without vigilance, oriental tyranny might one day govern France. Servitude, says Montesquieu, begins with sleep.[5]

III. THE GOOD GOVERNMENTS COMPARED

Several times Montesquieu writes of *les gouvernements modérés*. In Book XI he uses the term in a specific and rigorous sense; in Books III-VIII, however, the term is more loosely used. A moderate government there means any government other than

[1] *Lois*, VIII, 6.

[2] *Pensée* 1145 (Bkn. 1613); cf. *Pensée* 1122 (Bkn. lacks) and *Catalogue*, pp. 213–14.

[3] *Lois*, XII, 27. [4] *L.P.* 37. [5] *Lois*, XIV, 13.

despotism, that is, a republic or a monarchy, inspired by the principle, respectively, of virtue or of honour.

Virtue for Montesquieu is simply the love of one's country, and the preference of the interest of one's country to one's self-interest. It involves the love of what one's country stands for: equality and frugality in the democratic State. Faguet is writing intelligently when he insists that the reader persists in attributing to the word virtue its full sense and that he is right in doing so.[1] In spite of all that has been written to the contrary, by Montesquieu as well as by his commentators, Faguet's assertion is well founded. Virtue for Montesquieu means moral goodness:

> L'amour de la patrie conduit à la bonté des mœurs, et la bonté des mœurs conduit à l'amour de la patrie.[2]

Nor is Montesquieu saying anything different when he asserts that the form taken by virtue in the aristocratic State is moderation.[3] As it is love of equality and of frugality in a democracy, so it is moderation in an aristocracy, which prevents members of the government from exercising their power in their own private interest, and which causes them instead to seek to promote the general well-being. Already in 1725 he has defined virtue as a general affection for the human race.[4]

This spirit of patriotism and altruism is found more readily in republics than in monarchies, and it is found most notably in the republics of the ancient world. It is early in his career that the President wites:

> C'est l'amour de la patrie qui a donné aux histoires grecques et romaines cette noblesse que les nôtres n'ont pas.[5]

In the *Considérations* likewise love of equality is said to characterize the Roman republic more than the empire.[6]

The principle of honour is one which had been widely discussed. The customary law which had developed in France during the

[1] E. Faguet, *Dix-huitième siècle*, Paris, 1892, p. 156. [2] *Lois*, V, 2.

[3] *Lois*, III, 4. Those commentators who try to improve on Montesquieu by writing of the *four* principles of the *four* governments of *L'Esprit de lois* are distorting his meaning. Moderation in an aristocracy and love of equality and of frugality in a democracy are for him simply the two subordinate species of virtue in a republic.

[4] Nagel III, p. 213; Pléiade I, p. 47. [5] *Pensée* 221 (Bkn. 598).

[6] *Romains*, ch. IX (Nagel I, C, p. 413; Pléiade II, p. 118).

Middle Ages attached great importance to challenges and to duelling, and the code of rules governing these activities was based on a conception of honour. Usbek, in the *Lettres persanes*, mentions 'un certain je ne sais quoi, qu'on appelle point d'honneur', which he describes as the characteristic of each profession.[1] Honour, in *L'Esprit des lois*, is the prejudice of rank: the insistence, inspired by ambition, on privilege and distinction. The monarchical State necessarily rests on a hierarchical society, knitted together by the sentiment of honour:

> Chacun va au bien commun, croyant aller à ses intérêts particuliers.[2]

Scipione Maffei had elaborately discussed honour in his *Della scienza chiamata cavalleresca*—which Doria had regarded as pirated from his own *La Vita civile*.[3] Montesquieu generalizes the notion of honour and makes it the principle of all monarchies, as he had generalized the notion of republican virtue which was furnished to him by the ancient world.

Before his travels, the idealization of the republic based on virtue clearly characterizes the thought of Montesquieu; but the differentiation between honour and virtue is not yet rigid. In the *Lettres persanes* he had written:

> Le sanctuaire de l'honneur, de la réputation, et de la vertu semble être établi dans les républiques et dans les pays où l'on peut prononcer le nom de patrie.[4]

He adds that honour alone is the recompense of merit in Lacedemonia, among other countries. A few years later, but still before his travels, and treating again of Lacedemonia, he rebuts others' definition of honour as a thing separate from virtue:

> L'honneur n'est point parmi nous un être chimérique, inventé pour servir aux plus grandes erreurs des humains, qui s'obtient par hasard, se conserve sans dessein, se perd par un caprice, qui n'est presque jamais où il paraît être, et suit tantôt le crime et tantôt la vertu.[5]

But simultaneously with his disillusionment with the republican form of government, brought about when he actually sees republics in eighteenth-century Italy and Holland and learns how corrupt and dishonest they are, comes a clearer differentiation

[1] *L.P.* 90. [2] *Lois*, II, 7.
[3] Naples, Biblioteca nazionale, MS. Brancac. V. D. 2. [4] *L.P.* 89.
[5] Nagel III, p. 123; Pléiade I, p. 511.

between honour and virtue, and a fuller realization of the moral inferiority of honour. This is brought out in the *Histoire véritable*, where the speaker confesses:

J'ai trouvé que l'honneur n'a jamais dû m'empêcher de faire une mauvaise action. Je me suis aperçu que, dans les crimes qui déshonorent, il y a toujours une manière de les commettre qui ne déshonore pas.[1]

This is equally clear in *L'Esprit des lois*. Virtue, as it is found in the republic is a 'renoncement à soi-même', a constant preference of the public interest to one's own.[2] The spirit of monarchy, on the other hand, is war and aggrandizement.[3] Deceit and adulation are permitted.

On n'y juge pas les actions des hommes comme bonnes, mais comme belles; comme justes, mais comme grandes; comme raisonnables, mais comme extraordinaires.

Consequently, morals are never as pure in monarchies as in republics.[4]

This assertion of the moral inferiority of the monarchy to the republic is made by others in Montesquieu's own century. Doria once again is seen to argue in the same sense as Montesquieu when he writes:

Le repubbliche e i regni elettivi, per mantenersi, o per ingrandirsi, addimandano virtù più vere de' regni monarchici.[5]

In 1715 similar sentiments had been heard even in the Parlement of Paris. On St. Martin's Day the Procureur-général, later to be Chancellor of France, the illustrious D'Aguesseau, delivering his customary oration or *mercuriale*, took advantage of the increased freedom which had resulted from the death a few weeks before of Louis XIV and spoke of the nature of patriotism:

Lien sacré de l'autorité des rois et de l'obéissance des peuples, l'amour de la patrie doit réunir tous leurs désirs. Mais cet amour presque naturel à l'homme, cette vertu que nous connaissons par sentiment, que nous louons par raison, que nous devrions suivre même par intérêt, jette-t-elle de profondes racines dans notre cœur? Et ne dirait-on pas

[1] Nagel III, p. 314; Pléiade I, p. 425.

[2] *Lois*, IV, 5.

[3] *Lois*, IX, 2.

[4] *Lois*, IV, 2. This chapter, it may be noted, was copied out by Lord Chesterfield in a letter to his son of 11 June 1750 (*Letters*, IV, p. 1553).

[5] *La Vita civile*, p. 9.

que ce soit comme une plante étrangère dans les monarchies, qui ne croisse heureusement et qui ne fasse goûter ses fruits précieux que dans les républiques?[1]

Unpublished until after Montesquieu's death, this address contains sentiments so closely akin to this, that it must be asked whether he had knowledge of it. Though he did not hear the *mercuriale*, being at La Brède at the time, his interest in the affairs of the Parlement on the death of Louis XIV, attested by his transcription of the Regent's speech of 2 September 1715,[2] might well have led him to procure a manuscript copy of D'Aguesseau's address, either soon after its delivery or when he had made the acquaintance of its author. This similarity of sentiment makes readily comprehensible the protection which D'Aguesseau extended to *L'Esprit des lois* when it appeared.

The effect of Montesquieu's discussion of the republic in *L'Esprit des lois* is to inject a vigorous dose of idealism into the work. This enabled subsequent republicans to regard him as one of themselves. In the fourth year of the Republic a revolutionary named Goupil de Préfelne, bringing forward in the Conseil des Anciens a proposal that a bust of Montesquieu should be placed in their council chamber opposite a bust of Brutus, made a categorical claim that Montesquieu believed the best government and the only good government to be the republic;[3] and in the next year the more intelligent Barrère, while expressing a revolutionary's dissent from some of Montesquieu's propositions, none the less regards him as being a republican at heart, asserting that his accounts of other governments are satirical in intent.[4] Others, with more justice, have seen in his federative republic an expression of real internationalism.[5] Thus Louis-Sébastien Mercier, in his play *Montesquieu à Marseille*, puts into the mouth

[1] D'Aguesseau, *Œuvres*, Paris, 1759, I, pp. 207–8.

[2] *Spicilège* 278 (MS., pp. 220–2).

[3] *Le Moniteur*, XIV, 16 ventôse, an IV.

[4] B. Barrère, *Montesquieu peint d'après ses ouvrages*, s.l., an V, pp. 71–72.

[5] *Lois*, IX, 1–3. Montesquieu, developing an idea which he may have taken from Sidney (*Discourses concerning Government*, pp. 144–6), envisaged also a full-scale treatment of federal constitutions (Nagel III, pp. 600–7; Pléiade II, pp. 1004–10). The adjective *fédératif* was a neologism, not accepted by the Academy until 1798 and not recorded earlier than *L'Esprit de lois*. The compound *confédératif* appears to the best of my knowledge but once before Montesquieu: in the French translation, published in 1691, of Locke's *Civil Government*.

of the President a prediction of the establishment of the United States of Europe.[1]

The republic is a virtuous and admirable form of government; but at no point in *L'Esprit des lois* does Montesquieu offer the slightest suggestion that it has any relevance to eighteenth-century Europe. The examples of republics which he proposes are Rome, Athens, and Sparta. When he comments on modern republics, which he does most frequently in his *Voyages*, it is to disparage them. They are unsatisfactory anachronisms. The true republic was a thing of the past. Not only does he describe small republics as 'institutions singulières' and contrast them with ordinary institutions,[2] but he writes specifically:

> La plupart des peuples anciens vivaient dans des gouvernements qui ont la vertu pour principe; et lorsqu'elle y était dans sa force, on y faisait des choses que nous ne voyons plus aujourd'hui, et qui étonnent nos petites âmes.[3]

Republics flourished in a former age when men were greater, bolder, and better. The only good and effective government for the present day is monarchy. This, in the words of Montesquieu's admiring disciple Boulanger, the friend of Wilkes, is 'le seul gouvernement raisonnable, fait pour la terre'.[4]

IV. MONARCHY

Since monarchy has for Montesquieu a degree of actuality greater than that of any other form of government, he gives greater attention to its constitutional structure, and emphasizes particularly the role of fundamental laws.

The conception of fundamental law was one of great antiquity in France.[5] Its essential principle was that there existed certain

[1] F. Gaiffe, *Le Drame en France au XVIIIe siècle*, Paris, 1910, p. 285.

[2] *Lois*, XXIII, 7. [3] *Lois*, IV, 4.

[4] N.-A. Boulanger, *Recherches sur l'origine du despotisme oriental*, London, 1762, p. 262.

[5] See A. Lemaire, *Les Lois fondamentales de la monarchie française d'après les théoriciens de l'ancien régime*, Paris, 1907, M. Marion, *Dictionnaire des institutions de la France aux XVIIe et XVIIIe siècles*, Paris, 1923, s.v. *lois fondamentales*, and E. H. Price, 'Montesquieu's historical conception of the fundamental law' (*Romanic Review*, 1947).

laws by which the power of the monarch was limited. The nature of these laws and their origin were matters frequently discussed. Remote origins were always alleged for them; their terms varied according to their exponent and the case which he wished to prove. Belief in the existence of such laws is attested in the Middle Ages; it was strengthened and diffused by Hotman in the sixteenth century. During the reign of Louis XIV it was weakened but did not disappear; for so vigorous a proponent of royal power as the sovereign's apologist Antoine Bilain could write, with more than formal royal approval:

> La loi fondamentale de l'Etat [a] formé une liaison réciproque et éternelle entre le prince et ses descendants d'une part, et les sujets et leurs descendants de l'autre, par une espèce de contrat qui destine le souverain à régner et les peuples à obéir.[1]

And Bossuet himself was to declare that 'il y a des lois dans les empires, contre lesquelles tout ce qui se fait est nul de droit'.[2] In England the common law had been regarded as being, with Parliament, the most effective curb on arbitrary power. This view was particularly associated with Sir Edward Coke, who expressed it both in his *Institutes* and also, in the more extreme form that Parliament itself was subordinate to the common law, in his judgement in Dr. Bonham's case. Montesquieu shows himself to be aware of the writings of Coke.[3] An expression, closer to Montesquieu, of the doctrine of fundamental law is to be found in the *remontrances* of the Parlement of Paris issued on 26 July 1718. While the king is admitted to be the sole legislator, the Parlement insists that there are certain laws as old as the monarchy itself, fixed, invariable, and rigorously binding on the monarch.[4]

The list of fundamental laws is always subjectively determined. For Montesquieu, apart from his concern with the order of succession to the crown,[5] the fundamental law of monarchy is

[1] A. Bilain, *Traité des droits de la Reine très chrétienne*, Paris, 1667, p. 111.

[2] Bossuet, *Politique tirée des propres paroles de l'Ecriture sainte*, livre XVIII, II, 1 (Paris, 1709, p. 396).

[3] *Pensée* 1645 (Bkn. 1963).

[4] *Remontrances du Parlement de Paris au XVIIIe siècle*, ed. J. Flammermont, Paris, 1888–98, I, p. 95.

[5] He shows (*Lois*, XVIII, 22) that the French law of succession through males only is derived from the Salic law of succession to private property. Fundamental law has thus grown out of civil law. Cf. E. H. Price, loc. cit.

essentially the existence within the State of *pouvoirs intermédiaires*. The first sentence of his discussions of this topic[1] reads thus in the manuscript:

> Les pouvoirs intermédiaires constituent la nature du gouvernement monarchique, c'est-à-dire de celui où un seul gouverne par des lois fondamentales.

In the printed text he thought it wise slightly to attenuate his wording: the adjective *subordonnés* is inserted after *intermédiaires*. Montesquieu is anxious not to appear to be raising up other powers against the king. His caution led him to go further still. At the last stage of printing he used a cancel to insert yet another adjective and a whole new sentence, so that the beginning of the chapter in the published text runs as follows:

> Les pouvoirs intermédiaires, subordonnés et dépendants, constituent la nature du gouvernement monarchique, c'est-à-dire de celui où un seul gouverne par des lois fondamentales. J'ai dit les pouvoirs intermédiaires, subordonnés, et dépendants: en effet, dans la monarchie, le prince est la source de tout pouvoir politique et civil.

What are his intermediate powers? They are the nobility, the Church, and the Parlements.

The role of the nobility is of cardinal importance in a monarchy: 'point de monarque, point de noblesse; point de noblesse, point de monarque.' It is not for a moment suggested that their role is a legislative role. Nowhere do the three orders of the states-general appear in Montesquieu's system. The origin of the nobility is of great antiquity, and in later books of *L'Esprit des lois* Montesquieu will examine it in detail. But their function in a monarchy is limited and is a judicial function. The essential characteristic of a monarchy is that there should be a class of nobles, insistent on the privileges of their rank, and in particular administering seignorial justice. Those judicial appanages of feudal power, which Montesquieu possessed at La Brède, at Raymond, and at Clairac, are the distinctive feature of monarchy. With them removed, monarchy becomes either a despotism or a popular State, whether of the standard republican or the special English pattern.

The clergy too has a role in a monarchy, especially, the President argues, in a monarchy which is tending towards despotism,

[1] *Lois*, II, 4.

since ecclesiastical privileges, however little Montesquieu himself likes them (and he leaves no doubt about that), balance and restrain the monarch's power: the evil which limits and circumscribes despotic power is itself a good.

The nobility and the clergy are not enough in a monarchy, however. There must also be a *dépôt des lois*, a body which acts as custodian and interpreter of the laws. This function is discharged by the *parlements*, and once again the political doctrine of Montesquieu is seen to be moulded by the circumstances of his life.

The Parlements of France had both regarded themselves as the repositories of the fundamental laws of the realm, and maintained that among those laws were their own rights to refuse to register laws made by the monarch and to make representations or remonstrances to the monarch when they disapproved of his policy. As long before Montesquieu's day as 1616 the Parlement of Bordeaux itself issued remonstrances justifying their unwillingness to register a royal edict, and alleging in their support 'les lois fondamentales de l'Etat' and 'les lois les plus sacrées de l'Etat'.[1] Twelve years later, other remonstrances sought to define the function of the *parlements*:

> Sire, vos Parlements sont reconnus pour être les sphères plus prochaines du premier mobile de votre Etat . . . Ce sont facultés et puissances qui dépendent et coulent de la vôtre, qui communiquent la vie et mouvement à tous les membres de cet Etat.[2]

This same document condemns the practice of administering justice by means of commissaries.[3] Montesquieu echoes this view in *L'Esprit des lois*,[4] and after his death the Parlement of Bordeaux makes representations to the king to the same effect.[5]

The reign of Louis XIV had seen the eclipse of the *parlements*; but Orléans, in the first days of his regency, restored the right of remonstrance.[6] The *garde des sceaux* addressed the Parlement of

[1] C.-B.-F. Boscheron Des Portes, *Histoire du Parlement de Bordeaux*, Bordeaux, 1877, I, p. 393.

[2] Ibid., I, p. 459. Cf. *Lois*, II, 4: 'des canaux moyens par où coulent la puissance'.

[3] Ibid., I, p. 454.

[4] *Lois*, XII, 22.

[5] M. Lhéritier, *Tourny*, Paris, 1920, II, p. 354.

[6] Jourdan, Decrusy, Isambert, *Recueil des ancienne loiss françaises*, Paris, s.d., XXI, pp. 40–41.

Paris on the occasion of Louis XV's coronation, and speaking of the rights of the crown and the liberties of the kingdom, declared to the *parlementaires*, 'Vous en êtes, Messieurs, les dépositaires, le roi vous a confié cette portion de son autorité.'[1]

Not all the pronouncements of the *parlements* are in close accord with Montesquieu's opinions. He is not in harmony with them when they appear to accept a doctrine of social contract, or to regard themselves as having inherited the legislative functions of the states-general, now in desuetude. But[2] the similarity between the ideas of the former *président à mortier* and those of the *parlements* is sometimes striking. This is clearest of all in remonstrances addressed to Louis XV by the Parlement of Bordeaux a year after Montesquieu's death. The king, they admit, is the legislator and the fount of justice. The *parlements*, however, are the repositories of his supreme jurisdiction. To remove it from them is to offend the laws of the State and to overthrow the ancient legal structure of the kingdom; they cannot abandon it without prevarication and shame.

> Les lois sont autour de votre trône comme un rempart inébranlable; faire la moindre brèche à ce rempart, c'est montrer à l'infidélité qu'il peut être attaqué, c'est enhardir le prévaricateur, diminuer la confiance de vos peuples, et jeter l'alarme dans tous les esprits . . . Votre juridiction souveraine est immuable, elle a commencé avec la monarchie, elle est née avec la loi, et ne doit finir qu'avec elles; elle ne réside, Sire, et vos prédécesseurs ne l'ont exercée, que dans ces corps augustes, qui sous différents noms ont toujours été les organes de votre sagesse, les appuis de votre pouvoir, et les dépositaires de vos volontés sacrées.[3]

This tradition of the *parlements* inspired and was inspired by the political doctrine of Montesquieu; and when the President writes of the monarchy of his own day, albeit gothic in its origin, as being the best form of government that men have been able to imagine,[4] it is monarchy supported by this tradition which he has in mind.

[1] Flammermont, op. cit., I, p. 167.

[2] See R. Bickart, *Les Parlements et la notion de souveraineté nationale au XVIIIe siècle*, Paris, 1932.

[3] *Remontrances* of 16 January 1756 (*Recueil des mémoires, arrêts, remontrances, et autres pièces, concernant l'affaire présente du Parlement de Bordeaux*, s.l., 1756, pp. 119-47).

[4] *Lois*, XI, 8.

V. OTHER CRITERIA

From the doctrine of the principles of government another normative consequence is seen to arise in *L'Esprit des lois*. Montesquieu has said that if any government is corrupt it must be restored to health by a return to the principle. Adherence to the principle of government being then a preservative against corruption, it is a good in itself. States are more good or less good in proportion to their fidelity to their principles. Thus there is a non-tautological sense in which it can be said that the best republic is the republic in which there is most virtue; and it follows not only that the best monarchy is the monarchy in which there is most honour, but also, more awkwardly, that the best despotism is the despotism in which there is most fear.

This doctrine links several different notions: the claim of Hobbes and Spinoza that the preservation of one's own nature is a good; Bolingbroke's contention that 'there must be good in the first principle of every government or it could not subsist at all';[1] and the criterion of efficiency expressed in Pope's 'What'er is best administered is best' and already suggested by Montesquieu in the *Lettres persanes* where he argues that the best government is 'celui qui va à son but à moins de frais'.[2] But it presents serious problems in relation to despotism. If a man of goodwill is given charge of a despotic State, what ought his policy to be? Ought he to endeavour to mitigate the rigour of his government, either by the moderating effect of religion,[3] or by an educational system which might form a socially conscious citizen,[4] or by laws which might introduce a little liberty into the State?[5] These possibilities Montesquieu envisages. But he also insists that the principles of government must be observed and that if that is done few laws are bad,[6] and he argues that a despotic government without fear would be imperfect.[7]

This dualism in Montesquieu's thought is reflected when he advances the two reasons which may justify a policy of social assistance, to prevent the people from suffering, and to prevent it from revolting.[8] But it is nowhere more crucially seen than

[1] *Craftsman*, loc. cit. [2] *L.P.* 80. [3] *Lois*, V, 14.
[4] *Lois*, IV, 3. [5] *Lois*, XII, 29. [6] *Lois*, VIII, 11. [7] *Lois*, III, 11.
[8] *Lois*, XXIII, 29.

when he discusses slavery. Here he is torn between two preoccupations, to assert the wholly evil character of slavery, and to examine how, given that slavery exists, it should be ordered. At the last stage of this discussion he adds in his printed text words which were not in the manuscript:

> Je ne sais si c'est l'esprit ou le cœur qui me dicte cet article-ci.[1]

If by *esprit* he means intellectual decisions based on the calculated interest of the State and by *cœur* an emotional persuasion of the natural rights of mankind, it can be said that repeatedly in his work the reader finds a dialogue of the mind and the heart; and on such a dialogue Montesquieu makes his own comment:

> J'aime incomparablement mieux être tourmenté par mon cœur que par mon esprit.[2]

[1] *Lois*, XV, 8. [2] *Pensée* 1130 (Bkn. 19).

XIII
THE SYSTEM OF LIBERTY
I. THE ANALYSIS AND ITS TERMS

MONTESQUIEU had not always regarded political liberty as a good. The advantage of a free people over another, he had written soon after the *Lettres persanes*, is slight and largely illusory. It consists solely of immunity from arbitrary deprivation of life and property. A people ruled by a tyrant, but enjoying this immunity, would be as happy as a free people.

> Au reste (adds the President), je compte pour très peu de chose le bonheur de disputer avec fureur sur les affaires d'Etat, et de ne dire jamais cent mots sans prononcer celui de liberté, ni le privilège de haïr la moitié de ses citoyens.[1]

These words come surprisingly from the pen of the man who later was to define liberty as 'ce bien qui fait jouir des autres biens',[2] and in whom posterity was to see the great theorist of liberty.

The change in his attitude was brought about by his stay in England; and though his new ideas are reflected both in the *Considérations sur les Romains* and in the *Pensées*, it is in the eleventh book of *L'Esprit des lois* that they receive their complete expression.

The title itself of that book was striking to a Frenchman of 1748: *Des lois qui forment la liberté politique dans son rapport avec la constitution.* The word *constitution*, used in this sense and without a qualifying phrase, was a neologism and an anglicism. It was not accepted by the Academy's dictionary until 1798, and in the usage of Montesquieu's day the full phrase *la constitution du gouvernement* or *la constitution de l'Etat* was required. The word *Constitution* alone meant the Bull *Unigenitus*.

The substance also of the title of the eleventh book was new; for the idea that liberty could be secured by laws instead of being conceded by the good grace of a benevolent monarch was not widely appreciated in eighteenth-century France. Montesquieu himself, however, had already shown himself acquainted with that idea. In the *Lettres persanes* he had written of England as a

[1] *Pensée* 32 (Bkn. 1802). [2] *Pensée* 1574 (Bkn. 1797).

country where liberty is continually emerging from the flames of discord and sedition.[1] Nor was this his only reference, in 1721, to England: for Usbek reports the English opinion that kings are linked to their peoples by a reciprocity of duty, and that a prince who disobeys his people is guilty of treason.[2]

By the end of 1733—twelve and a half years after the publication of the *Lettres persanes*—Montesquieu, his stay in England being then a thing of the past, had written his essay on the English constitution.[3] Between that date and its publication in 1748 as chapter 6 of Book XI of *L'Esprit des lois*, the text underwent several changes. How extensive these were can be approximately ascertained.

Inspection of the Paris manuscript shows that the inclusion in *L'Esprit des lois* of the essay on the English constitution involved a physical incorporation of one manuscript, on different paper and in different hands, in the other. Of the 50 pages occupied by the chapter on England, 32 were written before 1739 and only one brief paragraph—the final one—as late as 1743. It appears from the vestiges of an early numbering of leaves and from some deleted catchwords that some of the later pages are no more than retranscriptions, with minor corrections, of the original text. Not more at most than one-sixth of the whole is likely to be subsequent in composition to 1741.[4] Three-quarters of the whole was written not later than 1738 and is likely to constitute the text of 1733. Thus most of the chapter as it now stands was written soon after Montesquieu's return from his travels, and under the immediate inspiration of English political life.

The first paragraph, theoretical and not practical in nature, was full of terminological novelty:

> Il y a dans chaque Etat trois sortes de pouvoirs: la puissance législative, la puissance exécutrice des choses qui dépendent du droit des gens, et la puissance exécutrice de celles qui dépendent du droit civil.

[1] *L.P.* 136. [2] *L.P.* 104. [3] Secondat, *Mémoire*, p. 401.

[4] The major post-1741 additions are four in number: (1) on the nature of Parliamentary representation (half of Nagel I, A, p. 211, *Comme dans un Etat* to p. 212, *volonté propre*; Pléiade II, pp. 399–400); (2) on the necessity for periodic dissolutions of Parliament (Nagel I, A, p. 215, paragraph beginning *De plus*; Pléiade II, p. 402); (3) on the relations between legislative and executive power (half of Nagel I, A, p. 218, *Si le monarque* to p. 219, *de la législation*; Pléiade II, p. 405); (4) on the corruption of the State (part of Nagel I, A, p. 221, *Elles ne sont point* to the end of the chapter; Pléiade II, pp. 406–7).

Puissance législative and *puissance exécutrice* were new terms, but unequally new. In 1652 *pouvoir législatif* had been used in French in a translation of Milton's *Eikonoklastes*; it reappeared in Andrew Michael Ramsay's *Essai de politique* and in Barbeyrac's translations of Pufendorf. *Pouvoir exécutif* had appeared in 1672, in a translation of Chamberlayne's *Angliae notitia.* But these phrases had not been accepted by the language; and *exécutif*, not recognized by the Academy until 1835, was so new that Montesquieu, although he had innovated to the extent of using *puissance* instead of *pouvoir*, found *exécutif*, though closer to the English, less suitable than *exécuteur* or its feminine *exécutrice*,[1] though these were not in ordinary use adjectivally.[2]

There was one place, however, where the phrases *pouvoir législatif* and *pouvoir exécutif* had appeared in juxtaposition before Montesquieu. This unique coincidence of his approximate terms indicates an almost certain source: Locke's *Second Treatise of Civil Government*, published in French translation at Amsterdam in 1691.

Locke had written of the legislative, executive, and federative powers, whose respective functions were the making of laws, the execution of the laws thus made, and the conduct of foreign policy. Montesquieu's *puissance législative* is the same as Locke's legislative power stripped of its paramountcy. Montesquieu's *puissance exécutrice des choses qui dépendent du droit des gens* corresponds as at first defined to Locke's federative power, but it is tacitly extended to include all ordinary executive functions of government, many of them classified by Locke under the headings of executive power and of prerogative. Montesquieu's *puissance exécutrice* [*des choses*] *qui dépendent du droit civil* is the judicial power. It corresponds directly to nothing in Locke's analysis, though it has some attributes of his executive power[3] and is perhaps named with these in mind—though its name is in fact rapidly abandoned in favour of *puissance de juger*. The similarity to Locke becomes increasingly faint, except in detail, as Montes-

[1] *Puissance exécutive* is found in the *Notes sur l'Angleterre* where it may be a corrupt reading of the 1818 editor. The manuscript is lost.

[2] Useful information on this and similar subjects has been assembled by F. Mackenzie, *Les Relations de l'Angleterre et de la France d'après le vocabulaire*, Paris, 1939, 2 vols.

[3] See E. De Marchi, 'Considerazioni intorno alla divisione dei poteri nel Locke' (*Occidente*, 1948).

quieu's arguments advance; and the chapter is still at its introductory stage when he redefines the three powers:

celui de faire des lois, celui d'exécuter les résolutions publiques, et celui de juger les crimes ou les différends des particuliers.

Here Locke is left far behind, and the doctrine of the division of powers receives what is to become its classical formulation. Interestingly, this definition, according to the handwriting of the manuscript, is anterior to that with which the chapter begins.[1] The closest resemblance to Locke and therefore Montesquieu's most attentive reading of Locke seem then to be subsequent to the first draft of the chapter, a fact which would suggest that Montesquieu sought theoretical support in Locke for an analysis which he had already formed on the basis of observation.

If in any State the legislative, executive, and judicial powers are in the same hands, the government is an intolerable despotism. If two of the powers are in the same hands but the third is separate, the government can be described as moderate. If all three are separate, then the State can be said to promote liberty. Liberty is not the power of doing as one likes, but rather the power of doing what one ought to wish to do; it is the right to do what the laws permit. It consists therefore of being governed by laws and of knowing that the laws will not arbitrarily be put on one side. Liberty is not restricted to, or necessarily found in, either a monarchy or a republic. It is not more distant from the throne than from a senate.[2] There is one country in which liberty is indigenous. It can perhaps be regarded as a republic with monarchical forms,[3] but it is not to be thought a monarchy as monarchy is defined by Montesquieu, activated by the principle of honour,[4] or in which abuse of power is guarded against by the seignorial rights of the nobility.[5] Its constitution is *sui generis*, and is of

[1] The later definition comes in the *premier jet* of the chapter and therefore dates most probably from 1733–4, while the opening of the chapter is an addition in hand *g* (1739–41).

[2] *Pensée* 884 (Bkn. 631). [3] *Lois*, V, 19.

[4] Montesquieu's disciple Blackstone endeavours to knit his system more closely together by attributing the principle of honour to the British monarchy (*Commentaries on the Laws of England*, fifth edition, Oxford, 1773, I, p. 157).

[5] Charles Yorke, in a letter to his father of 11 November 1749, reports a conversation with Montesquieu on the subject of seignorial rights. 'He said that he considered those rights as a barrier against the Crown, to prevent monarchy from running into despotism.' Yorke conceded that this might be argued in the

great antiquity. Tacitus describes it, having found it in Germany: 'ce beau système a été trouvé dans les bois'.

This State Montesquieu now proceeds to describe. He describes it in normative language: *il faut que* . . ., *il est nécessaire que* . . ., *on doit* . . . He names the State only in the title of the chapter and allusively at the end. But it is the English constitution which he is describing, and his account of it, accurate or false, is famous and was long held authoritative even in England.

II. CONSTITUTIONAL DETAIL

Beginning with the legal system, Montesquieu says that the judicial power must be given, not to a permanent court, but to an *ad hoc* tribunal whose members are selected from the people; and he asserts the right of a man to be tried by his peers. This is the English system of trial by jury. The procedure for the selection of jurymen is laid down by law. The accused can object to individual jurymen. The judgements rendered by the juries must be precise extracts from the text of the laws.

In relation to the right to object to members of the jury, Montesquieu has up-to-date knowledge. Chamberlayne's *Magnae Britanniae notitia* for 1729 asserts that

> the law [allows] any one of the commonalty, being arraigned for felony or treason, *in favorem vitae*, to challenge thirty-five of his jury, without shewing cause, and others by shewing cause.[1]

Recent legislation had confirmed this right.[2] With this exception, Montesquieu's discussion of the jury system is a gross simplification. There is no mention of the existence of professional judges or of the steps (very relevant to his theme) which had been taken to secure their independence. There is no mention

case of an absolute monarchy like that of France, but that in England 'all private rights, which encroached on the legal authority of the Crown, tended to erect tyrants at the expense of the people's liberty' (P. C. Yorke, *The Life and Correspondence of Philip Yorke Earl of Hardwicke*, Cambridge, 1913, II, pp. 172–3). Montesquieu had already written: 'Les Anglais, pour favoriser la liberté, ont ôté toutes les puissances intermédiaires qui formaient leur monarchie' (*Lois*, II, 4).

[1] See p. 162. All references to this work are to the edition of 1729, which Montesquieu possessed. It is cited, not as being (in most cases) a demonstrable source, but as evidence of contemporary usage and opinion.

[2] 3 Geo. II, c. 25.

of the different branches of the High Court, no mention of justices of the peace, no realization of the exact function of a jury or of the difference between a verdict and a sentence, no understanding, in what is said about a text of the law, of the unwritten nature of common law.

Such superficiality was doubtless intentional. Montesquieu shows himself elsewhere to be well acquainted with the working of the jury system,[1] and the former *président à mortier* was well enough informed about the nature of common law. He is barely concerned here with the judicial power in itself, which he hastens to proclaim 'invisible et nulle', and is interested in it only in its relation to the other powers. Thus his comment on the law governing imprisonment, with its insistence on early trial and its provision for bail except in the case of the gravest charges, shows a reasonably accurate knowledge of the law resulting from the Habeas Corpus Amendment Act of 1679. Similarly he shows himself well acquainted with the nature of the judicial functions of the House of Lords. The Lords' powers in relation to the trial of peers and the hearing of impeachments by the Commons are well understood; he realizes the existence of the appellate jurisdiction, but misunderstands its nature when he says that it is the duty of the House of Lords to mitigate the rigour of the law.[2]

The judicial power having been treated not more than summarily, Montesquieu addresses himself to his main interest, the legislative and executive powers.

The legislative power is vested in the people and exercised by them through representatives elected for individual boroughs (county constituencies not being mentioned).[3] All citizens are electors, except the most indigent who are deemed to have no will of their own: an idealized view of the great diversity of franchises to be found throughout the country,[4] though expressed

[1] *Lois*, VI, 3.

[2] 'Modérer la loi en faveur de la loi même, en prononçant moins rigoureusement qu'elle.'

[3] The eighteenth-century House of Commons consisted in fact of 432 representatives of boroughs, 122 representatives of counties, and 4 members for Universities.

[4] See E. and A. Porritt, *The Unreformed House of Commons*, Cambridge, 1903, I, pp. 20–84.

in words which Blackstone himself was to reproduce,[1] and a doubtless voluntary blindness to the existence of rotten and pocket boroughs. The representatives have a general mandate only from their electors, and do not need to receive from them specific instructions on individual issues, or to report back to them, wherein (says Montesquieu) they differ from the Dutch representatives who, according to Sidney, must render an account to those whom they represent.[2] This comparison with Holland was frequently made. Chamberlayne's *Magnae Britanniae notitia* says of the Member of Parliament that

> his power [is] absolute to consent or dissent without ever acquainting those that sent him, or demanding their assent, as the States-General of the United Netherlands are obliged to do in many cases.[3]

Instructions to members from constituents were not, however, unknown in the eighteenth century, and it has been thought that they were even frequent.[4] Here Montesquieu's language may be intended simply to deplore and not to describe.

The nobility, having a greater stake in the kingdom than the Commons, must be separately represented in the legislature. One of its functions is to hold the balance between king and Commons. This was often held to be one of the duties of the House of Lords, and Montesquieu is here in agreement with Bolingbroke who writes:

> I have spoken of this second estate in our government, as of a middle order, that are properly mediators between the other two, in the eye of our constitution.[5]

In relation to the raising of taxes, the nobles (though they may impose a veto) do not exercise a *faculté de statuer*, that is, they may not either initiate or amend proposals. This is the most detailed understanding shown by Montesquieu so far of technical minutiae. He could have cited Chamberlayne:

[1] '. . . To exclude such persons as are in so mean a situation that they are esteemed to have no will of their own' (*Commentaries on the Laws of England*, Oxford, 1773, 5th edition, I, p. 171).

[2] *Discourses concerning Government*, London, 1704, p. 385.

[3] See p. 88. Blackstone (op. cit., I, p. 159) makes a similar statement.

[4] Porritt, op. cit., I, pp. 263–6.

[5] *Dissertation upon Parties*, London, 1735 (possessed by Montesquieu), p. 177.

For levying of any money upon the subject, the Bill begins in the Commons' House, because from them doth arise the greater part of the monies; neither will they allow the Lords to make any alteration in a money bill.[1]

The legislature should meet frequently, but not continuously, and from time to time it should be dissolved and renewed. The time and duration of its sessions are to be regulated by the executive: Montesquieu shows no awareness of either the Triennial Act of 1694 or the Septennial Act of 1715.[2] It is by annual decision of the legislature that taxes are voted and the armed forces authorized; but the latter, once approved, are under the command of the executive. In both these matters Montesquieu's understanding of English constitutional practice is accurate.

The executive power is vested in a monarch, who may veto legislation but may not participate in debate, who is subject to the scrutiny but free from the control of the legislature. The monarch may not participate in the levy of taxes otherwise than by giving his consent: an error on Montesquieu's part, for by resolution of the Commons in 1706 the initiation of supply proposals was reserved to the Crown.[3] Should the executive power be vested not in a monarch but in a council of individuals drawn from the legislature, liberty would be imperilled: an assertion less strange than it seems when it is remembered that most ministers in the eighteenth century being peers were not members of the House of Commons,[4] and that Montesquieu sometimes thinks of the legislature as being simply the Commons.

III. THE PARTY SYSTEM

In his chapter on the English constitution Montesquieu makes no reference, direct or indirect, to the existence of political parties in England.

[1] Op. cit., p. 87. Cf. W. C. Costin and J. S. Watson, *The Law and Working of the Constitution*, London, 1952, I, pp. 153–4.

[2] His only clear reference to dissolution as opposed to prorogation occurs in a passage (Nagel I, A, p. 215, paragraph beginning *De plus*; Pléiade II, p. 402) written between 1740 and 1743 which a deleted catchword shows to be an addition and not a redraft. Montesquieu's interest may have been stimulated by the election of 1741 and the consequent fall of Walpole.

[3] See Costin and Watson, op. cit., I, p. 197.

[4] See B. Kemp, *King and Commons, 1660–1832*, London, 1957, p. 58.

This abstention is surprising, for Montesquieu held clear views about political discord and disunion. He had read in Machiavelli that disagreement between the Roman senate and the people had in fact, far from being harmful, promoted power and liberty in Rome,[1] could find the same view expressed by Algernon Sidney,[2] and in the *Considérations* had made it his own.[3] When discussing the republican form of government in *L'Esprit des lois* he insists that *brigue* is dangerous in a senate or among the nobles, but is positively desirable among the people.[4] But he makes no attempt in Book XI to apply this doctrine to England.

His silence surprises anyone acquainted with French discussions of English politics at this time. Other writers are fascinated by the terms Whig and Tory. The standard textbook on the subject, accepted as authoritative even in England, was written in French;[5] it scrutinizes the different shades of Whig and Tory opinion with great thoroughness and astuteness. Morery's *Grand Dictionnaire* devotes 1,500 words in its 1740 edition to a discussion of the two terms. At the time of Montesquieu's visit, a Swiss traveller writes:

> Ces deux partis sont si animés l'un contre l'autre et si enracinés, qu'on regarderait comme une espèce de miracle s'ils venaient à disparaître et à se réunir.[6]

Already in the *Pensées* Montesquieu himself had evinced some interest in the Whigs, noting that all the French refugees in England had joined that party;[7] Whigs and Tories were not unmentioned in the private *Notes sur l'Angleterre.*[8] Why do they not appear in *L'Esprit des lois*?

The reason may indeed be simple mystification, caused both by his reading and by his personal experience. A paragraph in the *Spicilège* discloses that in 1721 Montesquieu read at least one of the *Cato's Letters* of Thomas Gordon.[9] Here the intransigent

[1] *Discorsi*, I, 4. [2] *Discourses*, p. 105.

[3] *Romains*, ch. IX (Nagel I, C, p. 414; Pléiade II, p. 119). [4] *Lois*, II, 4.

[5] Rapin de Thoyras, *Dissertation sur les Whigs et les Torys*, The Hague, 1717.

[6] C. de Saussure, *Lettres et voyages*, ed. B. van Muyden, Lausanne, Paris, Amsterdam, 1903, p. 370 (letter dated 15 August 1729).

[7] *Pensée* 155 (Bkn. 1882). [8] Nagel III, p. 287; Pléiade I, p. 878.

[9] *Spicilège* 309 (MS., p. 260). The paper in question appeared on either 25 March or 8 April 1721, both of these answering to the description. Dedieu's arguments (*Montesquieu et la tradition politique anglaise en France*, Paris, 1909, pp. 284–304) for an influence of Gordon on Montesquieu receive some support from this reference in the *Spicilège*, to which he did not have access.

Whig had expressed his hatred of princes and his trust in the people. In other letters, as well as discussing themes dear to Montesquieu, such as the depopulation of the globe, the uselessness of Spanish gold, and the causes of the decline of Rome, he produced the most vigorous denunciation of arbitrary government and of corruption. These were sentiments traditionally expressed by Whigs. But what was Montesquieu to think when, during his stay in England, he found the opponents of the Whigs furiously publishing identical sentiments? Already his friend Ramsay had written:

> Les divisions et subdivisions parmi les Whigs et les Torys se multiplient chaque jour. Il y a souvent cinq ou six différentes espèces de Whigs et de Torys. D'ailleurs les chefs de ces différents partis changent souvent de principes. Les Whigs deviennent Torys et les Torys deviennent Whigs selon leur intérêt.[1]

This confusion received practical confirmation for Montesquieu when during his stay in England he witnessed the breach between Townshend and Walpole, discovered the Whig Pulteney to be the most violent of Walpole's opponents, and learnt of the duel fought in January 1730/1 between his two friends Pulteney and Hervey, both of them claiming to be Whigs.

Montesquieu's silence may well be occasioned by his failure to understand the complexities of party politics which he found in England. Nor is this to be wondered at. Although George II's first Parliament is as yet unexamined by the new techniques of structural analysis and biographical research devised by Sir Lewis Namier, some light is thrown on it by works dealing with neighbouring periods. Mr. R. Walcott, dealing with the first decade of the century, has shown how different issues provoked different alignments in Parliament. Instead of seeing the House of Commons divided on simple two-party lines, he claims that it can be regarded 'as a circle with four major segments: Court, Whig, Country, Tory', grouped now in one way and now in another, the task of Ministers being to attract to their permanent Court nucleus a sufficient number of either Whigs or Tories to create a majority.[2]

[1] *Essai de politique*, The Hague, 1719, p. 182.

[2] *English Politics in the Early Eighteenth Century*, Oxford, 1956, pp. 157–8 *et passim*.

Much closer to the Parliament known to Montesquieu is the third one of George II's reign, elected in 1741. It has been analysed in detail by Dr. J. B. Owen,[1] who finds its members readily divisible into two groups, the Old Corps of Whigs, supporting the administration and numbering 286, and the opposition, consisting of 268 members, almost equally divided between Tories and dissident Whigs. The Old Corps of Whigs comprises the dependent government supporters, forming largely the Court and Treasury Party of placemen, and the independents, mainly merchants and country gentlemen, who normally voted with ministers but did so freely. The term Whig has become so all-embracing (of all kinds there are 422 in the House) as to be incapable of definition. The Tories, however, can be readily defined: 'those whose ancestors were Tories, and who continued to behave as members of a country party opposed in general to the measures of the Court.'[2]

In approximate terms this description can be regarded as applicable also to George II's first house of Commons, of which Montesquieu had first-hand experience. The Whig-Tory demarcation, though it still survived, was becoming weaker as the issues on which it had been based became more remote in time. The Court-Country opposition was becoming increasingly significant, and was reinforced by the disappearance, after years of Whig patronage, of the Tory-Court group, and by the defection from the ministerial side of Pulteney and his supporters. The Government's interest in these circumstances was to consolidate the Old Corps and to rally the dissident Whigs by invoking as often as possible traditional Whig principles, the Protestant succession, the security of the régime, hatred of Jacobitism and of Popery, and by insisting that the Whig-Tory conflict was the really significant conflict in political life.[3] The interest of the Tories meanwhile was to detach as many Whigs as possible from support of Walpole. To do this it was necessary to argue that the old hostility between Whigs and Tories was a thing of the past, based on dead issues and no longer corresponding to political reality. The vital and

[1] *The Rise of the Pelhams*, London, 1957, pp. 41–86. [2] Ibid., p. 70.

[3] The ministerialist *London Journal* proclaimed that love of liberty and toleration were native qualities in 'a Whig, a Protestant, and an Englishman' and constantly urged loyalty to the Hanoverian dynasty while denigrating the Tories as Jacobites (see hereon Laprade, *Public Opinion and Politics in Eighteenth-Century England*, New York, 1936).

significant division for them was the division between Government and Opposition, or between Court Party and Country Party.[1]

The political conflict in England was then a Whig-Tory conflict if one saw it through ministerialist eyes, and a Court-Country conflict if one saw it through opposition eyes. In Chapter 6 of Book XI Montesquieu does not take sides and preserves a discreet silence about party conflict.

His silence, however, is not permanent. Some years later he begins another chapter on England,[2] which he regards as a pendant to the earlier one. In it he describes the manners and customs of the English and explains thus his intention:

> J'ai parlé au livre XI d'un peuple libre; j'ai donné les principes de sa constitution: voyons les effets qui ont dû suivre, le caractère qui a pu s'en former, et les manières qui en résultent.

It is in this chapter, rapidly recognized as important in England,[3] that Montesquieu gives a succinct account of English party politics. It was composed, according to the handwriting of the manuscript, in 1746 or 1747. He writes:

> Comme il y aurait dans cet Etat deux pouvoirs visibles: la puissance législative et l'exécutrice, et que tout citoyen y aurait sa volonté propre, et ferait valoir à son gré son indépendance, la plupart des gens auraient plus d'affection pour une de ces puissances que pour l'autre, le grand nombre n'ayant pas ordinairement assez d'équité ni de sens pour les affectionner également toutes les deux.

Since the executive controls all forms of public employment, it attracts many supporters, while it is attacked by those who can hope for no reward. Violent passions will be engaged on either side, and the hatred between the two parties, because it is impotent, Montesquieu paradoxically says, will be lasting. If one party is too much in the ascendant, the citizens will transfer their support to the other. Individuals will frequently change their party, and will even seek the alliance of their enemies. The monarch himself will sometimes transfer his support from his friends to his enemies.

[1] See K. Kluxen, *Das Problem der politischen Opposition*, Freiburg and Munich, 1956.

[2] *Lois*, XIX, 27.

[3] An English translation of this chapter, along with XI, 6, was published at Edinburgh in 1750.

These comments—in which the friends of the executive and the friends of the legislative clearly denote the Court and Country Parties—constitute an intelligent if arbitrary attempt to rationalize the English party system. Why should it be only after fifteen years from his return to France that Montesquieu puts them on paper?

A friend or perhaps more accurately a client of Montesquieu published in 1745 a book in which English party politics were extensively discussed. This was the Abbé Le Blanc, who has appeared already in the narrative of the President's life. His *Lettres d'un Français concernant le gouvernement, la politique, et les mœurs des Anglais et des Français*, written during his stay in England from 1737 to 1744, are one of the most interesting of French accounts of eighteenth-century England. Two of the letters are addressed to Montesquieu,[1] a fact which, combined with the sycophantic ambition of Le Blanc, makes it inevitable that the work should have been presented to the President. Here Montesquieu could read descriptions of the working of political parties in England, of the control over members of Parliament exerted by Ministers through the promise of places. He could read that English children imbibe the spirit of faction with their mother's milk and as soon as they can speak learn the words *corruption* and *opposition*. A letter to Nivernais expresses the new view of political alignments:

> Ces noms odieux de Whig et de Tory . . ., qui ont fait tant de bruit sous la reine Anne, sont presque aujourd'hui [*sic*] entièrement oubliés en Angleterre, mais les mêmes factions y subsistent toujours sous des dénominations différentes. Corruption et opposition sont les deux termes qui servent à distinguer celles qui sont pour ou contre le ministère.[2]

Whig and Tory are meaningless terms to Le Blanc. The Court and the Opposition are more real notions; and in writing in the same sense to Fréret he refers specifically to 'les lettres de milord B^{xxx}'.[3]

[1] The two letters inscribed to Montesquieu deal with English politics, and discuss the Court's control over both Houses of Parliament, the republicanism of some members of the opposition, the nature of liberty, the moral and physical causes which form national character, and honour as a principle of government. This, published three years before *L'Esprit des lois*, argues a closer association than has been suspected between Montesquieu and Le Blanc.

[2] *Lettres d'un Français*, The Hague, 1745, II, pp. 139–40.

[3] Ibid., II, p. 28.

Montesquieu was already acquainted with the products of Bolingbroke's fertile pen. During his stay in England he had read in *The Craftsman* the essays which later became the *Remarks on the History of England.* In the same journal there later appeared the *Dissertation upon Parties.* This work, in its first collective reprint of 1735, is in the library of La Brède. The handwriting in which its title is entered in the catalogue shows that Montesquieu himself acquired it between 1740 and 1743. Perhaps the author himself, who was in France during most of those years, conveyed it to the President.

At the beginning of the *Dissertation* Bolingbroke gives traditional definitions of the terms Whig and Tory, evoking the Whig acceptance of the majesty of the people, original contract, the supremacy of Parliament, and resistance to tyrants, and contrasting these with the Tory belief in divine right, passive obedience, and even slavery, and Popery. But all this, he insists, is superseded:

> These associations are broken; these distinct sets of ideas are shuffled out of their order; new combinations force themselves upon us.[1]

The greater part of both of the two old parties are united in defence of principles of liberty, and it is only remnants which remain divided on traditional lines. It is time for these archaic party hatreds to subside. Let there be no talk of Whigs and Tories: the only real party division is that between the Court Party and the Country Party:

> The principal articles of . . . the civil faith of the old Whigs are assented and consented to by the Country Party; and I say, upon good authority, that if this creed was made a test of political orthodoxy, there would appear at this time but very few heretics amongst us. How different the case is, on the other side, will appear not only from the actions, but from the principles of the Court Party, as we find them avowed in their writings; principles more dangerous to liberty . . . than even any of those, bad as they were, which some of these men value themselves for having formerly opposed.[2]

To illustrate the hollowness of the Tory-Whig analysis, he devotes the greater part of the book to a history of those parties, and ends by asserting that,

[1] *Dissertation upon Parties*, London, 1735, p. 4. [2] Ibid., p. 9.

as nothing can be more ridiculous than to preserve the nominal division of Whig and Tory parties, which subsisted before the Revolution, when the difference of principles that alone could make the distinction real exists no longer; so nothing can be more reasonable than to admit the nominal division of Constitutionists and Anti-constitutionists, or of a Court and a Country Party, at this time, when an avowed difference of principles makes this distinction real.[1]

The opposition between Whigs and Tories was by no means dead, or Bolingbroke would not have found it necessary so vigorously to assail it. In ignoring it, in abandoning his former silence, and in speaking in terms of the Court-Country analysis, Montesquieu is following the lead of Bolingbroke. He is also approaching more closely to the truth than a simple acceptance of the traditional Whig–Tory alignment would have brought him.

IV. SEPARATION OF POWERS

Montesquieu's indebtedness to Bolingbroke was still more extensive and was not unobserved in the eighteenth century. Pope had commented on the similarity between the *Considértions* and some of Bolingbroke's essays,[2] and Mrs. Thrale, reading in the manuscript of Spence's *Anecdotes* some observations by Bolingbroke on laws, declared—with less than complete truth—that they were 'word for word in Montesquieu'.[3] It was from Bolingbroke also that Montesquieu derived the doctrine of the separation of powers.[4]

The doctrine of the mixed State, which was exceedingly popular in seventeenth- and eighteenth-century England, is quite different from that of the separation of powers, though critics and commentators have often confused the two. The distinction between them can be defined thus:

The supporters of the mixed State urge that a desirable and lasting constitution can be obtained by assigning legislative power, which for them is regarded as sovereign, to king, nobles, and people, *jointly*, and by securing a harmonious balance between these three; while supporters

[1] *Dissertation upon Parties*, p. 239.

[2] J. Spence, *Anecdotes*, ed. S. W. Singer, London, 1820, p. 169.

[3] *Thraliana*, ed. K. C. Balderston, Oxford, 1951, I, p. 425.

[4] The detailed demonstration of the borrowing is to be found in my article 'Montesquieu, Bolingbroke, and the separation of powers' (*FS*, 1949).

of the separation of powers claim that liberty can be secured only by dividing political authority (which being divisible cannot be sovereign) into its three constituent functions, and by assigning these functions to different bodies or individuals, who will exercise their powers separately and without collusion.[1]

The eighteenth-century contenders for the mixed State (Bolingbroke sometimes, inconsistently, among them)[2] claim that in England King, Lords, and Commons represent monarchical, aristocratic, and democratic elements, and that since the legislative power is vested in these three, the English government is compounded of monarchy, aristocracy, and democracy. This is never Montesquieu's view. He argues instead for the mutual independence of the legislative power (entrusted to both Houses of Parliament), the executive power (in the hands of the monarch) and the judicial power; and since it is only in passing that he deals with the judicial power, his contention is essentially that the legislative and executive branches of government must be in separate hands.

This argument was the subject of vigorous debate during Montesquieu's stay in England between *The Craftsman* and the ministerialist *London Journal*. Bolingbroke asserts:

> In a constitution like ours, the safety of the whole depends on the balance of the parts, and the balance of the parts on their mutual independency on one another.[3]

The *London Journal* retorts:

> 'Tis plain to common sense and the experience of all the world, that this independency is a mere imagination; there never was really any such thing, nor can business be carried on or Government subsist by several powers absolutely distinct and absolutely independent.[4]

The governmental view is that legislative and executive must work together in harmony. The opposition view is that they must be separate, both for specific reasons relating to English politics and for general reasons expressed in these words:

> In every kind of government some powers must be lodged in particular men, or particular bodies of men, for the good order and preservation of the whole community. The lines which circumscribe these powers are the bounds of separation between the prerogatives of the

[1] R. Shackleton, loc. cit. [2] *Dissertation upon Parties*, p. 158.
[3] *Craftsman*, 27 June 1730. [4] 4 July 1730.

prince, or other magistrate, and the privileges of the people. . . . Thus we see how great a trust is reposed in those, to whom such powers are committed; and if we look into the heart of man, we shall soon discover how great, though unavoidable, a temptation is laid in their way. The love of power is natural; it is insatiable; almost constantly whetted; and never cloyed by possession.[1]

Side by side with this passage must be set a paragraph from the *Spicilège* of which this is a part:

13 juin 1730. La vigilance sur la liberté doit être proportionnée aux occasions. Les cent yeux d'Argus n'étaient pas toujours tous ouverts ou fermés. *The love of power is natural. It is insatiable almost constantly whetted never cloyed[2] by possession.*[3]

Holding already, as the allegory of the Troglodytes in the *Lettres persanes* shows, the belief, to which his training as a magistrate of a provincial *parlement* predisposed him, that political power is dangerous and a source of corruption, Montesquieu was the more ready to listen sympathetically to the arguments of *The Craftsman* when he read them, and to interpret the English constitution in their light. In the case of others among his ideas, there may be discussion about whether his mental process was *a priori* or empirical. Here there is no doubt. It is from his experience of the English Constitution and of political controversy in England that he empirically formed his theory of the separation of powers. He went on to generalize further and to enunciate the rule which is the most concise expression of his whole constitutional doctrine, 'pour qu'on ne puisse abuser du pouvoir, il faut que, par la disposition des choses, le pouvoir arrête le pouvoir'.[4]

In truth the vital characteristic of the British constitution, which was being shaped during Montesquieu's stay in England, was the solidarity and not the separation of the legislative and executive powers. It was Walpole's achievement, *per fas et nefas*, to promote that solidarity. This Montesquieu, readier to appreciate law than usage,[4] did not understand. He did not understand the

[1] *Craftsman*, 13 June 1730.

[2] 'Aiguisé, jamais empêché ou embarrassé' (Montesquieu's note).

[3] *Spicilège* 525 (MS., pp. 485–6). [4] *Lois*, XI, 4.

[4] This attitude, surprising in view of his stress on policy in his definition of the three governments, is shown too by his insistence on the royal power of veto in legislation. Had he realized that this had already fallen into practical desuetude and would never be used again, he would not have had to explain this slightly embarrassing infringement of the separation of powers.

developing cabinet system. He did not understand the role of a minister, still less of a leading minister like Walpole who was a personal link between the House of Commons and the Crown.[1] He did not understand that there might be some good, even a small, relative, or dubious good, to be gained from ministerial exercise of influence; he saw it simply as corruption, and predicted (again with Bolingbroke)[2] that the English State would perish when the legislative power became more corrupt than the executive.[3]

The separation of powers, during Montesquieu's stay in England, was no more than a partisan cry. It was he who dignified and rationalized the concept, linked it to a theory of liberty, and handed it to posterity as a doctrine far more practical than its proponents had known.

[1] An intelligent discussion of this aspect of Walpole's régime is given by J. B. Owen, *The Rise of the Pelhams*, pp. 37–40.

[2] *Craftsman*, 12 September 1730; *Dissertation upon Parties*, pp. 211–12.

[3] Montesquieu gives a detailed discussion of the nature of corruption in the draft of a letter to the Englishman Domville (*Pensée* 1960, Bkn. 1883).

XIV
CLIMATE AND CAUSES
I. TOWARDS A DOCTRINE

'AFTER ranging in vain through Grotius, Burlamaqui, and Pufendorf,' wrote an English pamphleteer, 'I read thirteen books of Montesquieu's *Spirit of Laws*, without making the least discovery. But at length the fourteenth book rewarded all my toils.'[1] No doctrine in *L'Esprit des lois* attracted more attention than did that of the influence of climate on mankind, set forth in Book XIV, and none provoked more surprise. It was said, reports Algarotti,[2] that as Malebranche saw everything in God, so Montesquieu saw everything in climate. A French versifier, René de Bonneval, writes in some lines egregiously entitled *L'Esprit des lois en vers*, that Montesquieu, indifferent to forms of government and religions, attributes all to climate, hence,

> On peut, dans le siècle où nous sommes,
> Par les seuls degrés du soleil
> Calculer la valeur des hommes.[3]

More serious writers also, some of them Montesquieu's disciples, have regarded the theory of climate as central in Montesquieu's thought. Buckle in England, Adam Ferguson in Scotland, Comte and Taine in France are seen to follow his lead. To define the importance of this theory in his system and to discover how it grew, are important tasks.[4]

The belief that climate is a major factor governing human societies is not found in the early writings of Montesquieu. Before his travels he had consigned a few remarks to the *Pensées*, and had put some sentiments into the mouths of Usbek and Rica, which show that he had thought about climate, and that his mind held elements of doctrines from which a full theory of climatic influence could be constructed. He had stressed the

[1] Richard Tickell, *The Project, a Poem*, London, 1778, dedication, p. [iii].

[2] *Opere*, Venice, 1792–4, IV, p. 253.

[3] *Œuvres de Montesquieu*, ed. E. Laboulaye, Paris, 1875–9, VI, p. 245.

[4] For a more detailed study of the growth of the theory see my article, 'The Evolution of Montesquieu's theory of climate" (*Revue internationale de philosophie*, 1955).

dependence of the mind on physical causes. One of the characteristics of his early materialist leanings was his acceptance of the doctrine of Galen, *Quod animi mores corporis temperamentum sequuntur*. When Usbek is made to report the conversation of a Parisian *bel esprit* who proclaims that his opinions depend absolutely on the constitution of his body,[1] Montesquieu is giving his reader a foretaste of the idea of the relativism of religion which is going to appear in Books XXIV and XXV of *L'Esprit des lois*. An appreciation of the role of climate in the economic condition of a country occurs early in the *Pensées*.[2] He had read the *Voyages* of Chardin, who declares that the cause or origin of the *mœurs* of the Orientals lies on the quality of their climate.[3] But he holds no systematic doctrine himself.

It is not until his visit to Italy that he shows serious interest in the effect of climate. Returned travellers had often given evil reports of the air of Rome, and guide-books seldom failed to comment on the noxious and even lethal effects of the atmosphere either of the city itself or of the Roman *campagna*. Rogissart's *Les Délices de l'Italie*, Misson's *Nouveau Voyage d'Italie*, and Addison's *Remarks on several parts of Italy*, all of them known to Montesquieu, cited by him, and possessed by him at La Brède, allude to the unhealthy qualities of the Roman air. Shortly before departing for Italy, he had made the acquaintance of the *Réflexions critiques sur la poésie et sur la peinture*, by the Abbé Dubos.[4] The learned Abbé asserts the influence of climate on national character, giving a fairly detailed analysis of its mode of operation. He even makes the assertion that climate can affect religious observance, and that it can draw men to vice or to virtue. Referring, as many eighteenth-century writers were to do later, to the large number of suicides found in England, he points out that fifty out of every sixty of them occur at either the beginning or the end of winter, when the wind comes from the north-east and engenders morose introspection and despair. He quotes Chardin in support, and also Fontenelle who, in his *Digression sur les anciens et les modernes* and, no doubt, in conversation also—he, Dubos, and Montesquieu were all three members of the salon

[1] *L.P.* 75. The passage in *L.P.* 121 describing the influence of air on the human body dates only from 1754.

[2] *Pensée* 312 (Bkn. 1981).

[3] Amsterdam, 1711, II, pp. 275–6.

[4] See above, p. 60.

of Madame de Lambert—had argued elegantly in favour of climatic influence.

Dubos was perplexed, and found his theory challenged, by the case of the Romans. How is one to explain the deterioration in their character, with no change of geographical location, since the days of Cato and Brutus? He meets this objection to his theory by declaring in the first place that the change in their character is more apparent than real, and then that the air of Rome has changed since those days:

> Il est arrivé de si grands changements dans l'air de Rome et dans l'air des environs de cette ville depuis les Césars, qu'il n'est pas étonnant que les habitants y soient à présent différents de ce qu'ils étaient autrefois. Au contraire, suivant notre système, il fallait que la chose arrivât ainsi, et que l'altération de la cause altérât l'effet.[1]

The reason for the present impurity of the Roman air is, he contends, that the soil of Rome contains large numbers of cavities, resulting from ancient drains and from ruined buildings now covered with earth, and that these cavities are filled with stagnant water. The heat of the summer sun causes exhalations to rise from these subterranean pools, and these exhalations pollute the air. To this first explanation Dubos adds two others: that the soil is no longer so carefully cultivated, and that subterranean deposits of alum, sulphur, and arsenic communicate noxious vapours to the atmosphere. The theory which Dubos makes most specifically his own is that of emanation, the nature of the air depending in large measure, in his view, on the presence in the soil either of minerals or of stagnant water.

During his travels, Montesquieu pays great attention to the problem of air and its effect on human beings. He was greatly interested in the mines of Hungary and of the Hartz and particularly comments on the impurity of the air inside them. In Rome, the first conversation he reports is with Polignac on the unwholesome nature of the air of Rome. The Cardinal offered three explanations: that the rivers no longer flowed as well as in time past; that cavities on the sea shore, when scorched in summer, produce insects and evil-smelling vapours; and that there are many mines of alum and other minerals, whence vapours rise. Montesquieu adds a reason of his own: the existence of hollows

[1] *Réflexions critiques* . . ., Paris, 1719, II, pp. 263–4.

in the ground, brought about by the subsidence of buildings. The winter's rain accumulates in these hollows and in the hot weather noxious vapours ascend to poison the air.[1] When visiting Polignac's excavations, he found confirmation for his theory;[2] and during his journey further south he found, in the ruined temples of Pozzuoli, at the Solfatara, in the slopes of Vesuvius, and even in the miracle of the liquefaction, new occasions for studying the effects of air.[3]

On his return to France Montesquieu sought to put on paper his observations already made, and to pursue his researches further by means of experiment. At an early date he read to the Academy of Bordeaux two papers on mines which he had inspected in Hungary; in a third paper read in December 1731, on the mines of the Hartz, he made some comments on the Roman air. A year later, perhaps relying on the works of Lancisi and Doni which he acquired about this time[4] he presented a paper entitled *Réflexions sur la sobriété des habitants de Rome comparée à l'intempérance des anciens Romains* in which he divides the causes of the changed character of the Romans into two groups, moral and physical.[5] His new enthusiasm seems soon to have been communicated to others, for the subject prescribed by the Academy of Bordeaux for the prize dissertation of 1733 was *La Nature et les propriétés de l'air*;[6] and if Montesquieu was disappointed by the quality of the entries, as he must have been if those still preserved in the Bordeaux library are a complete or a representative collection, at least he had the consolation of reflecting that several minds, both of candidates and of judges, had been exercising themselves on a problem dear to him, as, in time long past, it had been dear to his friend Navarre.[7]

He enthusiastically pursued experiments meanwhile. It was in 1737 that he consulted Mairan about microscopes[8] and it was probably about the same time that he undertook experiments,

[1] Nagel II, p. 1095; Pléiade I, p. 663.

[2] Nagel III, p. 459; Pléiade I, p. 906.

[3] Nagel II, pp. 1156–60; Pléiade I, pp. 724–8.

[4] Lancisi, *Dissertatio de nativis deque adventitiis Romani caeli qualitatibus*, in *Opera*, Geneva, 1718; Doni, *De restituenda salubritate agri Romani*, in Sallengre, *Novus thesaurus antiquitatum Romanarum*, The Hague, 1716.

[5] Nagel III, p. 358; Pléiade I, p. 910.

[6] P. Barrière, *L'Académie de Bordeaux*, p. 190.

[7] Ibid.

[8] See above, p. 211.

described in *L'Esprit des lois*, on a sheep's tongue under the microscope with the aim of discovering its reaction to changes in temperature.[1]

Montesquieu's interest in climate as a social factor is now beginning to emerge. It had been mentioned in the *Considérations* but only along with other factors and in passing. In the *Monarchie universelle* there is a little more evidence of it, since here he is seen to adopt a classification of nations into northern and southern —a division which, in the hands of Madame de Staël and Sismondi, was to be influential in forming the literary theory of Romanticism. The *Pensées*, from 1731 onwards, contain isolated references to the influence of climate, now in relation to literary taste, now to the status of women, to the character of the English, to celibacy, to the Russians.[2] These are but a few of many separate and unco-ordinated allusions.

He notes meanwhile in the *Spicilège*[3] that he must read John Barclay's *Icon animorum*, a character-book famous in its day (it was published at London in 1614), whose analyses are based on climate. He shows in the *Pensées*[4] that he is acquainted with the *Examen de ingenios* of the sixteenth-century Spaniard Juan Huarte. This book, which the President possessed in one of its several French translations, is an attempt to link Galenic medicine with Plato's educational theories. Huarte builds up a psychological system on the basis of the four humours, black bile, yellow bile, blood, and phlegm, and shows how distribution of these humours in the human body is controlled by climatic conditions. The *Examen de ingenios* was known to Montaigne also and it is interesting to see his fellow Bordelais drawing on the same source.[5]

The most significant French writer on political theory before Montesquieu was Jean Bodin, with whose general outlook the President has little in common. The theory of climatic influence plays a great part, however, in Bodin's works, and although it is linked there not only with obsolete medicine, but also with astrology, it provides some embryonic notions of the philosophy of history. Montesquieu's knowledge of Bodin's works has been

[1] *Lois*, XIV, 2.

[2] *Pensées* 717, 757, 889, 905, 1199 (Bkn. 853, 1088, 1436, 1926, 1389).

[3] *Spicilège* 562 (MS., p. 521). [4] *Pensée* 1191 (Bkn. 181).

[5] See P. Mauriac, 'Une source espagnole méconnue de l'*Esprit des lois*' (*Actes de l'Académie de Bordeaux*, 4e série, tome XV, 1958).

denied. He possessed them, however, including two copies of the *République*, and his copy of the *Methodus* is heavily marked, with asterisks and underlinings, at those precise points in the fifth chapter where Bodin's theory of climate is expounded.

Nor is Hippocrates, the progenitor of all exponents of climatic influence, absent from La Brède. For Montesquieu's papers include two extracts from his *De aere*,[1] the first of them being in the hand of a secretary who appears to have served the President between 1738 and 1741.

These precursors of Montesquieu are important. All of them probably inspired him, though a specific source has not, except in the case of Huarte, been established. More significant than these, however, are the Englishman John Arbuthnot and the Frenchman François-Ignace Espiard de La Borde. Arbuthnot published at London in 1733 *An Essay concerning the Effects of Air on Human Bodies*, in which the theory of the influence of climate is fully and systematically debated. Between this work, which was translated into French in 1742, and Book XIV of *L'Esprit des lois* there are many resemblances, to which the Abbé Dedieu was the first to draw attention.[2]

The likelihood of Montesquieu's being personally acquainted with Arbuthnot has already been alluded to. They were both friends of Chesterfield, Bolingbroke, and Hervey. They were both Fellows of the Royal Society. They were both freemasons. That they should meet in London was almost inevitable. Arbuthnot is twice cited by Montesquieu,[3] though not in connexion with climate. Arbuthnot's *Essay* was, it may be assumed, in progress of composition while Montesquieu was in England. Soon after

[1] Nagel III, pp. 712–14; not in Pléiade.

[2] *Montesquieu et la tradition politique anglaise en France*, Paris, 1909. Dedieu lists fourteen passages from the *Essay* and puts them side by side with as many passages from the *Lois*. These fourteen comparisons are not all of equal value. Six of them seem to me quite dubious, but seven are probable and one appears conclusive. One established borrowing will often serve to authenticate other possible ones from the same author. Arbuthnot writes (French translation, pp. 59–50): 'Un certain degré de chaleur, pas assez fort pour dessécher ou détruire les solides, *allonge et relâche* les fibres; de là l'*abattement* et la *faiblesse* qu'on sent dans les jours chauds.' Montesquieu writes (*Lois*, XIV, 2): 'L'air chaud *relâche* les *extrémités* des *fibres* et les *allonge*. Mettez un homme dans un lieu chaud, il souffrira une défaillance de cœur très grande; sa *faiblesse* présente mettra un *découragement* dans son âme.' This passage from the *Lois* dates, in the manuscript, from 1740–3.

[3] *Lois*, XVI, 4; *Spicilège* 781 (MS., pp. 790–1).

his return, and in the year of publication of the *Essay*, a similar subject was set in the Bordeaux Academy's annual competition. Montesquieu's friend the doctor Raulin, of Nérac, was an avowed disciple of Arbuthnot. The French translation, executed by Boyer de Pebrandié, published at Paris in 1742, and dedicated to the father of Helvétius, is a rare book, but it was possessed by the Academy of Bordeaux; it is still to be found in the municipal library of Bordeaux, bearing the stamp *Crescam et lucebo* of the Academy. That Arbuthnot greatly influenced Montesquieu in the development of his climatic theory cannot be doubted. It is by no means impossible that Montesquieu knew the *Essay* before its translation in 1742. That he knew it after 1742 is little less than certain.

Espiard de La Borde is far from being a literary giant. He was born at Besançon but came to live at Dijon. Here he became a protégé of Bouhier, to whom, in August 1742, with a request for help in finding a publisher, he sent the manuscript of a newly written work which he had prepared in the greatest secrecy.[1] The result of this approach was three volumes which appeared at Brussels in 1743 under the title *Essais sur le génie et le caractère des nations*. This work is exceedingly rare. It was republished in 1752 under the title *L'Esprit des nations* and in 1753 in English translation as *The Spirit of Nations*. In 1769 it was extensively plagiarized by Jean-Louis Castilhon in a work published at Bouillon under the title *Considérations sur les causes physiques et morales de la diversité du génie, des mœurs, et du gouvernment des nations. Tiré* [*sic*] *en partie d'un ouvrage anonyme*. He acknowledges making extensive use of Espiard's book, which he describes as very little known in France and of which he appears to know only the second edition.

If the second only were now known, it would be thought to plagiarize Montesquieu's writings. But the first edition precedes *L'Esprit des lois* by five years. The similarities between Espiard's work and the ideas of Montesquieu are too close to be accidental, from the opening words onwards: 'le génie des peuples peut être considéré comme un effet ou comme une cause.'[2] The *Considérations sur les Romains* are cited several times by Espiard, who professes many ideas dear to Montesquieu, some of them resembling ideas already held by the President and, though committed

[1] Espiard to Bouhier, 1 August 1742 (B.N., MSS. fr. 24421, ff. 48–49).
[2] *Essais*, I, p. 3.

to paper, unpublished in 1743, others very close, both in substance and in terminology, to what was later to appear in *L'Esprit des lois.*[1] A particularly persuasive resemblance is in relation to the word *climat.* Originally meaning specifically the area between two parallels on the earth's surface so distant that there is half an hour's difference in the length of their longest day, the word was extended to mean simply geographical situation. When Corneille, in 1666, writes

> Des climats différents la nature est diverse:
> La Grèce a des vertus qu'on ne voit point en Perse[2]

and La Bruyère, twenty-two years later, declares that 'la raison est de tous les climats'[3] they are using a word which means no more than geographical region. The connotation of atmospheric condition or weather is absent, as it is absent from dictionaries until the 1762 revision of the dictionary of the Academy.[4] Montesquieu is the first writer of any significance to use the word *climat* in the sense of weather; but Espiard precedes him. Having in his second chapter produced the specialized and traditional definition of a climate, he goes on thereafter to use the word *climat* in its modern meteorological sense. The numerous verbal resemblances of the two writers, fortified by this neological coincidence, argue a link between the two. Espiard might have been a runaway secretary of the President who plagiarized his former master; but more likely is the hypothesis that Montesquieu was the borrower: the very rare first edition of Espiard, absent from most French libraries, even (in its complete form) from the Bibliothèque Nationale, is present in the municipal library of Bordeaux where it bears the inscription *ex dono dom. praesidis Barbot.* Barbot was Montesquieu's oldest friend.

The development of Montesquieu's thought in relation to climate shows itself as being clearly inductive. Starting with an

[1] Some short textual comparisons are made in my article above-mentioned, 'The Evolution of Montesquieu's theory of climate'.

[2] *Agésilas*, vv. 1741–2.

[3] *Les Caractères*, ed. G. Servois, II, p. 88.

[4] Cf. also G. Cayrou, *Le Français classique*, Paris, 1924, s.v. *climat*. The modern sense of the English word *climate* (=weather) is not mentioned in B. Martin, *Lingua Britannica Reformata*, published in 1749, and Johnson in 1755 is still not admitting it when he records the popular meaning 'region or tract of land differing from another by the temperature of the air'.

examination of the specific problem of Roman air, enlarging his ideas by reading, by observation, and by experiment, he arrives in the end at his general theory of climatic influence.

II. THE DOCTRINE OF CLIMATE

The President begins his exposition of the influence of climate with an examination of the effect of heat and cold on man's body.[1] The fibres of the human frame are contracted by cold air and expanded by hot air. When they are contracted, their elasticity or *ressort* increases; for this reason, and because the blood then flows more easily to the heart, the strength of the body becomes greater. Men, then, are stronger in cold climates.

Cette force plus grande doit produire bien des effets: par exemple, plus de confiance en soi-même, c'est-à-dire plus de courage; plus de connaissance de sa supériorité, c'est-à-dire moins de désir de la vengeance; plus d'opinion de sa sûreté, c'est-à-dire plus de franchise, moins de soupçons, de politique et de ruses.

The nerves, on the other hand, end in little bundles on the skin. According as the skin is tense or relaxed, so are the ends of the nerves less or more open to external stimuli. The skin is tense in cold climates, relaxed in hot ones. External stimuli therefore are more readily responded to in hot climates than in cold. Sensations are more numerous then, in hot climates, and imagination, taste, sensitivity and vivacity, which depend on a multitude of sensations, are found in greater abundance where the sun shines more brightly.[2]

[1] The theory is embodied in Books XIV, XV, XVI and XVII, of which XIV is the most important and most famous. Several of the passages relating to climate belong to the earliest pages of the Paris manuscript and therefore date, at the latest, from the years 1739–41.

[2] The doctrine is paraphrased by Richard Tickell in lines which, as well as being amusing, illustrate the common reaction to Montesquieu:

The short'ning fibres braced by cold,
The blood flies back, the heart grows bold;
Relaxed by heat, their force declines,
The spirits droop, the being pines:
Till, quite o'erpowered, the sick'ning soul
Yields to the atmosphere's control.
(*The Project*, p. 2).

For what he had said, Montesquieu has experimental justification. He takes the tongue of a sheep, examines it under a microscope, and discovers little pyramids on its surface. He regards these pyramids as being, in all probability, the principal organs of taste. He then freezes the tongue, and finds that the pyramids are no longer visible. They have retreated into the tissues of the tongue, and it is only as the tongue gradually regains the temperature of the air that the pyramids begin to reappear.

After this digression, Montesquieu returns to his enumeration of the psychological results of heat and cold.

> Dans les pays froids, on aura peu de sensibilité pour les plaisirs; elle sera plus grande dans les pays tempérés; dans les pays chauds, elle sera extrême.

He has seen operas performed in Italy and in England. The same pieces, with the same actors, produce the most widely differing effects. The calmness of the one nation and the transport of the other can scarcely be believed. Pain, likewise, is variously felt in varied climates: 'il faut écorcher un Moscovite pour lui donner du sentiment.' The love of one sex for the other is far more intense in the south, where the seat of pleasure is the harem. The more vigorous natives of the north have for their delectation hunting, travel, war, and drinking; they have few vices; they are honest and open. But as one approaches the lands of the south, one seems to be moving away from morality itself.

What immediate consequences follow from the principle thus enunciated? Some peoples, notably the inhabitants of India, need the offices of a good legislator more than others. The intellectually indolent—to wit, the races of the Orient—are slow to change their ways; hence the same laws and institutions exist in their lands as existed a thousand years ago.[1] In these same lands speculation, rather than action, will be the habit of the people; hence monasticism will flourish. The number of dervishes in Asia increases with the heat of the climate, and this same phenomenon—it is recalled that monks, in the *Lettres persanes*, are called dervishes—is to be found in Europe.[2] Alcohol is drunk with more impunity in the north, where coagulation of the blood is less to be feared; in the south, therefore, the legislator Mahomet has been compelled to forbid the consumption of wine.[3] In England,

[1] *Lois*, XIV, 3. [2] *Lois*, XIV, 7. [3] *Lois*, XIV, 10.

the climate engenders weariness and disgust with everything, even life itself; it is therefore not expedient that the citizens should be able to vent their hostility to the government against a single man: it is better that laws rather than men should govern. Thus the government of England is what it ought to be.[1] In the hottest of countries, where courage is almost unknown, another stimulus has to take its place in urging men to do hard and painful things; the fear of punishment is that alternative; and therefore climate is one of the many causes of slavery.[2] In hot climates, since the early maturity of women cause them to marry while still infants, wives are in a position of clear subordination to their husbands; and since it costs less to maintain them than in cooler areas, a man can more easily afford more than one: hence polygamy.[3] Courage is the characteristic of the north, to the point that even within a single country remarkable differences are seen:

> Les peuples du nord de la Corée sont plus courageux que ceux du midi.[4]

It follows that northern races are more frequently free, and southern races often enslaved. Asia, according to the accounts of travellers, which Montesquieu elaborately examines, has virtually no temperate zone, whereas Europe's is very extensive. In Asia, therefore, races of widely different characteristics find themselves contiguous. The warlike and the weak are adjacent, and this contrast weakens the continent as a whole, and promotes war and servitude. In Europe, the more even balance of races is an element of strength and encourages liberty. The vast empires of conquest in Asia can be governed only despotically. In the smaller States of Europe freedom can flourish.[5]

These elements compose Montesquieu's theory of climate. It is not a rigorous and systematic doctrine. Certain effects on men's minds are in part caused by the climate, and as men's minds influence the forms of government under which they live, so climate, vicariously, influences those forms of government. This is a moderate and limited doctrine. It is only a part, and even a small part, of the doctrine of *L'Esprit des lois*; and the first

[1] *Lois*, XIV, 13. [2] *Lois*, XV, 7. [3] *Lois*, XVI, 3, 4.
[4] *Lois*, XVII, 2. [5] *Lois*, XVII, 3, 5.

impression one ought to retain of the theory of climate in Montesquieu's work is of the narrowness of the limits it occupies.

The first impression in the mind of the twentieth-century reader, however, may well be that of the *naïveté* of the doctrine; and that impression, if one is to judge by absolute scientific standards, is justified. But if one wishes to understand Montesquieu properly one must judge him in relation to the standards of his own day, and the theories of climate current in the seventeenth and eighteenth centuries often took odd forms. It was thought that the high temperatures of the south and east stimulated black bile and therefore strengthened the imagination, fostering in particular religious inspiration and literary genius. Hence new religions and literary *genres* were deemed to arise in the east. This view, going back to Cardano in sixteenth-century Italy, was expressed by Huet in modest form, and was not wholly dissented from by Fontenelle.[1] Others held that in cold climates the pores contract, the internal heat of the body cannot escape, and it is necessary to cool it: hence the notorious drunkenness of northern races.[2] For such views as these Montesquieu has no use,[3] and he marks a great advance on their exponents. He makes an effort to reject the *a priori* in relation both to the facts of climatic conditions and to the mode of influence. The seriousness of his attempts to discover experimentally the effect of heat and cold is surpassed only by the zeal with which he studies the accounts of travellers. He does not simply make assertions: he seeks evidence.

III. MORAL AND PHYSICAL CAUSES

The imputation of determinism or of fatalism has often been made against the author of *L'Esprit des lois* on the strength of his theory of climate. A reply to this charge can be based on the instruction which Montesquieu gives to the legislator when confronted with a people climatically disposed in a certain way. The good legislator, he says, must resist the vices of the climate. The bad legislator will accept them. In hot lands, for example,

[1] See Fontenelle, *De l'origine des fables*, ed. J.-R. Carré, Paris, 1932, pp. 30 and 84–91.

[2] *Inter alios*, Tassoni, *Pensieri diversi*, bk. VIII, ch. 13 (Venice, 1627, p. 392).

[3] There is a solitary exception: *Spicilège* 539 (MS., p. 498).

in order to overcome the idleness engendered by the climate, laws should seek to remove all possibility of living without work.[1]

But is this practical advice? Is Montesquieu simply constructing a *pons asinorum*? Is he not calling on the legislator to resist necessity, enjoining on him a course of action which is bound to fail? In answering this question one is examining one of the most important and most controversial problems which the study of Montesquieu provokes.

Already in the *Lettres persanes* Montesquieu has insisted on the importance of moral causes as well as physical. When discussing the reasons for the decline in the population of the world since ancient times, Usbek says to Rica, in a concluding paragraph of one of his letters:

> Je te ferai voir, dans une lettre suivante, qu'indépendamment des causes physiques il y en a de morales qui ont produit cet effet.[2]

Among the countless writers who, with one intention or another, had discussed causes, some had stressed the distinction between moral and physical causes: Samuel Clarke, who uses the terms 'moral motives' and 'causes physically efficient',[3] Dubos, who, dealing with literary history, by moral causes means patronage, and Espiard, whose notions are closer to Montesquieu's. The President develops his theory of causes gradually. He is enunciating his problem when in his own years of indecision, the later 1720's, he writes:

> Ce qui fait la plupart des contradictions de l'homme, c'est que la raison physique et la raison morale ne sont presque jamais d'accord.[4]

His ideas are fully developed only in the *Essai sur les causes qui peuvent affecter les esprits et les caractères*. This short work, published long after the death of Montesquieu, is of cardinal importance in his thought. Its genesis may have lain in an earlier dissertation on *La Différence des génies*, now lost,[5] but in its present form the *Essai* was begun soon after 1736 and was completed or abandoned soon after 1743.[6] It served Montesquieu as a storehouse

[1] *Lois*, XIV, 7. [2] *L.P.* 113.

[3] *Discourse concerning the being and attributes of God*, London, 1728 (the edition possessed by Montesquieu), p. 99.

[4] *Pensée* 241 (Bkn. 1208).

[5] Cf. *Pensée* 2265 (not in Bkn).

[6] See my article 'The Evolution of Montesquieu's theory of climate', which corrects my earlier dating (1736–41), given in Nagel III, p. 572.

of ideas. He conveyed into it ideas culled from his reading. He drew on it for *L'Esprit des lois*. He continued to add even after he had begun to take away: an unusual procedure, but one which he had already used in *Les Princes*.

The *Essai sur les causes* is important also in itself. The first part of this essay, dealing with physical causes, is a clear statement of the influence of climate and of temperament.[1] The description of the action of the fibres now found in *L'Esprit des lois* had originally been here. There is discussion of the effect of food—a subject which had been treated in a separate work by Arbuthnot[2]—and of the operations of 'un esprit ou suc contenu dans le nerfs', which is an echo of Descartes's animal spirits. Montesquieu shows himself to be among the many disciples of Locke in eighteenth-century France by his insistence on the dependence of the mind on external objects, and his language is at times reminiscent of La Mettrie, who gave a materialist distortion to Locke's ideas. After Plato, Bodin, and Montaigne, he considers the subtlety of the air of Athens; he discusses the effect of mountains, mentioning especially the Pyrenees and the Apennines; he compares the *sirocco* of Italy and the east wind of England; he alludes to the mental differences of the sexes, and to the effects of castration and of celibacy, of sleep and of fasting, and interjects, in characteristic mode, when dealing with this last topic that no one could suspect the ancient Fathers of the Desert of having been imbeciles. The position to which this debate leads him is largely materialistic, and is engagingly expressed: the soul in our body is like a spider in its web.

The second part of the essay is devoted to moral causes. These are as inseparable from the life of the individual as are physical causes. If his senses carry ideas to his brain, it is moral causes—of which the most important is education—which enable him to choose between different ideas presented to him, to evaluate them and compare them. It is education which keeps the brain active and efficient, which prevents it from falling, as otherwise it would certainly fall (witness Circassian and Mingrelian slaves) into atrophy. In this way it is true to say that education creates ideas for us, since it keeps alive the channel through which ideas

[1] The word "temperament" is here used in its old sense of the physical constitution of the body.

[2] *An Essay concerning the Nature of Aliments*, London, 1731.

come. Our educators are thus manufacturers of ideas. It is the function of moral causes to correct, control and supplement physical causes. Without physical causes life would not exist. Without the operation of moral causes, life would be worthless.

Physical causes then are controlled and directed by education, and education can be of two types:

> Nous venons de parler de l'education particulière, qui forme chaque caractère; mais il y a encore une éducation générale, que l'on reçoit dans la société où l'on est; car il y a, dans chaque nation, un caractère général, dont celui de chaque particulier se charge plus ou moins. Il est produit de deux manières: par les causes physiques, qui dépendent du climat, dont je ne parlerai plus; et par les causes morales, qui sont la combinaison des lois, de la religion, des mœurs et des manières, et cette espèce d'émanation de la façon de penser, de l'air et des sottises de la Cour et de la Capitale, qui se répandent au loin.[1]

The assembly of causes is one of the most important ideas of *L'Esprit des lois*, and it is an idea which had for long been germinating in Montesquieu's mind. In the fragment *De la politique*, which was a part of the *Traité des devoirs* of 1725, he had affirmed that in each society there is a common character or universal soul, whose mode of thinking is the result of an infinite sequence of causes which are multiplied through the ages.[2] In the *Considérations sur les Romains* he alluded again to this common character, calling it now the *esprit général*, and insisting that power is based on it and must not offend it.[3]

There are three places in which the factors of the *esprit général* are enumerated. There is first a passage in the *Pensées* dating from 1731–3, which lists five factors: religion, maxims of government, laws, *les mœurs*, and *les manières*.[4] A later passage, written between 1733 and 1738 and not susceptible of closer dating, discards maxims of government in order to make way for climate, which now enters the *esprit général*.[5] The third definition of the *esprit général* is penned after the subject has been further explored in the *Essai sur les causes*. It is found in the fourth chapter of Book XIX of *L'Esprit des lois*. This chapter, dating in the manuscript from 1740–3, is perhaps the most significant chapter of the

[1] Nagel III, p. 419; Pléiade II, p. 58.
[2] Nagel III, pp. 168–9; Pléiade I, p. 114.
[3] *Romains*, ch XXII (Nagel I, C, p. 519; Pléiade II, p. 203).
[4] *Pensée* 542 (Bkn. 645).
[5] *Pensée* 854 (Bkn. 1903).

whole work. It is also one of the shortest and it must be quoted in full:

Plusieurs choses gouvernement les hommes: le climat, la religion, les lois, les maximes du gouvernement, les exemples des choses passées, les mœurs, les manières; d'ou il se forme un esprit général qui en résulte.

A mesure que, dans chaque nation, une de ces causes agit avec plus de force, les autres lui cèdent d'autant. La nature et le climat dominent presque seuls sur les sauvages; les manières gouvernement les Chinois; les lois tyrannisent le Japon; les mœurs donnaient autrefois le ton dans Lacédémone; les maximes du gouvernement et les mœurs anciennes le donnaient dans Rome.

It is quite wrong, in view of this passage and its antecedents in the author's works, to say that Montesquieu recognizes but one cause in political societies. The fate of nations rests on a balance or equilibrium of these seven causes, on which the legislator must base his laws and the historian his analyses. Only one of these causes, climate, is physical. How, in Montesquieu's view, is the balance struck between them? Does he believe in the paramountcy of climate?

That he does not in his own opinion do so is made clear in a significant paragraph relegated to the *Pensées* between 1733 and 1738:

Je supplie qu'on ne m'accuse pas d'attribuer aux causes morales des choses qui n'appartiennent qu'au climat.[1]

He continues in a vivid, unfinished style:

Je sais bien que, si des causes morales n'interrompaient point les physiques, celles-ci sortiraient et agiraient dans toute leur étendue. Je sais encore que, si les causes physiques avaient la force d'agir par elles-mêmes (comme lorsque les peuples sont habitants de montagnes inaccessibles), elles ne détruisissent [*sic*] bientôt la cause morale: car souvent la cause physique a besoin de la cause morale pour agir.

He is afraid that he may be accused of having laid too small a stress on physical causes: a fear of which the tumultuous reception of *L'Esprit des lois* was very soon to disabuse him. He believes firmly in the concomitance of moral and physical causes.

What of the primitive condition of mankind? If one examines

[1] *Pensée* 811 (Bkn. 1209).

the *esprit général*, stripping off in turn like leaves from an artichoke those components which are the result of human activity, one sees laws, maxims, *mœurs*, and *manières* disappear. Religion itself is largely an artifact for Montesquieu, and the natural law which inspires the other, basic part of it, is not the first natural law in chronological order.[1] And when human activity is first starting, there can be no *exemples des choses passées*.

There remains climate: 'le premier de tous les empires'.[2] In the earliest societies, the least civilized communities, the physical cause is prepotent: 'la nature et le climat dominent presque seuls sur les sauvages'.

As society develops subsequently, religion is embraced, laws are made, precedents accumulate, *mœurs* and *manières* develop, maxims are pronounced. The further any society is from the moment of its original institution, the more important are the non-physical factors in the *esprit général*.

The political role of physical causes is thus seen to be quite different from that of moral causes. In value also, notwithstanding Brunschvicg's denial,[3] there is a great difference between them. The duty of the legislator, Montesquieu has declared, is to oppose the force of the climate. It is also his duty, however, to act in accordance with the *esprit général*, and of the *esprit général* climate is a part. This means that the good legislator must shift the emphasis, within the framework of the *esprit général*, from physical factors to moral factors. He must rely less than his predecessors on climate, and more on manners, morals, laws, religion, and the appeal to past usage.

Not only is it the duty of the good legislator so to act. Legislators as a whole do so act. With the passage of time the sole empire of climate becomes more remote, and as the moral factors necessarily increase in number, the role of climate is necessarily a dwindling role. Tradition, way of life, customs, religion, and opinion—above all opinion—are constantly gaining in importance as determining factors in society. They may not always be morally valuable, but they are more desirable than climatic influence and their growing predominance over climate is progress.

[1] *Lois*, I, 2. [2] *Lois*, XIX, 14.

[3] 'Entre "ces choses" hétérogènes, aucune hiérarchie préétablie' (L. Brunschvicg, *Progrès de la conscience dans la philosophie occidentale*, Paris, 1927, II, p. 496.

This conclusion is implicit in Montesquieu's doctrine of the *esprit général*. He does not make any intuitive generalization like the famous one of Turgot:

> La masse totale du genre humain, par des alternatives de calme et d'agitations, de biens et de maux, marche toujours, quoiqu'à pas lents, à une perfection plus grande.[1]

Montesquieu's theory is more tentative and more empirical. It is based on an attempt to synthesize the results of detailed study of scientific and historical fact. His documentation is incomplete. His synthesis is imperfect. He has omitted economic factors. Nevertheless, he has enunciated, not less than Turgot, a theory of progress, and far better than Turgot or any other contemporary, he has been able, in Gibbon's words, to conciliate the rights of liberty and of nature.[2]

[1] *Discours sur les progrès successifs de l'esprit humain* (1750), in *Œuvres*, ed. Daire and Dussard, Paris, 1844, II, p. 598.

[2] *Decline and Fall*, ed. Bury, IV, p. 596. Some of the preceding arguments were developed in my article, 'Montesquieu in 1948' (*FS*, 1949).

XV

THE HISTORY OF LAWS

I. ROMAN LAW OF SUCCESSION

THE presence at the end of *L'Esprit des lois* of four books of a largely historical nature, one of them dealing with the Roman law on successions and the other three treating French laws and institutions, has puzzled many commentators. The twenty-sixth book, *Des lois, dans le rapport qu'elles doivent avoir avec l'ordre des choses sur lesquelles elles statuent*, could reasonably have been followed by Book XXIX, *De la manière de composer les lois*, and *L'Esprit des lois* would have been a rounded whole. But that was not Montesquieu's design. It was not even his original design.

The great confusion of what is now the fifth volume of the Paris manuscript of *L'Esprit des lois*, where essential pages are missing and irrelevant pages have been inserted, makes difficult its utilization in the study of the last books of the work. The total absence from the manuscript of Book XXVI cannot be taken as proving that the composition of that book was subsequent to 1746, which is the final date of the manuscript. But the presence in the manuscript of Book XXVII in handwriting of the years 1741–3 is sufficient to show that the book on the Roman law of succession was not an afterthought. It was an integral and long-standing part of the text; and any attempt therefore to measure the unity of *L'Esprit des lois* must take account of, and not exclude, this book and with it the other historical books XXVIII, XXX, and XXXI.[1]

D'Alembert, in his *Analyse de l'Esprit des lois*, claims that Montesquieu, having in the rest of the work enunciated his principles, seeks now to illustrate them by examples drawn from the history of the world's most famous race, the Romans, and from that of the race which most concerns his readers, the French.[2]

[1] It is surprising that Barckhausen, in his highly ingenious attempt to systematize *L'Esprit des lois*, excludes these books, the more so since it would not have been impossible to relate them to the fourth of his constitutive elements, *les patrimoines* ('Le Désordre de l'*Esprit des lois*' in his *Montesquieu, ses idées et ses œuvres*, Paris, 1907).

[2] Nagel I, A, p. li.

Lanson, not incompatibly with this, argues for a division of the work into three parts, dealing respectively with *les choses en soi*, with *les choses dans l'espace* (discussed in the geographical books), and with *les choses dans le temps*.[1]

Montesquieu himself throws light on the question in a passage taken from the *Pensées*. He is dealing only with the book on Roman law, but his words explain also the books on French antiquities, and indeed illuminate also the whole of *L'Esprit des lois*.

Il y a des lois principales et des lois accessoires, et il se forme, dans chaque pays, une espèce de génération de lois.[2] Les peuples, comme chaque individu, ont une suite d'idées, et leur manière de penser totale, comme celle de chaque particulier, a un commencement, un milieu et une fin.

Cette matière n'aurait point de bornes si je n'en mettais. J'ai pris un exemple qui est de l'origine et de la génération des lois des Romains sur les successions, et cet exemple servira ici de méthode.

Je n'ai point pris la plume pour enseigner les lois, mais la manière de les enseigner. Aussi n'ai-je point traité des lois, mais de l'esprit des lois.

Si j'ai bien donné la théorie des lois romaines sur les successions, on pourra, par la même méthode, voir la naissance des lois de la plupart des peuples.[3]

Montesquieu's interest in the specific problem of succession in Roman law may have been stimulated by his former preoccupations as a parliamentary president. For example, in Salviat's *La Jurisprudence du Parlement de Bordeaux*,[4] published after the death of Montesquieu but based largely on cases decided during his lifetime or before, it is pointed out that whereas the Roman law of succession gives no preference to the eldest son over his brothers, in the custom of Bordeaux the eldest son, if his parents die intestate, enjoys a *préciput* or additional share over and above his equal portion. This is simply one of many problems

[1] G. Lanson, 'L'Influence de la philosophie cartésienne sur la littérature française' (*Revue de métaphysique*, 1896, reprinted in his *Etudes d'histoire littéraire*, Paris, 1929).

[2] Book XXVII was originally (in an early draft of the manuscript) entitled *De quelques dépendances des lois* and subsequently *De la dépendance des lois*.

[3] *Pensée* 1794 (Bkn. 398). An intelligent discussion of the relevance of this passage to *L'Esprit des lois* is to be found in C. Oudin, *De l'unité de l'Esprit des lois*, Paris, 1910, pp. 130–2.

[4] Paris, 1787, pp. 36–37.

involving the relationship between Roman and French customary law; for though the province of Guyenne was a *pays de droit écrit* in which Roman law, in its surviving form, was predominant, there was nevertheless a large number of local customs which limited its sway. The duty of the magistrates was to understand and differentiate between these different bodies of law; and a magistrate with a curious or inquisitive mind could not fail to ask questions about the reasons for these differences.

In relation to the Roman law of succession, Montesquieu is enterprising. He is not content to examine the *Corpus iuris civilis*, which he already knew well, as the closely written pages of his *Collectio juris* testify. He discusses the earliest laws of the Kings and of the Republic, and in doing so was entering a field into which few had ventured before him. Beginning with a division of land which he claims to have been effected by Romulus, he attempts to determine the nature of the law before the Twelve Tables, relying for this purpose on Dionysius of Halicarnassus and Plutarch. He discusses next the Twelve Tables, the Voconian and the Papian Laws, seeking at each stage to relate them to the general history of the Roman people, and tracing out the reasons for the laws. He is at his best in explaining the law of wills, with its original distinction between the public and the private will. There is an air of modernity about his argument; and if the substance of what he says is now to be found, pruned of some of its suppositions but resting essentially on the same evidence, in legal textbooks, this does not mean that he was in his own day writing ordinary commonplaces.

For writers before Montesquieu were not in most cases interested in this sort of problem. Domat and Pufendorf, both of them utilized by Montesquieu, were descriptive and not historical in approach. Heineccius, though more interested than they in the evolution of the law, did not consider it in relation to the civilization of the Romans in general, and was still overawed by Justinian.[1] Of the two best known histories of Roman law most closely preceding Montesquieu, neither addresses itself to the problems studied by Montesquieu. Doujat, whose *Historia iuris civilis Romani* appeared shortly before Montesquieu's birth,[2]

[1] I. G. Heineccius, *Antiquitatum Romanarum iurisprudentiam illustrantium syntagma*, Utrecht, 1745, 6th edition.

[2] Paris, 1678.

devotes but some ten pages to Roman law before Tiberius, while Ferrière's *Histoire du droit romain* (Paris, 1718), though stressing the importance of a historical approach and recommending that law should be studied in relation to forms of government, is ill at ease in the pre-Justinian period and deals mainly with the simple outlines of the external history of law.

Even Gravina, more modern than these in spirit, and attestedly studied by Montesquieu, is of little use to him in Book XXVII; for what Montesquieu is doing is to have recourse to the ancient authorities, to bring together and compare different pieces of evidence, and to apply an acutely analytical mind to the problems. He produces intelligent personal explanations, and pursues a more rigorous and more efficient historical method than he has been seen to do previously.

He also, on an obscure point of substance, arrives at a conclusion which could not but seem new to his contemporaries.

This related to the relative antiquity of intestate and testamentary succession. The jurists of the past age had seen testamentary succession as the original and normal mode of succession to property, being based on the law of nature.[1] Montesquieu will not have this. The rules governing intestate succession he sees as older. Personal posthumous disposal of one's property by will he sees as involving a departure from normal legal procedure, necessitating a quasi-legislative act:

> L'ordre de succession ayant été établi en conséquence d'une loi politique, un citoyen ne devait pas le troubler par une volonté particulière; c'est-à-dire que, dans les premiers temps de Rome, il ne devait pas être permis de faire un testament . . . On trouva un moyen de concilier à cet égard les lois avec la volonté des particuliers. Il fut permis de disposer de ses biens dans une assemblée du peuple; et chaque testament fut, en quelque façon, un acte de la puissance législative.[2]

In this argument Montesquieu, though following a line of thought suggested by Domat, is innovating. He is throwing an interesting light on the relation between private and public law. In emphasizing the greater antiquity of intestate succession he is foreshadowing a conclusion which later researches have done much to

[1] See Sir H. S. Maine, *Ancient Law*, p. 207; H. F. Jolowicz, *Historical Introduction to Roman Law*, p. 125; Pufendorf, *Droit de la nature et des gens*, I, p. 565 sq.

[2] *Lois*, XXVII.

substantiate. He has also illustrated the truth of Sir Henry Maine's later dictum, that no department of law would serve better than testaments or wills to demonstrate the superiority of the historical method of investigation over other methods.[1]

II. ORIGINS OF FRENCH LAW

It was not only or mainly the early stages of Roman law which commended themselves to the eighteenth-century scholars; and though most of them sought to examine the law which governed Rome at the height of its power, there were some whose ambitions were more exacting. In the pages of Giannone's history of Naples Montesquieu had been able to read arduous directives:

> A sort of a history of the Roman Jurisprudence has been compiled by some excellent writers; nevertheless they have all laboured to make it clear and evident in relating its origin and progress in the times when the Roman Empire had its rise, growth, and when it came to the highest pitch of grandeur; but its various turns of fortune, when the empire afterwards began to fall from its glory, its declension, extinction, and restoration, the use and authority that it had in the new dominions established in Europe after the inundations of so many nations, when by the new laws it was in a manner extinct, and when, being restored, it eclipsed these, cannot surely be described by any one man in the whole world.

Therefore, exclaims Giannone, 'how much better it is for a man to toil himself in searching after the various fortune and chance of the Roman laws, and of those of his own at home, than to go wandering up and down doubtful, and with little certainty, in a foreign country.'[2]

Montesquieu had been impressed by Giannone's work.[3] He was already interested in the history of the French reception of Roman law.[4] It is not surprising that, after treating the Roman law of succession, he turned to the obscure problems presented by the growth of the French legal system out of the debris of Roman law and the tangled mass of barbarian customs. 'Les livres précédents', he had thought to write in *L'Esprit des lois*,

[1] Op. cit., p. 186.
[2] *The Civil History of the Kingdom of Naples*, London, 1729, I, p. iii.
[3] See above, pp. 113–14. [4] *Spicilège* 266 (MS., pp. 210–12).

'ont conduit à celui-ci où je donnerai un petit essai de l'histoire des lois de la France, comme je viens de donner l'histoire de quelques lois romaines.'[1]

Two questions inevitably sprang to the mind of the historically minded jurist: whence arose the division of France into two zones of which one was governed by written or Roman law, the other by customary law? what was the origin of French customary law itself?

These are the questions which he examines in Book XXVIII. He was already well supplied with books. The catalogue of La Brède lists thirty-one books under the heading *De consuetudinibus scriptores*, while legal works in general are very numerous. While in Paris, being deprived of access to his own principal library, he borrows from the Bibliothèque du Roi, sometimes taking books, such as, on 27 April 1747, *Le Grand Coutumier*, which he possesses himself at La Brède.

His early legal training is now seen to stand Montesquieu in good stead. Now no longer can we reproach him with lending too uncritical an ear to travellers' tales, or treating the exceptional as representative. He plunges with prudent zeal into discussions of the differences between the laws of the Visigoths and the Burgundians, and those of the Franks. He discusses trial by ordeal and by single combat, the point of honour, the *Etablissements* of Saint Louis, the limits of ecclesiastical and lay jurisdiction, and the extraordinary diversity of French customs. He prolongs this discussion through almost 70 quarto pages, marshalling his varied and obscure authorities, and ends Book XXVIII with an apology for his brevity:

> Je suis comme cet antiquaire qui partit de son pays, arriva en Egypte, jeta un coup d'œil sur les pyramides, et s'en retourna.

But this apology minimizes his toil. A better appraisal of his task comes nearer the end of the work:

> Quand on jette les yeux sur les monuments de notre histoire et de nos lois, il semble que tout est mer, et que les rivages mêmes manquent à la mer. Tous ces écrits froids, secs, insipides et durs, il faut les lire, il faut les dévorer, comme la fable dit que Saturne devorait les pierres.[2]

The standard and recognized authority, in Montesquieu's day, on the history of French law was the Abbé Fleury's *Histoire du*

[1] *Pensée* 1795 (Bkn. 399). [2] *Lois*, XXX, 11.

droit français. First published in 1674 and possessed by Montesquieu in the first edition, it was often reprinted, being prefixed to several editions of Argou's *Institution au droit français*. The article on French law in the 1740 edition of Morery's *Grand Dictionnaire historique* consists simply of extracts from this work.

Fleury draws a rigid distinction between what he calls the old law and the new, with the tenth century as the dividing line between the two. The Roman conquest imposed on Gaul the system of Roman law, as embodied primarily in the Theodosian Code. The barbarian invasions introduced barbarian law which, however, in all its forms, is little more than custom which has been written down. Under the Merovingian dynasty, the Franks were governed by the Salic law, the Burgundians by Gondebaud's compilation, the Visigoths by Gothic law, and all other inhabitants of Gaul—and notably all ecclesiastics—by Roman law. But these various forms of law were not equal partners. Roman law, according to Fleury, predominated under the first race and was used in all cases except those where barbarian law had a specific contrary provision. The advent of the Carolingians caused no great change, except that to the Roman and barbarian systems was added the new legislation, in the form of capitularies, of the French kings. In the tenth century the troubles from which France suffered caused the country to recede into a barbaric state. Law itself disappeared, and gradually, obscurely, and incomprehensibly customs emerged. They were the creation of the tenth and eleventh centuries and from them arose eventually the *droit nouveau* which was French customary law.

Fleury's hesitant hypotheses were far from dispelling the obscurity of the dark ages. Montesquieu illuminates the whole period. The first five chapters of Book XXVIII are among his most skilful and most vigorous.

In each of the three parts of Gaul there existed, under the first race, barbarian and Roman law side by side. Everywhere the Gallo-Romans were subject to Roman law while the barbarians were governed by their own usages: the Salic law in the Frankish zone, Gothic custom as written down by Euric in the region of the Visigoths, the compilation of Gondebaud in Burgundy. These laws were in all cases personal and not territorial in their application. A child followed his father's law, a wife her husband's, a freedman his master's. This fact, extremely important in legal history and now a commonplace, was not unknown in Montesquieu's day. But it was the President who pointed to it when others had forgotten it and who handed it down to posterity as a sound and approved doctrine.

He insists, however, that the hereditary basis of personal law was not unshakable. Each individual had the right to select the law under which he would live. He naturally chose the law which would be most beneficial to him. In the Frankish area, the Salic law discriminated savagely against those who were subject to Roman law. The Gallo-Romans in the Frankish area therefore opted, in large numbers, to place themselves under the barbarian law and to procure for themselves the benefits of the Salic rule. Roman law, therefore, began to decline in this area, and barbarian law advanced at its expense. The laws both of the Visigoths and of the Burgundians did not discriminate against those subject to Roman law; and therefore there was no inducement to the Gallo-Romans to abandon their own law in order to embrace either Gothic or Burgundian law. Roman law thus remained strong and valid in these two areas. Thus arose the distinction between *pays de droit coutumier* and *pays de droit écrit*, which survived until the Revolution and which Montesquieu sees attested as early as 864 in the Edict of Pistes.

He does not, however, equate customs and barbarian laws. Customs were often imposed by barbarian laws but were distinct from them. They arose from the conflict of laws: from judicial decisions made in accordance with one system of law in areas where another system was the law of the majority (for example, where a Burgundian was tried in accordance with Burgundian law in an area where the majority of the population was subject to Frankish law); and from lacunae in the different legal systems. Customs thus developed side by side with and as a rival to barbarian law, which they eventually ousted. They challenged Roman law also, and the capitularies; and though their triumph comes later, they are abundantly attested in the reign of Pippin and there is evidence of their existence under the first race.[1]

This was a new claim. The Abbé Fleury had not accepted an earlier origin for French customs than the tenth or the eleventh century. Montesquieu sees them already existing and acknowledged in the ninth, and announced his discovery four years

[1] *Lois*, XXVIII, 12.

before the learned Grosley, archaeologist, traveller, and historian, expressed a similar conclusion in his *Recherches pour servir à l'histoire du droit français* (Paris, 1752).[1]

In his assertion that each citizen could choose the law by which he would be governed Montesquieu was treading on more dangerous ground and is advancing a theory which later historians, starting with Savigny, have rejected.[2] If he errs, however, he errs in the most respectable company, for Muratori shares the same opinion, basing himself among other documents on the laws of Liutprandus which Montesquieu knew as he knew the *Rerum italicarum scriptores* of Muratori, two volumes of which he borrowed from the Bibliothèque du Roi in August, 1747.[3] And more important than an authority, he has a text which he alleges in support. This is the constitution of the Emperor Lotharius I, which lays down that the people must be asked to say under which law it chooses to live.[4] Subsequent commentators have been embarrassed by this text and have interpreted it differently. Montesquieu, even in error, is judicious and his interpretation deserves respect.

III. ORIGINS OF THE FRENCH NOBILITY

It was after *L'Esprit des lois* had been completed according to its original design that Montesquieu decided to add to the work a discussion of feudal origins. It was a matter of pride that he should add his own decisive word to the discussions of this difficult problem. Giannone had written of fiefs that,

like the Nile [they] had their head so hidden and their origin so

[1] Grosley congratulates himself in his preface (p. vi) on being in agreement with Montesquieu, and rebuts in advance any charge of plagiarism. Montesquieu wrote to Grosley on 3 July 1752 to express his delight at their agreement.

[2] They have not, however, been unanimous. The theory of free choice has been defended by Italian scholars (A. Giorgetti, 'Il Cartulario di S. Quirico in Populonia,' *Archivio storico italiano*, 3rd series, XVII, 1873).

[3] The text of Liutprandus ('si unusquisque de lege sua discedere voluerit') is printed by Muratori (vol. I, pt. ii, p. 69). Montesquieu had made an analysis of part of this volume (Nagel III, p. 1579). He refers twice to Liutprandus in *L'Esprit des lois* (XXVIII, 1; 18).

[4] 'Volumus ut cunctus populus Romanus interrogetur, quali lege vult vivere, ut tali lege quali vivere professi sunt vivant' (*Capitularia Regum Francorum*, ed. S. Baluzius, Paris, 1677, II, p. 319; possessed by Montesquieu). The text is cited in *Lois*, XXVIII, 2.

concealed, that among the writers of the ages past, it was reputed so difficult and desperate a task to find it out, and their accounts were so different and inconsistent, that the thing in question was rendered more obscure and dark, than clear and evident.[1]

The former associate of Fréret, Alary, and Boulainvilliers could not fail to be tempted by this investigation; and Montesquieu begins Book XXX of *L'Esprit des lois* with the assertion that there would be an imperfection in his work if he passed over the growth of feudalism in silence. Feudal laws he likens to an ancient oak tree whose branches spread far and wide, but whose roots are hidden: it is necessary to pierce the ground to find them.

The problem was not only difficult; it was extremely significant. It led ineluctably to the great question of the origins of the French nobility and of the French State, the subject of more than a century of heated debate in which myth and prejudice had been more eloquent than historical research.

The traditional explanation of the origin of the French traced their descent back to Francus, son of Hector of Troy, the vicissitudes of whose fate were sung by Ronsard in his epic poem *La Franciade*. Etienne Pasquier had treated this opinion with respect, and though clearly not holding it, had refused specifically to disclaim it.[2] Mézeray, at the end of the seventeenth century, abandoned it completely, and endeavoured to show through what corruption of texts it might have arisen.[3]

Fréret's contribution, contained in a dissertation entitled *De l'origine des Français et de leur établissement dans la Gaule*,[4] is to assert that the Trojan hypothesis is universally rejected, and that the Franks are a nation or a league of different peoples of Germany, who made a series of aggressive entries into Gaul and eventually settled in Gaul before the year 358. This explanation of French origins, later to be regarded as a historical axiom by Augustin Thierry,[5] was in conflict with the officially approved doctrine, represented by the Jesuit Daniel, who refused to accept

[1] *The Civil History*, I, p. 192.

[2] *Les Recherches de la France*, Paris, 1665, pp. 35–36.

[3] He suggests that the Latin name of *Kellen* near Cleves, Colonia Traiana, was read as Colonia Troiana (*Histoire de France avant Clovis*, Amsterdam, 1696, pp. 227–8).

[4] Fréret, *Œuvres complètes*, Paris, 1796, 20 vols., V, p. 155—VI, p. 227; cf. *Spicilège* 585 (MS., pp. 539–42).

[5] *Récits des temps mérovingiens*, Paris, 1846, 3rd edition, I, pp. 45–46

any Frankish settlement in Gaul before the reign of Clovis at the end of the fifth century; and Fréret was imprisoned in the Bastille for having added 280 years to the antiquity of the French monarchy.

After his incarceration Fréret turned to less controversial subjects, but this discussion of French origins was continued by others. Two rival doctrines are associated with the names of Boulainvilliers and Dubos.

The first of these, vigorous, proud, and independent, claimed that the Franks or French were of German origin. They were all free and equal. They entered Gaul as conquerors and enslaved the Gallo-Roman population which they found there. They elected one of themselves as king. The French nobility of modern times was descended from the invading Franks, while the proletariat had the enslaved Gallo-Romans as ancestors.

Dubos, more learned but less bold than Boulainvilliers, advanced a different hypothesis. It was not as conquerors that the Franks entered Gaul, but as the friends and allies of the Romans. It was by prudence, not violence, that Clovis gained possession of Gaul, and he and his successors left the Roman institutions largely intact. Serfdom in medieval France, far from having been imposed by victorious Franks on defeated Gallo-Romans, was a survival of Roman serfdom. The authority of the Kings of France was the direct descendant of the authority of the Caesars: it was an absolute authority beneath which all ranks were equal. No aristocratic privileges were legitimate.

These doctrines were expressed in the three quarto volumes of Dubos's *Histoire critique de l'établissement de la monarchie française dans les Gaules* (Paris, 1734), a work whose influence in the realm of historiography was described by Montesquieu's friend Hénault as not less revolutionary than that of Descartes on the philosophy of the previous century.[1]

Boulainvilliers appears to have been known to Montesquieu;[2] Dubos was his colleague for twenty-eight years in the French Academy. The works of each were well known to him and he maintains a clear position in relation to their doctrines.

The first part of Montesquieu's exposition is a refutation of

[1] *Histoire critique de l'établissement des Français dans les Gaules*, Paris, an IX, I, p. 1.

[2] See above, pp. 12–13.

Boulainvilliers. It is untrue, he declares, that fiefs were established in Gaul by the invading Franks. It is likewise untrue that the servitude of the glebe was established by them. Anxious not to simplify the facts of history, he emphasizes that there were three barbarian invasions of Gaul, not a single one, and that the invaders did not all follow the same method. The Visigoths and the Burgundians, it is true, took for themselves two-thirds of the land of the Gallo-Romans; but this land lay only in areas which had been assigned to them. They took also one-third of the serfs: serfdom therefore existed already in Roman Gaul, and Boulainvilliers was wrong. The institutions of Frankish Gaul were continuations of Roman institutions.[1]

The President's criticisms of Boulainvilliers do not mean that he is a disciple of Dubos. On the contrary: he embarks on a formal refutation of the Abbé.[2] He asks what the presuppositions of the Roman thesis of Dubos are, and deals with them one by one.

The contention that the Franks entered Gaul as allies of the Romans implies that Clovis was invited to enter Gaul. By whom was he invited? If by anyone, it was (according to the Abbé's premises) either by the Romans who lived in the Armorican Confederation or by those Romans who were still subject to imperial authority. But he does not succeed in proving the existence of the Armorican Confederation (a criticism in which Montesquieu was later to be approved by Gibbon)[3] and produces no evidence at all of an invitation to Clovis from the Romans within the Empire.

Dubos lays stress on the continuity implied by the cession of political authority made by Justinian to the offspring of Clovis. But, retorts Montesquieu, the kingdom of the Franks was now so securely established that Justinian had nothing to give.

By similar arguments to these, Montesquieu says he could prove that the Greeks never conquered Persia.[4]

Montesquieu describes the system of Boulainvilliers as a conspiracy against the *tiers état*, and that of Dubos as a conspiracy against the nobility. Citing from Ovid the sun's words to Phaeton, urging him to go neither too high nor too low, neither too far to

[1] *Lois*, XXX, 5–11. [2] *Lois*, XXX, 23–24.

[3] *Decline and Fall*, ed. J. B. Bury, III, p. 353.

[4] Montesquieu adds a refutation, based on Thegan's life of Louis the Debonair, of Dubos's claim that only one social class existed in Frankish society (*Lois*, XXX, 25).

the left nor too far to the right,[1] he argues for an intermediate course. But his own doctrine is not a compromise.

For Montesquieu the significant event which founded French nobility was not the establishment of fiefs; it was the making hereditary of fiefs. Only then did a powerful and organic class of nobles develop. The generally held view in Montesquieu's day was that fiefs became hereditary in the tenth century with the accession of Hugh Capet.[2] The President's view is quite different. He insists that the perpetuity of fiefs began earlier in France than in Germany.[3] He asserts that some fiefs were hereditary already under the kings of the first race,[4] while a century after the death of Charles Martel several of the fiefs which he had granted had become hereditary, and perhaps had been so from their establishment.[5] A capitulary of 877, made by Charles the Bald, shows that fiefs were then generally hereditary. The nobles had thus become independent of the crown, and had become an intermediate order between the crown and the freemen.[6]

The establishment of this doctrine by Montesquieu gives an answer to other questions also. There had been hot debate in the decades preceding *L'Esprit des lois* on the problem of whether the ancient French monarchy had been hereditary or (as asserted by Hotman,[7] with practical and modern consequences of extreme importance) elective. Montesquieu's claim is that under the first race succession was hereditary, with partition of the domain between brothers;[8] that under the second race, succession was hereditary in one family but based on election within that family;[9] and that under the third race, succession was purely hereditary, with discrimination between brothers on the basis of primogeniture.[10] A question which had previously been discussed mainly on the basis of prejudice and in pursuit of a particular solution was thus settled by Montesquieu objectively and dispassionately.

[1] *Lois*, XXX, 10.

[2] Morery, *Grand Dictionnaire*, Amsterdam, 1740, s.v. *fief*; the authority relied on is H. Spelman, *Glossarium archaiologicum*, London, 1664.

[3] *Lois*, XXXI, 30. [4] *Lois*, XXXI, 7. [5] *Lois*, XXXI, 14.

[6] *Lois*, XXXI, 28.

[7] 'Ceux qui estoyent appellez à la couronne de France, estoyent eleus pour estre rois sous certaines loix et conditions qui leur estoyent limitees' (*La Gaule françoise*, Cologne, 1574, p. 63).

[8] *Lois*, XXXI, 33. [9] *Lois*, XXXI, 16. [10] *Lois*, XXXI, 33.

There was also an important theoretical consequence. Hugh Capet had gained the throne by uniting the crown and the greatest fief in the kingdom. The mode of succession to a fief became thus the mode of succession to the throne: constitutional law was shaped by private law, 'la disposition de la loi civile força la loi politique'.[1]

This example of the way in which civil and political law are bound up together illustrates the significance of feudalism as a historical concept. The definition of this concept and the acceptance of it as a basis for history-writing are largely the work of Montesquieu: an achievement to which the principles of *L'Esprit des lois* readily led him. Others, though not many, had written of feudalism before him. It was he who, as Marc Bloch has said, gave the concept *droit de cité* in historical literature and caused history to advance from a narrative based on empires and dynasties to the observation of social phenomena.[2]

IV. THE SKILL OF ERUDITION

Towards the end of a valuable discussion of the historical writings of Montesquieu, Friedrich Meinecke lists three favourite themes which the President treats with enthusiasm: republican Rome, constitutional England, and the Germano-French Middle Ages.[3] These three constant and beloved preoccupations he treats with varying degrees of skill. The historical method followed in the *Considérations* is naïve and his information about England is derived in part from tendentious sources. One can fittingly apply to his study of Rome and of England the tribute which he himself applied to Boulainvilliers:

> Il avait plus d'esprit que de lumières, plus de lumières que de savoir; mais ce savoir n'était point méprisable, parce que, de notre histoire et de nos lois, il savait très bien les grandes choses.[4]

In relation to Frankish antiquities, however, he is in different case. Although criticized not only by his enemies but also by his

[1] *Lois*, XVIII, 22.

[2] M. Bloch, *La Société féodale: la formation des liens de dépendance*, Paris, 1939, p. 2.

[3] *Die Entstehung des Historismus*, Munich and Berlin, 1936, I, p. 175.

[4] *Lois*, XXX, 10.

friends, like Lauraguais who wrote that Montesquieu 'n'a jamais fait qu'enluminer de mauvaises estampes',[1] Montesquieu displays in his chapters on French history a spirit of rigorous investigation and research which does not characterize his writing on Rome and on England. Writing late in his life, when he might have been expected to seek relaxation and when his eyes were giving him serious trouble, he shows a new and surprising faculty for textual criticism.

Two examples will illustrate this skill.

In a passage from Gregory of Tours[2] there occurs the word *ingenui*. Dubos translates this as *affranchis de tributs*. Montesquieu regards this rendering with disgust, exclaiming that there is no grammarian who would not grow pale on seeing it. He himself translates the term as 'not serfs'.[3]

Dubos, however, was not alone in his rendering. Before his day there had been two French translations of Gregory. The earlier of these produces the translation, *francs de toute charge*,[4] while the second follows with *exempts de toute charge*.[5] The text contained in Bouquet's *Recueil des historiens*, published shortly after the work of Dubos, appends to the passage in question the note, *ingenui, id est, tributo immunes*.[6] The glossary of Du Cange does not greatly help. The first edition, like the Frankfurt edition of 1710 which Montesquieu owned, after defining *ingenui* unobjectionably as 'free men, as opposed to serfs or any others of servile condition'[7] proceeds at once to add *hi a tributis immunes erant, quod secus erat de servis*, citing as sole evidence the precise passage in question from Gregory of Tours. In 1746 or 1747 Montesquieu acquired a new and revised edition of Du Cange (Paris, 1733, 6 volumes folio), but found here simply the same entry for the word *ingenui*; and indeed the paragraph has remained substantially unchanged in subsequent editions up to the present day. Montesquieu had a heavy battery of opinion arrayed against him; its leaders were specialists while he was but an amateur.

[1] Louis de Brancas, comte de Lauraguais, *Mémoire pour moi, par moi*, London, 1773, p. xxxi.

[2] *Historia Francorum*, VII, 15.

[3] *Lois*, XXX, 12.

[4] *Histoire françoise*, tr. C. Bonet, Paris, 1610, f. 290v.

[5] *Histoire des françois*, tr. Marolles, Paris, 1668, p. 455.

[6] Vol. II, Paris, 1739, p. 299.

[7] *Liberi, quibus opponuntur servi aut quivis obnoxiae conditionis.*

Subsequent editors of Gregory have however accepted Montesquieu's interpretation. Guadet and Taranne, editing the text for the Société de l'histoire de France, though in their translation they oddly follow Dubos, append a note explaining that he was wrong and Montesquieu right,[1] while a more recent English editor translates simply 'free men.'[2]

In another case, Montesquieu upsets the attribution of a document against the most respectable authorities. A capitulary existing in two manuscript versions, beginning with the words *Clodacharius rex Francorum*, had been published for the first time in the seventeenth century by the illustrious Sirmond, who had attributed it to Clotaire I and had assigned to it the date 560.[3] Baluze, whose edition was used by Montesquieu, maintained this attribution.[4] Many a professional scholar, having before his eyes an edition which was a recognized monument of learning, would have accepted its text without question. Montesquieu does not do this. Where Sirmond had relegated any slight doubt he felt to a remote appendix[5] and Baluze had not expressed any doubt at all, Montesquieu does not hesitate to impugn their attribution. He assigns the capitulary to Clotaire II for three reasons: the grandfather of the author of the edict appears to be a Christian, which Clotaire I's grandfather was not; the abuses which the edict seeks to remedy are known to have survived the reign of Clotaire I; and the edict implies a weakness in the royal power which is known to have marked Clotaire II's reign though not that of Clotaire I.[6]

These arguments have been found convincing. When the capitularies were next seriously edited, the attribution to Clotaire II was maintained, and Montesquieu was cited as the responsible authority.[7]

There are other cases, some of them not unimportant, in which Montesquieu's views have not commanded general acceptance;[8]

[1] *Histoire ecclésiastique des Francs*, Paris, 1837, III, pp. 45 and 403.

[2] *The History of the Franks*, ed. O. M. Dalton, Oxford, 1927, II, p. 297.

[3] *Concilia antiqua Galliae*, ed. J. Sirmondus, Paris, 1629, I, pp. 318–19.

[4] *Capitularia regum Francorum*, Paris, 1677, I, col. 7.

[5] Op. cit., I, p. 611. [6] *Lois*, XXXI, 2.

[7] *Capitularia regum Francorum*, ed. A. Boretius, Hanover (*Monumenta Germaniae historica*), 1883, I, p. 18.

[8] Savigny, for instance, has questioned him on several details (*Geschichte des römischen Rechts im Mittelalter*, 2nd edition, Heidelberg, 1834–50, I, pp. 31–32, 117, 178, 251; II, p. 105).

but they have been treated with respect and regarded as worthy of argued refutation. After 1748, indeed, his position in the world of erudition was secure. It was a new situation for him, and one which he found to his taste. He formed projects for treating other learned themes, notably the life of Theodoric,[1] and though he did not realize them, he had already, in *L'Esprit des lois*, done enough to earn for himself a title to be regarded not simply as a philosophical historian, but also as a scholar.

[1] *Lois*, XXX, 12.

XVI
RELIGION
I. THE CAUSES OF RELIGION

RELIGION was one of the seven factors in the assembly of second causes which Montesquieu called the *esprit général.* It was itself, as Montesquieu points out at the beginning of *L'Esprit des lois*, caused by nature:

> Cette loi, qui, en imprimant dans nous-mêmes l'idée d'un créateur, nous porte vers lui, est la première des lois naturelles par son importance, et non pas dans l'ordre de ces lois.[1]

This explanation, however, as the reservation contained at the end of the sentence suggests already, was too simple to give complete satisfaction to Montesquieu. Having spent much time in the society of such men as Fréret and Fontenelle, he was deeply interested by the problem of the psychological basis of religion. The *Pensées* and the *Spicilège* contain, at different periods of his life, discussions or oracles, where the influence of Van Dale and Fontenelle shows itself clearly, of miracles, both before and after his witnessing the Naples liquefaction, and of religion itself. The *Lettres persanes* contain a multitude of comments on religious practices and beliefs of which Montesquieu tries to discover an explanation.[2] After their publication his interest in these problems continues. He shows himself fascinated by the title of a book mentioned by Athenaeus, *De iis quae falso creduntur*. He discusses the belief in miracles, attributing it to human pride, and though he writes, 'false miracles', his example is taken from the Old Testament. He contrasts the foolish elements present in false religions with the absence of such elements in the sciences, accounting for this difference by pointing to the different origins, religions being created by the people and systematized by the élite, while sciences are the creation of the enlightened, who hand them on to the people.[3]

Montesquieu's views on the source of religious sentiment are summed up in the second chapter of Book XXV of *L'Esprit des*

[1] *Lois*, I, 2. [2] See above, pp. 40–42.
[3] *Pensées* 13, 22, 46 (Bkn. 882, 2191, 2192).

lois.[1] In the eighteenth century there were several discussions of this problem ranging from the intelligent analyses of Fontenelle and the Président de Brosses, to the naïve hypotheses of Montesquieu's own disciple Boulanger. Montesquieu's personal contribution is a valuable one.

He lists seven different reasons for adherence to a religion, and more specifically for adherence to the Christian religion: pleasure at our own intelligence in having selected a non-idolatrous faith (or in other words, intellectual vanity); the gratification afforded to our senses and emotions by the ceremonies of religion; the pride we feel in being able to regard ourselves as selected individuals; the frequency of occupation imposed on us by religious practices; the satisfaction given to our natural tendency to hope and to fear by the belief in heaven and in hell; the attractiveness of the morality taught by the Church (because 'les hommes, fripons en détail, sont en gros de très honnêtes gens'); and finally, the great appeal made by the magnificence and wealth of the visible Church, even to those who can but contrast it with their own poverty.

If the elements of religion evoke in this way a response in men's hearts and minds, religious institutions also can be explained similarly. All civilized peoples live in houses: what is more reasonable than to believe that God, too, must have his house, larger and more magnificent than the houses of individuals? What is more natural than that the temple should be deemed to offer immunity from pursuit to those who seek asylum there? Proper care for the temple, and adequate attention to the worship of God, require more constant application than ordinary men can give: what more reasonable, then, than to create a caste of priests who will devote themselves exclusively to the cult of God? If there are many priests, what more sensible than to appoint a pontiff to preside over them?[2]

These are general and universal causes of religion; but there are also local and particular causes. Religion is in important measure dependent on the political and social background, on existing political institutions and traditions, on *mœurs*. So a

[1] This chapter was subjected to frequent revision. In the Paris manuscript it appears in a hand which dates from very shortly before 1746; but it is likely to have been originally composed several years previously.

[2] *Lois*, XXV, 3, 4, 8.

country which has a tradition of liberty, like England, will find either that there is great indifference in the matter of religion, or that there are a large number of rival religious sects.[1] So a despotically governed land, inadequately provided with laws, will need another sanction and will rely greatly for this purpose on religion.[2] So, since the organization of a religion must bear some analogy to the system of government of the State, it will be found that the people of the south will embrace more readily Roman Catholicism, while those of the north will turn to Protestantism, preferring Lutheranism if they are governed by princes, and Calvinism if they live in republics.[3] As political institutions are themselves in part determined by climate, so too does climate influence religions. Montesquieu here abstains, as he abstained when discussing the general influence of climate, from producing a rigorous and systematic theory like that of Charron; he contents himself with examples of its effect on feasts, taboos, and practices: food growing more readily in the south, leisure is more easily socially practicable, and the number of feast days may be greater; the meat of the pig being extremely rare in Arabia, it is expedient that its consumption should be forbidden; hot climates make frequent bathing in rivers salutary, and Islam and Hinduism have therefore vested it with religious significance.[4] There are two cases in the writings of the President where he assigns accidental causes to theological doctrine itself, coming nearer here than elsewhere to full psychological determination. He asserts that Moslems see in their daily lives so many examples of the unforeseen and the extraordinary, caused by the arbitrary civil power which oppresses them, that they are perforce driven to believe in the rigid control of external fate; while Christians, living under moderate governments which are controlled by human prudence, believe that their own actions also are so controlled and that their wills are free.[5] The other example is afforded by metempsychosis, which Montesquieu suggests was invented in the hot climate and parched countrysides of India, in order to protect from slaughter

[1] *Lois*, XIX, 27.

[2] *Lois*, II, 4. The political role of religion had already been discussed by Montesquieu in his *Dissertation sur la politique des Romains dans la religion*, read to the Academy of Bordeaux in 1716.

[3] *Lois*, XXIV, 5.

[4] *Lois*, XXIV, 23–26.

[5] *Pensée* 2157 (Bkn. 2186).

the few cattle which can live there, by teaching that human souls have passed into their bodies.[1]

Montesquieu was not a builder of systems. He did not write what was later, with Hume, to be known as the natural history of religion. But in his examples, his *obiter dicta*, and his occasional generalizations, he produces the elements of such a history. In enumerating the causes of religion he is not fired with a desire to discredit it. He does not see religion as the invention of dishonest priests; it is not a fraud. Herein he differs from men like D'Holbach, who regarded organized religion as an imposture, and were anxious first to discredit religion, and then to extirpate it. Montesquieu was concerned to explain it; to understand rather than to judge was his aim as it is necessarily the aim of the historian.

An important consequence arises from this. If it is the historian's duty to discover the causes of religion, as of other institutions, it is the statesman's duty to respect these causes. Montesquieu, as has been seen already, never wholly abandoned the principle of Spinoza, that that which is has a right to continue to be, and he cannot avoid applying that principle to religion. 'Le paganisme devait nécessairement être,' he writes in the *Pensées*.[2] It is climate, he says in *L'Esprit des lois*, which has prescribed limits, humanly speaking, to the Christian and Moslem religions.[3] It is impossible that Christianity should ever succeed in China.[4] The religion of the Hindus is indestructible.[5] Few people ever so persistently sought the society of missionaries, and so assiduously read their works, while believing all the time that their activities were bound to fail. Not content with having frequented Fouquet and Ripa, missionaries who had returned from China to Italy, he encountered others also in France: Stephen Evodius Assemani, titular Archbishop of Apamea in Syria, proved in conversation to be an expert in things Chinese.[6] He had also known one Solus, a missionary returned from Siam, who reported the opinion that elephants had a language and a religion.[7] In his notebooks, he carefully analysed the published narratives written by Jesuits in

[1] *Lois*, XXIV, 24. [2] *Pensée* 417 (Bkn. 2130). [3] *Lois*, XXIV, 26.
[4] *Lois*, XIX, 18.
[5] *Lois*, XXI, 1. The words 'qui est indestructible' were later changed to 'qui a sur eux tant d'empire'.
[6] See above, p. 176. [7] *Spicilège* 348 (MS., p. 311).

the Far East. Meanwhile, doubting already before his travels about the chances of success of Christian missionaries in Turkey,[1] he was preparing the doctrine enunciated in *L'Esprit des lois*, that since proselytizing faiths are usually intolerant, a State which is satisfied with its existing religion would do well to forbid the establishment of any other.[2]

II. MORALITY AND FAITH

Pierre Bayle, in his *Pensées diverses sur la comète*, had devoted one of his monumental digressions to an examination of the relative merits of atheism and idolatry; approaching this problem from the social point of view, he had argued in favour of atheism, claiming that ideas of morality existed independently of religious faith. Montesquieu dissents from this contention. He insists that all religions have social and moral consequences, and in Book XXIV especially he sets out to examine them:

> Comme on peut juger parmi les ténèbres celles qui sont les moins épaisses, et parmi les abîmes ceux qui sont les moins profonds, ainsi l'on peut chercher parmi les religions fausses celles qui sont les plus conformes au bien de la société.

He considers also the Christian religion, but hastens to protect himself against censure by saying that he writes only as a political writer and not as a theologian.

His first attack[3] on Bayle takes the form of a declaration that even if it were useless for the subjects in a State to have a religion, it would still be expedient that the prince, standing above all earthly sanctions, should be placed under this restraint. This is summed up in one of those vivid sentences which make *L'Esprit des lois* significant in the history of French style as well as in the history of ideas:

[1] *Spicilège* 382 (MS., p. 332). [2] *Lois*, XXV, 10.

[3] Montesquieu's opposition to Bayle on this point is of old standing. The *Spicilège* (415; MS., pp. 355–7) contains an anecdote about a Turkish merchant, who having goods to transport by sea, chose a Catholic rather than a Protestant shipowner, since the necessity to confess would be a deterrent from fraud to the Catholic, which the Protestant would lack. One must be blind, adds Montesquieu, to agree with Bayle. On Montesquieu's attitude to Bayle, see my article, 'Bayle and Montesquieu,' as cited.

Un prince qui aime la religion et qui la craint, est un lion qui cède à la main qui le flatte, ou à la voix qui l'apaise: celui qui craint la religion et qui la hait, est comme les bêtes sauvages qui mordent la chaîne qui les empêche de se jeter sur ceux qui passent: celui qui n'a point du tout de religion, est cet animal terrible qui ne sent sa liberté que lorsqu'il déchire et qu'il dévore.[1]

But the moderating consequences of religion are not less desirable on the part of the people than on that of their ruler. Spinoza had claimed that even the superstitions of the Turks were useful;[2] and Montesquieu enumerates the merits of Islam as well as those of Christianity. Though the faith of Mahomet tends to favour despotism, since it is a fear added to the fear which is the principle of that government, it may help to temper some of its evils, perhaps by modifying the will of the prince,[3] perhaps by modifying the penal code.[4]

The effect of Christianity is different. It opposes despotism. It has improved the lot of human beings in many parts of the world, in Ethiopia, in spite of the climate, as well as in Europe. Its principles, if followed, would be infinitely stronger than honour, virtue—the purely human virtue of the republic—and fear. The effect of Christianity has sometimes been harmful: Lucretius's lamentation over the ills which religion has inspired can sometimes be justly applied even to the Christian religion;[5] witness the crippling effect on commerce of the Church's condemnation of usury.[6] But for good or for ill the historical significance of Christianity is seen by Montesquieu as transcendently great, and in no case more pregnant with consequence or more praiseworthy than in its effect on slavery: Plutarch in his life of second King of Rome declares that when men were governed by Saturn there was neither master nor slave. Christianity, says the President,[7] has in our lands brought back that age.[8]

[1] *Lois*, XXIV, 2. [2] *Opera*, II, p. 87.
[3] *Lois*, III, 10. [4] *Lois*, XII, 29. [5] *Pensée* 207 (Bkn. 1573).
[6] *Lois*, XXI, 20. [7] *Lois*, XV, 8.
[8] Occasional passages, consigned to the *Spicilège* or the *Pensées*, express different views; for example, 'aujourd'hui le Mahométisme et le Christianisme, uniquement faits pour l'autre vie, anéantissent toute celle-ci. Et pendant que la religion nous afflige, le despotisme, partout répandu, nous accable' (*Pensée* 1606, Bkn. 588). The praise given to Christianity in Ethiopia, mentioned above, accords oddly with a satirical portrait of the form that Christianity assumes there, given in the *Spicilège*, 643 (MS., pp. 607–8).

The social and historical importance of Christianity, as of other religions, is a result of its moral teaching and not of its articles of belief. Montesquieu agrees with most of the thinkers of the Enlightenment in prizing morality more highly than faith. The manuscript of *L'Esprit des lois* contains at the beginning of Book XXV a passage never incorporated in the work, and unpublished:

> Dans les gouvernements modérés les hommes sont plus attachés à la morale et moins à la religion, et dans les pays despotiques ils sont plus attachés à la religion et moins à la morale.

For Montesquieu the value of morality is more evident than the truth of doctrine, and religions can be compared more easily in point of morality than in respect of their faith. The moral inferiority of Islam to Christianity is immediately obvious.[1] In those countries which do not enjoy Christianity, it is imperative that religion should accord with morality.[2] Three examples of non-Christian religions which do this are given by Montesquieu:[3] the simple moral faith of the inhabitants of Pegu in Burma; that of the Jewish sect of the Essaeans; and the Stoics, in praise of whom Montesquieu extracts a paragraph from his *Traité des devoirs* of many years before, adding to it a sentence eulogizing Julian the Apostate. The social utility of religion, proclaims the President in as many words, is irrelevant to the truth of its doctrine; false doctrines may be useful, true and sacred doctrines may be harmful in social life.[4]

An early paragraph in the *Pensées* gives a simple analysis of duty as it arises from religion. God has given laws to men, and these laws are of two sorts: moral precepts and sacred precepts. The first of these are based on the necessity of preserving society, or in some cases simply on their own ease of execution; sacred precepts are either based on eternal reason, such as the injunction to love God; or they are arbitrary and relate to ceremonial.[5]

[1] *Lois*, XXIV, 4. [2] *Lois*, XXIV, 8. [3] *Lois*, XXIV, 8–10.

[4] Montesquieu's greater interest in morality than in faith leads him to disapprove of the contemplative life of religious orders. Monasticism in general he frowns on, even though climate may sometimes encourage it; his strictures in the *Lettres persanes* on 'Christian dervishes' are repeated, in more serious form, in *L'Esprit des lois* (XXIII, 29; XXIV, 11).

[5] *Pensée* 205 (Bkn. 1928).

This strange mixture of Spinozism and orthodoxy, coeval roughly with the *Traité des devoirs*, does not represent the final attitude of Montesquieu. In *L'Esprit des lois*, using the Catholic terminology of precept and counsel, he insists that precepts should be given by the civil law. It is the function of religion to give the more general and the more elevated guidance, to point to ideals rather than to prescribe sanctions:

quand par exemple elle donne des règles, non pas pour le bien, mais pour le meilleur; non pas pour ce qui est bon, mais pour ce qui est parfait, il est convenable que ce soient des conseils et non pas des lois.[1]

Man-made rules are concerned rather with the possible and the expedient.

III. JANSENISM

The importance of religion in human society was manifest to Montesquieu. It is now necessary to discover what religion meant to the President himself, and in view of the age and society in which he lived, it is useful to begin by examining his attitude to the controversies about Jansenism. It is in the *Pensées* and in his minor works, rather than in *L'Esprit des lois*, that his views on this subject are disclosed.

The eighteenth-century heirs of Saint-Cyran and Arnauld differed greatly and strangely from the founders of their cause. No longer in the forefront of their minds were the doctrine of grace, the interpretation of Saint Augustine, or the rigorous moral system practised and prescribed by the solitaries of Port-Royal. The cardinal theme of debate was now the Bull *Unigenitus*, reluctantly and under heavy governmental pressure accepted by the Parlements of France, among them, protesting like the others, the Parlement of Bordeaux. The aim of the eighteenth-century Jansenists was to overthrow this Bull, by means of a General Council of the Church, and the pursuit of this objective brought them allies who were far removed in character and in outlook from Pascal, from La Mère Angélique and La Mère Agnès.

In his early years of literary activity Montesquieu shows himself to be opposed to the Bull *Unigenitus*, as was fitting in a practising *président à mortier*. The shafts of his wit in the *Lettres*

[1] *Lois*, XXIV, 7.

persanes are directed against the Bull which forbids reading of the Bible, and against the Tartuffe-like bishop who publishes a *mandement* against it.[1] He appears to have despised the immediate issues. He had a very low opinion of Quesnel's *Réflexions morales sur le Nouveau Testament*, the work condemned in the Bull: 'jamais tant de pensées basses, jamais tant d'idées puériles'.[2] The appeal to the future Council he thought ridiculous, saying that perhaps there would never be another General Council of the Church,[3] as indeed there was not until 1869. On the other hand, he disapproves when in 1721 the appellant doctors of the Sorbonne were driven into exile, and insists that opinions cannot be changed by the exercise of force.[4] He comments on the liberties of the Gallican Church, which the Jansenists claimed to defend, saying, 'on devrait plutôt dire la *servitude* de l'Eglise gallicane', because the so-called liberties, far from promoting the independence of the church, increase its subservience to political control. The liberties in question are the liberties of the people of France, founded on *ius gentium*, which asserts a nation's right to be free of alien control, on divine right, which places a General Council above the Pope, and on reason.[5] Montesquieu, though making common cause with the Jansenists, was inspired by motives very unlike theirs. Indeed, another paragraph of the *Pensées*, admittedly difficult of interpretation, suggests that one of his motives was the desire to see the regular clergy disendowed.[6]

His travels did not mean that Montesquieu's interest in Jansenism was interrupted. It is reported that at Vienna Prince Eugene

[1] *L.P.* 24, 101. [2] *Pensée* 166 (Bkn. 901).
[3] *Spicilège* 286 (MS., pp. 226–7). [4] *Spicilège* 322 (MS., pp. 278–9).
[5] *Pensée* 215 (Bkn. 2039).
[6] *Pensée* 273 (Bkn. 2056): anti-Papal sentiment might, he says, give rise to a move for disendowment. 'Quoique je n'approuve nullement une pareille entreprise, voici comment je m'imagine qu'elle sera exécutée.' Then Montesquieu explains how all religious institutions except bishoprics, cures of souls, hospitals and universities, would be deprived of their endowment on the death of their present members. The careful description of the procedure to be followed and the insistence that the people of France would support this policy, suggest that Montesquieu's protestation of disapproval is the ironical device so often found in eighteenth-century writers. He goes on to say that we must take care never to depart from what has been defined by 'le sacré concile de Trente'. Montesquieu's real views on the Council of Trent at this time are shown to be hostile by *Pensée* 214 (Bkn. 2057) and by his asking Desmolets to procure him a copy of Fra Paolo Sarpi's history of that Council (Montesquieu to Desmolets, s.d.; Nagel III, p. 889).

interrogated him on the affairs of the Constitution in France, and the President replied that as a result of the ministry's policy Jansenism would be extirpated in France and that in a few years it would no longer exist. Prince Eugene disagreed with this view:

> Vous n'en sortirez jamais; le feu roi s'est laissé engager dans une affaire dont son arrière-petit-fils ne verra pas la fin.[1]

Proceeding to Rome, the President found himself, as has been seen, moving in circles sympathetic to Jansenism, which in Italy was the ally of the Enlightenment to a much greater extent than ever in France. While at the Papal capital Montesquieu made a serious attempt to study the administrative machinery of the Holy See. He discovered that the personal policy of Benedict XIII was less hostile to Jansenism than the policy of the Congregation of the Holy Office, or indeed than that pursued in France by Fleury. It was his delight to learn details of the secret history of the relations between the French court and Rome, and above all from Polignac he was able to acquire much information about the motives behind Louis XIV's opposition to the Jansenists. His Roman acquaintances do not appear to have given him any sympathy for the theological or moral ideas of the disciples of Arnauld, unless the Jansenist belief in reading the Bible lies behind a note inserted in the *Spicilège* soon after the President's return to France: 'livres originaux que j'ai à lire: *Scriptura sacra.*'[2]

During Montesquieu's absence there had been some Jansenist activity in Bordeaux. In 1730 the Bishops of Agen and of Limoges had published anti-Jansenist pastoral letters, and the Parlement of Bordeaux had thought it its duty to denounce these letters to the Government. A year later, an appellant priest living in Bordeaux had had the sacraments refused to him by his parish priest, the Curé of Saint-Projet. He appealed to the Parlement, which passed on his request, with favourable comment, to Cardinal Fleury, but Fleury referred the whole matter to the Archbishop of Bordeaux, which was tantamount to intervening in opposition to the Jansenist.[3] Though absent during the first of these crises,

[1] Secondat, *Mémoire*, pp. 399–400.

[2] *Spicilège* 561 (MS., p. 521).

[3] C.-B.-F. Boscheron Des Portes, *Histoire du Parlement de Bordeaux*, II, pp. 267, 270.

and though not exercising his office, Montesquieu cannot have failed to hear much of them and to have discussed them with his friends of the Parlement. It is about two years later that he writes in his notebook, 'les Jésuites défendent une bonne cause, le molinisme, par de bien mauvaises voies,'[1] and soon afterwards complains that the Jansenists would deny us all pleasures except that of scratching ourselves.[2] He reproduces a simple argument, which Polignac had taught him, to prove the liberty of the will,[3] and later in the *Pensées*, in a place where his secretary is largely occupied in recopying older fragments, there is to be found what, though without naming the Jansenists, is a formal denial of their theology:

> S'il arrive quelquefois que Dieu prédestine (ce qui ne peut arriver que rarement: car il n'arrive que rarement que Dieu nous ôte la liberté), il ne peut jamais nous prédestiner qu'au salut. Ceux qui sont prédestinés sont sauvés. Mais il ne s'ensuit pas que ceux qui ne sont pas prédestinés soient damnés.[4]

This opinion he supports by prolonged argument from Saint Paul.

The interest of the public, meanwhile, was being more closely drawn to Jansenism by the activities of the convulsionaries. The Deacon François de Pâris, a cleric of great sanctity and asceticism, a true disciple of the great Arnauld, and an appellant who had never accepted the Bull, had died in 1727, and was interred in the churchyard of Saint-Médard near the Rue Mouffetard on the left bank of the Seine. Numerous miraculous cures of the crippled and infirm, it was claimed, had occurred on his tombstone, and these were interpreted as evidence of God's condemnation of the Bull and approval of its opponents. The cures, which often involved their subjects in involuntary contortions and convulsions, were described in innumerable pamphlets, and their history was eventually written by Carré de Montgeron, counsellor of the Parlement of Paris, and himself a former libertine converted by the miracles. The convulsionaries were discussed throughout France, but in Bordeaux opinion was somewhat sceptical, if credence is to be given to the intendant's report to the central government:

[1] *Pensée* 730 (Bkn. 1326).
[2] *Pensée* 852 (Bkn. 1337).
[3] *Pensée* 437 (Bkn. 2175).
[4] *Pensée* 1945 (Bkn. 674).

Dans cette généralité, on n'est pas fort crédule sur ce qu'on appelle miracles, à cause de la différence des religions, surtout à Bordeaux où il aborde un grand nombre d'étrangers, et même les églises y sont peu fréquentées.[1]

Montesquieu comments on Carré de Montgeron's arrest and incarceration in 1737, but is interested only in the problem of Parliamentary privilege which arose;[2] he discussed the miracles with Martin Folkes, and the Englishman and the Frenchman appear to have agreed in scepticism.[3] The activities of the convulsionaries did not increase the President's sympathy for Jansenism.

Montesquieu was still mainly interested in the political aspect of the conflict, but his attitude was changing. Writing still at the time of the convulsionaries, he laments that he has almost never heard sense spoken on the conflict. It has not for more than ten years been the Bull which was at stake, but now the question is whether or not there is to be a schism in France, an eventuality which neither the Court nor the Parlement desires. The Jansenists seem to desire only to be hanged, while the Molinists are busily occupied preparing the ropes with which to hang them—or to hang themselves. The Papal Court meanwhile exacerbates the struggle. Montesquieu is nostalgically filled with admiration for Fleury, whose handling of the situation he regards as having been masterly, but Fleury is no more; he is none the less completely loyal to the spirit of the Parlement of Paris which he declares to be the spirit of the entire magistracy. The great need is for men's minds to be calmed and for counsels of moderation to prevail, and to a man who asks him if the King cannot suppress the Parlement, he replies, 'Monsieur, apprenez de moi que le roi ne peut pas faire tout ce qu'il peut.'[4]

In 1753 the conflict became more serious and the Parlement of Paris was banished to the provinces. In this critical situation Montesquieu's attitude becomes more clearly defined. Jansenism he describes as a dying superstition: it would be foolish to use unnecessary violence to dispatch it.[5] The Bull *Unigenitus* must now be accepted as a part of French law, and then forgotten. The sick man who thinks it necessary to tell his priest that he rejects

[1] A. Grellet-Dumazeau, *La Société bordelaise sous Louis XV*, p. 95.
[2] *Spicilège* 775 (MS., pp. 783–4). [3] *Spicilège* 669 (MS., pp. 638–9).
[4] *Pensée* 1226 (Bkn. 2049). [5] *Pensée* 2158 (Bkn. 2052).

the Bull must be treated as a disturber of the peace; but likewise a disturber of the peace is the priest who asks the sick man if he accepts it. The Bull is not an article of faith. This practical and undoctrinaire attitude, attested by Jean-Baptiste de Secondat in the memoir of his father's life,[1] is expressed by Montesquieu in a letter to a member of the exiled Parlement of Paris.[2] It is also outlined from a different standpoint in a memorandum which he drew up for possible submission to the government.[3] Here he shows how greatly exercised he is by the strife which is lacerating the religious life of France. He urges the acceptance of the Bull as an accomplished fact, but appeals forcibly to the King to show a spirit of magnanimous toleration. Montesquieu's attitude to the conflict in its last, bitter days is not that of a partisan of either Parlement or Court; it is not that of a friend or of an enemy of the Bull. It is the attitude of a lover of peace and advocate of toleration. In him, in the eighteenth century, is continued the tradition illustrated during the religious wars of 200 years before, by that other Gascon, Montaigne, and that other magistrate, L'Hôpital.[4]

IV. MONTESQUIEU'S PERSONAL FAITH

In considering the religion of any individual two separate things must be considered: external practice and internal conviction. The first of these is usually more easily defined than the second;

[1] Secondat, *Mémoire*, p. 405.

[2] Montesquieu to a member of the Parlement of Paris, 9 July 1753.

[3] *Mémoire sur la Constitution* (Nagel III, pp. 469–76; Pléiade II, pp. 1217–21).

[4] It should be added that Montesquieu had, though in milder degree, something of the Jansenist opinion of the Society of Jesus. He is at all times greatly interested in it as an organization. He asserts that the Jesuits would have ruled the world, had they come into existence before the Reformation (*Pensée* 11, Bkn. 1325); he admires their political talent (*Pensées* 453, 544, Bkn. 1335, 1329), observes that they govern Venice (Pléiade I, p. 560; Nagel II, pp. 992–3), and—unlike many other writers—praises their government of Paraguay (*Lois*, IV, 6). At one time Montesquieu entertains the project of writing a history of their order (*Pensée* 237, Bkn. 537). But, although he sends his son to be educated by them, he distrusts them and fears them (*Pensées* 393, 482, Bkn. 1331–2). Of Tournemine he says, 'Il n'avait aucune bonne qualité, et il était même mauvais Jésuite' (*Pensée* 1223, Bkn. 921); two Jesuits he regards as quite enough in the Academy of Bordeaux (Montesquieu to Barbot, 20 December 1741); and perhaps most conclusive of all in *Pensée* 715 (Bkn. 1330): 'une chose que je ne saurais concilier avec les lumières de ce siècle, c'est l'autorité des Jésuites.' See on this subject P. Bastid, 'Montesquieu et les Jésuites' (*Congrès 1955*).

it rests usually on evidence which is straightforward and unfallacious. Internal conviction is less easily ascertained, especially in an age where powerful inducements to apparent orthodoxy were provided by civil authority and by a still militant Church; and historians have sometimes assumed that light was thrown on intimate conviction by evidence which simply attests external and nominal allegiance. Death-bed repentances are of this order. That a man, physically weakened and morally intimidated by the prospect of eternity before him, confesses and dies fortified by the last rites of the Church, is a fact which may tell one how, in Catholic theology, his soul stands in relation to its creator; it may tell one what his mind, in its moment of final humility, thought about the Church. But it tells one nothing about the intellectual convictions which guided his life. The last hours of the President's life, which will be discussed at a later stage, do not concern this immediate inquiry.

Montesquieu's external profession was of loyalty to the Roman Church.[1] His family was one in which religion was respected. There had been nuns and ecclesiastics in each generation. The President had two sisters who were nuns. An uncle had been Abbot of Faize, and was succeeded in this living by Montesquieu's much respected brother and godson, Charles-Louis-Joseph, who held it in plurality with other offices, the most important of them being that of dean of the Collegiate Church of Saint-Seurin in Bordeaux, in whose sacristy his austere portrait hangs to this day. Joseph, who was no *abbé de cour* but a man of devotion, maintained very amicable relations with his brother the President, who lived in the deanery during his visits to Bordeaux for a period of almost thirty years. Montesquieu had many friends in the Church: Cerati, Niccolini, Polignac (in whom however he saw the ambassador and the author of the *Anti-Lucretius* rather than the man of God), François de Fitz-James, Jansenist son of the devout Berwick, and Bishop of Soissons. There were many others of Montesquieu's close acquaintance whose holy orders were graced with learning and whose scholarship adorned the Church, such as Conti and Desmolets, not to mention the many *abbés* of fortune whom Montesquieu inevitably met, and of whom Guasco was the prince. Nor above all should it be forgotten

[1] See my article, 'La Religion de Montesquieu' (*Congrès 1955*), in part reproduced here.

that the young Montesquieu was educated in the diocese of Bossuet and under the shadow of Malebranche, whose name he venerated even when he disagreed with his ideas. The background of Montesquieu's life was that of an orthodox Roman Catholic, with one striking and almost startling exception: his wife was a Calvinist and remained to the end of her days loyal to her original faith.[1]

The first thing that must be said about the religious conviction of Montesquieu is that he believes firmly in the existence of God. This belief he holds early in his life and late in his life. Il est bien vrai que Dieu a été de toute éternité,' he writes before his travels;[2] and one of his chief concerns in the *Traité des devoirs* is to refute the atheist. A long discussion in the *Pensées*, originally intended for that treatise, contains vigorous arguments for the existence of God.[3] It is true that some of them are based on the psychological utility of the idea of God, as a consolation when men think of death; what is at issue, however, is not whether Montesquieu's reasons for belief were beyond logical reproach, but whether he believed, and this passage leaves no possibility of doubt. His belief in God was the foundation of his notions, as they then existed, of morality. The hopes and fears of mankind are derived from the existence of God, and if God were proved not to exist, the whole economy of the human mind would be destroyed. Nor is this belief the passing fancy of the young man dallying with metaphysics: there is no place in the *Pensées* where eloquence is more elevated, and where sincerity seems more indubitably its companion, than in a passage where Montesquieu laments his inability to revise and improve *L'Esprit des lois*:

Mes lectures ont affaibli mes yeux, et il me semble que ce qui me reste encore de lumière n'est que l'aurore du jour où ils se fermeront pour jamais. Je touche presque au moment où je dois commencer et finir, au moment qui dévoile et dérobe tout, au moment mêlé d'amertume et de joie, au moment où je perdrai jusqu'à mes faiblesses mêmes . . . Dieu immortel! le genre humain est votre plus digne ouvrage. L'aimer, c'est vous aimer, et en finissant ma vie je vous consacre cet amour.[4]

[1] F. Hardy, *Memoirs of Charlemont*, I, p. 66; *Arch. hist. Gironde*, XXIII, p. 539.

[2] *Pensée* 156 (Bkn. 2061).

[3] *Pensée* 1266 (Bkn. 615).

[4] *Pensée* 1805 (Bkn. 206).

The author of these words was a spiritually minded man, to whom a great respect for religion and an appreciation of its spirit cannot be denied.

That is not to say, however, that he had a firm Christian conviction. He had been educated as a Christian and had never formally renounced his faith. In the *Lettres persanes* he had betrayed but meagre sympathy with either faith or Church. During his travels he confesses that he feels more attached to religion after seeing Rome and its treasures; but he prefaces this confession with the words, 'Les hommes sont grandement sots!'[1] Montesquieu the believer is thus mocked by Montesquieu the rationalist. In the *Considérations* he pays at least some formal tributes to Christianity.

Some thirteen years later, Book XXIV (which Lacordaire described as the finest apology for Christianity of the eighteenth century)[2] gives what the index of the 1757 edition will describe as a *beau tableau* of the Christian religion:

> Une religion qui enveloppe toutes les passions; qui n'est pas plus jalouse des actions que des désirs et des pensées; qui ne nous tient point attachés par quelques chaînes, mais par un nombre innombrable de fils; qui laisse derrière elle la justice humaine, et commence une autre justice; qui est faite pour mener sans cesse du repentir à l'amour, et de l'amour au repentir; qui met entre le juge et le criminel un grand médiateur, entre le juste et le médiateur un grand juge.[3]

It is hard to imagine that this description of Christianity came from the pen of a man to whom its beliefs were always foreign. This is more than a formal act of homage to Christianity. It is a retrospective and perhaps nostalgic glance at the beliefs which first his mother, and later the fathers of the Oratory, had nurtured in him. It is a vestige of an earlier certainty, now elusive and external to Montesquieu, but still worthy to receive respect and praise.

It is in deism that is to be found the real religious belief of Montesquieu.

Many definitions of deism have been given, but in *L'Esprit des lois* Montesquieu gives his own. Plato, he says, declared

[1] Nagel II, p. 1273; Pléiade I, p. 867.
[2] Lacordaire, *Discours de réception à l'Académie française*, Paris, 1861, p. 8.
[3] *Lois*, XXIV, 13. This chapter, not found in the manuscript, probably therefore dates from 1747.

impious alike those who deny the existence of the gods, those who admit their existence but maintain that they are unconcerned with earthly events, and those who think the gods can be appeased by sacrifices. *La lumière naturelle*, avers the President, has never said anything more sensible about religion.[1] This deistic sentiment is completely consonant with the personal religion of Montesquieu, who unites it with an ecumenical outlook when he asserts that God is a monarch to whom all nations bring tribute, each with its own religion.[2]

It should not be forgotten that deism in the eighteenth century had more than one aspect. In tone and in emphasis there is little in common between the negations of Voltaire's poem *Le Pour et le contre* and the constructive ideas of his *Poème sur la loi naturelle*; nor should the hostility between deism and Christianity be exaggerated. In England in particular the line between low Churchmanship and non-conformity on the one hand, and constructive deism on the other, is not a straight line and it is sometimes blurred. Thus an Englishman, visiting La Brède in 1754, is able to say of its *châtelain*, 'He certainly was not a Papist; but I have no evidence to believe that he was not a Christian.'[3]

It is in that same year that the President, writing to an English bishop, makes a statement about religion which shows in clear relief what his opinions were. He confesses to Warburton that it is always possible to attack revealed religion, because it has a factual basis and facts can be assailed. But natural religion is in different case. It is based on the nature of man, and on the internal sentiment of man, two factors which cannot lend themselves to debate. Revealed religion in England, however, has assumed an aspect such that no man of goodwill would wish to attack it. But if a man did none the less attack the English religion,

> cet homme, quand il réussirait, *quand même il aurait raison dans le fond*, ne ferait que détruire une infinité de biens pratiques pour établir une vérité purement spéculative.[4]

The man who wrote those words was not an uncharacteristic member of the deistic literary society of the Enlightenment. He can most fitly be compared with Alexander Pope. Like Pope,

[1] *Lois*, XXV, 7. [2] *Pensée* 1454 (lacking in Bkn.).
[3] F. Hardy, op. cit., I, p. 71.
[4] Montesquieu to Warburton, May 1754 (Nagel III, pp. 527–9). (My italics.)

Montesquieu was born a Roman Catholic; like Pope, he made his peace with the Roman Church on his death-bed; like Pope again, he was more concerned with morality than with dogma, and his own allegiance throughout his life was primarily to the rational principles of natural religion.

V. RELIGIOUS TOLERATION

One element in the religious outlook of Montesquieu has so far been mentioned only in passing, but it is the belief to which he clung more tenaciously than to any other, and in support of which he engaged to the limit his powers of eloquence. This is his belief in the necessity of religious toleration, a belief which he shared with Voltaire, and which he held more consistently than did Rousseau. It has been said that a man's support for religious toleration varies inversely with the vigour of his own religious conviction. Montesquieu does nothing to disprove such a contention.

Before his travels he deplored already the revocation of the Edict of Nantes and the massacre of Saint Bartholomew.[1] The ideal of liberty which his stay in England revealed to him included, as it did for Voltaire, liberty of conscience; and no Spinozist acceptance of the right of the existing to exist ever destroyed the integrity of his belief in religious toleration: God must be honoured, not avenged.[2] The principle of toleration must be accepted by the State, and imposed on all religions found within the State's frontiers.[3] In a moment of unfounded optimism he had written, soon after his travels, that the Jews were now saved, and superstition would not return. and that their persecution had ended.[4] He was wrong. Persecutions continued in his lifetime, and an *auto-da-fé* at Lisbon inspired Montesquieu's most impassioned piece of writing. This is an open letter, styled *Très Humble Remontrance*, to the Inquisitors of Spain and Portugal. It constitutes the thirteenth chapter of Book XXV of *L'Esprit des lois*. In this letter a Jew appeals to the Inquisitors to spare his race. Their sole error is to have remained faithful to the creed which the Christians of the present day

[1] *Spicilège* 456 (MS., p. 409); *Pensée* 207 (Bkn. 1573).
[2] *Lois*, XII, 4. [3] *Lois*, XXV, 9. [4] *Pensée* 913 (Bkn. 2159).

believe once to have been the true creed. We believe, he says, that those beliefs are still dear to God; you think not, and therefore

vous faites passer par le fer et par le feu ceux qui sont dans cette erreur si pardonnable, de croire que Dieu aime encore ce qu'il a aimé.

Christians appeal to the blood of martyrs to prove the divine mission of their faith; but they have become themselves the Diocletians of their day:

Vous voulez que nous soyons chrétiens, et vous ne voulez pas l'être.

The age they live in is an age of enlightenment greater than has been known before; but in time to come men will look back and consider the persecutions which were then practised. By the persecutors, the reputation of the age will be for ever tarnished. They, and with them their contemporaries, will be viewed with hatred. This remonstrance, a useless document, says Montesquieu ('quand il s'agit de prouver des choses si claires, on est sûr de ne pas convaincre'), is comparable with the *Areopagitica* and with the *Declaration of the Rights of Man.* It reveals the principal and inviolable article of Montesquieu's faith.

XVII

THE QUARREL OF *L'ESPRIT DES LOIS*

I. THE EARLIEST ATTACKS

THE first person to write to Montesquieu about *L'Esprit des lois* was Madame de Tencin. She had received the first copy, unbound and unsewn, to reach Paris. She had read no more than a little of it, with the intensest pleasure, when she had to surrender her copy to Fontenelle, who, she says, would have eaten out her eyes had she refused.[1] About three weeks later she writes again. She has now read the book through, and declares that philosophy, reason, and humanity had assembled to compose it while the graces had taken thought to bedeck its erudition.[2]

Other friends were slower to receive their copies. Immediately before publication, a new edition of the *Considérations* had appeared (on this occasion at Paris and with royal privilege), and letters came to the President thanking him for this work. But before long his friends wrote in the most admiring language about *L'Esprit des lois*: Helvétius, speaking also for Saurin, Duclos, and others, calling it 'le plus grand, le plus bel ouvrage du monde'; Aydie, who says it will make kings, ministers, and peoples wiser; Madame Geoffrin, with glowing hyperbole; Formey, who tells Montesquieu that he is the first man since Adam to write two quarto volumes without one word too many. The only person to dissent from the chorus of praise is Richer d'Aube, nephew of Fontenelle, the author himself of an *Essai sur les principes du droit et de la morale* and therefore resentful of Montesquieu's success.

Others unknown, or at best slightly known, to Montesquieu, were not less impressed. The Président de Brosses writes to a friend:

> Oh que cela est beau! Que d'idées, que de feu, que de précision (et trop!) Que de pensées neuves et lumineuses!

When he has read it twice, he will reflect on it, and will discuss

[1] Mme de Tencin to Montesquieu, 14 November 1748.
[2] Mme de Tencin to Montesquieu, 2 December 1748.

it when he has learnt it by heart.[1] A nephew of the learned Bouhier, meanwhile, on reading it for the first time, was so transported, he said, with enthusiasm, that his liberty of judgement was destroyed.[2] Admirers were not lacking outside France. Horace Walpole was categorical in his description: 'the best book that ever was written'.[3] Cerati meanwhile, having borrowed the work for twenty-four hours from Solar, writes from Pisa of his ecstasy of admiration.[4]

In the same letter Cerati gives the President a warning. He had heard a few weeks previously news from Paris which caused him to fear some hostile activity against Montesquieu: 'quelque tempête contre votre ouvrage'.

His warning was well founded and before long opposition to Montesquieu had become violently articulate.

The first to give tongue were the Jesuits. Castel had resented not being presented with a copy of *L'Esprit des lois*. He had been asked to write an analysis of the work for the *Mémoires de Trévoux*, but not having it had to refuse.[5] Montesquieu replied that he would prefer Castel not to read the work, saying, to the Jesuit's anger, that it was not within his competence.[6] An article by another appeared in the *Mémoires de Trévoux* in April 1749.[7] Its reputed author was one Père Plesse, a Breton with very few publications to his name, and it took the form of an open letter to Père Berthier, editor of the periodical. A short time had passed since the day of publication, but Plesse describes *L'Esprit des lois* as already famous among men of letters. He pays it many compliments before discussing the respects in which it is offensive to religion. He objects to Montesquieu's statement that God must be honoured but not avenged, to his natural explanation of suicides in England, to his attitude to polygamy and celibacy, his praise of Julian the Apostate, to his stress on the disadvantages of a change of religion

[1] De Brosses to Gemeaux, 24 February 1749 (in Y. Bézard, 'Le Président de Brosses d'après une correspondance' in *RHLF*, 1923).

[2] Marquis de Maleteste, *Œuvres diverses d'un ancien magistrat*, London, 1784, p. vii.

[3] H. Walpole to H. Mann, 10 January 1750 (*Letters of Horace Walpole*, Oxford, 1903–5, II, p. 419).

[4] Cerati to Montesquieu, 18 February 1749.

[5] Castel to Montesquieu, 1748–9 (Nagel III, pp. 1153–9).

[6] Castel, *L'Homme moral*, p. 186.

[7] Reprinted in *Œuvres complètes de Montesquieu*, ed. E. Laboulaye, VI, pp. 101–13.

in a State. He ends by saying that he respects the author's great talents and would be very willing to listen to his arguments were he to speak in his own defence.

Later in the same year there appeared the first full-scale book directed against Montesquieu. Entitled *Réflexions sur quelques parties d'un livre intitulé De l'esprit des lois*, it fills two octavo volumes. The *Avis au lecteur* is silly: quoting for the first time the epigram that the work is really *de l'esprit sur les lois*, it says that the lack of method in the work has created the impression that it is but a pleasantry like the *Espion turc*, the *Lettres juives*, or the *Lettres persanes*. This is followed by a foreword which is a curious mixture of praise and blame. The text of the work is of little merit. Montesquieu is attacked for being paradoxical and arbitrary. His definition of law is said to lead the reader into the work by the gate of darkness. The writer attacks Montesquieu's principles of government and would substitute others. He attacks the scientific inadequacy of the chapters on climate. He denies the freedom of the English, saying that on the other hand they are continuously menaced by revolution.

No author's name appears on the title-page of this crude refutation of Montesquieu. It came, however, from the pen of one who passed as his friend, the financier Claude Dupin. Montesquieu had been warned that Dupin was writing an attack on *L'Esprit des lois*. Rousseau was the scribe who wrote the manuscript,[1] and it is he who furnishes the information that Père Berthier collaborated with him in this task.[2] It is probable that Plesse also was involved, and that Madame Dupin wrote the preface.[3]

This attack on Montesquieu was abortive. No more than eight copies were printed and most of these—all but three according to some accounts[4]—were destroyed. One copy only is known today. It belonged to the Marquis d'Argenson and is found now in the Bibliothèque de l'Arsenal in Paris. The circumstances which caused Dupin to withdraw his work are obscure. Guasco's

[1] The manuscript was acquired by the Bordeaux Library in 1960 and bears the shelfmark MS. 2111.

[2] Rousseau, *Confessions*, p. 326.

[3] A. G. Du Plessis, 'Notice biographique, historique, et littéraire sur Claude Dupin' (*Bulletin du bibliophile*, 14e série, 1859). Cf. Marquis d'Argenson, *Journal et mémoires*, VI, p. 74, where it is suggested that the work was about to appear under the name of Mme Dupin.

[4] Du Plessis, loc. cit.

account is that Montesquieu was indignant at the distortions which the author had caused his thought to undergo, that Dupin withdrew the work in order to prepare a corrected edition.[1] Maupertuis claims that on the eve of publication Dupin was advised by his friends to reread *L'Esprit des lois*, did so, saw his error, and withdrew the work.[2] The author of the *Nouveau Dictionnaire historique*, the eighteenth century's best biographical dictionary, relates another story. Angered by Dupin's criticisms, Montesquieu addressed himself to the Marquise de Pompadour and sought her aid. She sent for Dupin, and informed him that she had taken *L'Esprit des lois* and its author under her protection. Dupin thereupon withdrew the copies which had been placed in circulation and burnt the entire edition.[3]

Which of these accounts is truthful is uncertain. Guasco and Maupertuis were both writing in praise of Montesquieu and had therefore a motive for suppressing an unworthy incident. Chaudon, the author of the dictionary, on the other hand, was an *anti-philosophe* and had been associated with such enemies of the Enlightenment as the Abbé Nonnotte. An anecdote showing that Montesquieu acted on other principles from those he professed would be welcome to him. The answer to the problem is in doubt; but a letter from Dupin to the *sous-précepteur* of the Dauphin, written on 10 June 1759 and published in part,[4] suggests that Dupin withdrew the edition of his own choice. All that is certain is that Dupin's critique was a failure.

The attack of the *Mémoires de Trévoux* was not more than half-hearted. That of Dupin, with Jesuit assistance, had failed. Montesquieu was personally on good terms with several Jesuits. He even dined with Père Berthier.[5] The Jesuit Lombard of Toulouse wrote to Venuti in enthusiastic praise of *L'Esprit des lois*.[6] In these circumstances the Jansenists sprang into action.

The Abbé de La Roche had from 1729 been editor of the

[1] *Lettres familières*, XXXVIII (Nagel III, p. 1276).
[2] *Éloge de M. de Montesquieu*, Berlin, 1755, p. 46.
[3] 7th edition, Caen and Lyons, 1789, VI, p. 308.
[4] Vian, pp. 360–1.
[5] Castel to Montesquieu, 14 February 1750.
[6] Lombard to Venuti, 22 April 1749 (Cortona, Biblioteca etrusca, MS. 497, ff. 141–2): 'le nom de [Bordeaux] me rappelle l'ouvrage du président de Montesquieu, dont le génie honore la province. Je dévore son livre qui me frappe par l'étendue des vues et de la plus brillante érudition. Quand désormais on me parlera du royaume de Loyola dans le Paraguay, je renverrai les censeurs à l'*Esprit des lois*.'

Jansenist *Nouvelles ecclésiastiques*, and was a controversialist practised more in violent denunciation than in gentle persuasion. On 9 October 1749 he devoted an article to *L'Esprit des lois*. He begins by saying that about a year previously there has appeared one of those irreligious works with which the world has been inundated for some time and which have been so prodigiously multiplied since the Bull *Unigenitus*. This is *L'Esprit des lois*. The author in his preface had said that he pursued his object without forming a plan; and it is not surprising then that he has had the fate of those who lose their way. Never was he better advised than when he consigned to the flames his first attempts. *L'Esprit des lois* is based on the system of natural religion: the system of Pope and the system of Spinoza. Religion for the author is simply a political device. Man and God alike are governed by fate. Virtue is declared unnecessary and out of place in monarchy. Irreligion is to be found in the author's pronouncement on climate, on polygamy, on divorce, on usury, on celibacy. The author seeks throughout to bring religion into disrepute.

A week later he resumes his theme. Though Bayle is refuted in *L'Esprit des lois*, the author describes him as a great man, and thus unsays his refutation. The praise given to the Stoics cannot come from the pen of a Christian. The entire book serves to argue that religion must be based on the customs, manners, usages and climate of a country. The writer concludes that those whom he calls 'Messieurs de la religion naturelle' have no religion at all, and that *L'Esprit des lois* is not less opposed to sound maxims of government than to the religion of Jesus Christ.[1]

Montesquieu did not allow this fierce and unbalanced attack to perturb him publicly. A few hornets, he writes to a friend, are buzzing around him; but if the bees can gather a little honey, he will not mind.[2] Nor was a feeble critique published early in 1750 by the Abbé de La Porte of a nature to worry him.[3] But in private, under pressure from Guasco,[4] he was active, and early

[1] The two articles from the *Nouvelles ecclésiastiques* are reprinted in *Œuvres de Montesquieu*, ed. Laboulaye, VI, pp. 115–37.

[2] Montesquieu to Cerati, 11 November 1749.

[3] *Observations sur la littérature moderne*, III (Amsterdam, 1750), art. V, pp. 73–96. After having described *L'Esprit des lois* as the most interesting book written for a long time, he ends with the assertion that he condemns the entire work. Cf. Montesquieu to Guasco, 1749–50 (Nagel III, pp. 125–6 and Castel to Montesquieu, 14 [=15] February 1750.

[4] Montesquieu to Guasco, 4 October 1752.

in February 1750, with the false imprint of Barrillot at Geneva, he published the *Défense de l'Esprit des lois*.[1]

II. THE *DÉFENSE*

Like Montesquieu's other works the *Défense de l'Esprit des lois* appeared without mention of the author's name and all references to him in the text are in the third person. He declares that the occasion for the work is provided by two articles in a journal which made against him the most grave imputations. He was accused of being a Spinozist and a deist, and though these two accusations are in themselves contradictory and cannot both be true, they serve to make him appear odious.

He rebuts the charge of Spinozism. Beginning each with the words 'Il est donc Spinoziste', paragraph follows paragraph in refutation of the charge. He had differentiated the material from the spiritual world. He had assailed atheism. He had expounded the creative role of God. He had asserted that justice and equity preceded all positive laws. He had declared that the belief in God was the most important of all natural laws. He had, with all his strength, sought to refute the paradox of Bayle.

There follow replies to three specific objections. The most simple and not the least effective is shown in the second:

Objection. L'auteur cite Plutarque, qui dit que la loi est la reine de tous les mortels et immortels. Mais est-ce d'un païen, etc.
Réponse. Il est vrai que l'auteur a cité Plutarque, qui dit que la loi est la reine de tous les mortels et immortels.

Some 40 pages follow on the charge of deism. Montesquieu cites many passages in reply. Each one of them, not surprisingly in view of his own outlook, deals with the social influence of Christianity, none of them with his personal belief. Specific objections are then considered. To the charge that he had described Bayle, though refuting him, as a great man, Montesquieu retorts that if he had denounced Bayle as an abominable man he would have succeeded in showing, not that Bayle had argued rightly or wrongly, but simply that he himself could write insults. He rejects the criticism that he had not mentioned original sin because he was writing a political and not a theological treatise.

[1] The coincidence of *fleurons* and other decorations show that it was published in reality at Paris by Huart and Moreau.

To the charge of following the system of Pope, he retorts that the system of Pope is not mentioned in the entire work. To the initial assertion that *L'Esprit des lois* and other irreligious works were the result of the Bull *Unigenitus*, he replies that the Bull *Unigenitus* was not the occasional cause of *L'Esprit des lois*, but that the Bull *Unigenitus* and *L'Esprit des lois* were the occasional causes which led to this puerile reasoning on the part of the critic.

There follows a section filling more than a hundred of the tiny pages of the *Défense* in reply to minor and specific charges of heretical opinion: polygamy, climate, toleration, celibacy, and usury are the themes discussed. Montesquieu replies with skill, resilience, and learning. A short third part contains sensible and balanced reflections on the method of criticism: one must not attack a part by arguments which are really directed against the whole; one must not attribute to an author ideas which are not directly expressed in his words; and in the concluding paragraphs—the last pages which Montesquieu published—he writes what can be taken as his final message:

> Quand on écrit sur les grandes matières, il ne suffit pas de consulter son zèle, il faut encore consulter ses lumières.[1]

Never was Montesquieu's style better than in the *Défense*; never were grave and moderately gay more skilfully mixed; never were his statements more precise, or his command of his pen more complete; never were his arguments more telling.

Nor was he ever more firm in his convictions. At various moments in his life he had shown a lawyer's readiness to compromise, and had been willing to yield to pressure. And in his remaining years this was to happen again. He had been ready to modify the text of the *Lettres persanes*, he had submitted the *Considérations* to clerical censorship, and had excised controversial passages. He had introduced cancels into the text of *L'Esprit des lois*. There is nothing of this sort with the *Défense*.[2] The bitterness of the attacks made on him inspired courage in him. He withdrew nothing and apologized for nothing.

It was bound, therefore, to stimulate rather than to silence criticism, and the alignment of forces became more rigid.

[1] Nagel I, B, p. 488; Pléiade II, p. 1162.

[2] There is one cancel in the first edition, inserted in order to correct a false reference and a spelling mistake.

III. THE SKIRMISH

An article in the *Mémoires de Trévoux* on 16 February 1750 dealt with one point only in the *Défense*, the use made of Diodorus Siculus. The previous day, however, Castel had written to Montesquieu at his usual inordinate length but with much more asperity than was his wont:

> Ou vous êtes un ennemi théologique ou vous ne l'êtes pas. Si vous ne l'êtes pas, il faut la défense complète; si vous l'êtes—*quod Deus avertat!*—mon amitié, très vive, très pure assurément, ne peut ni ne veut vous absoudre.

The Jansenists remained firm in their previous position. La Roche published two further articles in the *Nouvelles ecclésiastiques*, on 24 April and 1 May 1750.[1] They add little, except further invective (Montesquieu now is *cet impie*; he *vomit des blasphèmes*) except a reasoned reiteration of the charge of Spinozism, with direct reference to the text of Spinoza; and here he succeeds in some measure in making his point.

Montesquieu now gained an ally, temporary but powerful, and unexpected. Voltaire, dating his work 14 May 1750, published a short pamphlet ironically entitled *Remerciement sincère à un homme charitable.*[2] You have saved the world from the poison of Pope, he tells the Jansenist pamphleteer, but you must not stop now. The works of Pope, Locke, Bayle, and Montesquieu must all be burnt. Add to them all the pagan sages of antiquity. You are right when you say that their beliefs were based on the light of reason. You must thank God that you have nothing in common with them.

Voltaire was not always Montesquieu's literary friend, but he supported him generously in this controversy where their enemies were the same.[3]

The next recruit to Montesquieu's side is a surprising one. It was the chief opponent of the *philosophes*, Elie-Catherine Fréron. He had refrained from reviewing *L'Esprit des lois* in his

[1] Reprinted in *Œuvres de Montesquieu*, ed. Laboulaye, VI, pp. 209–37.

[2] Voltaire, *Œuvres complètes*, ed. Moland, XXIII, pp. 257–61.

[3] Voltaire alluded to the controversy again in a note to his preface to the *Poème sur le désastre de Lisbonne* (1756), where he says that the *Nouvelles ecclésiastiques* took one page to prove Montesquieu an atheist, and another to prove him a deist.

journal, *Lettres sur quelques écrits de ce temps*, but had alluded to it briefly with eulogistic adjectives ('profond ouvrage', 'grand ouvrage')'[1] He made an attack, wholly in character, on Voltaire's *Remerciement sincère.*[2] Six weeks later he is on Montesquieu's side.[3] He describes *L'Esprit des lois* as a work of so great learning that one is surprised to see it come from the amiable pen of the author of the *Lettres persanes*. Every page bears the mark of a publicly minded citizen. Those who assert that the work lacks a plan are in error. Those who seek to denigrate it are pursuing a useless aim. Of criticisms made so far the best is that of La Porte (who was Fréron's colleague on more than one journal); but he has his shortcomings and has been replied to by 'un homme d'esprit'.

The critique by La Porte was a new one, entitled *Observations sur l'Esprit des lois, ou l'art de lire ce livre*,[4] in which, at the length of 198 pages, the author discerns flaws and beauties in Montesquieu's work: nothing in it, he says, is mediocre; there are beauties which demonstrate Montesquieu's greatness, and faults which one would not tolerate in an ordinary man. The reply is the *Apologie de l'Esprit des lois* by Boulanger de Rivery,[5] a non-practising doctor unknown to Montesquieu. His conclusion is that 'l'auteur de l'*Esprit des lois* est partout ce qu'il faut être'. Another reply, almost simultaneous, is the *Réponse aux observations sur l'Esprit des lois* by François Risteau,[6] a merchant of Bordeaux, well known to Montesquieu, and whose daughter was eventually to achieve some modest renown as a novelist under the name Madame Cottin.

The controversy was widened by the Jansenist Gautier's bitter book, *Les Lettres persanes convaincues d'impiété*. Otherwise the year 1751 saw four other items in the discussion. Criticism on a number of points in ancient history is made by Johann August Ernesti in his *Animadversiones philologicae in librum franciscum De caussis legum*,[7] who claims that Montesquieu was very far from having an accurate knowledge of Latin and impugns his

[1] I, *Lettre XVI*, 4 September 1749, and II, *Lettre VI*, 20 October 1749.
[2] III, *Lettre VIII*, 9 November 1750.
[3] IV, *Lettre VII*, 19 December 1750. The letter is shown by internal allusions to have been completed in the course of 1751.
[4] Amsterdam, 1751. [5] Amsterdam, 1751.
[6] s.l., 1751: reprinted as an appendix to *Lettres familières*, Florence, 1768.
[7] Reprinted in his *Opuscula philologica critica*, Leyden, 1764.

historical method in relation to a few detailed points. The *Mercure de France* takes him to task about the meaning of the word *honneur*.[1] The Abbé de Bonnaire published his *L'Esprit des lois quintessencié par une suite de lettres analytiques*.[2] He was a foolish, sententious man, and his book resembles its author. He sees in the work of Montesquieu 'des imaginations sans consistance, des chimères réduites en systèmes.'[3] The *Suite de la Défense de l'Esprit des lois*[4] is a work of a different order. Its author is the protestant La Beaumelle, a friend of Montesquieu and himself a minor *philosophe* of merit. He assails Montesquieu's adversaries with great gusto. He praises *L'Esprit des lois* as the triumph of humanity, the masterpiece of genius, the Bible of politicians. In it are united in the highest degree 'le bon sens, l'esprit, et le génie'.

The corner for Montesquieu was now turned, so far as pamphlets, broadsheets, and occasional pieces were concerned. A volume of *Pièces pour et contre l'Esprit des lois* appeared in 1752 with the imprint Geneva. It contained more for than against Montesquieu, and to place the Jansenist attacks beside Voltaire's *Remerciement sincère* and the Jesuit attacks beside La Beaumelle's *Suite de la Défense* was to argue in Montesquieu's favour. Fréron gives a reasoned bibliography of the controversy in his *Idée de toutes les critiques qui ont été faites du livre de l'Esprit des lois*.[5] His comments are favourable to the President's friends and hostile to his enemies. Véron de Forbonnais in his *Extrait du livre intitulé de l'Esprit des lois*[6] though occasionally hostile is fair and reasonable. And though Dupin's work appeared again, under the title *Observations sur un livre intitulé de l'Esprit des lois*, and now in three volumes, its strictures on Montesquieu were much attenuated.

Outside France his fame was growing. The Italian Cataneo shows great admiration for him in his *La Source, la force, et le véritable esprit des lois*;[7] the Florentine Bertolini composed in 1753, though it was not published until 1771, an *Analyse raisonnée de l'Esprit des lois* which won the President's approval; the Danish author Holberg was respectful and admiring in his *Remarques sur quelques positions qui se trouvent dans l'Esprit des*

[1] July, 1751. [2] s.l., 1751, 2 vols. [3] P. 24. [4] Berlin, 1751.

[5] *Opuscules*, Amsterdam, 1753, III, pp. 313–431.

[6] Contained in Fréron, *Opuscules*, III. [7] Berlin and Potsdam, 1752.

lois.[1] These successes could not, however, efface for Montesquieu the bitterness of the controversy that had raged. Neither Voltaire, nor Diderot, nor even La Mettrie, whatever official disapproval the most daring of their works had provoked, had been the victims of comparable literary persecution. The tumult against Montesquieu drew Voltaire, for a short time, to his side. It evoked the sympathy of D'Alembert, and led him to add a glowing tribute to Montesquieu in a revised edition of the *Discours préliminaire de l'Encyclopédie*.[2] It was described by Maupertuis as an 'opprobre éternel'.[3]

IV. OFFICIAL ATTITUDES

Although attacked by many pamphleteers, *L'Esprit des lois* did not involve its author in trouble with political or legal authority. In England it was cited as authoritative in Parliament.[4] In Austria, though clerical influence tried to secure its proscription, it was widely read and its diffusion was encouraged by the imperial librarian.[5] The King of Sardinia ordered his son to read it and make notes from it.[6]

Opposition in Paris could have come from the Parlement or from the Government. It would have been surprising if the Parlement had turned on the former *président à mortier*, and though there was a whisper of hostility on the part of two counsellors,[7] it did not develop and no more was heard of it. On the part of the Government, represented by the Chancellor, then D'Aguesseau, there was some hesitation. An advance copy had been sent to D'Aguesseau.[8] His initial reaction seems to have been one of hostility, and he forbade the sale.[9] He admired the work never-

[1] Copenhagen, 1753.

[2] D'Alembert to Mme Du Deffand, 4 December 1752 (*Correspondance de Mme Du Deffand*, ed. Lescure, I, p. 154).

[3] *Eloge de M. de Montesquieu*, Berlin, 1755, p. 45.

[4] By Bath (Hume to Montesquieu, 10 April 1749) and by Granville (Mme de Tencin to Montesquieu, 7 June 1749).

[5] Jameray Duval to Nivernais, 26 June 1750 (Nagel III, pp. 1544–7).

[6] Marquis d'Argenson, *Journal et Mémoires*, VI, p. 11.

[7] Montesquieu to Guasco, 1749–50 (Nagel III, p. 1276).

[8] Vernet to Montesquieu, 4 November 1748.

[9] Mme de Tencin to Montesquieu, 9 January 1749; *fiche de police* (B.N., MSS. n.a.f. 10782, f. 169).

theless,[1] and eventually was prevailed on not only to permit its sale, but to allow an edition to be printed in Paris on condition (as was usual in such cases) that the name of some foreign town appeared on the title-page.[2] Many subsequent editions appeared at Paris without impediment.

Ecclesiastical institutions in France presented more difficulty to Montesquieu. The first of these was the General Assembly of the Clergy of France. The first meeting of this body to occur after the publication of *L'Esprit des lois* began on 25 May 1750, under the presidency of the Cardinal de La Rochefoucauld.[3] On 24 July La Rochefoucauld was asked to make representations to the King about anti-religious works with a view to having action taken against them.[4] Three days later the Cardinal reported that the King was scandalized and would do his best. The *procès-verbal* does not enumerate the works in question. It is Montesquieu himself who discloses that *L'Esprit des lois* was one of them and that the individual who denounced it was Languet de Gergy, Archbishop of Sens, and his colleague in the Academy, the principal charge being that he had not spoken of revelation, in which, Montesquieu adds succinctly, 'il errait, et dans le raisonnement et dans le fait.'[5]

On 26 August the Cardinal returned to the assembly with his report. He announced that the task of examining all works contrary to religion and morals would be enormous. He urged the expediency of dealing with one work only—namely, the *Lettres, Ne repugnate vestro bono* of Daniel Bargeton, which argued against the clergy's immunity from taxation. These letters, which end with a six-line quotation from the preface to *L'Esprit des lois*, had appeared surreptitiously after the opening of the assembly.

[1] Bulkeley to Montesquieu, 13 January 1749.

[2] Huart and Moreau *fils* to Montesquieu, 8 January 1749. It was they who published the 1749 edition, the second to have been approved by the author. On the title-page appears *Genève, chez Barrillot et fils.*

[3] An account of the proceedings is to be found in A. Duranthon, *Collection des procès-verbaux des assemblées générales du clergé de France*, Paris, 1767–8, VIII, pt. I, and in greater detail in the MS. proceedings in the Archives Nationales (G^{8x} 688).

[4] The MS. account has many deletions at this point (pp. 265–6). One passage crossed out, and annotated in the margin 'approuvé la rature', is in the address to the King, who was asked 'd'arrêter le torrent d'impiété qui inonde et sa cour et la ville et toutes les provinces.'

[5] Montesquieu to Nivernais, 8 October 1750.

They had been attributed to Silhouette, and were thought to express the views of the anti-clerical *contrôleur-général* Machault. The clergy's privileges were in jeopardy, and it was thought possible that their general assembly might never meet again.[1] This preoccupation was Montesquieu's salvation. A commission, headed by the archbishops of Sens and Vienne, was at once appointed to deal with the anti-clerical letters, and *L'Esprit des lois* received no more attention from the assembly.

While Montesquieu's fate at the hands of the General Assembly of the Clergy was still in doubt, he was denounced to the Sorbonne or more accurately to the Faculty of Theology of the University of Paris. The fullest account of the proceedings, though a tendentious one, is given by the *Nouvelles ecclésiastiques* of 23 January 1752. It was on 1 August 1750 that the Faculty of Theology decided to take action against books hostile to religion, and to this end appointed a committee of twelve deputies, presided over by the Abbé Tamponnet. Their first act was to equip themselves with the *Nouvelles ecclésiastiques* in order to establish a list of books to be considered. Their list when drawn up included two translations, by Du Resnel and by Silhouette, of Pope's *Essay on Man*, the *Histoire naturelle* of Buffon, and *L'Esprit des lois*. The translators of Pope readily retracted whatever was reprehensible in their work. Buffon did likewise, and published the retraction in the fourth volume of the *Histoire naturelle*. But *L'Esprit des lois* had another fate.[2]

Montesquieu, on being approached by the Sorbonne, was angry and uncompromising, and was unable to understand the coolness of Buffon in this situation.[3] He took the step of appealing to François de Fitz-James, Bishop of Soissons, an old friend who was Berwick's son and nephew to Bulkeley. Fitz-James, who did

[1] On Bargeton and the *Lettres*, see Barbier, *Journal*, III, p. 145, and D'Argenson, *Journal et mémoires*, VI, pp. 208 and 258.

[2] For Montesquieu's reactions, see C. J. Beyer, 'Montesquieu et la censure religieuse de l'*Esprit des lois*' (*Revue des sciences humaines*, 1953).

[3] Buffon reports that Montesquieu was furious. ' "Qu'allez-vous répondre?" me disait-il. "Rien du tout, Président"; et il ne pouvait concevoir mon sang froid' (Hérault de Séchelles, *Voyage à Montbar*, Paris, an IX, p. 38). Another report agrees: 'Les députés, me disait Buffon, me parlèrent très honnêtement, et je me rétractai; Montesquieu, plus vif, s'y refusa' (*Mémoires et correspondance de Mallet du Pan*, ed. A. Sayous, Paris, 1851, I, p. 124). Cf. also Buffon to Le Blanc, 21 March 1750 and 24 April 1751 (Buffon, *Œuvres*, ed. J.-L. de Lanessan, Paris, 1883, XIII, pp. 67–68, 78–79).

not believe in the censoring of works and had no confidence in the Sorbonne's committee, said he would speak to the Archbishop of Paris and ask him to intervene, though he was doubtful about both his willingness to act and his efficacity in action.[1]

The Archbishop, who was Christophe de Beaumont, sought to mediate, according to the *Nouvelles ecclésiastiques*, and a committee of two, Millet who was then Syndic and Regnault, was appointed to negotiate a settlement. The committee met both Beaumont and Montesquieu. But Montesquieu lost interest and departed for Bordeaux, leaving the Archbishop and the doctors to conclude an operation for which he showed 'une indifférence philosophique'. The censure thus failed and (according to the Jansenist journal) no list of censurable propositions was published. This account is approximately confirmed by Montesquieu, who writes to Nivernais on 3 March 1751 that 'il n'y aura point de condamnation et cette affaire est tombée'.[2] It was late in May 1751 that Montesquieu returned to Bordeaux. There had been a list of censurable propositions, however, and though remaining unpublished it had been printed, for copies of it survive.[3] It had been submitted to Montesquieu,[4] and it must be assumed that he gave replies which could be regarded as adequate.

This was not, however, the end of the conflict between Montesquieu and the Sorbonne. The rest of the story is told in the manuscript *procès-verbal* kept in the Archives Nationales.[5] It appears that Montesquieu's reassurance was premature. For on 1 July 1752 the Syndic of the Faculty of Theology asked his colleagues what they wished done in relation to *L'Esprit des lois*, so that from the great diversity of opinion expressed some judgement might be reached.[6] It was decided that the committee should be strengthened by the addition of eight new deputies and, taking

[1] Fitz-James to Montesquieu, 29 September 1850. Montesquieu's letter of 27 September is not extant.

[2] Nagel III, p. 1363. For the date, see my article 'Montesquieu's correspondence: additions and corrections' (*FS*, 1958).

[3] In the Bodleian Library (Mason GG. 48) and the Bibliothèque Mazarine (12,222 B). The text was published by Vian (pp. 283–5) but without the judgements. Three propositions were described as heretical, three as false, and the rest as offensive to pious ears or as injurious either to religion, or to the State, or to natural law.

[4] Nagel III, p. 656; Pléiade II, p. 1178.

[5] MM 257.

[6] 'Ut ex tanta multitudine opinionum ac varietate circa censuram libri, cui titulus *Mens legum*, aliqua sacrae facultatis sententia exsurgeret' (p. 400).

account of the many learned observations that had been made, should recommend additions and deletions in the two lists or *indicula* which had been prepared.[1]

A special meeting of the Faculty on 17 July 1752 received the committee's report, recommending four new propositions and new censorial notes on the first eight propositions, and approved it. Then, on 1 August 1752 the regular Faculty meeting accepted the proposals, with two amendments, and ordered their publication. Once again, however, the list appears not to have been published. It was submitted to Montesquieu, who drew up replies.[2] These came before the Sorbonne on 15 June 1754, either Montesquieu or the Faculty having been slow to act.[3] They were then rejected, publication once again was ordered, and once again did not occur. The Sorbonne never published its censure. It had waited too long and Montesquieu's renown was then assured.

V. THE HOLY SEE

Letters in praise of *L'Esprit des lois* had come to Montesquieu from Italy. The Duc de Nivernais, French ambassador to the Holy See, known to Montesquieu through their common membership of the Brancas salon, and Solar, now ambassador of Malta in Rome, wrote in glowing praise of the work. Cerati likewise was filled with enthusiasm, and his attitude is of particular interest. For he was a man of Jansenist leanings, as were many of his friends, and his attitude to *L'Esprit des lois* stands out in striking contrast to that of the French Jansenists expressed in the *Nouvelles ecclésiastiques*. The voice of Jansenism in Italy was very different from the voice with which it spoke in France. Beyond the Alps it had become, with many of its spokesmen, the ally of the Enlightenment, an alignment which is one of the most remarkable events in ecclesiastical history. The principal two Jansenist journals of Italy both mention *L'Esprit des lois* in the course of 1750. The Roman *Giornale de' letterati*, edited by Foggini, has a review of 8 pages in January. It makes several critical observations on the obscurity of the work. The moderately

[1] Presumably the list of reprehensible propositions and the list of judgements on them, which were separate.

[2] Nagel III, pp. 649–74; Pléiade II, pp. 1172–95.

[3] Archives Nationales, op. cit., p. 441.

learned, it is said, may feign to understand it and they will certainly admire, but their attitude is like that of the Romans when first they passed the Ciminian Mount: the immense gnarled trees cast over them black and impenetrable shadows, and they thought this darkness was divine. So the vulgar (defined as 'any kind of man who is not free from prejudice') have been bemused by *L'Esprit des lois*. The work is full of contradictions and obscurities.[1] But none the less it is a masterpiece of supreme greatness. It is written with elegance, it is filled with new and brilliant thoughts, it reveals great erudition. The reviewer, among his various individual criticisms, nowhere makes the slightest imputation of irreligion against the work, and his objections are made with good humour. On 20 March of the same year, Giovanni Lami allows his *Novelle letterarie* of Florence to describe *L'Esprit des lois* as worthy to be daily in the hands of everyone, and as most useful in teaching the duties of civil life. Nor were Lami and Foggini inspired by personal friendship for Montesquieu. He did not know them. In 1728–9 Lami was abroad and Foggini was a mere child.

Early in 1750 Montesquieu learnt that *L'Esprit des lois* had been denounced to the Holy See, and that an attempt was being made to place it on the Index of Prohibited Books.[2] He wrote at once to the Duc de Nivernais at Rome and told him of the threat to *L'Esprit des lois*. He explained the nature of the criticisms made against him in France, announced that the *Défense* would appear in four days' time and silence his adversaries, and declared that he was preparing a new edition of *L'Esprit des lois* from which the passages objected to would be withdrawn. He expressed surprise that measures should be taken against his book under so enlightened a pontiff as Benedict XIV and with such cardinals as

[1] The contradiction which the reviewer chooses as his main example is this: we are told by Montesquieu that the superiority of Christianity over Islam is immediately apparent, to the extent that we should embrace the one and reject the other. Yet we are told that if one is satisfied with the religion generally held in the State, it must not be changed. What then, satisfied as they are with their faith, are the Turks to do?

[2] Accounts of the negotiations in Rome have been given by E. Dammig, *Il Movimento giansenista a Roma nella seconda metà del secolo XVIII*, Rome, 1945 (*Studi e testi*, 119) and L. Bérard, '*L'Esprit des lois* devant la Congrégation de l'Index' in *Deuxième centenaire de 'l'Esprit des lois' de Montesquieu*, Bordeaux, 1949 (also in *La Revue*, 15 August 1949). Bérard has added no manuscript evidence to that discovered by Dammig.

Valenti and Passionei *in curia*; and he begged Nivernais to intervene on his behalf.[1]

From whom the denunciation came is not known.[2] The Congregation of the Index had already been seized of the affair, and had appointed as reviser Mgr Bottari, who was a celebrated scholar, intimate with the Pope, a close personal friend not only of the Corsini family, but also of Cerati and Niccolini. He was also, to Montesquieu's good fortune, a man who had already read and praised *L'Esprit des lois*, and had recommended it as an admirable work to Bartolomeo Corsini.[3]

Nivernais was not slow to act.[4] He began a series of interviews; he wrote a memorandum expressing Montesquieu's views: his humility, his regret at the distortions his work had suffered, his innocence of the charges raised against him, and his intention to publish a corrected edition. He presented this memorandum to Passionei on 1 February 1750,[5] and he asked Montesquieu to send him twelve copies of the *Défense*.

Solar meanwhile was seconding Nivernais in making diplomatic *démarches*. Cardinal Passionei, who was a man of great learning and considered himself a patron of scholars, exerted himself vigorously in order to ensure that Montesquieu should be able to speak in his own defence, an unusual concession on the part of the Congregation. The Secretary of State Valenti also was well disposed; for though Durini, the Nuncio in Paris, sent him a copy of the *Défense* with the accompanying comment that it was full of errors against the Christian religion, which it treated as the

[1] Montesquieu to Nivernais, 26 January 1750.

[2] There is no indication in the official correspondence that it came from the Nuncio (Archivio segreto Vaticano, Nunziatura di Francia, supplt. XII) although the making of such denunciations was part of his function (cf. letters to Secretary of State of 13 and 27 October 1749); and Vian's assertion (p. 287) that it came from the editor of the *Nouvelles ecclésiastiques* is unsupported by evidence. P. Bastid ('Montesquieu et les Jésuites' in *Congrès 1955*) argues that the denunciation was probably of Jesuit origin.

[3] Bottari to Bartolomeo Corsini, 13 July 1749 (Biblioteca Corsiniana, MS. 1910, f. 307).

[4] Nivernais to Montesquieu, 18 February 1750 (L. Perey, *Un petit-neveu de Mazarin*, Paris, 1890, pp. 153–5).

[5] Printed by Perey, op. cit., p. 561, and also at Nagel III, pp. 647–8, where it is suggested that it was Montesquieu's reply to Bottari's criticisms. This, however, is incompatible with its date as given by Perey, and its text does not in fact constitute a reply to Bottari.

equivalent of Mohammedanism,[1] Valenti had already handed a copy of the same work to Bottari in order to advance Montesquieu's prospects.[2] The President meanwhile sent Nivernais the twelve copies of the *Défense* for which he had asked. The Ambassador gave one of these to the Pope, along with Montesquieu's other works, with the prudent exception of the *Lettres persanes*. Benedict was greatly gratified at this mark of esteem, and said that the author would not have acted in vain.[3]

Bottari did not take long to make up his mind which passages were censurable. He committed his observations to paper. Passionei insisted on seeing them, on discussing them, and (although told this was unnecessary) having them translated into French. Finally Nivernais was able to transmit them to Montesquieu. He told the President that he must write and thank Passionei and must do so in the language of extreme adulation: 'éloges, admiration, et remerciements excessifs, c'est là son régime'.[4] Montesquieu did not fail to rise to this occasion.[5]

On Friday 28 August 1750 Passionei wrote a letter to Bottari in a tone very different from that of leisurely badinage which he normally used. He had just learnt that the Congregation could wait no longer, and that Bottari would be called on to submit his report the following Monday.[6] The next day Nivernais sent Montesquieu's complete reply to Bottari, conveying the President's complete trust in Bottari's judgement.[7] Bottari now appeared before the Congregation and, apparently not yet having studied Montesquieu's reply, asked for and procured an adjournment.

All was not well, however. Nivernais was afraid that the publication, pending at Naples, of an Italian translation of the book might be regarded as a provocative move. He had it stopped. Opinion was building up against Montesquieu. Daniel Concina, a Dominican, noted for his exposition of moral rigorism and for

[1] Durini to Valenti, 20 July 1750 (Archivio segreto Vaticano, Nunziatura di Francia, supplt. XII).

[2] Solar to Montesquieu, 4 March 1750.

[3] Nivernais to Montesquieu, 24 March 1750.

[4] Nivernais to Montesquieu, 4 May 1750 (Nagel III, pp. 1304–5).

[5] Montesquieu to Passionei, 2 June 1750.

[6] Passionei to Bottari, 28 August 1750 (Biblioteca Corsiniana, MS. 2054, ff. 95–96; Dammig, op. cit., p. 79, refers).

[7] Nivernais to Bottari, 29 August 1750 (Biblioteca Corsiniana, MS. 1569, ff. 341–2). Montesquieu's reply is not extant.

his opposition to the Jesuits, made a vigorous attack on *L'Esprit des lois*, especially Book XXVI, in the sixth volume of his *Theologia Christiana dogmatico-moralis*. Innumerable things in this work, he says, are worthy of severe censure. The author wanders through all laws, both sacred and profane, he discusses the religious and political governments of the most numerous nations, he approves, condemns, and according as his fancy defines. His little reflections, he says, and moderately witty comments are now adorned with the flowerets of learning, now besmeared with paint. The whole work is pernicious and reprehensible.[1] Almost simultaneously the Barnabite religious Giacinto Sigismondo Gerdil, later to become a cardinal, and a friend of Benedict XIV before his elevation to the Papacy, delivered a lecture to the Royal Academy of Turin, in which he alluded to 'some recently published commentaries, which enjoy great and continuous fame, on the intimate force and meaning of the laws, or if you will have it literally, on the Spirit of the Laws'. Their author, he continues ironically, is most learned, to the point that being versed in the study of the laws, institutions, judgements, and customs of all ages and of all peoples, he endeavours to trace all these back to their sources: an egregious enterprise, and one that leads him into many errors. Gerdil goes on to deal with the notion that virtue is peculiar to republican governments, and vigorously rebuts it, both in his lecture and in the twenty-five questions which are examined in the appendix.[2]

The opposition to Montesquieu was mounting in Italy, when another meeting of the Congregation was called shortly before Christmas 1750. Nivernais on this occasion appealed to the Pope himself, who in response to his request ordered that no decision should be made. Sentiment in the Congregation was becoming increasingly hostile, though a new ally for Montesquieu appeared in the person of Cardinal Querini.[3] The President exchanged letters with his new advocate, who was prefect of the Congregation of the Index; but he was urgently warned by Nivernais to conceal this correspondence, since Querini was

[1] Pp. xi–xii.

[2] The lecture, delivered on 5 November 1750, was published in the ensuing year under the title *Virtutem politicam ad optimum statum non minus regno quam reipublicae necessariam esse oratio*.

[3] Nivernais to Montesquieu, 23 December 1750.

exceedingly ill thought of by the Pope who, if he knew that Montesquieu and he were in touch, would change forthwith from white to black.[1] Nivernais, in order to gain time, caused Bottari to be replaced as rapporteur by one Aimaldi, his own personal friend, and an avowed admirer of Montesquieu.

The move was in vain, however. On 29 November 1751 *L'Esprit des lois* was placed on the Index of Prohibited Books, and all that Nivernais could obtain by a personal appeal to the Pope was that the decree by means of which this was done should not be published separately.[2] The decree was in fact published on 2 March 1752. Along with *L'Esprit des lois* were condemned the *De officio hominis* of Pufendorf, the *Comte de Gabalis* in Italian, a work, entitled *Examen impartial des immunités ecclésiastiques*, written by the Abbé Chauvelin, and a doubtless scurrilous publication called *La Guerre séraphique*.

Why was *L'Esprit des lois* placed on the Index? The criticisms produced by Bottari were modest indeed and expressed with a degree of courtesy and moderation very different from those of the *Nouvelles ecclésiastiques*.[3] Objections are raised only to points of detail, and often a remedy is suggested. Montesquieu had described as tyrannical the Jewish law which permitted men to repudiate their wives, but gave no reciprocal right to women. The word *tyrannique*, says the censor, is too strong; it is better to say, *la legge è dura*. *Indestructible* is too strong a word to describe the religion of the Indians; a weaker epithet should be found. Nor should the scholastics as a whole be blamed for the unhappy effects on commerce of their teachings concerning usury; this should be limited to bad scholastics. Henry VIII eliminated from his realm the monks, 'nation paresseuse elle-même'. It is unfortunately true that many monks are lazy, says the censor; but the author should either make it clear that he is not referring to all monks, or should put the words in the mouth of Henry

[1] Nivernais to Montesquieu, 24 April 1751.—Relations between the Pope and Querini were so bad in 1751 that the Cardinal wrote a memorandum in justification of his personal conduct (Biblioteca Vaticana, MS. vat. lat. 8430, ff. 390–4).

[2] Nivernais to Montesquieu, 8 December 1751.

[3] *Note sopra lo Spirito delle leggi* (Biblioteca Vaticana, MS. Ottob. lat. 3157, ff. 5–9). The fact that several of the corrections proposed here were later made by Montesquieu, and a comparison with the references to Bottari's criticism in Nivernais to Montesquieu, 4 May 1750, leave no reasonable doubt that this MS. is Bottari's report.

VIII. The only categorical censure which is pronounced is against Book XXVI, chapter 11, which deals with the Inquisition. The whole chapter must be deleted.

These were mild criticisms. The Pope was favourable to Montesquieu, and three cardinals were active in his behalf. But though his supporters were prominent and celebrated, and his opponents for the most part unnamed, it was the opponents who triumphed. A possible reason for their triumph was the publication in 1751 of an unrevised edition. Another, suggested by Nivernais,[1] was that the Congregation may have been offended by the publication of La Beaumelle's *Suite de la Défense de l'Esprit des lois*. But more likely is the simple fact that *L'Esprit des lois* contained much that the eighteenth-century Church, operating within its traditional framework of doctrine and of practice, was bound to censure. The acceptance by some ecclesiastics of the newly circulating ideas, the personal friendship of others for Montesquieu, could at best disguise but could not alter the incompatibility with the Church's teaching of some elements in his book. This was specifically recognized by Cerati, Montesquieu's close friend, who wrote to Bottari in the middle of the crisis. He describes *L'Esprit des lois* as the achievement of a most lofty genius who does honour to his age, but insists that it definitely cannot escape some theological censure.[2] Not very differently had Montesquieu's old and intimate friend, Père Desmolets, written even before the first Jansenist attacks in the *Nouvelles ecclésiastiques*: the work deserved the greatest praise but was bound to be condemned because it proclaimed truths which must be kept from little minds.[3] The divergence between the outlook of Montesquieu and other *philosophes* and the outlook of the Church was too great for the goodwill of Lambertini, Passionei, Valenti, and Querini to bridge it.

The discovery of this fact was an unwelcome event for Montesquieu. He was extremely anxious that his work should not be condemned. In his letters to Nivernais, when he gives or seeks advice, he writes with a lack of control and a diffuseness which are

[1] Nivernais to Montesquieu, 8 December 1751.

[2] Cerati to Bottari, 31 January 1751 (Biblioteca Corsiniana, MS. 1590, f. 4; Dammig, op. cit., p. 79, refers).

[3] Desmolets to Mme xxx, 26 September 1749 (Bx, MS. 1867). The subject matter suggests that the addressee was perhaps Mme de Tencin. The letter is unsigned but the handwriting is Desmolets's.

most uncharacteristic. He realizes this himself, even saying in one letter[1] that he writes like a child and he hopes that Nivernais will give his letter no more attention than it deserves. In this same letter, however, he is lucid enough to confess that he is doing more harm to himself than other people are doing:

> Je me fais plus de mal que l'on ne peut m'en faire, et . . . le mal même qu'on peut me faire cessera d'en être un sitôt que moi, jurisconsulte français, je le regarderai avec cette indifférence que mes confrères les jurisconsultes français ont regardé les procédés de la Congrégation dans tous les temps.

Lofty indifference was, however, far from being Montesquieu's attitude in this crisis. Not remembering that his companions on the Index included Montaigne and Descartes, he was anxious to avoid the stigma of censure. His anxiety led him to view ecclesiastical censure more seriously, if Nivernais is to be believed, than the censors themselves; for the Ambassador told him, when announcing the condemnation, 'ces gens-ci ne croient pas vous avoir fait grand mal.'[2]

[1] Montesquieu to Nivernais, 8 October 1750.

[2] Nivernais to Montesquieu, 8 December 1751—It may be noted that the *Lettres persanes* were placed on the Index in 1761.

XVIII

RENOWN, 1748–55

I. APPEARANCE AND CHARACTER

MONTESQUIEU'S life before 1748 offers to his biographer only meagre documentation. It is for the most part only after the publication of *L'Esprit des lois* that encounters with him were deemed worthy of being placed on record, that his witticisms were written down, that his letters were treasured. Almost half the extant correspondence comes from the years 1748–55.

Even his physical appearance becomes reliably known only towards the end of his life. In the apartments of the Academy of Bordeaux there survives an oil painting which has been attributed with some plausibility to Jean Lapenne the elder, of Toulouse, who painted six pictures for the Academy in 1739.[1] Montesquieu is dressed in the red robe of a *président à mortier* (though he had not sat on the bench since 1726 and had sold his office); the *mortier* is in his hand, and he is wearing a full wig. His appearance, which is surprisingly old for a man who was barely fifty, is one of placid dignity. His face is elongated with a pointed chin. His jaw is firm. His eyes are blue. His nose, though he is not shown in profile, is prominent, and there is a swelling to the right of the left eye. It is a formal portrait with all the shortcomings which that implies. It tells one much more about the full-dress costume of a parliamentary magistrate than about the character of Montesquieu.

Guasco, some years later, after much pleading, succeeded in persuading Montesquieu to allow himself to be painted by an Italian artist who was passing through Bordeaux on his way back from Spain.[2] This portrait is lost. It was kept for a time by Guasco, but appears subsequently to have entered the collection of Niccolini. An engraving made from it by Carlo Faucci and

[1] R. Mesuret, 'Le Portraitiste de Montesquieu' (*RHBx*, 1954).

[2] Guasco, *Lettres familières*, pp. 258–9 (Nagel III, p. 1553). Guasco and Montesquieu were together at La Brède from September 1744 to August 1746, and from April 1748 to April 1749. The portrait was therefore probably painted in one of those periods, but it is barely possible that it was executed earlier (though not before 1738).

published in 1767 gives a very poor representation of the President. He is shown in simple day clothing, with white *jabot* and full wig; but his face is wholly expressionless and the general impression is of insignificance.[1]

Montesquieu was hostile to the notion of being painted, partly through modesty, partly (as his son relates) through economy.[2] He rejected repeated requests from Quentin de La Tour, the most celebrated portrait painter of the day. There was one invitation, however, to which he yielded towards the end of his life.

His friend the merchant Risteau, who had sprung to his defence in the quarrel of *L'Esprit des lois*, relates that during a visit to Paris he met the Swiss medallist Jacques-Antoine Dassier who was extremely anxious to meet Montesquieu.[3] Dassier, who had been employed by the London mint, and had executed medals of a number of prominent English noblemen, had come to Paris expressly to see Montesquieu. Risteau approached the President, who proposed the next day, at eight in the morning, for a rendezvous. Dassier and Risteau presented themselves at that hour at Montesquieu's house in the Rue Saint-Dominique and found the President breakfasting on a crust of bread, water, and wine. After general conversation, in the course of which Dassier displayed a medal which he had made of Chesterfield, the request was addressed to Montesquieu that he should sit for his portrait. After a moment's hesitation the President replied that what he had not done for La Tour and others he would do for Dassier, adding that he would be standing on pride if he refused, more than if he accepted. The result was a medal which gives the best representation of Montesquieu which is known. The President was so gratified by it that he indited a poem of ten lines to the artist.[4]

The medal shows a left profile of Montesquieu. He has a thin neck, firm chin, elongated but sensitive nose, and fearless eyes,

[1] It has been claimed that two drawings at La Brède, one in red chalk, the other in charcoal, are living portraits (Meaudre de Lapouyade, 'De l'iconographie et des origines chevaleresques de Montesquieu', in *Bulletin de la Société des bibliophiles de Guyenne*, 1948). I am not convinced that the second of these is a living portrait or that Montesquieu is the subject of the first.

[2] Secondat, *Mémoire*, p. 403.

[3] Risteau to Jean-Baptiste de Secondat, 1778 (Bernadau, *Le Viographe bordelais*, Bordeaux, 1843, pp. 259–62, and reprinted in Vian, pp. 390–1). Risteau dates this episode in 1752, which is impossible since Montesquieu was not in Paris in that year. 1753 is the most probable date.

[4] Nagel III, pp. 563–4; Pléiade II, p. 1473.

with thick and disarranged hair: it is a magnificent Roman head. It has been likened to Cicero[1] but much more resembles Caesar, especially Caesar as he appears in the Chiaramonti Gallery; but Montesquieu is more resilient, subtle, and lively.

He is especially more lively, and liveliness is one of his most frequently commented on characteristics. The Italian artist who painted him said that he had never had a subject whose face changed so much from one moment to another.[2] His son and D'Alembert alike speak of his extraordinary vivacity.[3]

He was short, thin, and fair.[4] His eyes, to the last, gave him trouble. And though he faced the threat of blindness with courage and adaptability, insisting, as Chesterfield reports, 'Je sais être aveugle',[5] this affliction was a great impediment in social life as well as in his researches.

Montesquieu had been absent-minded in his early days. In his old age this characteristic was intensified, partly by the deterioration of his sight, and was the subject of anecdotes both during and after his life. The story lingered in Bordeaux, and was noted there by Miranda in 1789 and by Stendhal in 1838, that Montesquieu, driving with his wife through the streets of Bordeaux, left her for a moment in order to pay a very short visit to a lady. He stayed in fact for three or four hours, forgetting that Madame de Montesquieu was waiting in the carriage; and the situation was made the more embarrassing by the fact that the lady visited was reputed to be his mistress.[6] On another occasion he set off from Fontainebleau, following his carriage on foot for exercise. Through inadvertence he walked as far as Villejuif, thirty-two miles away and in the outskirts of Paris, thinking he had walked only five miles to Chailly.[7] Of another example there is a first-hand account given by Lord Charlemont:

1 Bernadau, *Tableau de Bordeaux*, Bordeaux, 1810, p. 188.

2 Guasco, loc. cit.

3 Secondat, p. 405; D'Alembert, *Eloge* (Nagel I, A, p. xxviii).

4 *Fiche de police* (B.N., MSS. n.a.f. 10782, f. 169); Bernadau, loc. cit. Secondat told Miranda that his father's height was five feet two inches (*Archiva del general Miranda*, IV, p. 244).

5 Chesterfield to Richard Chenevix, Bishop of Waterford, 7 October 1762, and to Mme de Monconseil, 7 December 1762 (*Letters*, ed. Dobrée, VI, pp. 2441 and 2457).

6 *Archiva del general Miranda*, IV, p. 246; Stendhal, *Voyage dans le midi*, p. 76.

7 Voisenon, *Anecdotes littéraires* (*Œuvres complètes*, IV, p. 112).

I remember dining in company with him at our ambassador's, Lord Albemarle, where, during the time of dinner, being engaged in a warm dispute, he gave away to the servant who stood behind him seven clean plates, supposing that he had used them all.[1]

Charlemont adds the comment that this was only in the heat of controversy, when he was carried away by 'lively and impetuous earnestness' and that at other times, and especially in the society of women, he was perfectly collected.

He had the reputation with some, however, of being uneasy and awkward in society. Vauvenargues, not knowing him, expected his conversation to be inferior to his writings.[2] Without relying on the apocryphal memoirs of Madame de Créquy where it is asserted that, unable to remember names, he continually punctuated his conversation with the word *chose*, to the point that Madame Geoffrin called him *le Président chose*,[3] one can find reliable evidence that he did not always shine in society. A future Bishop of Salisbury, travelling in 1749, observes that Montesquieu

is remarkably short-sighted, which is a great disadvantage to him in company and makes him appear shy, because he is not able to distinguish those who speak to him.[4]

D'Argenson who knew him well says that there was more wit in his works than in his conversation, because he did not wish to shine and did not take trouble; and he reproaches him with having kept his Gascon accent.[5]

Others, however, assert that his conversation was brilliant. D'Alembert says that his conversation resembled the *Défense de l'Esprit des lois*—and there could be no higher praise than that; and he goes on to be more specific: it was light, agreeable, and instructive, staccato, 'pleine de sel et de saillies', free from bitterness and from satire.[6] Maupertuis found him even more remarkable in his conversation than in his works: 'simple, profond,

[1] F. Hardy, *Memoirs of Charlemont*, p. 36.

[2] Vauvenargues to Mirabeau, 24 December 1738 (*Œuvres posthumes et œuvres inédites de Vauvenargues*, ed. D.-L. Gilbert, Paris, 1857, p. 109).

[3] *Souvenirs de la marquise de Créquy*, Paris, 1834–5, III, p. 186.

[4] John Douglas, *Select Works*, Salisbury, 1820, p. 150.

[5] Marquis d'Argenson, *Les Loisirs d'un ministre*, Liége, 1787, II, pp. 62–63.

[6] D'Alembert, *Eloge* (Nagel I, A, pp. xxiv and xxviii).

sublime, il charmait, il instruisait, et n'offensait jamais'.[1] Madame Du Deffand found him original,[2] Chesterfield found his speech natural and free from conceits, and acknowledged his pre-eminent position in French society.[3]

It is Chesterfield's biographer, Maty, who explains best the contrasting praise and blame accorded to the President's conversational powers:

> It is said that Montesquieu, in mixed companies, did not appear equal to the idea conceived of him; but he is universally allowed to have been most amiable, sprightly, and universal, in select societies.[4]

Certainly Montesquieu preferred small to large gatherings, and it was when he was in the presence of a few intimate friends that he was most able to apply the principles which he himself had, in the *Essai sur les causes*, laid down for conversation: not always to be producing flashes of wit, because three-quarters of the time they are out of place, not always to be aiming at accuracy, because gay conversation consists of a succession of false arguments, which are pleasing on account of their falsity and their singularity.[5] It is sad that no record of such a conversation survives, but this conversational principle explains why Montesquieu sometimes was censured by the slow and dull. It is not surprising that his brilliant talk at the English court, comparing the English and French nations, provoked an ambassadorial rebuke.

II. DIVERSE OCCUPATIONS

After *L'Esprit des lois* Montesquieu's popularity in the salons did not decline.

> Qui n'aimerait pas cet homme, ce bon homme, ce grand homme, original dans ses ouvrages, dans son caractère, dans ses manières, et toujours digne d'admiration ou adorable?

[1] Maupertuis, *Eloge*, p. 55.

[2] Mme Du Deffand to Carl Fredrik Scheffer, 21 February 1754 (G. von Proschwitz, 'Lettres inédites de Mme Du Deffand, du président Hénault, et du comte de Bulkeley au baron Carl Fredrik Scheffer, 1751–6', in *Studies on Voltaire and the Eighteenth Century*, X, 1959).

[3] Chesterfield to his son, 24 December 1750 and 22 April 1751 (*Letters*, ed. Dobrée, IV, pp. 1631 and 1716).

[4] Maty, *Memoirs of [Chesterfield's] life*, in *Miscellaneous Works* of Chesterfield, London, 1777, I, p. 42. The word 'mixed' is to be taken in a general sense.

[5] Nagel III, p. 418; Pléiade II, p. 57.

wrote the Chevalier d'Aydie to Madame Du Deffand.[1] And of that same lady Montesquieu said:

J'aime cette femme de tout mon cœur; elle me plaît, elle me divertit; il n'est pas possible de s'ennuyer un moment avec elle.[2]

In her house appeared Pulteney, now Earl of Bath, bearing a gift of tea and meeting Montesquieu at her table.[3] In the salons or elsewhere many young Englishmen on the grand tour sought Montesquieu's company. Bath's son, Lord Pulteney, was among them, accompanied by his tutor John Douglas, subsequently Bishop of Salisbury.[4] Lord Hyde came talking of Bolingbroke, of religion, of the Pope, before he ended an intense career of dissipation by falling from his horse and dying in 1753.[5] The eccentric Scot, Robert Clerk, later to be a general and described by Hume as a meteor, came to talk about education and reported that Montesquieu preferred private education to a school.[6] The tenth Earl of Pembroke, whose grandfather is mentioned by Montesquieu, visited him and afterwards bought wine of Rochemorin.[7] James Caulfield, Viscount and subsequently Earl of Charlemont, came accompanied by Edward Eliot, later to be a friend of Gibbon, and saw Montesquieu both in Paris and at La Brède. His account is now one of the major sources of information about Montesquieu's life.[8]

Another young English visitor, dear to Montesquieu's heart, was Charles Yorke, a young man of great promise—in the event unfulfilled—who moved with equal assurance among the great and the learned. His father, Lord Hardwicke, was Lord Chancellor and had been attorney-general when Montesquieu was in England. He himself was already a correspondent of Warburton, and was later to become F.R.S., trustee of the British Museum, correspondent of King Stanislas, and finally, immediately before

[1] D'Aydie to Mme Du Deffand, 28 January 1754 (*Correspondance de Mme Du Deffand*, I, p. 192).

[2] Ibid.

[3] Bath to Mme Du Deffand, 25 April 1751 (ibid., I, pp. 126–8) and cf. Montesquieu to Trudaine, 26 September 1749 (*FS*, 1948).

[4] See above, p. 381.

[5] Hénault to Carl Fredrik Scheffer, 1 May 1753 (*Studies on Voltaire*, X, 1959).

[6] George Dempster to Sir Adam Fergusson, 14 August 1799 (*Letters of George Dempster to Sir Adam Fergusson*, ed. J. Fergusson, London, 1934, p. 278).

[7] Montesquieu to Guasco, 3 November 1854.

[8] Hardy, *Memoirs of Charlemont.*

his death, Lord Chancellor. He came to Paris in 1749 and reported thus to his mother:

M. le président Montesquieu was so good as to admit me into his acquaintance in half an hour. Today I had the pleasure of a long conversation with him. He has a great deal of good nature and vivacity as well as understanding; admires the constitution of England and the genius of the people; and I should not forget to add, that he is penetrated with the honour my Lord Chancellor has done him in reading and approving his book. If he ever returns into England, it will be his ambition to acknowledge it. I have been told, said he to me, that during a Chancellorship of thirteen years, not one of his judgements have [*sic*] been reversed, nor above two or three appealed from. 'Tis true, answered I. Ah! replied he, *C'est un éloge au-dessus de toute la flatterie.*[1]

The President and Yorke met again in 1750,[2] and failed to meet during three subsequent visits of the young man. But they exchanged ideas by letter as well as by talk. Yorke supplied Montesquieu with books, including Warburton's *Divine Legation of Moses* and his own *Discourse on the Law of Forfeiture for High Treason*, and discussed with him, in relation to the English constitution, the problem of seignorial rights.[3]

It is not surprising that Montesquieu in his last years was proposing to travel abroad again.[4]

Social life reduced the amount of time which he was able to give to the affairs of the Academy. In 1749 and 1750 he attended for elections and receptions, in 1751 and 1752 not at all, being most of the time away from Paris. On 2 April 1753 he was elected *directeur* and began to attend more frequently. During his period of office occurred a vacancy to which the worthy poet Piron was about to be elected. The king, learning through episcopal delation of a licentious poem, *A Priape*, of which Piron had been guilty years before, sent for Montesquieu and vetoed the election. The vacancy was now filled by a reluctant Buffon, and Montesquieu appealed through Madame de Pompadour for an act of royal

[1] Charles Yorke to Lady Hardwicke, 13 October 1749 (B.M., Add. Mss. 35353, ff. 88–89; partially quoted in P. C. Yorke, *The Life and Correspondence of Philip Yorke, Earl of Hardwicke*, II, p. 481).

[2] Charles Yorke to Lord Hardwicke, 21 October 1750 (B.M., ibid., f. 109).

[3] See above, pp. 287–8.

[4] Montesquieu to Charles Yorke, 6 June 1753; cf. his will, dated 26 November 1750 (Nagel III, pp. 1573–4).

generosity towards the unfortunate poet. His plea was successful; a pension of 1,000 *livres* was accorded to Piron, whom Montesquieu thereafter addressed as 'mon cher confrère' and who was able to compose his celebrated epitaph:

> Ci-gît Piron, qui ne fut rien,
> Pas même académicien.[1]

Montesquieu was in fact well thought of at court, and when by Voltaire's migration to Berlin the office of historiographer-royal fell vacant, it was thought by some, and notably by the Papal Nuncio, that Montesquieu would be appointed.[2] The notion was in fact erroneous, and Duclos received the honour. In the following year Montesquieu received a mark of royal favour, but from Stanislas Leszczynski, exiled king of Poland. Hearing that Stanislas had established an academy at Nancy, Montesquieu solicited a place, which was very readily accorded to him.[3] He did not visit the Polish court again, but he wrote for it the last work which he published during his lifetime. This was *Lysimaque*, a short prose narrative of which the idea had occurred to him twenty years before.[4] Reminiscent of his *Dialogue de Sylla et d'Eucrate* for the style, and of the story of the Troglodytes for the theme, it has an allegorical substructure applicable to the exiled Polish monarch, for it described the eventual triumph over a capricious despot of an enlightened ruler who was the friend of a philosopher. There are fine phrases in *Lysimaque*, as when the philosopher Callisthène says that if the gods have made men only for pleasures of the senses, 'ils ont plus exécuté qu'entrepris'; but it is no more than an elegant essay by a courtier.

The other literary activities of Montesquieu in his last years were to prepare new editions of *L'Esprit des lois* and of the *Lettres persanes*, to take up again old materials to write his *Essai sur le goût* and the *Mémoire sur la Constitution*, and to begin to

[1] The sources of information for this episode are *Registres de l'Académie française*; Secondat, *Mémoire*, pp. 402–3; Grimm, *Correspondance littéraire*, II, pp. 261–2; R. de Juvigny, 'Vie de Piron' (*Œuvres complètes d'Alexis Piron*, Neuchâtel, I, pp. 126–30); Montesquieu to Mme de Pompadour, [14] June 1753.

[2] Nuncio to Secretary of State, 7 September 1750 (Archivio segreto Vaticano, Nunziatura di Francia, supplt. XII).

[3] Montesquieu to Stanislas, 20 March 1751; Stanislas to Montesquieu, March 1751 (Nagel III, p. 1371).

[4] *Pensée* 563 (Bkn. 439).

prepare a work on Theodoric;[1] it has been claimed that manuscript fragments were at La Brède after his death;[2] but they have disappeared and no trace remains to show that this intention, which was praised by Gibbon,[3] bore fruit.

III. MONTESQUIEU AND THE *PHILOSOPHES*

Is Montesquieu to be considered one of the *philosophes*?

The term *philosophe* had a chequered history in the eighteenth century. It is least ambiguous in the 1760's, and the question acquires greatest precision if it is put in this form: do Montesquieu's works and ideas resemble those of the group of thinkers of the 1760's who surrounded and included Diderot, Helvétius, D'Alembert, and Duclos? to what extent did he socially belong to this group, so far as it existed during his lifetime? how far did he share the sense of common purpose which came to mark them?

In ideas Montesquieu is very close to the deist wing of the *philosophes*. His belief in religious toleration and his love of liberty resemble theirs, and theirs were in fact in large measure shaped by his. The strength of his influence is most clearly attested by Italy's characteristic *philosophe*: 'Je date de cinq ans l'époque de ma conversion à la philosophie, et je la dois à la lecture des *Lettres persanes*.'[4] The factor which differentiates him most from many of the figures of the Enlightenment is the extent of his learning; and in his later years he is certainly, after Gibbon and Fréret, the most erudite of them.[5] But erudition in Montesquieu's life was almost an afterthought. The *Considérations* were no great monument of learning, and the doors of the Académie des Inscriptions were never opened to him. He never belonged to the party of anti-philosophical scholars. His ideas and his work make him one of the *philosophes*: both they and their enemies thought so.

Nor do his personal relationships argue differently. It is true

[1] *Lois*, XXX, 12.

[2] *Nouveau dictionnaire historique*, Caen and Lyons, 1789, VI, p. 310.

[3] *Decline and Fall*, ed. Bury, IV, p. 180.

[4] Beccaria to Morellet, 26 January 1766 (*Illuministi italiani*, ed. F. Venturi, III, Milan and Naples, 1958, p. 205.)

[5] On the general question of the relationship between erudition and *la philosophie*, see J. Seznec, *Essais sur Diderot et l'antiquité*, Oxford, 1957.

that the vigorous enemy of the *philosophes*, Lefranc de Pompignan, a close friend of Filippo Venuti[1] and of Barbot, though Barbot admitted it reluctantly,[2] maintained amiable relations with the President and translated into French some verses addressed to his daughter Denise by Guasco.[3] It is true that for Voltaire, though meeting him socially, Montesquieu did not conceal his distaste.

But that is not all and it is not decisive.

The Academy, in the last years of Montesquieu's life, contained nine members who could with justice be described as being in some sense *philosophes*: Fontenelle, Mairan, Du Resnel (the translator of Pope's *Essay on Man*), Mirabaud, Maupertuis, Voltaire, Buffon, D'Alembert, and Duclos. Of these he had known from his youth Fontenelle and Mairan. Maupertuis was a friend and ally, Du Resnel little better than a client.[4] He was greatly esteemed by Buffon who, though he expressed some scarcely veiled criticism of *L'Esprit des lois* in his *Discours sur le style*, was none the less wont to declare that there were but five great men, Newton, Bacon, Leibniz, Montesquieu, and himself.[5] Though it is true that Voltaire and Montesquieu were mutually hostile, each had some respect for the other. Voltaire praised the *Considérations* in his *discours de réception* and defended *L'Esprit des lois* in his *Remerciement sincère à un homme charitable*. Montesquieu did not deny Voltaire's talent.[6] D'Alembert and Duclos were later to be the most energetic leaders of the philosophical cause in the Academy.[7] For D'Alembert the President had a great regard. He writes to him in the gay language of familiarity, warmly praises the *Discours préliminaire* to the *Encyclopédie*,[8] and seeks to promote his candidature for the Academy.[9] The younger man's reverence for Montesquieu is magnificently

[1] Cortona, MS. 497, *passim*.

[2] 'Vous êtes donc l'ami de M. Lefranc?—Hélas, oui, me dit-il' (Marmontel, *Mémoires*, Paris, 1891, II, p. 167).

[3] *Mercure de France*, February 1745 (cited by Grellet-Dumazeau, op. cit., p. 120).

[4] Mme Dupré de Saint-Maur to Montesquieu, 23 November 1748.

[5] Hérault de Seychelles, *Voyage à Montbar*, p. 54.

[6] See above, p. 212.

[7] See especially L. Brunel, *Les Philosophes et l'Académie française au XVIIIe siècle*, Paris, 1884.

[8] Montesquieu to D'Alembert, 16 November 1753.

[9] Montesquieu to Mme Du Deffand, 13 September 1754.

attested in his *Eloge*. Through their friendship Montesquieu became, in the literal sense, an encyclopedist, for at D'Alembert's request he produced for the *Encyclopédie* an article on *goût*, published posthumously in 1757. Duclos was an older friend, perhaps a very old one, and at least from the days of the Brancas salon their association was a close one.

Outside the ranks of the Academy was Helvétius, the most outspoken, in his day, and the most audacious of the *philosophes*: he was a close friend of Montesquieu and his literary confidant. Nor was Raynal unknown to the President: they met, among other places, at the modest dinners given by the aged and benevolent poet Titon du Tillet in his small house in the Faubourg Saint-Antoine.[1] Raynal wrote years later to an eminent Scottish friend:

> Ayant eu le bonheur d'être connu particulièrement [de Montesquieu,] il m'a inspiré ces nobles sentiments, que la plus grande vertu et la meilleure religion consistait à se rendre utile à ses semblables: mais dans quel siècle la nature produira un si grand homme?[2]

The most amiable and most loyal of the encyclopedists, Louis de Jaucourt, was the President's very close friend, being linked to him through the Vivens family of Clairac. Diderot was to honour Montesquieu at his interment.

Of the scientific writers of the Enlightenment, in addition to Mairan and Buffon, there were of his acquaintance Réaumur, the Swiss biologist Abraham Trembley and (by correspondence only) Charles Bonnet, as well as La Condamine, a gay scientist with limitless curiosity. Nor were the Swiss the only foreigners whose intellectual activities appealed to Montesquieu in his last years. He maintains a correspondence with Warburton who, though his situation in England was far different, was regarded in France as a friend of the *philosophes*; he exchanged several letters with Hume and found him a congenial spirit. He even reports a conversation with a philosophically minded Spanish colonel, hostile to the Jesuits and well disposed to Feijóo, the pioneer of the Spanish Enlightenment.[3] Montesquieu does not name him: very possibly this was Aranda, who was in France in

[1] Titon du Tillet to Filippo Venuti, 7 August 1752 (Cortona, MS., 497, ff. 149–50).

[2] Raynal to William Hunter, 16 April 1772 (Hunter–Baillie Collection, Royal College of Surgeons of England).

[3] *Spicilège* 779 (MS., pp. 786–9).

1753 and is said to have lived in the society of Diderot, D'Alembert, and Montesquieu. He was to become, in Spain, one of the most prominent political figures of the age.[1]

To have had these friends and acquaintances is testimony enough. The society in which Montesquieu lived in Paris in his last years, the salons he frequented, the houses in which he was invariably welcome, were the society, the salons, and the houses in which philosophical ideas circulated. D'Holbach had not yet reached his ascendancy, Galiani's conversational gifts had not yet been deployed, Hume, Walpole, Beccaria, and the Verri brothers had not yet annexed themselves to the *conversazioni* of Paris; but the society of the *philosophes* existed already and Montesquieu was one of its most valued members.

To what extent was there consciousness of a common purpose or the realization of forming a movement?

It was the enemies of the *philosophes* who threw them together into something like a movement. If they had possessed the freedom of expression which they sought, they might not have had any corporate existence. Each of his major works had shown Montesquieu that he had enemies. The *Lettres persanes* had involved him in serious difficulties, but the work had never actually been banned. The *Considérations* had caused trouble, but the precaution of submitting the manuscript to Castel's censorship had averted the gravest consequences. With *L'Esprit des lois* the situation was different. The wave of persecution of advanced works, which started with Voltaire's *Lettres philosophiques*, had gained momentum. Duclos had been a victim in 1745 with his *Histoire de Louis XI*, and Diderot in the next year with the *Pensées philosophiques*. Early in 1748 *Les Mœurs* of Toussaint was consigned to the flames. In 1749 Diderot was imprisoned at Vincennes on account of his *Lettre sur les aveugles à l'usage de ceux qui voient*. The crisis provoked by the thesis of the Abbé de Prades at the end of 1751 resulted in the suppression of the *Encyclopédie* for the first time in the following year. It was in these circumstances that *L'Esprit des lois* appeared and was discussed. The philosophical party was being created in battle. And the writers who went to prison and whose books were burnt

[1] A. Morel-Fatio, *Etudes sur l'Espagne*, 2e série, Paris, 1890, p. 143; Horace Walpole, *Memoirs of the Reign of King George III*, ed. Sir D. LeMarchant and G. F. Russell-Barker, London and New York, 1894, III, p. 7 n.l.

were expressing ideas almost all of which were to be found, in veiled or embryonic form, in the *Lettres persanes* a generation earlier. The alignment of forces caused by the quarrel of *L'Esprit des lois* makes Montesquieu a *philosophe* before the *philosophes* had formed a party.

Another relevant factor is Montesquieu's friendly solicitude toward young and unestablished thinkers. In his relations with them he appears in a most favourable light. For he carried his fame exceedingly well. Kindly throughout his life, in his youth and middle age he did not escape the torments of ambition. He suffered from being misunderstood and inadequately valued. But when his fame was established, his character was consolidated and his natural benevolence had greater scope. To the literary novice, especially if poor and a provincial, he showed himself thoughtful, generous, and patient. Fourteen years after his death it was still said in Paris how anxious he had been to learn from anyone.[1]

The young Suard, working for Raynal on the *Mercure*, wrote something which pleased Montesquieu, who asked Raynal to arrange a meeting. They met, and Suard, at ease before Montesquieu, conceived a reverent affection which remained with him to the end of his days.[2]

A young Protestant, Angliviel de La Beaumelle, who had gone to Denmark as a private tutor, founded a periodical to which he gave the name *La Spectatrice danoise*. It lasted but one year, starting in March 1749, but in that year appeared five *Lettres sur l'Esprit des lois* which were exceedingly eulogistic. It was not to be wondered at if, when the young man returned to Paris and established himself at the Café Procope, Montesquieu took notice of him. The President did not content himself with the simple civility of inviting La Beaumelle to dinner, he caused him to meet his friends, notably La Condamine, and maintained amiable contact with him. La Beaumelle was responsive to this kindness, for, shocked and perturbed by the attacks on *L'Esprit des lois*, he himself wrote and published the admirable *Suite de la Défense de l'Esprit des lois*. An exceedingly bitter literary quarrel with

[1] Alessandro to Pietro Verri, 16 September 1769 (*Carteggio di Pietro e Alessandro Verri*, ed. G. Seregni, III, Milan, 1911, p. 67).

[2] Mme Suard, *Essais de mémoires sur M. Suard*, ed. M. de Lescure, Paris, 1881, p. 133; Garat, *Mémoires historiques sur la vie de M. Suard, et sur le XVIIIe siècle*, Paris, 1820, I, pp. 102–3.

Voltaire led to his being incarcerated in the Bastille on 24 April 1753. He remained there almost six months, and his release was largely due to an intervention on the part of Montesquieu, who subsequently offered him money if he stood in need.[1]

The encouragement given by Montesquieu to Raulin, the simple country doctor of Nérac, has already been mentioned.[2] Another doctor of the south-west who received the thoughtful protection of Montesquieu from his earliest years was Augustin Roux. A Bordelais, he has been described on his way to school, dragging himself through the streets of Bordeaux in the snow and ice of winter, looked down on by his school-fellows, neglected by his masters. Barbot and Montesquieu smiled on him, however; Montesquieu found for him a situation as a private tutor in Paris, saying, when objection was raised to his lack of experience, 'Monsieur Roux n'est pas un homme qui doive faire deux fois ce métier'.[3] In later life he travelled to England, translated into French some articles in the *Philosophical Transactions*, edited the *Journal de médecine* for fourteen years, contributed to the *Encyclopédie*, and collaborated with D'Holbach.

Roux, in his early years, presented to Montesquieu one of his contemporaries, Jean Darcet, born at Douazit in the Landes. The President took Darcet into his care, and appointed him secretary, allowing him sufficient leisure to pursue his own studies. Darcet became a chemist of note and a member of the Académie des Sciences.[4]

Another young Gascon who obtained Montesquieu's patronage was Alexandre Deleyre, a *quondam* Jesuit who embraced the principles of the *philosophes*. While the *Encyclopédie* was appearing, he published an *Analyse de la philosophie de Bacon*, Bacon being the greatest single inspiration of its basic conception. He contributed to the *Encyclopédie*. He translated Goldoni in order to exculpate Diderot from a charge of plagiarism. He was and claimed to be an all-embracing *philosophe*, free from exclusive partisan attachments. He was a friend of Diderot and Rousseau alike, and published a synopsis of Montesquieu's thought with the title *Génie de Montesquieu*.

[1] See especially A. Taphanel, *La Beaumelle et Saint-Cyr*, Paris, 1898.

[2] See above, p. 223.

[3] A. Deleyre, *Eloge de M. Roux*, Amsterdam, 1777.

[4] M.-J.-J. Dizé, *Précis historique sur la vie et les travaux de Jean d'Arcet*, Paris, an X.

It is the thought of such men as Darcet, Roux, and Deleyre, young and poor together but brought by Montesquieu, partly through his innate kindness but partly through his sense of handing on a torch, to positions of influence and responsibility, that gives the ring of authenticity to some sentences of Montesquieu towards the end of his life, which are reported by Suard:

Allons, Messieurs, disait-il un jour à l'abbé Raynal, à Helvétius, au docteur Roux et à M. Suard, vous êtes dans l'âge des grands efforts et des grands succès: je vous invite à être utiles aux hommes comme au plus grand bonheur de la vie d'un homme; je n'ai jamais eu de chagrin dont une demi-heure de méditation n'ait adouci l'amertume. Je suis fini, moi; j'ai brûlé toutes mes cartouches; toutes mes bougies sont éteintes. Vous commencez, vous; marquez-vous bien le but: je ne l'ai pas touché; je crois l'avoir vu. L'homme n'a pas voulu ou n'a pas pu rester dans son instinct, où il était assez en sûreté, quoique très près des animaux. En cherchant à s'élever à la raison, il a enfanté et consacré des erreurs monstrueuses; ses vertus et ses félicités ne peuvent pas être plus vraies que ses idées. Les nations s'environnent de luxe des richesses et de luxe d'esprit; et les hommes manquent très souvent de pain et de sens commun. Pour leur assurer à tous le pain, le bon sens, et les vertus qui leur sont nécessaires, il n'y a qu'un moyen: il faut beaucoup éclairer les peuples et les gouvernements: c'est là l'œuvre des philosophes; c'est la vôtre.[1]

III. DEATH

'I have but two things to do,' wrote Montesquieu in old age, 'to learn to be ill, and to learn to die.'[2]

From July to December in 1754 he had been at La Brède. In August his brother Joseph had died, and was succeeded as Dean of Saint-Seurin by the son of Tourny.[3] Before the end of the year the President travelled to Paris, with the intention of winding up his affairs. He terminated the lease of his house and gave notice to Mademoiselle Betty the housekeeper. He had decided to spend the rest of his days at La Brède.[4] He was not destined, however, to see his vineyards again.

In the first months of 1755 Paris suffered from an epidemic of

[1] Garat, op. cit., pp. 103–4.
[2] *Pensée* 2242 (Bkn. 67).
[3] Arch. dép. Gironde, catalogue, série G2, p. 33.
[4] Montesquieu to Latapie (Nagel III, p. 1531).

fever which in some cases became malignant.[1] Montesquieu contracted this fever on 29 January. For two days he ignored it and as a result his condition became critical. The doctors bled him excessively. He became delirious, and the signs of approaching death were unmistakable. He saw its approach, however, without fear; and in one of his moments of lucidity declared, 'Ce moment n'est pas si affreux que l'on pense.'[2]

Two doctors, Bouvard and Lorry, were in attendance in his house. Two secretaries, Darcet and Saint-Marc, were present. The house was thronged with visitors. The Duchesse d'Aiguillon scarcely left the bedroom. Madame Dupré de Saint-Maur was not less assiduous. The Chevalier de Jaucourt and Ulrik Scheffer, the Swedish ambassador, were there continuously. The nearest relative present was Marans, himself barely recovered from an illness in the course of which Montesquieu had looked after him. He was accompanied by his son, the Comte d'Estillac. The Fitz-James family was represented and the faithful Bulkeley was in attendance. The Duc de Nivernais was sent to inquire by the king, and the sick man, learning this, succeeded in writing a note of thanks to the Marquise de Pompadour, to whom he recommended his son. In another moment of lucidity he learned that his parish priest, the curé of Saint-Sulpice, had been excluded, and he ordered that when he next came he should be admitted without delay. He asked Bulkeley to say frankly what his condition was. He was told that he was gravely ill, but that the doctors had not despaired of him. 'Cela suffit,' he responded, 'j'entends ce langage. Je voudrais bien avoir un confesseur.' When the parish priest entered, Montesquieu said to him that he intended to do all that an *honnête homme* should do in the situation in which he found himself. The choice of a confessor was discussed. Neuville, a fashionable Jesuit, was proposed, but Montesquieu preferred his old friend Castel, who had been the educator of his son and the critic of his published works. Castel thereupon was sent for.[3]

[1] Hénault to Scheffer, 1 March 1755 (*Studies on Voltaire*, X, 1959).

[2] Devienne, *Histoire de la ville de Bordeaux*, Bordeaux, 1771, p. 505, citing a first-hand but unnamed witness.

[3] The narrative so far is conflated from various accounts which differ only in minor detail: Mme d'Aiguillon to Maupertuis, February 1755 (Nagel III, p. 1550, first published in Maupertuis, *Eloge de M. de Montesquieu*, Berlin, 1755, pp. 57–58); Marans to Gardès, 15 February 1755 (Nagel III, pp. 1549–50,

The events which followed attracted the attention of all Europe. Montesquieu was on his death-bed, and the Jesuit sought to effect an unforgettable conversion. In the house in the Rue Saint-Dominique a famous battle in the war between the Church and the *philosophes* was being fought.

The Pope himself was impatient to know the issue. A month after Montesquieu's death, Valenti, Secretary of State, wrote at the express wish of Benedict XIV to the Paris Nuncio, asking for a full account of the President's death.[1] The reply which he obtained contains one of the fullest accounts of the last days of Montesquieu.[2]

The message to Castel was borne by a secretary of the President. The Jesuit preferred that another of his order should confess Montesquieu, and selected Bernard Routh, an Irishman who was already known to the dying man. The two Jesuits arrived at the Rue Saint-Dominique. It was 5 February. 'Père Castel,' said Montesquieu, 'I am departing first.' Castel withdrew and Routh received the confession of the sick man.

It might have been expected that the canonical seal of secrecy would for all time cover the terms of Montesquieu's confession. This was not to be. Routh required of the sick man that he

from a MS. at Bordeaux); Saint-Marc, secretary of Montesquieu, to Suard, February 1755 (Nagel III, pp. 1547–8; this letter was first published, from the MS., in E. Mennechet, *Matinées littéraires*, Paris, 1846, IV, pp. 156–8, which is the sole source; Laboulaye's arbitrary attribution to Mme Dupré de Saint-Maur, though followed by later editors, is not justified); and Duc de Luynes, *Mémoires*, Paris, 1860–5, XIV, pp. 36–37. The first three were present in Montesquieu's house, while Luynes's testimony is detailed enough to suggest that it was based on a first-hand informant, most probably Nivernais. Two unsigned letters to Navarre, of 12 February 1755 (Nagel III, pp. 1548) and 3 March 1755 (P. Courteault, *Un ami bordelais de Montesquieu*, Bordeaux, 1938, p. 12), give information about the progress of his illness and about the letter to Mme de Pompadour.

[1] Valenti to Gualtieri, 12 March 1755 (Archivio segreto Vaticano, Nunziatura di Francia, 447, ff. 16–17).

[2] The answer to the Papal inquiry, written by Bernard Routh, S.J., is absent from its expected place in the Vatican Archives, having been doubtless passed on to the Pope; but the covering letter from the Nuncio is in place (Nunziatura di Francia, 492, f. 240). The Bibliothèque Calvet at Avignon has three copies of a printed text of the document, and it was reprinted in Chaudon, *Dictionnaire anti-philosophique*, Avignon, 1767. It has been recently reprinted in O. R. Taylor, 'Bernard Routh et la mort de Montesquieu' (*FS*, 1949). This article gives the fullest discussion so far available of Montesquieu's death, though its conclusions are not in my view wholly decisive.

should permit his final sentiments to be published, and he communicated them to the Nuncio. The confessor interrogated Montesquieu about his attitude to the great mysteries proposed to the faithful by the Catholic Church and about his submission to the Church's decisions. Routh reports that he received, with an edifying and touching simplicity and candour, complete satisfaction. He asked if Montesquieu had ever been in a state of unbelief. The sick man replied that he had not, that clouds and doubts had passed through his imagination, as might happen to any man, but that he had never had any fixed or defined intellectual objection to the articles of faith. Routh now inquired by what principle Montesquieu had expressed in his words ideas which cast doubt on the faith. He replied that it was from his liking for the new and the singular and his desire to rise above prejudice and accepted maxims, to win the approval of those who shape public opinion and who approve most readily freedom and independence from constraint. The Jesuit observed that the strain of speaking had greatly exhausted the sick man, and thought that the last sacrament should not be delayed. He required of him public conformity in the event of recovery, public reparation in whatever terms the confessor should think fit, and permission to make publicly known his last sentiments just now expressed. These conditions Montesquieu accepted with the best grace imaginable, whereupon Routh sent for the parish priest.

Of the conversation between Routh and the dying man, Routh is naturally the sole narrator. There are other witnesses of what now passed between Montesquieu and the curé of Saint-Sulpice.

The parish priest returned at three o'clock. He approached the bed and, according to both Routh and the secretary Darcet,[1] sought assurance about the sentiments of the dying man. Montesquieu referred him to Routh: 'Monsieur, j'ai pris avec le Révérend Père des arrangements dont je me flatte que vous serez content.'

Routh assured the curé that Montesquieu had given satisfaction.

The curé now turned to Montesquieu: 'Monsieur, vous comprenez mieux qu'un autre combien Dieu est grand . . .'

'Oui, Monsieur,' came the reply, 'et combien les hommes sont petits.'[2]

[1] Darcet, *Note*, in *Œuvres de Montesquieu*, Paris (Plassan), 1796, IV, p. 483.
[2] Ibid.

The host was now brought to the President, and the priest asked him if he believed that it was God.

'Oui, oui,' he responded, 'je le crois, je le crois.'[1]

The priest asked him to perform an act of adoration; and Montesquieu raised to heaven his eyes and his right hand, which was grasping his nightcap. He received extreme unction and the viaticum.

Montesquieu was to survive for five days more. He lay in almost continuous delirium,[2] but had some moments of lucidity. During some of these he interrogated the doctors about his condition, in others he expressed gratification at the interest shown in him by the public. In one moment of consciousness he uttered words which show both the extent and the limits of his religious belief:

> J'ai toujours respecté la religion; la morale de l'Evangile est une excellente chose, et le plus beau présent que Dieu pût faire aux hommes.[3]

Routh meanwhile did not leave the house. He remained there to inform visitors of the condition of Montesquieu, and spoke in particular to Cardinal de La Rochefoucauld and the Archbishop of Paris. He stayed also, as he himself declares, to take advantage of any return of lucidity in order to engage Montesquieu further in the path of devotion.

One step which he endeavoured to take in that direction related to a manuscript containing corrections which the President proposed to make to the *Lettres persanes*. The Duchesse d'Aiguillon relates that, pressed by the Jesuits to surrender this manuscript to them, Montesquieu gave it instead to her and to Madame Dupré de Saint-Maur, saying:

> Je veux tout sacrifier à la raison et à la religion, mais rien à la Société; consultez avec mes amis et décidez si ceci doit paraître.[4]

Accordingly to Collé, who was not an eye-witness, as he handed the manuscript to Madame Dupré, he said:

> Les bons Pères voulaient me l'attraper, pour le défigurer le plus saintement qu'ils auraient pu; mais je n'ai point cédé.[5]

Guasco, no more an eye-witness than Collé but better connected,

[1] Saint-Marc, loc. cit. [2] Marans, loc. cit.
[3] Mme d'Aiguillon to Maupertuis, as cited. [4] Ibid.
[5] Charles Collé, *Journal historique*, ed. H. Bonhomme, Paris, 1868, II, p. 4.

adds further information, probably derived from the Duchesse d'Aiguillon.[1] One day during the illness, when the duchess had gone out to dine, Routh entered the sickroom, ordered out the secretary who was there, and remained with Montesquieu. When Madame d'Aiguillon returned, she heard Montesquieu's voice raised within the room. She knocked and to the Jesuit who opened the door exclaimed, 'Why do you torment this dying man?' Montesquieu complained that Routh was bullying him into surrendering the key to the cupboard where his papers were kept. The Jesuit defended himself against the duchess's reproaches by saying that he was required to obey his superiors.

Where the detailed truth lies is not certain. There was clearly conflict between the Duchesse d'Aiguillon and Routh.[2] Routh was clearly anxious to procure and make manifest a literary repentance on the part of Montesquieu. That his zeal carried him too far is probable, and it is only normal that he should not have recorded his own excesses. In 1767 the Duchesse d'Aiguillon herself said that she found his narrative credible.[3] Nor is there, on the other hand, any reason to disbelieve her own account. Jean-Baptiste de Secondat, who came to Paris immediately after his father's death received the manuscript from her, accepted her story and, though himself a devout Catholic, described as extraordinary the efforts of the Jesuits to lay hands on them.[4]

More important to the reader and to the biographer, however, is the attitude of Montesquieu. As the rival parties contended

[1] Guasco, *Lettres familières*, LX (Nagel III, pp. 1551–2).

[2] A former wine-merchant of Bordeaux, writing almost a century later, knew an Irishwoman who, in her youth, had been a servant in Montesquieu's Paris house and claimed to have assisted Routh against Mme d'Aiguillon, who was resisting him at the instigation of D'Alembert (James Roche, *Critical and miscellaneous Essays by an Octogenarian*, Cork, 1850, I, p. 28.

[3] Marquis de Cambis-Velleron to Mme d'Aiguillon, 6 April 1768 (referring to a letter from her in the previous year): 'Le ci-devant Père Routh, dites-vous, a eu apparemment de bonnes raisons pour écrire cette lettre' (Avignon, Bibliothèque Calvet, MS. 3487, f. 37v). Routh was in fact separately known to Mme d'Aiguillon, and is shown by the Stuart Papers at Windsor to have corresponded with her.

[4] This was reported on 12 April 1789 by Miranda, who met Montesquieu's son on that day: '[Secondat] me aseguró que la anecdota del Jesuita Rooth y la duquesa de Eguillon era sierta . . ., que él llegó immediatamiente depues de su muerte à Paris, y que dhs manuscritos le fueron entregados; siendo increible las promesas y empeñas que los Jesuitas le avian hecho por obtenerlos' (*Archiva del general Miranda*, IV, p. 245, the anecdote itself being reported on p. 241).

around him, he sought to give some satisfaction to each, and to die without offending religion and without betraying his convictions as they had been disclosed in his works.

He expired on Monday, 10 February 1755, St. Scholastica's day, in the presence of his kinsman Marans, Marans's son Estillac, his own grandson D'Armajan, Rolland, curate of Saint-Sulpice, and three other witnesses.[1] The Duchesse d'Aiguillon and Madame Dupré de Saint-Maur were there almost to the end, and the Chevalier de Jaucourt, with characteristic fidelity, left him only at the last moment.[2]

The Pope received Routh's account of his last days, read it with the deepest reverence, and ordered it to be circulated to all nuncios and to the governors of the principal cities in the Papal States.[3] The Academy of Bordeaux broke its custom of silence on the death of a member and, though insisting that a precedent was not being created, sent a letter of condolence to Secondat.[4] In Bordeaux, the members of the Parlement paid a state visit of condolence to Madame de Montesquieu after a memorial service in the cathedral of Saint-André; and as they entered her darkened room, failing to observe a step, they all fell prostrate in their robes.[5]

Meanwhile, at five o'clock in the afternoon on the day after his death, Montesquieu was interred in the chapel of Saint-Geneviève in the church of Saint-Sulpice.[6] Of all the *philosophes*, Diderot alone was present.[7]

The tomb was profaned during the Revolution and Montesquieu's remains are lost.

Diderot, resenting the attacks he sustained, imagined for him the Virgilian epitaph:

> alto
> quaesivit caelo lucem ingemuitque reperta.[8]

[1] Certified copy of the certificate of burial, at La Brède; cf. A. Jal, *Dictionnaire critique de biographie et d'histoire*, Paris, 1872, p. 888.

[2] Mme d'Aiguillon to Guasco, as cited.

[3] Archivio segreto Vaticano, loc. cit., and Cambis-Velleron to Mme d'Aiguillon, as cited. Cambis-Nelleron's interpretation of this measure as the first step in a process of canonization is not to be taken seriously.

[4] Bx MS, 1699, I, p. 151.

[5] MS. account at La Brède.

[6] Bernadau, *Tableau de Bordeaux*, Bordeaux, 1810, p. 188.

[7] J.-J. Rousseau to Perdriau, 20 February 1755 (*Correspondance générale*, ed. T. Dufour and P.-P. Plan, Paris, 1924–34, II, pp. 159–60).

[8] *Encyclopédie*, V (1755), p. 284 (s.v. *Eclectiques*).

But Lord Chesterfield looked further ahead when he published in the *London Evening Post* a notice of his death which ended with the words:

> His work will illustrate his name, and survive him as long as right reason, moral obligation, and the true spirit of laws, shall be understood, respected, and maintained.[1]

[1] *The Letters of Chesterfield*, ed. Dobrée, V, p. 2137.

BIBLIOGRAPHY OF MONTESQUIEU

In respect of each work an indication is given, whenever possible, of the location of the manuscript and of the dates of composition, of first publication, and of any critical edition existing. In the case of unpublished works of which the manuscript is lost, mention is made of the evidence for the work's existence.

Further abbreviations used:

Mélanges	*Mélanges inédits de Montesquieu*, ed. Baron de Montesquieu [and R. Céleste], Bordeaux and Paris, 1892.
Pensées et fragments	*Pensées et fragments inédits*, ed. Baron Gaston de Montesquieu [and H. Barckhausen], Bordeaux, 1889–1901, 2 vols.
Plassan	*Œuvres de Montesquieu*, Paris, an IV—1796, 5 vols.
Voyages	*Voyages de Montesquieu*, ed. Baron Albert de Montesquieu [and R. Céleste, H. Barckhausen, and R. Dezeimeris], Bordeaux, 1894–6, 2 vols.

I. ORIGINAL WORKS BY MONTESQUIEU

(in chronological order of composition)

1700–5 *Britomare* (a verse tragedy written at Juilly)
[MS. lost; unpublished; fragments in *Pensée* 359 (Bkn. 477)]

1711 *Les Prêtres dans le paganisme*
[MS. lost; unpublished; Secondat, *Mémoire*, p. 397, and *Pensée* 2004 (Bkn. 591) refer]

1716 *Discours de réception à l'Académie de Bordeaux*
[MS.: Bx MS. 828 (6), no. 5; read 18 April; first publ., Plassan, IV]

1716 *Dissertation sur la politique des Romains dans la religion*
[MS.: Bx MS. 828 (6), no. 6; read 16 June; first publ., Plassan, IV]

1716 *Discours sur le système des idées*
[MS. lost; unpublished; Bx MS. 1699 (3), p. 281, refers; read 16 November]

1716c *Mémoire sur les dettes de l'Etat*
[MS.: Bx 2104; first publ., *Mélanges*, 1892; cf. F. K. Mann, 'Montesquieu, homme d'Etat' (*Revue économique de Bordeaux*, 1911) and B.N., MSS. fr. 7767]

1717 [*Mémoire sur la Constitution*] (see under 1752)

1717 *De la différence des génies*
[MS. lost; unpublished; Bx MS. 1699 (3), p. 332, refers; read 25 August]

1717 *Discours prononcé à la rentrée de l'Académie de Bordeaux*
[MS.: Bx MS. 828 (3), no. 1; read 15 November; first publ., Plassan, IV]

1717c *Discours sur Cicéron*
[MS.: Bx MS. 2099; first publ., *Mélanges*, 1892; Montesquieu says written 'dans ma jeunesse']

1717c *Eloge de la sincérité*
[MS.: Bx MS. 2100; first publ., *Mélanges*, 1892, q.v. for discussion of date]

1717–21 *Lettres persanes*
[MS. lost, but MS. corrections are in B.N., not yet shelf-marked; first publ., Cologne (=Amsterdam), 1921; for date see R. Shackleton, 'Moslem Chronology of *Lettres persanes*'; critical editions by H. Barckhausen (1897, 1913), E. Carcassonne (1929), A. Adam (1954), P. Vernière (1960)]

1718 *Discours sur les causes de l'écho*
[MS.: Bx MS. 828 (3), no. 2; read 1 May; first publ., Plassan, IV]

1718 *Discours sur l'usage des glandes rénales*
[MS.: Bx MS. 828 (6), no. 7; read 25 August; first publ., Plassan, IV]

1719 *Projet d'une histoire physique de la terre ancienne et moderne*
[MS. lost; first publ., *Journal des savants* and *Mercure de France*, 1719]

1719–21 *Essai d'observations sur l'histoire naturelle*
[MS.: Bx MS. 828 (6) no. 8; read on 16 November 1719 and 20 November 1721; first publ., Plassan, IV]

1720 *Discours sur la cause de la pesanteur des corps*
[MS.: Bx MS. 828 (3), no. 3; read 1 May; first publ., Plassan, IV]

1720 *Discours sur la cause de la transparence des corps*
[MS.: Bx MS, 828 (3), no. 4; read 25 August; first publ., Plassan, IV]

1723 *Dissertation sur le ressort*
[MS. lost; unpublished; read to Académie de Bordeaux on 18 November; Nagel III, p. 6 refers]

1723*c* *Epître au curé de Courdimanche*
[MS.: Bx MS. 693, pp. 389–90 (*sottisier* of Barbot); first publ., *Correspondance de Montesquieu*, ed. F. Gebelin and A. Morize, Bordeaux, 1914, I, pp. 36–37 (in part previously, Vian pp. 182–3)]

1723*c* *Chanson*: 'Nous n'avons pour philosophie'
[MS. lost; first publ., Plassan, V]

1723*c* *A Madame de Prie*: 'Les dieux que vous vîntes surprendre'
[MS.: Bx MS. 693, p. 599 (*sottisier* of Barbot); first publ., Vian, p. 183]

1723 *Dissertation sur le mouvement relatif*
[MS. lost; unpublished, but a synopsis appears in Desmolets, *Nouvelles littéraires*, 1724; read 18 November to Académie de Bordeaux]

1724*c* *Lettres de Xénocrate à Phérès*
[MS. sold at Hôtel Drouot, 14 March 1957; first publ., *Mélanges*, 1892; date from death of Regent (December 1923) which preceded composition]

1724 *Le Temple de Gnide*
[MS. lost; first publ., *Bibliothèque française*, 1724, and separately, Paris (with privilege), 1725]

1724 *Céphise et l'amour*
[appended to *Le Temple de Gnide*, q.v.]

1724 *Dialogue de Sylla et d'Eucrate*
[MS. lost, having in 1817 been in Villenave's collection (*Œuvres de Montesquieu*, Paris (Belin), 1817, I, p. xxi); Bx MS. 828 (3), no. 5, is a copy; first publ., *Mercure de France*, 1745; date from Barbot to Montesquieu, July 1724]

1725 *De la considération et de la réputation*
[MS.: Bx MS. 2101 (subsequent to composition); first publ., in synopsis, *Bibliothèque française*, 1726, in full, *Mélanges*, 1892; read to Académie de Bordeaux, 25 August 1825]

1725 *Discours prononcé à la rentrée du Parlement de Bordeaux* (or *Discours sur l'équité qui doit régler les jugements et l'exécution des lois*)
[MS.: Bx MS. 828 (39), no. 13; first publ., 1771, as a separate brochure; read to Parlement, 12 November]

1725 *Discours sur les motifs qui doivent nous encourager aux sciences*
[MS.: autograph, Bx (Arch. de l'Académie), and copy, Bx MS. 828 (6) no. 9; first publ., Plassan, IV; read to Académie de Bordeaux, 15 November]

1725 *Traité général des devoirs*
[MS. lost; extracts read to Académie de Bordeaux, 1 May; these extracts first publ., *Bibliothèque française*, 1726; description of MS. (with table of contents) in 1818 list of MSS. (Nagel III, pp. 1575–6); cf. R. Shackleton, 'La Genèse de l'*Esprit des lois*' (*RHLF*, 1952)]

1725 *De la politique*
[MS.: Paris, Bibliothèque de l'Assemblée nationale; first publ., *Mélanges*, 1892; appears to have been annexed to *Traité des devoirs*]

1725*c* [*Essai touchant les lois naturelles et la distinction du juste et de l'injuste*]
[MS., formerly in Leningrad, lost; MS. copy in Arch. mun. Bx; first publ. in Nagel III; of dubious attribution to Montesquieu]

1726 *Discours contenant l'éloge du duc de La Force*
[MS.: Bx MS. 828 (6) no. 10; read to Académie de Bordeaux 25 August; first publ., Plassan, IV]

1726 *Discours sur la cause et les effets du tonnerre*
[MS. lost; unpublished; Nagel III, p. 7 refers]

1726 [*Essai sur le goût*] (see under 1753–4)

1726–7*c* *Considérations sur les richesses de l'Espagne*
[MS. in possession of executors of Dr. M. Altmann, London; first publ., *RHLF*, 1910; date from handwriting]

1727 *Mémoire contre l'arrêt du conseil du 27 février 1725*
[MS.: Bx MS. 2105; first publ., *Mélanges*, 1892, q.v. for date]

1727 [*Voyage à Paphos*]
[MS. lost; first publ., *Mercure de France*, 1727; attribution to Montesquieu dubious]

1727*c* *Dialogues*
[MS. lost; unpublished; *rejet* only in *Pensées* 330–8 (Bkn. 478–86); date from place in *Pensées*]

1727*c* *Dialogue de Xantippe et de Xénocrate*
[MS. sold at Hôtel Drouot, 14 March 1957; first publ., *Mélanges*, 1892; *rejet* in *Pensées*, whence date]

1728 *Discours de réception à l'Académie française*
[MS. lost; read 24 January; first published as brochure, 1728]

1728 *Voyage en Autriche*
[MS. in collection of R. Schuman; first publ., *Voyages*, I, 1894]

1728 *Adieu à Gênes*
[MS. lost; first publ., *Lettres familières*, 2nd ed., 1767]

1728–9 *Voyage en Italie, en Allemagne, et en Hollande*
[MS. in collection of R. Schuman; first publ., *Voyages*, I and II, 1894–6]

1728–9 *Florence*
[MS. in collection of R. Schuman; first publ., *Voyages*, II, 1896]

1729–31 *Notes sur l'Angleterre*
[MS. lost; first publ., *Œuvres*, Paris (Lefèvre), 1818, V]

1729–31 *Voyage en Angleterre*
[MS. lost; unpublished; 1818 list of MSS. refers (Nagel III, p. 1575)]

1731*c* *Lettre sur Gênes*
[MS. in collection of R. Schuman; first publ., *Voyages*, II, 1896]

1731 [*Lysimaque*] (see under 1751)

1731–2 *Mémoires sur les mines*
(the first of these five *mémoires* is entitled *Description de deux fontaines de Hongrie*)
[MS. in collection of R. Schuman; first publ., *Voyages*, II, 1896; read to Académie de Bordeaux on 25 August and 2 October 1731 and 3 February 1732]

1731–3 *Réflexions sur la monarchie universelle en Europe*
[MS. lost; first publ., 1734 (unique copy which was withdrawn, now at La Brède); next publ., *Deux Opuscules*, 1891]

1731–3 *Considérations sur les causes de la grandeur des Romains et de leur décadence*
[MS. lost; first publ., Amsterdam, 1734; critical editions by C. Jullian, s.d., and H. Barckhausen, 1900]

1731–3 *Réflexions sur le caractère de quelques princes et sur quelques événements de leur vie*
[MS. sold at Hôtel Drouot, 14 March 1957; first publ., *Mélanges*, 1892; date from reference in *Pensées*]

1731*c*–8 *Histoire véritable* (or *Le Métempsychosiste*)
[version A: MS. lost (sold in 1939); first publ., *Mélanges*, 1892; version B: MS. lost (sold in 1924); first publ., Bordeaux, 1902; critical edition of both by R. Caillois, 1948; for date, see *Mélanges*]

1732 or earlier *Lettres de Kanti*
[MS. lost; unpublished; *rejet* in *Pensées*, whence date]

1732 or earlier *Histoire de la jalousie* (or *Réflexions sur la jalousie*)
[MS. lost; unpublished; *rejet* in *Pensées*, whence date]

1732 *Réflexions sur la sobriété des habitants de Rome comparée à l'intempérance des anciens Romains*
[MS. in collection of R. Schuman; first publ., *Voyages*, II, 1896; read to Académie de Bordeaux, November 1732]

1734 *Discours sur la formation et le progrès des idées*
[MS. lost; unpublished; read to Académie de Bordeaux, 14 November 1732 (Bx MS. 1699 (3), p. 471 refers)]

1734*c* *La Liberté politique*
[MS. lost; unpublished; *rejet* in *Pensées*, whence date]

1734*c* *De la manière gothique*
[MS. in collection of R. Schuman; first publ., *Voyages*, II, 1896; date from sources]

1734*c*–48 *De l'esprit des lois*
[MS.: B.N. n.a.f. 12832–6; first publ., Geneva, 1748; critical edition by J. Brethe de La Gressaye, 1950 sq.; for date see R. Shackleton in 'Le Manuscrit de la Bibliothèque nationale' (Nagel III, pp. 567–77) and above, and Brethe]

after 1734 *Ebauche de l'éloge historique du maréchal de Berwick*
[MS. lost; first publ. in *Mémoires* of Berwick, 1778; date from death of Berwick]

1736–32 *Essai sur les causes qui peuvent affecter les esprits et les caractères*
[MS. sold at Hôtel Drouot, 14 March 1957; first publ., *Mélanges*, 1892; for date see R. Shackleton, 'The Evolution of Montesquieu's theory of climate' (*Revue internationale de philosophie*, 1955)]

1738 *Pour Madame Geoffrin* (quatrain)
[MS.: Bx MS. 1868, p. 335; first publ., Nagel III; the quatrain is dated; an earlier version was written in 1734; its attribution to Montesquieu is less than certain]

1738 *Pour Madame Le Franc*
[MS. at La Brède; first publ., Nagel III; the poem is dated; one stanza of the poem constitutes an earlier version (of 1735); its MS. is Bx MS. 1868, p. 331, first publ., *Correspondance de Montesquieu*, ed. Gebelin and Morize, 1914]

1738*c* *Histoire de France*
[MS.: large fragments in *Pensées* 1302, 1306 (Bkn. 595, 596); first publ., *Pensées et fragments inédits*, I, 1899; uncertain whether anything else existed]

1739–40 *Histoire de Louis XI*
[MS. lost (destroyed inadvertently by secretary); unpublished; *Lettres familières*, XXIV (Nagel III, p. 1097) refers]

1740 or later *Portrait* [de Madame de Mirepoix]
[MS. lost; first publ., *Œuvres*, 1758, III (a *carton*); also in *Opuscules*, 1765; date from marriage of Mme de Mirepoix]

1742 *Arsace et Isménie*
[MS. at La Brède; first publ., *Œuvres posthumes*, 1783, also separately in same year; date from Montesquieu to Barbot, 8 September 1742]

1742 *Etrennes de la Saint-Jean*
[MS. lost; first publ., 1742; for attribution to Montesquieu, see above, pp. 184–5]

1743 [*Les Netturales, ou la Liceride*]
[MS. lost; first publ., 1743; attribution to Montesquieu very dubious, based on MS. annotation on B.N. copy]

1745*c* *A Madame de Boufflers*
[MS. lost, previously owned by Vian; first publ., *Œuvres*, ed. Laboulaye, VII, 1879; date from his acquaintance with Mme de Boufflers]

1745*c* *Madrigal: à deux sœurs qui lui demandaient une chanson*
[MS. lost; first publ., Plassan, V; date from Montesquieu's acquaintance with Mme de Boufflers, it being probable that she and Mme de Mirepoix were the addressees]

1747 *Souvenirs de la cour de Stanislas Leckzinski*
[MS. in collection of R. Schuman; first publ., *Voyages*, II, 1896; date from date of visit to Lunéville]

1747 *Invocation aux Muses*
[MS. in B.N. MS. of *Lois* (a later copy); first publ., Saladin, *Mémoire sur Vernet*, 1790; Mussard to Montesquieu, 8 July 1747, refers]

1748 or later *Dissertation sur l'action possessoire*
[MS. at La Brède; unpublished; date from handwriting; unfinished]

1750 *Défense de l'Esprit des lois*
[MS. lost; first publ., Geneva (=Paris), 1750]

1750 *Eclaircissements sur l'Esprit des lois*
[MS. lost; first publ., with *Défense*, 1750]

1750 *Réflexions sur le rapport de Mgr Bottari*
[MS. lost; first publ., Vian, p. 291; Montesquieu to Passionei, 2 June 1750, refers]

1751 *Lysimaque*
[MS. lost; first publ., *Mercure de France*, 1754; Montesquieu to Solignac, 4 April 1751, refers; *rejet* in *Pensées* shows that part of this work existed in 1731*c*]

1751*c* *Remarques sur certaines objections que m'a faites un homme qui a traduit mes 'Romains' en Angleterre*
[MS.: Bx MS. 2103; first publ., *Mélanges*, 1892; date from translation in question]

1752*c* *Mémoire sur la Constitution*
[MS.: Bx MS. 2103; first publ., *Mélanges*, 1892, q.v. for date; the work appeared to have been first written in 1717*c*)

1752–4 *Réponses et explications données à la Faculté de théologie*
[MS. at La Brède; first publ., H. Barckhausen, *Montesquieu, l''Esprit des lois', et les archives de La Brède*, Bordeaux, 1904; for date see above, pp. 369–70]

1753 *A Dassier*
[MS. lost; first publ., *Opuscules*, Copenhagen, 1765; date from execution of medal (see also p. 379)]

1753–5 *Essai sur le goût*
[MS. lost; first publ., *Encyclopédie*, VII, 1757; additional chapters: MS.: B.N., n.a.f. 717; first publ., in part, Plassan, III; in full, *Annales littéraires*, 1804; Montesquieu to D'Alembert, 16 November 1753, refers; *rejet* in *Pensées* shows that work existed in embryo in 1728]

Works which cannot be dated

Chanson (Amour, après mainte victoire)
[MS. lost; first publ., *Œuvres*, 1758, on a cancel]

Cyropédie, ou monarchie d'Espagne
[MS. lost; unpublished; 1818 list of MSS. refers (Nagel III, p. 1575)]

Dissertation sur la manière d'apprendre ou d'étudier la jurisprudence
[MS. lost; unpublished; G. Labat, 'La Château de La Brède' (*Recueil des travaux de la Société d'agriculture, sciences et arts d'Agen*, 1834), refers and cites a paragraph (cf. J. Delpit, *Le Fils de Montesquieu*, Bordeaux, 1888, p. 183)]

Dissertation sur les satyres

Les Dieux animaux
[MS. lost; unpublished; Nagel III, p. 7 refers, on basis of note by Lamontaigne; fragments in *Pensée* 2254 (Bnk. 592)]

Traité de Westphalie
[MS. lost; unpublished; 1818 list of MSS. refers (Nagel III, p. 1581)]

II. EXTRACTS AND ANALYSES MADE BY MONTESQUIEU

1. *Collections*
(in approximate chronological order)

Historia Romana (a schoolboy's notebook, arranged by question and answer)

[MS. at La Brède; a brief extract in Pléiade II, pp. 1443–5; 1701–5 (Montesquieu's stay at Juilly)]

Collectio juris (notes on Roman Law)

[MS. in Bibliothèque Nationale, n.a.f. 12837–42, 6 vols. 4°; unpublished; Nagel III, p. 716 refers; 1716–21, from handwriting and allusions]

Résomptions (analyses of papers read by others to the Académie de Bordeaux)

[MSS. in Bibliothèque municipale de Bordeaux; first published (with exception of *résomption* of Navarre *sur l'ivresse*) in F. Jouannet, *Statistique du département de la Gironde*, I, Paris, 1837, pp. 423–9; Nagel III; various dates between 1717 and 1726]

Spicilège

[MS. in Bibliothèque municipale de Bordeaux, no. 1867; first published by André Masson, Paris, 1944; Nagel II, pp. 681–919; Pléiade II, pp. 1265–1438; 1715–55]

Mes Pensées

[MS. in Bibliothèque municipale de Bordeaux, no. 1866; various fragments published in *Œuvres*, Paris (Plassan), 1796, IV; first complete edition, in rearranged order, H. Barckhausen, *Pensées et fragments inédits*, Bordeaux, 1899–1901; reprinted in Pléiade I, pp. 974–1574, with *rejet* of different works printed after those works; first edition in order of MS., Nagel II, pp. 1–677; *c.* 1722–55]

Extrait de mes extraits: Ridicula

[lost; unpublished; *Pensée* 326 (Bkn. 952) refers to this as a project; 1818 list of MSS. however mentions it as if complete and as an early collection (Nagel III, p. 1576)]

Recueil d'airs

[MS. in Royal Library, Windsor; unpublished; 1729–32, from handwriting]

Prince

Princes

Bibliothèque
Bibliothèque espagnole
Journal
Journal espagnol
[lost; unpublished; several references in *Pensées*, where coincidences of cross references show that this was a single collection referred to by different names; 1731–3, though some material was collected earlier; the *Journal de livres peu connus* mentioned in 1818 list of MSS. (Nagel III, 1576) is perhaps the same]

Geographica I
[lost; *Pensées* 1810 and 1845 (Bkn. 384 and 299) refer; see Frézier below; before 1738, since prior to *Geog. II*]

Geographica II
[MS. at La Brède (see my article, 'Montesquieu: two unpublished documents', *FS*, 1950); extensive extracts in Nagel II, pp. 923–63; 1733–43]

Politica I
[lost, unpublished; existence inferred from *Politica II*]

Politica II
[lost; unpublished; *Pensées* 1502, 1767–8, 1776, 1880 (Bkn. 1501, 431, 240, 215, 268) refer; includes Aristotle]

Politica–Historica
[lost; unpublished; *Pensée* 1834 (Bkn. 376) refers; includes Fredegar (Continuation), and probably Barbeyrac]

Juridica I
[lost; unpublished; existence inferred from *Juridica II*]

Juridica II
[lost; unpublished; *Pensée* 2055 (Bkn. 1814) refers; includes Vitriarius]

Mythologica et antiquitates
[lost; unpublished; *Pensée* 906 (Bkn. 709) refers]

Anatomica I
[lost; unpublished; *Spicilège* 347 (MS. p. 311) refers; includes Riquet]

Histoire universelle
[lost; unpublished; *Pensée* 2191 (Bkn. 168) refers; includes Constantine Porphyrogenitus]

Commerce
[lost; unpublished; contents of *Geog. II* refer (Nagel II, p. 923)]

Pièces diverses
[lost; unpublished; *Pensées* 1752 and 1765 (Bkn. 369 and 385) refer]

Recueil pour des dissertations
Matériaux de dissertations
[some MS. fragments at La Brède, others referred to in 1818 list of MSS. (Nagel III, pp. 1577–80); some fragments published in H. Barckhausen, *Montesquieu, l' 'Esprit des lois', et les archives de La Brède*, Bordeaux, 1904; Nagel III, pp. 600–25; Pléiade II, pp. 1004–35; others, referred to in 1818 list of MSS. (Nagel III, pp. 1577–80) are lost and unpublished; all fragments known consist of *rejet* from *Lois*]

Réflexions
[lost; 1818 list of MSS. refers (Nagel III, pp. 1577–9); unpublished; contained *rejet* of *Lois* (Nagel III, p. 1577, line 8 should read 'ou pour mes *Réflexions*')]

Pièces justificatives sur l'usure
[MS. at La Brède; unpublished; 1751–5, from handwriting]

2. *Individual Works*

(arranged in alphabetical order)

The sign + prefixed to a work indicates that it was possessed by Montesquieu in the edition named, but not necessarily that the extract was made from that edition.

Aboul Gazi Bahadour Khan, *Histoire généalogique des Tatares*, Leyden, 1726
[*Geog. II*; extracts in Nagel II, pp. 951–3; 1734–42]

+Addison, *Remarks on Several Parts of Italy*, London, 1705
[*Geog. II*; unpublished, but see Nagel III, pp. 923–4; 1735–8]

+Amelot de La Houssaie, *Histoire du gouvernement de Venise*, Paris, 1676
[lost; *Pensée* 1842 (Bkn. 291) and Nagel III, p. 619 (Pléiade II, p. 1019) refer]

+Ammianus Marcellinus, *Histoire*, Paris, 1672
[lost; *Pensée* 716 (Bkn. 1262) refers; before 1733]

Anson, *Voyage autour du monde*, Amsterdam, 1749–51 (or Paris, 1750)
[MS. of 42 pp. at La Brède; unpublished; 1751–5, from handwriting]

+Aristotle, *Politique*, tr. Oresme; or tr. Le Roy, Paris, 1576
[lost; in *Politica II*; *Pensées* 1501–2 (Bkn. 1502 and 1533 refer; before 1745]

+Arrian, *De expeditione Alexandri* (various editions)
[lost; Bernadau, *Tableau de Bordeaux*, Bordeaux, 1810, refers]

+Aulus Gellius, *Noctes Atticae*, Lyons, 1659
[lost; *Essai sur les causes* refers (Nagel III, p. 412; Pléiade II, p. 51); before 1743]

+Barbeyrac, *Supplément au corps universel diplomatique*, Amsterdam and The Hague, 1739
[lost; *Pensée* 1834 Bkn. 376) refers]

+Beaumanoir, *Coutumes de Beauvaisis*, Paris and Bourges, 1690
[lost; *rejet* of *Lois* refers (Nagel III, p. 638; Pléiade II, p. 1036)]

+Bernier, *Voyages*, Amsterdam, 1709–10, 2 vols.
[*Geog. II*, ff. 287–302; extracts published in Nagel III, p. 953–5; 1738–40]

Bernis (Abbé, later Cardinal de), *Œuvres mêlées*
[MS. of 4 pp. at la Brède; unpublished; 1751–5, from handwriting]

+*Bibliothèque universelle*, XXIV, 1693
[lost; *Pensée* 41 (Bkn. 1461) refers; *c.* 1725]

Bochart, *Geographia sacra*, Caen, 1646
[MS. in collection of R. Schuman; extracts in Nagel III, pp. 714–16; 1743–6, from handwriting]

+Bonet (Théophile), *Polyanthes sive thesaurus medico-practicus*, Geneva, 1690, 3 vols.
[MS. at La Brède; unpublished; Nagel III, p. 714 refers]

+Brisson, *De regio Persarum principatu*, Paris, 1595
[MS. at La Brède; unpublished; Nagel III, pp. 717-18 refer; 1716–31, from handwriting]

Cassiodorus, *Variae*
[lost; *Voyages* refer (Nagel II, p. 1164; Pléiade I, p. 732)]

+Chardin, *Voyages en Perse*, Lyons, 1687, 2 vols., or Amsterdam, 1711, 10 vols.
[lost; *Pensée* 41 (Bkn. 1461) refers; probably before 1725)

Chassepol (F. de) (or Chassipol), *Traité des finances et de la fausse monnaie des Romains*, Paris, 1739
[MS. of 18 pp. at La Brède; unpublished; 1740–1, from handwriting]

Commerce des Hollandais, ch. III (unidentified)
[MS. at La Brède; unpublished; 1739–41, from handwriting]

Conringius, *De habitu corporum Germanorum*
[lost; *Pensée* 396 (Bkn. 1464) refers; 1731–3]

+Conringius, *De imperii Germanici Republica*, Yverdun, 1654
[lost; *Pensée* 1918 (Bkn. 394) refers]

Constantine Porphyrogenitus, *Excerpta de virtutibus et vitiis*
[in *Hist. univ.*, lost; *Pensée* 2191 (Bkn. 168) refers]

+*Coran*, tr. Du Ryer, Paris, s.d. (or in Italian, s.l., 1547)
[lost; *Pensée* 41 (Bkn. 1461) refers; probably before 1725]

Craftsman, The
[*Spicilège* contains several extracts from the period 1729–31]

Cragius, *De republica Lacedemoniorum*
[lost; *Pensée* 1755 (Bkn. 211) refers]

+Dampier, *Nouveau Voyage autour du monde*, Amsterdam, 1711
[*Geog. II*; unpublished except for very brief extracts in Nagel II, pp. 925–6; 1733–8]

Daniel, *Histoire de la milice française*, Paris, 1721
[*Spicilège* 544 (p. 502 of MS.); 1733–8]

Deslandes, *Essai sur la marine et le commerce*, Paris, 1743
[MS. of 10 pp. at La Brède; unpublished; 1743–6, from handwriting]

+Desmarets (Nicolas), *Mémoire sur l'administration des finances*, s.l., s.d.
[*Spicilège* 441 (MS., pp. 377–86); unpublished; *c.* 1726–8]

Dexippus, *Historia* [in *Pièces diverses*, lost; *Pensée* 1752 (Bkn. 369) refers]

+Diodorus Siculus, *Histoire universelle*, Paris, 1737, (also *Opera*, Bâle, 1526 and 1548)
[lost; *De la manière gothique* and *Mémoires sur les mines* refer (Nagel III, pp. 282 and 465–7; not in Pléiade) giving extracts; *c.* 1731]

+Domat (Jean), *Les Lois civiles dans leur ordre naturel*, Paris, 1689
[lost; Labat, 'Le Château de la Brède' (*Recueil des travaux de la Société d'agriculture, sciences et arts d'Agen*, III, 1834) refers]

Du Halde, *Description . . . de la Chine*, Paris, 1735
[*Geog. II*; unpublished except for extracts in Nagel II, pp. 943–51; 1735–8]

Dutot, *Réflexions politiques sur les finances et le commerce*, The Hague, 1738
[MS. at La Brède; unpublished; 1738, from handwriting and date of book]

Eutropius, *Historia Romana* (in Muratori)
[lost; *Voyages* (Nagel II, p. 1164; Pléiade I, p. 732) refer]

+Fénelon, *Télémaque*, The Hague, 1705
[MS. at La Brède; short extract in Nagel III, p. 707; 1751–5, from handwriting]

Fontaines (Pierre de), *Le Conseil*
[MS. at La Brède; unpublished; Nagel III, p. 717 refers; 1748–55, from handwriting]

Fortifications ('petit traité par demande et réponse')
[*Spicilège* 469 (MS., pp. 432–3); 1728]

Frédégaire (*Continuation de*)
[in *Polit. Hist.*; lost; *Pensées* 1834 and 1930 (Bkn. 376 and 430) refer]

Fréret, *De l'origine des Français et de leur établissement dans la Gaule*
[*Spicilège* 585 (MS., pp. 539–42); Fréret's dissertation was not yet published; 1734–8]

+Frézier, *Relation du voyage de la Mer du sud aux côtes du Chili et du Pérou*, Paris, 1716
[in *Geog. I*; lost; *Pensée* 1810 (Bkn. 384) refers; before 1738 (*Geog. I* being held to precede *Geog. II*, which starts between 1733 and 1738)]

+Galen, *De alimentorum facultatibus* and *De differentiis febrium* (in *Opera latine*, Bâle, 1549)
[MS. at La Brède; unpublished; Nagel III, p. 714 refers]

+Gaya (Louis de), *Cérémonies nuptiales de toutes les nations*, Paris, 1680
[*Geog. II*; unpublished; Nagel II, p. 924 refers; 1733–8]

Gazettes
[The *Spicilège* contains very numerous extracts at different dates from the *Gazette de France* and the *Gazette de Hollande*]

+Giraldus (Lilius), *Opera omnia*, Bâle, 1580
[lost; *Pensées* 860–9 (Bkn. 2136, 2139–45) refer and give extracts; 1734–8]

Gordon (George), *The History of our national Debts and Taxes*, London, 1751
[MS. at La Brède; unpublished; Nagel III, p. 718 refers; 1751–5]

Gravina, *Origines iuris civilis*
[lost; *Pensée* 1912 (Bkn. 255) refers; before 1743 (date of *Lois*, I, 3, which utilizes Gravina]

+Gregory of Tours, *Historia Francorum*. Paris, 1610
[lost; *Pensée* 1932 (Bkn. 431) refers]

+Herodotus, *Historiae* (H. Estienne, 1592, or Frankfurt, 1608; or French translations, Paris, 1556 and 1645)
[in *Hist. univ.*, lost; *Essai sur les causes* refers (Nagel III, p. 399; Pléiade II, p. 1481); before 1743]

Hippocrates, *De aere, aquis et locis*
[two extracts; both MSS. at La Brède; first, published in Nagel III, pp. 712–13; second, unpublished but Nagel III, p. 714 refers; date of first, 1738–43]

+*Histoire des ouvrages des savants*, 1690
[lost; *Pensée* 198 (Bkn. 1700) refers; *c.* 1725]

+Homer, *Iliade*, tr. Mme Dacier, Paris, 1709, or tr. La Motte, Paris, 1714
[MS. at La Brède; extracts in Nagel III, pp. 703–6; 1751–5, from handwriting]
Homer, *Odyssée*, tr. Du Souhait, Paris, 1627, or tr. Mme Dacier, Paris, 1709
[MS. at La Brède; extracts in Nagel III, pp. 706–7; 1751–5, from handwriting]
Hyde (Thomas), *Historia religionis veterum Persarum*, London, 1700
[lost; *Pensée* 41 (Bkn. 1461) and *Spicilège* 402 (MS., p. 348) refer; before 1725]
+*Journal des savants*, 1689
[lost; *Pensée* 182 (Bkn. 2054) refers; *c.* 1725]
Journal des savants, 1736
[lost; *Pensée* 1354 (Bkn. 1171) and *Essai sur les causes* (Nagel III, p. 419; Pléiade II, p. 58) refer; 1737–43]
+Justinus, *Historiae*, Leyden, 1640
[lost; *Pensée* 41 (Bkn. 1461) refers; before 1725]
+Kämpfer, *Historia imperii Japonici*, London, 1727
[*Spicilège* 517 (MS., pp. 476–81); 1728–34]
Kolbe, *The Present State of the Cape of Good Hope*, London, 1731
[*Spicilège* 539 (MS., p. 498); 1731–4]
+La Loubère, *Du royaume de Siam*, Paris, 1691
[*Geog. II*; two very brief extracts in Nagel II, p. 926; 1734–8]
La Mottraye, *Voyages*, The Hague, 1727
[*Spicilège* 538 (MS., pp. 493–7); 1728–34]
+La Thaumassière, *Anciennes et nouvelles coutumes locales de Berry et de Lorris*, Bourges, 1679
[MS. at La Brède; unpublished; Nagel III, p. 717 refers; 1742–6, from handwriting and watermark]
Le Bret, *Ordo perantiquus iudiciorum civilium*, Paris, 1604
[MS. at La Brède; brief extracts in Nagel III, pp. 719–20; after 1742, from watermark]
+Le Gendre, *Mœurs et coutumes des Français dans les différents temps de la monarchie française*, Paris, 1686
[lost; *rejet* of *Lois* refers (Nagel III, p. 642)]
Lettres édifiantes et curieuses . . . par quelques missionnaires de la Compagnie de Jésus, Paris, 1703–41
[*Geog. II*; extracts in Nagel II, pp. 955–62; *c.* 1738–42]
+Lindenbrogius, *Codex legum antiquarum*, Frankfurt, 1613
[lost; *Pensée* 1826 (Bkn. 404) refers and gives extracts]

+Livy, *Historia*, Paris, 1553 and other editions; tr. Du Ryer, Paris, 1653, and Amsterdam, 1722

[lost; *Pensée* 1809 (Bkn. 283) refers]

Meursius, *Themis Attica*, Utrecht, 1685

[lost; *rejet* of *Lois* refers (Nagel III, p. 626; Pléiade II, p. 1546)]

Muratori, *Rerum italicarum scriptores praecipui*, Milan, 1723 sq., vols. I and II

[lost; *Voyages* refer to vol. I (Nagel II, p. 1164; Pléiade I, p. 723); 1818 list of MSS. refers to vol. II (Nagel III, p. 1579), and cf. *Lois*, XXVIII, 36]

Nouveaux Mémoires des missions de la Compagnie de Jésus, Paris, 1715

[*Geog. II*; unpublished; Nagel II, pp. 962–3 refers; 1738–40]

Ouanges (Arcadio), conversations with Montesquieu analysed in *Quelques remarques sur la Chine que j'ai tirées des conversations que j'ai eues avec M. Ouanges*

[MS. of 96 pp. in Bibliothèque municipale de Bordeaux, no. 1696, t. 32; extracts published by L. Desgraves in RHBx, 1958; conversations occurred in 1713; other extracts are in *Geog. II*]

+Ovid (Montesquieu possessed in all fourteen editions of different works)

[lost; *Pensée* 2180 (Bkn. 879) refers; unpublished]

+*Pandects* (several editions)

[lost; Labat, 'Le Château de La Brède' (Agen, 1834) refers]

+Petronius, *Satiricon*, Paris, 1601

[*Spicilège* 206 (MS., p. 157); 1715–24]

+Philostrates, *Les Images ou tableaux de plate peinture*, Paris, 1629

[*Spicilège* 272 (MS., pp. 217–18); before 1726]

+Plato, *De legibus* (in *Opera omnia graec. lat.*, Geneva, 1578)

[lost; *Pensée* 1766 (Bkn. 359) refers]

+Pliny, *Historia naturalis*, Paris, 1723, bk. II

[MS. at La Brède; unpublished; after 1734]

Plumard de Dangeul (pseud. Nickolls), *Remarques sur les avantages et les désavantages de la France et de la Grande-Bretagne par rapport au commerce*, Leyden, 1754

[MS. at La Brède; unpublished; Nagel III, pp. 718–19 refers; 1754–5]

+Plutarch, *Illustrium virorum vitae*, Bâle, 1553 (and other editions, including three of Amyot's translation)

[lost; *Pensée* 665 (Bkn. 710) refers; 1731–3]

+Plutarch, *Moralia* (several editions)

[lost; *Pensée* 1789 (Bkn. 309) refers; the allusion, *pace* Barckhausen, is to Plutarch's *Quaestiones Romanae*]

+Pomponius Mela, *De situ orbis*, Paris, 1540
[*Spicilège* 241 (MS., pp. 185–8); probably before 1721]

Pothier (R.-J.), *Coutumes des duché, bailliages, et prévosté d'Orléans*, Orléans, 1740
[lost; Labat, 'Le Château de La Brède' (Agen, 1834), refers; identification uncertain]

+Procopius of Caesarea, *Histoire de la guerre des Goths*, Lyons, 1578 (or from Muratori, I)
[lost; some extracts in *Pensées* 2051–2 (Bkn. 2158 and 434); probably before 1733]

+Procopius of Caesarea, *Historia arcana*, Lyons, 1623
[lost; in vol. *Pièces diverses; Pensée* 1765 (Bkn. 385) refers]

+Pufendorf, *Introduction à l'histoire des principaux royaumes et Etats dans l'Europe*, Leyden, 1710
[lost; *Pensée* 380 (Bkn. 1626) refers; before 1733]

+Ramazzini, *De fontium mutinensium admiranda scaturigine* (in *Opera omnia*, Geneva, 1717)
[lost; *Pensée* 44 (Bkn. 687) refers; after 1728]

+Renaudot, *Anciennes Relations des Indes et de la Chine de deux voyageurs mahométans*, Paris, 1718
[*Geog. II*; unpublished; Nagel II, pp. 926–7 refers]

Riquet, *Traité de la digestion* (unidentified)
[in *Anatomica*, lost; *Spicilège* 347 (MS., pp. 310–11); *c.* 1726]

Sainte-Palaye, *Mémoires sur l'ancienne chevalerie* (*Mémoires de l'Académie des inscriptions*, XX, Paris, 1753)
[*Spicilège* 782 (MS., pp. 791–800); 1753–5]

Sidney, *Discours sur le gouvernement*, The Hague, 1702, 3 vols.
[lost; *Pensée* 626 (Bkn. 1659) refers; probably *c.* 1734]

Sloane (Sir Hans), *Histoire de la Jamaïque*, tr. Raulin, London, 1751, 2 vols.
[MS. of 26 pp. at La Brède; unpublished; 1751–5]

+Strabo, *Geographia*, Geneva, 1587
[lost; *Pensée* 166 refers]

Vertot, *Apologie de l'histoire de Frédégaire* (*Mémoires de l'Académie des inscriptions*, I, Paris, 1717)
[lost; *Pensée* 324 (Bkn. 1453); refers]

+Virgil, *Aeneid*, VII and VIII (Montesquieu possessed five editions and one MS. of works)
[MS. at La Brède; extracts in Nagel III, pp. 708–9; 1748 or later, from handwriting]

+Virgil, *Georgics*, I and II
[MS. at La Brède; extracts in Nagel III, pp. 710–11; 1748 or later, from handwriting]

+Vitriarius, *Institutiones iuris naturae et gentium*, Leyden, 1734
[*Juridica II*; lost; *Pensée* 2055 (Bkn. 1814) refers]

+*Voyages du nord*, Amsterdam, 1715 sq., I–VIII
[I–VII in *Commerce*; lost; Nagel II, p. 924 refers; before 1738; VIII in *Geog. II*; extracts in Nagel II, pp. 924–5; 1733–8]

INDEX